Advance Praise for Trave
A Guide to Exploring Ou

"Jack Hanrahan's *Traveling Freedom's Road* is a must read. The physical and cultural landscape of civil rights historic sites and memory are rapidly changing. Hanrahan's book provides the most up-to-date material to help travelers navigate this space. I highly recommend this book to anyone interested in learning more about our country's rich history."

Patrick Weems, **Executive Director, Emmett Till Interpretive Center, Sumner, Mississippi**

"Written with intentionality, passion, and precision, Hanrahan's debut is both an historical account and a travel guide, published to illuminate civil rights and African American history....Readers will gain a snapshot of the lives behind some of the historical activists, the courageous people commemorated in the landmarks featured in this guide. Hanrahan also offers practical recommendations for travel planning, including sample checklists and trip itineraries, alongside meticulously detailed information about historical destinations located primarily in the southern United States.

...This impressive guide belongs on the shelves of historians, teachers, travelers, and any readers interested in taking a meaningful, life-changing trip through civil rights history."

BookLife Reviews, **a division of *Publishers Weekly***

"For most of us there will be moments of "Aha!" or "I never knew that!" or even "Why haven't I heard of this?" This enhanced guide will, if you allow it to, excite your spirit of inquiry, lead to growth in your fund of information, and provide a clearer picture of how the continuing battle for civil rights for all can help us form that more perfect union alluded to in our national narrative. ... such a book is sorely needed!"

Dr. Terrence Roberts, **Little Rock Nine member and author of *Lessons from Little Rock***

"*Traveling Freedom's Road* has all that you need to hit the road. Combining solid history, practical guidance, and connections to local resources along the way, the book provides everything you need to visit our country's most important civil rights sights. But *Traveling Freedom's Road* is more than directions; it also provides a picture of the people and places that animated the movement. The snapshots are quick and compelling—once you read, you'll want to hit the road!"

Dave Tell, **Co-Director of the Emmett Till Memory Project and the author of *Remembering Emmett Till***

"...what you have put together is outstanding."

Dr. Shelley Murphy, **Descendant Project, University of Virginia, and Library of Virginia board member**

"Those who journey in history's footsteps will benefit from this book whether they do it by car or from their armchair. ...The book is packed with social, political, and cultural observations that examine...the atmosphere of historical impact and change associated with them....

This approach provides both a 'you are here' feeling to the narrative and emphasizes why each civil rights landmark... continues to be relevant and important to modern audiences. Sidebars on civil rights history and many footnoted references provide scholarly readers with the source materials documenting civil rights events, politics, and their interpretation. The lively tone of this sojourn invites even non-history readers to imbibe, creating an important survey that's very highly recommended to audiences of American history buffs and travelers alike."

D. Donovan, **Senior Reviewer, Midwest Book Reviews**

"This wonderful guide takes you on an adventure to must-see places and explains why they are important to the past and present..."

Wanda Howard Battle, **CEO and Founder, Legendary Tours, Montgomery, Alabama**

"...hope lots of people read your book."

Jerry Mitchell, **investigative reporter and author, *Race Against Time: A Reporter Reopens the Unsolved Murder Cases of the Civil Rights Era***

TRAVELING FREEDOM'S ROAD

A Guide to Exploring Our Civil Rights History

John J. Hanrahan

Freedom's Road Press
Charlottesville, Virginia

Published by
Freedom's Road Press
Charlottesville, Virginia
Jack@justice4all.org

ISBN: 979-8-9855010-0-1 (paperback)
979-8-98555010-1-8 (ebook)
Library of Congress Control Number: 2021925583

Text and cover design and formatting by Mayapriya Long, Bookwrights
Cover photo top © "1-The U.S. Civil Rights Movement" by U.S. Embassy The Hague is licensed with CC BY-ND
Cover photo middle © DiAnna Paulk
Cover photo bottom © Federal Highway Administration, Public domain via Wikimedia Commons

The profits from this book will be shared by two organizations which continue to fight tirelessly for social justice today: the **Equal Justice Initiative** in Montgomery, Alabama and the **Legal Aid Justice Center** in Charlottesville, Virginia.

This book is dedicated to all those who spoke up, marched, sat in, stood in line to register to vote, refused to be moved and otherwise acted to make the US civil rights movement a beacon of true American patriotism and a high point of the human spirit's determination.

In every human Breast, God has implanted a Principle which we call Love of Freedom; it is impatient of Oppression, and pants for Deliverance.

— Phillis Wheatley, February 11, 1774

Contents

PART ONE: Getting Started

PART TWO: Traveling Freedom's Road on the Civil Rights Loop

PART THREE:
Traveling Freedom's Road Elsewhere within the Loop States

PART FOUR:
Traveling Freedom's Road Elsewhere in the South

PART FIVE:
Traveling Freedom's Road Elsewhere in the United States

PART ONE

GETTING STARTED

CHAPTER 1

A Journey Calls

James Baldwin had lived in Paris since 1948. By 1979, Mr. Baldwin realized there was a book he needed to write. Three of his friends had been assassinated. The deaths of Medgar Evers, Malcolm X, and Dr. Martin Luther King Jr. pushed Baldwin to speak of writing *Remember This House* as an unwanted mission, telling his literary agent Jay Acton that he proposed the book "in a somewhat divided frame of mind."[1]

Remember This House, a book that never came to pass, would have had Baldwin returning to the United States, going to the American South, and interviewing the widows, brothers, and sisters of his murdered friends. He knew that would take a high personal emotional toll.

Baldwin used the word "journey" to describe what he felt in proposing his book. As he wrote to Jay Acton,

> "I am saying that a journey is called that because you cannot know what you will discover on the journey, what you will do, what you will find, or what you find will do to you."[2]

The journey that *Traveling Freedom's Road* asks you to consider is one where you do not know going in all that you will discover. You also don't realize up front everything you will do or find on the way. Above all, you cannot predict the effect the journey will have on you.

That was certainly true with my experience. I didn't intend to write a book. That true confession is probably a horrible way to start.

My intent was to take a two-week car trip with my wife. The goal was to travel to several southern states; to explore some parts of the country that we had never visited; to see firsthand places where civil rights history was made, where tragedies and triumphs happened; and to try to better understand the issues that the nation grappled with then and still is dealing with decades later.

This trip would bring us to big cities, medium-sized towns, small hamlets, and even single-street neighborhoods of significance during the 1950s and 1960s civil rights era. Along the way, we would visit the modest homes where leaders like Dr. Martin Luther King Jr. and Medgar Evers once lived as well as museums of every size and sophistication, many of which have opened in the past few years to satisfy a growing interest in civil rights tourism and African American history.

The trip would be much more than standing around restored homes of civil rights legends and walking through new, information-rich museums. It became a collection of places and experiences that triggered strong reactions and difficult questions:

- Some of the places, like Little Rock Central High School, would present just as they were decades ago. Others—like Bryant's Grocery in Money, Mississippi, a key part of the Emmett Till murder—would not even be close to their original look. It was barely standing. Why wasn't this historic place preserved?
- Some of the places, like the Lorraine Motel in Memphis or the Edmund Pettus Bridge in Selma, are locations where well-known history happened. Others presented as historically important like the Glendora Gin (another part of the Emmett Till murder case) may or may not be the scene of any historical event at all . . . even though a marker in front of it makes that claim. Who decides when a place merits an historical marker and what goes on it?
- Still other locations, like where the bodies of Freedom Summer civil rights workers Michael Schwerner, James Chaney, and Andrew Goodman were recovered in Philadelphia, Mississippi, are not memorialized at all with any type of marker. Neither is the spot near the Bogue Chitto swamp where their burned-out station wagon was pulled from a blackberry thicket. Why not?

Why was this trip important to us? Both of us grew up in the Northeast, in mostly white suburbs of two large cities. In my case, I was getting ready for second grade when fourteen-year-old Emmett

Till was murdered in 1955 in the Mississippi Delta. In 1961, I was twelve years old—just like Jamie Forsyth—who brought buckets of water to the choking Freedom Riders who had just escaped the firebombed Greyhound bus burning in front of her father's store in Anniston, Alabama. I was starting tenth grade when four little girls were killed by a bomb at the Sixteenth Street Baptist Church in Birmingham, Alabama, on September 15, 1963.

By the time I was in college, I was more aware that I was living at a time in the nation's history when brave people (both well-known and not) were holding a mirror up before the country and pushing it to fulfill the words of the Declaration of Independence . . . that all men are created equal. Taylor Branch, the author of the definitive trilogy on Martin Luther King, summed up the civil rights movement by saying it was "the essence of patriotism. It was modern founders doing what the original Founders had done, confronting systems of hierarchy and oppression and moving toward equal citizenship."[3]

Now retired, I wanted to learn more about the people who advocated for change those many decades ago, to experience the places where triumphs and tragedies occurred, and to grow in my understanding of this important era. In short, there was a reversible imbalance between what I knew about the civil rights movement compared to the impact of that movement on the country's history. Taking this trip was one way to address that imbalance.

I learned that this would be easier said than done. Three obstacles are worth mentioning:

Logistically, the trip is complicated to plan. I enjoy planning trips and buy into the notion that one needs to do the requisite homework to make any trip successful. However, this tour was especially challenging. The distances between the dozen or so principal cities we wanted to see meant a lot of driving. We knew the entire trip required over thirteen hundred miles (not including what it would take to drive to the trip's starting point) and easily twenty-five hours of driving once we began the trip in earnest. (It turned out to be more miles *and* more hours of driving.) Besides sleep, three activities must be accommodated every day and typically in different cities: driving, visiting places of interest, and basics like meals and relaxation. It didn't seem like a trip where we could just wing it. Planning was essential.

No recent books on cross-regional civil rights travel are available. As I planned our trip, which we took in 2018, I bought three excellent books about civil rights travel in the Southeast. The problem was that they were published in 1999, 2004, and 2008. New options for the civil rights tourist had come into existence since the most recent book. State-specific and destination-specific resources existed and helped. However, destination and state resources understandably have limited focus.

Online resources are scattered. Pulling off this trip without a guide like *Traveling Freedom's Road* requires hours of internet searching. Dozens and dozens of websites need to be accessed for the information needed to plan the trip and avoid surprises, which can include changes in

- Days opened or closed for museums
- Hours of operation
- Admission fees charged
- Exact addresses
- How to arrange an appointment, when required

I know this is true because it is what I had to do. My intent is to bring this all together. By doing so, you will know how to arrange a visit to historic Sisters Chapel on the closed campus of Spelman College and you won't bypass the National Park Service facility in Lowndes County, Alabama, as you drive from Montgomery to Selma.

Importantly, the book also shares some less well-known spots that merit a stop. For example, I'll encourage you to visit Carver Avenue in Philadelphia, Mississippi. A recommended stop on the driving loop offered in the book, Philadelphia is where civil rights workers Schwerner, Chaney, and Goodman were murdered during Freedom Summer 1964. The Carver Avenue neighborhood was the center of organizing activities in Neshoba County, Mississippi, in the 1960s. There, be sure to stop in McClellan's Café for coffee and conversation with owners Beverley and Randy Gill. Beverley is the daughter of Mamie McClellan, who ran the popular café in the 1960s. That was a memorable part of our trip—one not mentioned on any website.

The Goal of the Book

The overarching goal of this book is get you on Freedom's Road and, thus, increase your knowledge and understanding of civil rights and African American history by detailing places where you can learn about the quest for equality—in short, to come face-to-face with that history. While some of highest-profile events of the civil rights movement of the 1950s and 1960s occurred in the South in places like Montgomery, Memphis, and Money, not every success, not every setback, and not every hero or heroine was associated with only a handful of states. The fight for civil rights was nationwide.

If that is true of civil rights history, it is also the case for the broader topic of African American history. Thus, the overall objective of *Traveling Freedom's Road* is to get you on the road, whether it is a multiweek tour of major sites in the South, a weekend trip within your state, or simply a day trip to a local museum or historical marker.

To that end, the book has five parts:

Following this opening chapter in part 1, chapter 2 presents how the book is organized. Then chapter 3 addresses the elephant in the room when civil rights tourism is promoted: namely, that the very states that jailed protesters, denied voting rights, spied on citizens, and worse today are among the biggest economic beneficiaries from that tourism.

The next two chapters offer advice on planning a multiday civil rights journey. Chapter 4 provides two planning checklists: the first spells out actions to take three to four months prior to departing on the journey, while the second lists steps to take within two months of getting on Freedom's Road. Chapter 5 offers a detailed way to lay out the trip day-by-day. The approach is certainly not a requirement, but offered as one way to see what you want to see in a manner consistent with your personal travel style.

The final chapter in part 1 offers some resources for those responsible for exposing children and teens to the violent realities experienced not only by civil rights–era activists but earlier generations of African Americans. Hold off reading chapters 4, 5,and 6 if you are anxious to get to the destination chapters.

Part 2, "Traveling Freedom's Road on the Civil Rights Loop," guides readers city by city on a thirteen-day journey to some of the most well-known civil rights sites in five southern states. It is the longest of the book's five parts. Cities like Atlanta, Montgomery, Selma, Little Rock, and Memphis are part of this loop, so-called because they lay out in an imperfectly shaped oval. While the entire loop requires a two-week commitment, it can be customized to fit shorter time frames. Two examples of one-week itineraries, one using Atlanta as the starting point and the other originating further west in Jackson, are presented in chapter 4.

Part 3, "Traveling Freedom's Road Elsewhere within the Loop States," covers sites in other cities in Georgia, Alabama, Mississippi, Arkansas, and Tennessee. Readers will learn of the disappointment Dr. King experienced in Albany, Georgia as well as the important role the Nashville Student Movement played and the leadership it provided. Those are just two examples of the rich history that can be found beyond the loop in these five states.

In part 4, "Traveling Freedom's Road Elsewhere in the South," chapters cover the nine states that border the five states previously covered. All nine have important history to share, relevant places to visit, and extraordinary people to meet.

Finally, part 5, "Traveling Freedom's Road Elsewhere in the United States," shows that you don't have to tour the South to connect with the freedom movement. This final part of the book notes potential places to visit from the coast of Maine to the shores of Hawaii. In all, twenty-four additional states plus the District of Columbia are covered.

The four location-focused parts support the overall goal of encouraging readers to connect to heritage history when and where they can. For example, part 2 concentrates largely though not exclusively on the civil rights movement. Ida B. Wells, a crusader for equality in the late nineteenth and early twentieth centuries, is mentioned in chapter 14 on Memphis. In addition, chapter 19 covers her Mississippi birthplace, and chapter 30 relates how Chicago honors this pre–civil-rights-era crusader for justice.

The book's lens in the last three parts broadens to include more content on slavery, the Underground Railroad, Reconstruction, and the Jim Crow era that led into the civil rights movement.

The comprehensive geographic coverage within the book gives readers flexibility and options in how they connect with this important and moving history. The easiest and least expensive way to connect is "closer to home"—no long trip, no overnight stays, and far less planning. The wide geographic scope of the book provides opportunities to discover important events, people, and places in many communities across the country.

Another way to use the book is to plan a side adventure or two during other travel. A family on a trip to Orlando's Disney World, for example, could give their feet and wallet a rest by traveling about an hour to Daytona Beach to visit locations associated with three Black legends: Mary McLeod Bethune, Howard Thurman, and Jackie Robinson. They could also take time to visit the relevant (though oddly spelled) Wells'Built Museum in Orlando.

This guide also offers possibilities for weekend trips focused on exploring historical sites. For example, residents of Atlanta who have already visited the main civil rights museums and other sites in their hometown could plan a weekend trip to other sites in Georgia (like Savannah, Macon, or Albany) or cross the state line to Tennessee or South Carolina for more exploring. Any type of travel opens the chance to see civil rights history along the way.

Many of those taking the full tour of the major civil rights locations described in the Atlanta to Anniston chapters may live outside the South. So, they will drive several hundred (or even thousand) miles just to arrive at one of the entry points on the loop. The book also helps these travelers find relevant history along the way to their chosen starting point. For example, a family from Baltimore heading to Atlanta to begin the loop tour could break up the drive to Atlanta with a stop at the Robert Russa Moton Museum in Farmville, Virginia, to learn of its role in the landmark 1954 *Brown v. Board of Education* desegregation case. On the way home, a visit to Greensboro's International Civil Rights Center and Museum, the site of the historic 1960 lunch-counter sit-in could be a possibility.

To accomplish the goal of encouraging readers to explore our nation's civil rights history, the book first needs to succeed as a travel book. If you are like me planning this trip, you want to visit places that you have read about that were instrumental in the civil rights movement. You want to sit in a church where Dr. King preached, stand on the street corner where Rosa Parks boarded that bus, or walk up to the school where nine high school students made history in Little Rock. The book gets you to those places, allowing you to be where courageous icons made their famous stands.

However, the book is more than a travel book. You'll learn the stories behind some of the people and events that made the history highlighted in museums and memorialized on historical markers. There are moving tales of courage, persistence, selflessness, and achievement that I often did not know before writing this book. In particular, the text shares the stories of people and events that don't get much or any attention in the history books, especially many of the women who had such a significant impact on the freedom movement—like Unita Blackwell, Jo Ann Robinson, Irene Morgan, Sarah Mae Flemming, and Modjeska Simkins.

Along with my education came the erasure of several misimpressions I held. Three examples illustrate my own prior incomplete understanding:

- An armed coup in the United States? Never thought there was one until I learned what occurred in Wilmington, North Carolina, in 1898. White supremacists overthrew the city's duly elected mixed-race government, killing an undetermined number of Black citizens and displacing many others.

- The Greensboro lunch-counter sit-in in 1960, as important as it was to ignite similar actions in the early 1960s, wasn't the first such protest by a long shot. Not taking an ounce of credit away from the four brave young men at the F. W. Woolworth's in Greensboro, but lunch-counter protests were led by Edna Griffin in Des Moines, Iowa, in 1948; Mary Church Terrell in Washington, DC, in 1950; and Clara Luper in Oklahoma City in 1958. These three women's stories appear later.

- The Selma-to-Montgomery marchers were certainly heroic and produced important social change when they walked 50-plus miles in that historic 1965 action. A few years later, Robert Hicks and A. Z. Young led six hundred marchers into Baton Rouge, Louisiana, to protest racial violence in a 106-mile march from their hometown of Bogalusa. Again, taking nothing away from the Selma-to-Montgomery marchers but the Bogalusa-to-Baton Rouge march and its two leaders deserve more ink—and they get it in chapter 26 when we travel Freedom's Road in Louisiana.

As I wrote, I also became more consciously aware of how much of this history has not been taught. An imbalance may always be there, but I have found immense satisfaction in filling my own knowledge gaps. I hope that sense of discovery comes through in the pages in the book.

Thinking back on the trip and reflecting on the knowledge gained while researching this book, another thought constantly came to mind: *What patriotism the leaders and participants in the civil rights movement displayed!*

Take Dr. King's words at the Holt Street Baptist Church on December 5, 1955, the first night of the Montgomery Bus Boycott. After his opening sentence greeted those packed into the church (and hundreds more listening outside) and his second statement told them they were there for "serious business," Dr. King tied the actions of that day and the next 380 days to the meaning of citizenship, a love of democracy, and a belief that American democracy had to be more than "thin paper."

Said Dr. King that night,

> We are here in a general sense because first and foremost we are American citizens, and we are determined to apply our citizenship to the fullness of its meaning. We are here also because of our love for democracy, because of our deep-seated belief that democracy transformed from thin paper to thick action is the greatest form of government on earth.[4]

Three other periods in the nation's history, all military conflicts, stand out in calling on true patriots to "thick action":

- The Revolutionary War, when patriotism led to the country's creation.
- The Civil War, when soldiers in Union Blue preserved the country as one.
- World War II, when patriotic women and men defended the country and the concept of democratic rule against foreign aggression.

My father was an airman in the Second World War. I have always considered him and all those who served in that war to be patriotic, courageous, and important to our history. Those who participated in the civil rights movement deserve the same feelings of admiration of commitment and respect of sacrifice. If those three past patriotic periods created, preserved, and defended the nation, then the civil rights movement held the Founding Fathers' unrealized ideals in front of the country, challenging the United States to live up to its unfulfilled aspirations. That is just as patriotic as any actions taken in those three wars.

Speaking at the fiftieth anniversary of Bloody Sunday in Selma, Alabama, in 2015, President Barack Obama captured this sentiment. The president noted the enormous well of faith and patriotism that resided in those who held the mirror of the Founders' vision up to America in the civil rights years. President Obama may have been remarking about the men and women who crossed the Edmund Pettus Bridge on March 7, 1965, but his words aptly describe the patriotic actions of decades in the drive to social justice:

> "What enormous faith these men and women had. Faith in God, but also faith in America. . . . What could be more American than what happened in this place? What could more profoundly vindicate the idea of America than plain and humble people—unsung, the downtrodden, the dreamers not of high station, not born to wealth or privilege, not of one religious tradition but many, coming together to shape their country's course?
>
> " . . . What greater expression of faith in the American experiment than this, what greater form of patriotism is there than the belief that America is not yet finished, that we are strong enough to be self-critical, that each successive generation can look upon our imperfections and decide that it is in our power to remake this nation to more closely align with our highest ideals?"[5]

While I'd like to think that such feelings lay within me before traveling Freedom's Road, this trip amplified those emotions and changed me. My bet is that such a trip will change you too. Get on Freedom's Road. As the James Baldwin quote that led off this chapter noted, you don't know "what you will discover on the journey . . . or what you find will do to you."[6]

CHAPTER 2

How the Book Is Organized

The first chapter spelled out that the book has four parts following this initial one. Part 2, the longest section lays out a two-week trip to cities and towns that played a major role in our civil rights history. These places certainly are not the only ones to play a role—not by a long shot—yet they fall geographically in a fashion that fills a two-week driving trip. The route can be shortened when less time is available. Moreover, other cities could be substituted into the route, making the journey easier or meeting the traveler's interests better.

That's one way to use the last three parts of the book. They present hundreds of options to connect with civil rights and African American history outside of the stops recommended for the five-state loop.

Part 3 focuses on locations within Georgia, Alabama, Mississippi, Arkansas, and Tennessee that were not in cities and towns on the two-week tour, places like:

- Midway, Georgia, where Dr. King and his colleagues planned the 1963 Birmingham Campaign after his efforts in Albany, Georgia, did not go as planned.
- Scottsboro, Alabama, which gave the infamous "Scottsboro Boys" case its name.
- Hattiesburg, Mississippi, where selfless hero Vernon Dahmer paid with his life for his work to register voters in his community.
- Elaine, Arkansas, the site of a 1919 massacre of an unknown number of Blacks.
- Monteagle, Tennessee, where the Highlander Folk School not

only provided nonviolence training to people including Rosa Parks but also played a role in the evolution of the civil rights–era rendition of "We Shall Overcome."

Part 4, which covers nine bordering states, illustrates how important civil rights and African American history can be explored outside the five core tour states. Here are three examples of heroic women from these other states whose stories are shared in this section:

- South Carolina's Septima Clark had an impact felt across the movement. Her grassroots education initiative called Citizenship Schools began in the Lowcountry of her home state. Her successful approach was adopted by Dr. King's Southern Christian Leadership Conference (SCLC) and implemented across the South.
- Born in Virginia and raised in North Carolina, Ella Baker's leadership skills benefited multiple civil rights organizations. Her combination of drive and maturity was critical when the Student Nonviolent Coordinating Committee (SNCC) was founded at Shaw University in Raleigh, North Carolina, in 1960.
- Barbara Johns was sixteen years old when she led a student walkout at her high school in Farmville, Virginia, in 1951, the year Dr. King began his studies at Boston University and four years before Rosa Parks refused to move from her seat on a Montgomery bus. So, as you read about Barbara Johns in the Virginia chapter, think about how bold her actions were in the context of the times, especially in the rural South.

Part 5 covers twenty-four of the remaining thirty-six states. I self-imposed a limit of three locations per state to keep this last section at a manageable length (though another location or two occasionally sneaks into the discussion). Part 5 also presents relevant sites in Washington, D.C. There is too much heritage history in our nation's capital to impose the three-location limit, so the district received a pass.

That's a broad look at the entire book. In addition to the city-specific and state-specific content in these four sections, three chapters are designed to help readers before they set out on Freedom's Road. Two of these, chapters 4 and 5, focus on travel planning and are most relevant to those who decide to take an extended, multistate trip. Chapter 6 deals with introducing young people to the realities of African American history—calling attention to free content from major civil rights museums as well as a variety of other useful resources available to parents and others tasked with explaining this history to children and teens.

Selecting a Starting Point

The five-state loop tour suggests visits to the following cities and towns in these states:

- Alabama: Montgomery, Tuskegee, Selma, Marion, Birmingham, and Anniston
- Mississippi: Philadelphia, Jackson, and the Mississippi Delta region (e.g., Money, Glendora, and Sumner)
- Arkansas: Little Rock
- Tennessee: Memphis
- Georgia: Atlanta

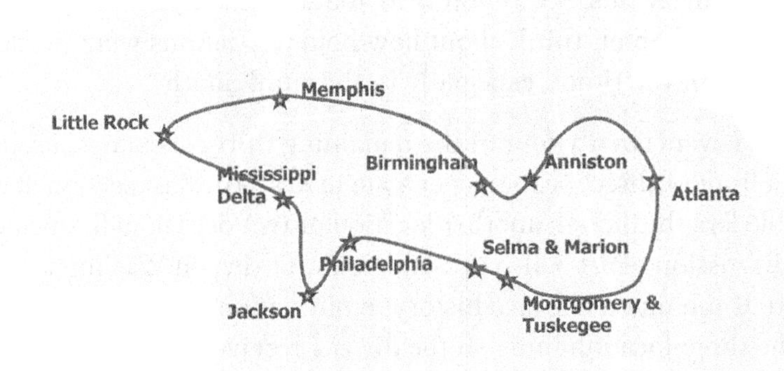

Travelers can start their trip anywhere they want on the recommended route. Some cities are within a day's drive of one of the many possible starting points. For example, Richmond, Virginia, is less than eight hours from Atlanta; Roanoke, Virginia, Tampa, Florida; and Cincinnati, Ohio are less than seven. Memphis could be a starting point for those from Chicago, Indianapolis, and Kansas City—all are a one-day trip to the home of the National Civil Rights Museum at the Lorraine Motel. The same is true if some from Houston or Manhattan (Kansas, that is) selected Little Rock as a jumping-off point.

While readers can begin their trip anywhere they would like, a book needs to start somewhere. This book leads with Atlanta. Why?

First, it's the most likely starting point for US residents and international visitors who choose to fly in and rent a car. Atlanta's Hartsfield-Jackson International Airport (named after two civil rights–era luminaries) has the most direct connections with US and international cities of any of the loop cites, by far.

Second, civil rights history enthusiasts driving in from cities in the Northeast, from a large part of the Midwest, from North and South Carolina, and from most of Florida will find Atlanta to be the shortest drive from home.

Third, it's almost unimaginable that someone taking a journey into our civil rights past would not include Atlanta. The city is a terrific way to kick off the trip, in large part due to the connections between the city and the life of Dr. Martin Luther King Jr.

Atlanta is the location of Dr. King's birthplace, his high school, his college, one of the churches he pastored, and his burial site. The National Park Service's Historical Park honoring him, based in the Sweet Auburn neighborhood where he grew up, is clearly a must-see. The other recommended area of Atlanta for a one-day visit is the campuses of the historically Black colleges of Morehouse (Dr. King's undergraduate Alma Mater), Spelman, and Clark Atlanta. Just three miles from the NPS Historical Park, these campuses were central to the organizing activities during the early 1960s.

From Atlanta, subsequent chapters guide readers west into Alabama, where Montgomery, Selma, and Marion are recommended stops. We exit Alabama to enter Mississippi for several chapters (and days). We cover Philadelphia, Jackson, and the Mississippi Delta, with an emphasis in the Delta on places related to the murder of Emmett Till and the sham trial of his killers (spoiler alert: they eventually confessed their guilt to a journalist after their trial ended with a not-guilty verdict).

Little Rock, Arkansas, is our westernmost stop before heading two hours back east to Memphis, Tennessee, the site of Dr. King's assassination and one of the country's major civil rights museums. From Memphis, the chapters here travel south, reentering Alabama for a visit to Birmingham and a final stop in Anniston, Alabama, the site of a fiery attack on a bus carrying Freedom Riders in May 1961.

If Atlanta was your starting point and you need to return there to catch a plane, Hartsfield-Jackson Airport is less than two hours from Anniston. That's less than two hours, in theory; it is, after all, Atlanta, where traffic jams are almost as ubiquitous as Waffle Houses. (If you don't know the Waffle House restaurant chain, you will see more than a few on this trip!) Remember that Alabama is in the Central Time Zone while Georgia is in the Eastern Time Zone—a critical fact to remember in making a flight in Atlanta.

How the Loop Tour Destination Chapters Are Structured

Ten chapters cover the destinations recommended for consideration on the two-week tour. These chapters follow a common structure:

- Background: The purpose here is to provide some context for each destination. What happened here? Who were the key players? The commentary for each chapter, however, follows no template.

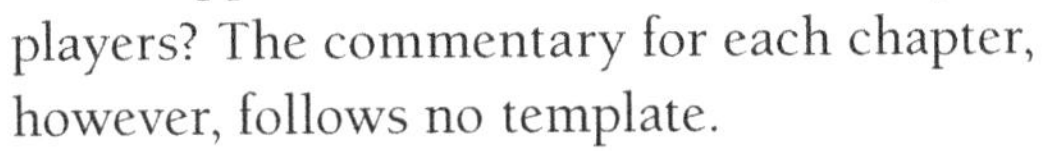

In Selma, for example, my belief is that readers know the history that draws them to want to come here. As such, the background in Selma starts with events that took place in nearby Marion, Alabama, a month before the Bloody Sunday events of March 7, 1965. Then the focus shifts to Turnaround Tuesday, a lesser-known event that happened in Selma on March 9, 1965.

In the background for the chapter on Philadelphia, Mississippi, the appropriate context seemed to be a grounding in the goals and training of Freedom Summer volunteers. The chapter begins by taking readers to Oxford, Ohio, where the instruction occurred. There we meet the inspirational Robert "Bob" Moses as he gives the summer volunteers a reality check on what their time in Mississippi is going to be like.

- The Plan for ———: The blank there is the destination that is the focal point of the chapter ("The Plan for Selma," for example). In every case, "The Plan for ———" text is limited to three hundred words or less. This self-imposed brevity allows the recommended stops to be summarized, as travelers gain a quick sense of what they will see. What follows goes into much more detail.
- Specific destination recommendations: For each possible stop within each city, the chapter makes sure you know how to find the location. In most cases, entering the address provided into your GPS software should take you there without hassle. In a few instances, longitude and latitude data are provided when a precise address isn't available. In a few instances, we guide you through accessing a location turn by turn. In addition, if the stop is a museum, a National Park Service (NPS) site, or the like, the book provides its operating days and hours, costs to visit, and other relevant visitor information.

For many locations, knowing some history is important, which is where the storytelling comes in. I am not a historian, but I have benefited from reading some of the leading writers on the events that defined the civil rights movement. I try to concisely weave in what I have learned in researching people, places, and events so that you can judge whether a specific place interests you. Sources used appear in the notes.

For museums, homes, churches, and other go-inside visits, we cover the highlights and provide a sense of what you will experience: main exhibit halls, degrees of audiovisual usage, special exhibits, and so on. If there are films to see, I mention the ones you shouldn't miss. The desire is to provide a flavor of each place but not stifle your own sense of discovery.

- More Options: In some places, you'll will want to stay longer than the book recommends. The Mississippi Delta region is a case in point. The book has you spending a day there; that may be enough just to visit the principal sites related to Emmett Till's murder, but it won't exhaust all the Delta's possibilities. The book presents plenty of opportunities for those who want to go deeper.

Non–civil rights activities or diversions may prompt you to spend added time in one or more places. The book doesn't cover those kinds of general tourism diversions (sports, outdoor activities, other types of museums, casinos, etc.). There are plenty of places to get help on that front. Information on state and city tourism and visitors' bureaus in the core states are referenced in chapter 4.

CHAPTER 3

The Controversy around Civil Rights Tourism

An elephant stands prominently in the room when writing a book encouraging civil rights tourism. Considering our planned itinerary, perhaps this thought crossed your mind: *The very states and cities that were the among the most egregious offenders in denying the rights of all their citizens would now be benefiting from an influx of tourists seeking to visit the significant civil rights museums and memorials which have emerged across the South.*

Do these former slave states indeed profit from the actions they took against their African American residents? After all, the argument goes, where do the taxes for lodging, meals, shopping, and attractions that tourists pay go? Right into the revenue coffers of those same states.

When the Mississippi Civil Rights Museum opened in Jackson in December 2017, several veterans of the civil rights movement chose not to attend, objecting to the state gaining tourism dollars from decades of neglect and violence against Black people. For example, Congressman John Lewis—a giant of the movement, a veteran of the 1961 Freedom Rides, the 1965 Selma-to-Montgomery March, and more—did not attend. However, the congressman's decision to stay away may have had more to do with President Donald Trump choosing to attend the museum's opening. Other heroes of the civil rights era, however, did attend, including Myrlie Evers-Williams, wife of slain Mississippi civil rights leader Medgar Evers.

Objections to civil rights tourism are not just a recent phenomenon. Before there was much interest in civil rights travel or ways to satisfy such an interest where it existed, there was controversy. In 1988, the Lorraine Motel, the Memphis site where Dr. King was assassinated, was closed to allow the work to begin to convert it into the National Civil Rights Museum.

The motel at the time was a single-room-occupancy building, providing housing to the very people whom Dr. King fought for when he was alive. The last tenant evicted was Jacqueline Smith. She had lived there for fifteen years.

Ms. Smith believed that evicting long-term residents at the Lorraine to build a museum would not have met with Dr. King's approval. She began to protest her eviction across from the motel at the corner of Butler and Mulberry and kept it going for over thirty-two years. As late as March 2020, Ms. Smith could be still found at that corner asking people to boycott the museum.

Concerns about states that supported enslavement and segregation benefiting from the type of tourism covered here are understandable. However, I don't think that's a sufficient reason to negate these benefits derived from civil rights tourism:

- Tourism dollars benefit all citizens, white and Black—or at least they should.
- Some of the places we suggest for a visit are Black-run or Black-owned organizations. For example, the National Voting Rights Museum and Institute in Selma, Alabama, was cofounded by Joanne Bland, a witness to and participant in many of the events that took place in Selma in the 1960s. She is also the owner of Journeys for the Soul, a company offering tours of civil rights sites in and around Selma.
- Perhaps most importantly, everyone benefits when this type of history is uncovered and discussed. Through honest, blunt, and often upsetting reminders, these museums, memorials, and markers educate. Education is the best avenue to enlightenment. Positive social change has a chance when people are enlightened by understanding and dealing honestly with their history.

As I researched the book and began to write it, events occurred that resurrected the past, in ways both uplifting and disturbing. The line in William Faulkner's *Requiem for a Nun* kept popping into my head: "The past is never dead."

This often-paraphrased line seemed to fit some reprehensible killings of Black citizens that took place across the country as I entered the final stages of writing the book in 2020:

- In March, Breonna Taylor, a twenty-eight-year-old emergency medical technician, was shot eight times and killed by Louisville police as they executed a search warrant, a search that found none of the named contraband.
- In May, a video of Ahmaud Arbery, out jogging in February, was posted by a Georgia radio station showing how Mr. Arbery was accosted by two men in a pickup truck and shot to death.
- Later in May, George Floyd was murdered on the streets of Minneapolis when a police officer held him down with his knee on Mr. Floyd's neck for over nine minutes, while three other officers did nothing to stop their colleague.
- Rayshard Brooks was shot in the back and killed by an Atlanta policeman just weeks after George Floyd's death.

Sadly, that is not a complete list of these types of tragedies that took place in 2020. In a very dark way, the past did not seem to be dead as I came closer to the book's end.

During the same period, more uplifting parts of the past also seemed to come alive again.

- In January 2020, Jefferson County, Alabama, voted to preserve a jail in the county courthouse. What made the jail so special? It was the last jail cell where Dr. King was held, serving three days there in 1967 for a contempt charge for demonstrating without a permit years earlier. This jail time was served only months prior to Dr. King's assassination, the last of the leader's twenty-nine times behind bars. The seventh-floor lockup was being used for storage. Someone looked at the booking records from the 1960s and noted that Dr. King was held here.
- In February 2020, Chicago's DuSable Museum announced that it was opening a unique virtual reality (VR) exhibit on the

1963 March on Washington. Thanks to VR technology and the attention to detail by the creators of this experience, visitors would find themselves on the steps of the Lincoln Memorial as Dr. King delivers his "I Have a Dream" speech. The historic twentieth-century past had been re-created with twenty-first-century tech, only to be delayed by this century's first pandemic.

- In June 2020, the struggle for racial equality of decades ago basked once again in its proud and historic legacy. The employment rights of gay and transgender people were found to be protected by the Civil Rights Act of 1964 in the highly consequential *Bostock v. Clayton* County, Georgia decision by the US Supreme Court.

For reasons both distressing and uplifting, the past did not seem to be dead.

A few years ago, my wife and I traveled to Berlin, Germany. We visited places like the Memorial to the Murdered Jews of Europe. The memorial's title alone tells you that there is no sugarcoating here of what happened during the Third Reich. The different-sized rectangular slabs of concrete (technically referred to as "stelae" in the design world) and the pitch of the land on which these 2,711 slabs sit allow a visitor to see someone else across the memorial. In a split second, that person will suddenly disappear. This gave me the discomforting sense of what it must have been like in Germany under Hitler: to be with a friend or relative one moment and suddenly they were taken away by the Nazis.

The Germans are not trying to hide the ugliness of their past with a memorial like this. They were bringing past atrocities to a visitor's consciousness. The same was true of the brutal frankness of the Topography of Terror museum, set in the same building out of which the Gestapo operated. Again, there was no whitewashing of the Nazi past.

I had similar reactions during our own two-week-long trip though the southeastern United States as I had in Berlin. The past was not dead. The jars of earth from lynching sites across the country on display at Montgomery's Legacy Museum brought that reality from our nation's past to light vividly. The incessant sounds of taped anti-Black insults and cracking whips at the Mississippi Civil Rights Museum in Jackson provided an aural representation of what it must have been like to be an African American in many places during Jim Crow.

The impressions I had on the realism presented throughout my own travels in the Southeast were shared by others. Consider the headline of a *New York Times* article written by Holland Cotter, reviewing the Mississippi Civil Rights Museum in 2017: "The New Mississippi Civil Rights Museum Refuses to Sugarcoat History."[7]

Cotter's review, while focused on the museum in Jackson, also connected his museum experience with events in contemporary America. For Cotter, a Pulitzer Prize–winning critic, the past did not seem to be dead:

> "The story it [the museum] tells is still in progress: from 1960s Jackson, to Ferguson, Mo., Charlottesville, Va.,

> and the 2017 White House. That the new museum says this outright, and leaves us upset, its story unresolved, is what makes it work. We don't need our museums—any of them—to calm us down; we need them to sound alarms."[8]

These alarms need to be heard; these places need to be seen by all people. This journey that the book encourages is certainly not just for African Americans. People of my (white) race especially need to travel Freedom's Road. As Andrea Taylor, the former chief executive of the Birmingham Civil Rights Institute noted, "It's a part of American history, not just African-American history."[9] That's why the book's subtitle is a "A Guide to Exploring *Our* Civil Rights History." Like it or not, Americans alive today all own a piece of this part of our history.

Earlier, I wrote that education can lead to enlightenment, and that can lead to positive change. Bryan Stevenson, founder and executive director of the Equal Justice Initiative in Montgomery, struck a note of optimism on what squarely confronting the past can do. Speaking at the end of a *60 Minutes* segment on the National Memorial for Peace and Justice in Montgomery, Stevenson said,

"America can be a great nation, even though there was slavery, even though there was lynching, even though there was segregation. But if we don't talk about those things we did, we don't acknowledge those things, we're not going to get there."[10]

The past is not dead. However, you must search it out. It's certainly worth the trip. This book hopefully gets you out traveling Freedom's Road.

CHAPTER 4

Planning Your Trip: The Basics

This chapter and the next can help you plan the multistate journey that part 2 suggests. This chapter covers the basics—providing a checklist of items to think through a few months before you travel—and poses a variety of questions to help you prepare for a trip with as many components as the civil rights journey.

If, at the end of reading this chapter, you realize that you cannot just hop in the car and head out for two weeks traveling Freedom's Road, I'll consider it a mission accomplished.

Chapter 5 helps you fill in the details. Essentially, it allows you to plan wisely, sightsee comfortably, and avoid disappointment.

You don't have to read these two chapters now if you are anxious to delve into the destination chapters. If that's the case, skip or skim chapters 4 and 5 now. However, coming back to them at some point will make for a better trip experience. Still thinking about skipping ahead? Just read the next few paragraphs.

This isn't likely to be your first vacation, nor your first lasting over a week. It may not even be your longest road-trip vacation. However, it may be your first long road-trip adventure where you will

- Travel well over fifteen hundred miles, not counting what it will take to get to one of the starting-point cities and back home again.
- Be on the road almost every day, averaging hundreds of miles of driving on those days.
- Need to maximize how you spend daylight hours every day.
- Have set appointments at certain places you want to see.

The length of this trip, the amount of driving required, and the necessity of booking certain experiences in advance all scream out for preparation. Winging it may be your usual approach to trip planning, but don't do it on this trip.

Take something as common as hotel reservations. You may be used to pulling into a place to stay when you get tired of driving for the day. That may work well on some vacations. For this one, having a predetermined goal destination for the night lets you know the driving distances that you will face for two days: the day you arrive at the hotel and the day you depart the hotel for the next day's touring. Having confirmed lodging reservations also eliminates one concern from each day of your trip, and is one element I urge you to take care of before you hit the road.

Driving distances are key on Freedom's Road. If you stay too far from a destination of interest and leave a lot of driving to do the morning of your visit there, you may not have enough time to see all you want to see. Proper advance planning results in less stress during your trip, delivers deeper learning, and generates less disappointment.

Advance planning also compels you to make choices at home, not on the road. For each city, you must decide at least three basic things:

- What do you want to see?
- How much time to spend at each place?
- What is the best sequence in which to see everything?

Assume for the moment that you plan on eight hours of site visiting time each day, say from 10 a.m. to 6 p.m. What do I mean by "site visiting time"?

This includes the time you plan to spend at all the places you want to see in a given city or section of a state *plus* the time it takes to get from one place to another *within* that destination, including driving and walking within that destination.

Site visiting time *excludes* driving to the destination city and driving on to the next city. The eight hours earmarked for site visits thus must accommodate the time spent at places that interest you in and around that city or region of the day (museums, National Park

Service sites, churches, cemeteries, markers, neighborhoods, etc.) plus the driving or walking you need to do within that city.

Suppose you lay out all the places you want to see on a given day, how much time you think you will need at each one, and how much in-city travel time is needed. Suppose that total comes up to twelve hours and you planned for eight. Something must give. Your options:

- Cut down on the time spent at certain places of interest.
- Cut out some of the places of lesser interest or greater distance entirely.
- Start earlier or leave later on this particular day.

This is where planning ahead ensures that you visit what you want, see all the sites efficiently, and get on the road and arrive at your next lodging destination in a manner that fits your travel style (more on travel style in chapter 5). Everything on any trip may not always go according to plan, but having a plan improves the odds in your favor.

I recognize there are different types of trip planners, which is why this chapter offers some basic considerations and a bare-bones planning template. Chapter 5 is more detailed. The increased level of detail is a suggestion, not a requirement.

Let's divide the preparation elements for the type of extended day trips proposed into two time frames:

- Preparations to complete *prior to two months* before departure
- Preparations to complete *within two months* of departure

The choice of two months as a dividing line is arbitrary. The point is to do some planning far enough out to avoid cramming all of that work into a compressed time frame. This is particularly important should you need to contact places where you an appointment to visit is required or if you are planning for a large group. Start early; avoid disappointment.

Trip Planning: Two or More Months from Departure

I started researching and laying out the trip my wife and I took about four months prior to getting on the road. While there was no doubt we would take this two-week journey, I knew devoting full time to the planning tasks wasn't in the cards for me at the time. Rather, working in planning spurts was more my style. Also, I didn't have the benefit of all the information in this book. So, while I don't believe you need to start four months out, I would still start to design the trip, using this book, two to three months ahead of travel.

The planning checklist presents eight items discussed in this chapter. The two questions to ask yourself first are:

- How long can we be away?
- What day of the week can we begin?

Planning Checklist: Two or More Months from Departure

√ **How many days?**

√ **What day will I start?**

√ **What's my starting point?**

√ **Build a basic trip template.**

√ **Check "closed on" dates.**

√ **Build a detailed template.**

√ **Make reservations.**

√ **Request travel information.**

How Long Can We Be Away?

The full trip of the ten suggested locales laid out in the loop from Atlanta to Anniston—no matter where you choose to begin—requires about two weeks. Thirteen days of touring are spelled out in chapters 7 to 16. In addition, another day likely needs to be added to drive to or fly to your starting-point city. If you started the five-state trip as presented in this book, your last day will end in Anniston, Alabama. As you will read in the Anniston chapter, all the sites you probably want to see there require about a half day. The city is modest in size, so the civil rights sites are not far from one another.

Anniston is about a ninety-minute drive from Atlanta, but with the change back to Eastern time, it is two-and-a-half hours on the clock). So if you flew into Atlanta and rented a car to start the trip, you could finish Anniston touring by early afternoon and catch an evening flight back home the same evening. Be sure to plan for Atlanta's traffic if you are flying home.

Anniston is also a reasonable end point for drivers from a wide swath of the eastern and central parts of the United States. For some, leaving Anniston by early afternoon could mean they would be tucked into their own bed the same night.

What if you can't carve out two weeks or so for this trip? Work with what you have available. Use the basic planning template to lay out a trip that fits the time you have.

Suppose you can only spare a week. This is a common trip length for church groups, fraternities and sororities, work groups, and others. The solution: build a mini loop.

Below are just two possible mini loop examples. Each lays out six days of touring in a fashion that mimics a (somewhat) circular trip—one that gets you back close to or at your starting point.

Take, for example, the trip labelled Mini Loop 1 in the table. After spending a day in Atlanta, this loop moves on to provide two days in Montgomery and Tuskegee (versus three in the two-week trip), then Selma and Marion, Birmingham, and ending in Anniston. These cities would highlight major civil rights events like the Montgomery Bus Boycott, the Selma march, and the tragic bombing of the Sixteenth Street Baptist Church in Birmingham. Moreover, you'd have a chance to visit some important museums and National Park Service (NPS) sites and spend significant time tracking some events and places associated with Dr. Martin Luther King Jr. And since this mini loop begins in Atlanta, it may be the best option for those who only have a week available and plan to fly in.

What if starting a weeklong trek in Atlanta isn't convenient? Perhaps if you lived in east Texas or in Louisiana, a mini loop that began in Jackson, Mississippi, might be an easier starting point. Notice with this option (Mini Loop 2 in the table), we start and end with a day in Jackson. That gives you more options in touring Jackson's major sites, such as the Medgar and Myrlie Evers Home or the Mississippi Civil Rights Museum (closed on Monday). Ending in Jackson on Day 6 also puts you in a position to be home by the seventh day of your vacation.

Note that Little Rock is also under seven hours away from Houston, so this mini loop could have started in Little Rock and ended in Jackson, if one day in Jackson was viewed as sufficient. The point is to explore your options and make your available time work.

If your schedule driving home from Jackson allowed, you could plan a stop or stayover in or near New Orleans to visit sites presented in the Louisiana chapter, such as Whitney Plantation to experience the unforgettable *1811 Slave Revolt Memorial* or the school that six-year-old Ruby Bridges desegregated in 1960.

Mini Loop 1: Atlanta to Anniston	Mini Loop 2: Jackson to Jackson
Day 1: Atlanta	Day 1: Jackson
Day 2: Montgomery/Tuskegee	Day 2: Mississippi Delta
Day 3: Montgomery/Tuskegee	Day 3: Philadelphia
Day 4: Selma and Marion	Day 4: Birmingham
Day 5: Birmingham	Day 5: Selma and Marion
Day 6: Anniston	Day 6: Jackson

What if you have more than a week but end up a day or two shy of having two weeks available? Well, you can see more than someone on a mini loop, but you will have to make some adjustments from the full tour route, probably painful ones. If something must give, here are some considerations:

- Before cutting any city out or reducing the recommended number of days in a city, look over each city's schedule and reexamine your driving times.
    - Are you packing too much into one city, causing you to leave there later than necessary and shortchanging the next stop?
    - Could you drive a little more on any given day to create more time for site visits?
    - Could you stay closer to the city you are visiting the next day to turn morning drive time into site visiting time?
- In the two-week tour, we suggest three days in Montgomery, the only city with a three-day stay. That could make it the place to look at closely to determine whether two days might be enough.

- In the chapter on Little Rock, I explain how I wondered about going there. Was it worth the drive west when Memphis was so much closer, given our plan to explore the Mississippi Delta area (particularly, Emmett Till–related sites) the day before? We had the luxury of two weeks, so we included Little Rock. We were glad we did. However, you may decide to save Little Rock for another trip.

The bottom line: When you may find yourself with a longer civil rights tour wish list than available vacation time, you'll make some tough choices. Talk it over with your travel mate(s). Don't feel that you must do it all in one trip. Plan it out so that you are rewarded with ample time to appreciate each stop and enrich your understanding of people and events—and so the trip isn't stressful because of the travel alone.

What Day of the Week Will You Begin Touring?

Let's be clear what this question asks: It's about when your tour itself begins, not when you depart your home. This detail might seem unnecessary to consider. Why should it matter whether the first day of site visits in your initial loop tour city starts on a weekend or some weekday?

The reason is simple. Every place may not be open every day. This is not only the case in that first city but every city thereafter, so thinking about your tour's start date (and where you begin it; that's coming up next) is quite important.

Suppose you select the thirteen-day timeline laid out in the book. Once you pick what day to begin your tour on and where you start, the schedule for where you will be on every one of the following days falls into place. Remember, all the days are interdependent. Unless you make some changes to the number of days in each city, change the order of visiting cities, or insert a day for some other reason, the puzzle forms once you lay down the first piece.

Suppose further that you decide to begin in Atlanta on a Saturday. If you follow the plan over the next two weeks, if Day 1 is Atlanta, then Day 5 would be Selma, and Day 11 is Memphis. If Day 1 is a Saturday, then Day 11 would be a Tuesday. What's wrong with being in Memphis on a Tuesday? Nothing, unless you were planning on visiting the National Civil Rights Museum at the Lorraine Motel. It is closed on Tuesday. Basic planning beforehand avoids such a problem. It can be remedied in any number of ways, all of which are best done as you plan. For example,

- Shift the Atlanta start to Friday; now Day 11 in Memphis is a Monday.
- Tour Atlanta at the end of your travels, not on Day 1.
- Cut out a day between Atlanta and Memphis.

Advance planning catches this kind of problem before you depart. Importantly, you catch it early in the process following the two-plus-months-out checklist, long before you book hotel rooms or appointments at destinations requiring them.

Knowing closed-on days is key to planning this trip. To understand closed-on days, consult the table. Most places are open Wednesday, Thursday, and Friday. However, depending on the specific museum, church, or NPS site, you may find it closed on one or more other days.

The chart on page 35 does not include places that are by appointment only, such as two important churches in Selma: First Baptist Church and Brown A.M.E. Chapel. Also, some spots never close, like roadside historic markers or sites with outdoor exhibits, like the Southern Poverty Law Center (SPLC) and the Freedom Rides Museum (both in Montgomery). The Xs in the table refer to inside access only.

Check for special events on the websites of places that you plan to visit. Some special events may interest you and cause you to add some time to your visit there. On the other hand, some events may result in an early closing or even the total closing of a museum or historic place. An example of this would be the tours that typically go inside Little Rock Central High School. Those tours do not occur on dates when the school is closed (e.g., school vacation periods, national holidays). When we get to the planning checklist within two months of travel, we include this late check of museum websites on the to-do list.

City	Place	Sunday	Monday	Tuesday	Wednesday	Thursday	Friday	Saturday
Atlanta	Martin Luther King Jr. National Historical Park	Open daily (ex. some holidays)						
Montgomery	Legacy Museum			X				
Montgomery	Southern Poverty Law Center (inside exhibits)	X						
Montgomery	Freedom Rides Museum	X	X					
Montgomery	National Memorial for Peace & Justice			X				
Montgomery	Rosa Parks Museum	X						
Montgomery	Dexter Avenue King Memorial Baptist Church	X	X					
Montgomery	Dexter Avenue King Memorial - Parsonage	X	X					
Montgomery	Montgomery NPS Interpretive Center	X						
Tuskegee	Tuskegee Airmen National Historical Site	X						
Tuskegee	Tuskegee Institute National Historical Site	X						
Lowndes County	Lowndes NPS Interpretive Center	X						
Selma	National Voting Rights Museum	AO					AO	AO
Selma	Selma NPS Interpretive Center	X						
Jackson	Mississippi Civil Rights Museum		X					
Jackson	Mississippi State Capitol	X						X
Jackson	Smith Robinson Museum	X						
Glendora	Emmett Till Historic intrepid Center	X	AO					
Sumner	Emmett Till Interpretive Center	AO						AO
Little Rock	Little Rock Central High School Nat'l. Hist. Site	Open daily (ex. some holidays)						
Memphis	Nat'l. Civil Rights Museum at the Lorraine Motel			X				
Birmingham	Birmingham Civil Rights Institute		X					
Birmingham	Sixteen Street Baptist Church	X	X					
Key:	X = Closed on these days; AO = Appointment Only on these days							
Note:	Closed on days of the week do change; check websites for any changes.							

Where Should I Begin the Trip?

This may seem like a no-brainer. Why not select the starting point that is the shortest point from your home city? That may, in fact, be the best choice. However, consider this choice as you try to avoid two possibilities:

- Ending up in a city on a day of the week when a place of interest is closed
- Having a long drive home on the last day of your tour

The easiest way to illustrate these points is with some real-world examples. Let's start with someone living in the Nashville, Tennessee, area who planned on setting out from home on a Monday with the goal of beginning their touring on the following day. Departing the Nashville area, both Memphis and Birmingham are about three hours away. Does it matter where this person starts touring?

Alarm bells should go off every time "Tuesday" and "Memphis" come up together. As noted earlier, the National Civil Rights Museum at the Lorraine Motel is closed on Tuesday so starting on Tuesday in Memphis would likely lead to disappointment. Birmingham is the smarter choice in this case.

In that example, both starting cities were about the same distance from the person's home. Would it ever be smarter to begin your tour in a city that's a longer drive from home? It could if it allows you to keep important civil rights locations on your itinerary.

Suppose someone was leaving from the west coast of Florida, say Tampa. The two closest starting points are Atlanta and Montgomery. However, Montgomery is an hour farther from Tampa than Atlanta is (seven and a half versus six and a half hours). Let's assume both drives are too time consuming to allow much touring time on the day of arrival. Thus, the following day will be the first day of this traveler's tour.

Does it matter which city is chosen for Day 1 of the loop tour? It could. Montgomery can be tricky given that two key sites associated with Dr. King are closed on Sunday and Monday. This may mean that the longer drive to Montgomery is a better choice, again depending on what day you plan to begin visiting sites. A decision for the longer drive to Montgomery to begin touring would be smart if you leave Tampa on Friday and you had decided that two days in Montgomery were sufficient. Leaving for Montgomery on Friday makes Saturday and Sunday your two touring days there. That will avoid possible disappointment from missing some must-see places in Montgomery:

- By being in Montgomery for two days and arriving to tour on Saturday and Sunday, you can try to book a tour the inside of Dr. King's Dexter Avenue Baptist Church and the parsonage on Saturday.
- If you drove to Atlanta first, toured there on Saturday and toured Montgomery on Sunday and Monday, you would miss

those two Dexter Avenue Baptist Church sites. Both are closed on the two days you are in the city.

As such, the longer drive to Montgomery to start the tour is the smarter choice here.

A longer drive on the front end has another benefit. It means a shorter drive home when your final full day of touring is done, likely a welcome outcome after a lengthy trip.

Takeaway: Think about what's closed and the drive home when deciding where to begin your tour.

Build a Basic Template of Your Trip

It's time to start working with some of the decisions made so far. This template is simple, focusing solely on the where and when aspects of the journey, and this step won't take long. Chapter 5's detailed day-by-day template builds on the bare bones one suggested here and takes more time to complete.

The basic template to build at this stage relies on decisions you have already made:

- How many days are allotted for the trip?
- What day of the week will my touring begin?
- What city will lead off my touring, and what cities will I visit?

This doesn't have to be fancy. Just note these decisions in an organized way on a piece of paper. If you want to do an electronic spreadsheet, knock yourself out. However, right now you just need three columns reflecting the items above.

Let's use the schedule of that person from Nashville who was leaving home on Monday to begin site visits on Tuesday. Let's call her Nadine. Recall that one of her must-see locations in Memphis is the National Civil Rights Museum and it is closed on Tuesday. Nadine opted to start in Birmingham. She also decided on the thirteen-day tour as recommended in the book.

Her trip's basic layout would look like this:

Day #	Day of Week	City
1	Tuesday	Birmingham
2	Wednesday	Anniston
3	Thursday	Atlanta
4	Friday	Montgomery
5	Saturday	Montgomery
6	Sunday	Montgomery
7	Monday	Selma
8	Tuesday	Philadelphia
9	Wednesday	Jackson
10	Thursday	Jackson
11	Friday	Mississippi Delta
12	Saturday	Little Rock
13	Sunday	Memphis

Check the "Closed-On" Dates

With the basic schematic of your trip in place, check the closed-on-days reference presented in this chapter. Are the sites you want to visit open on the day you are in town? It will be a lot easier to juggle things at this stage than after you make reservations for lodging and at appointment-only destinations. Remember that appointment-only destinations are not listed on the closed-on chart. Theoretically, they could be closed any day of the week, so make calls to the appointment-only spots important to you before getting locked in on a schedule.

In general, pay close attention to where you plan to be on Sunday and Monday. Those days have the most closed museums, churches, and NPS sites. Wednesdays through Fridays tend to have the fewest closures.

Tuesdays can be tricky if your draft schedule has you in Memphis or Montgomery. Two major Montgomery destinations, the Legacy Museum and the National Memorial for Peace and Justice, respectively, are closed on Tuesday. However, the book recommends three days in Montgomery so this shouldn't pose a problem unless you limit your trip to a single day in Montgomery and it happens to be Tuesday.

In some cities, you have nothing to worry about on any day of the week. The NPS sites in Atlanta and Little Rock are open every day. In the case of Philadelphia, Mississippi, there are no museums. In these three locales, any day is a good day to visit.

On the other hand, pay closer attention when you visit Montgomery, Jackson, and Birmingham. The chapter on Montgomery suggests structuring your three days here to be able to see all the recommended locations and at least one NPS facility in nearby Tuskegee. Because two major sites in Birmingham and one in Jackson are closed on Monday, these two cities can be an issue if you are there on a Monday. However, the issues are solvable:

- Solve the Monday problem in Jackson by devoting a second day (or part of a second day) here, as recommended in the book.
- Solve the Monday problem in Birmingham by visiting Anniston (an hour away) on Monday and coming back to Birmingham on Tuesday.

Considering where you plan to be each day against closed-on days before you travel helps avoid disappointment during your travels. Be sure to also note the hours of operation; some sites may not open as early on weekends as they do on weekdays.

Note: the pandemic played havoc with the operations at the sites covered in this book. Some museums and other facilities cut back on days and/or hours opened; others closed all together. All museums contacted expressed their intent to return to the normal operating schedule presented here in 2022. That said, check with any site you plan to visit to make certain that conditions have not forced them to alter their options for visitors.

Build a Detailed Plan For the Trip

Now you need to put some specifics down to build out your plan day by day. You know where you want to be on each day of the journey. Now it is time to fill in what places you want to visit each day and where you want to stay each night. If you already have a way of planning multistop driving trips, terrific: use it. If you don't, one is suggested in the next chapter.

Everyone's travel style isn't the same. Some travelers aren't bothered by hour after hour in an outstanding museum; others have legs that scream *no más* after two hours. Driving tolerance is another point of difference. Some drivers aren't bothered a whit by two to three hours of driving after a long day of sightseeing; others would balk at that, especially if it meant driving after the sun goes down.

Respecting these differences, the book does not lay out an ideal trip in detail, yet the next chapter offers a template to use in building your detailed plan, one that fits your personal travel style.

Make Reservations

Once your trip layout has been reviewed against the closed-on days, it's time to make some reservations. The two kinds of reservations to take care of before your departure are reservations at certain civil rights locations that require appointments or where advanced ticketing is recommended and lodging reservations. Handle booking at the civil rights sites first. You might learn of a closing that causes an adjustment to the basic template.

Civil Rights Locations

Most locations covered in the book do not require a reservation for individual travelers. This is true of most large museums and NPS sites. One exception would be if you wanted to be part of a special tour offered at one of these sites, like the ranger-led tours at the NPS site in Little Rock.

Many museums request advance reservations for large groups. The Rosa Parks Museum in Montgomery requires reservations for groups of twenty or more seeking a guided tour. Even if prior notice is not required for groups, a phone call ahead of time is still smart for no other reason than for advice on where to park the tour bus.

While most large museums are fine with solo travelers or small groups of visitors simply showing up, one major museum likely high on your must-see list asks visitors to have a timed entry ticket: the Legacy Museum in Montgomery. The National Museum of African American History and Culture also has a timed entry ticket policy. Some historical churches and homes require a prior appointment to take a tour or see the inside. In addition, medium-sized or smaller museums or interpretive centers have limited hours but are available by appointment outside of normal operating hours if you call—as is the case, for example, with the Emmett Till Interpretive Center in Sumner, Mississippi.

While you can always stop at an appointment-only place and see if they will accommodate you, don't take this chance. Some of the best experiences you will have on this trip are the small group tours led by passionate and knowledgeable docents at places requiring an appointment. For these homes or churches, it is always possible to stop by to see the place from the outside. Often there are markers or other information boards to tell you the story behind the location, but an informed and engaged docent does a much better job than a physical marker.

The book notes which locations require or permit booking in advance as well as information on how to arrange it. Make reservations at your highest-priority appointment-only locations as soon as your preliminary trip plan is done.

Lodging

The book doesn't make any lodging recommendations, viewing this as a matter of personal preference. However, where you exercise that personal preference—in the city or on the highway—may impact how far you must drive the next day.

As you read the book and especially as you build a more detailed plan, you will note the range of driving distances between cities you are likely going to visit. Depending on how late you tour in one city before heading to where you will spend the next day, it might be smart to stay just outside the city or even between cities to avoid an arrival time at in-city lodging that you see as too late.

My own experience in developing our plan anticipated a long, one-day stop in Memphis. The next stop was Birmingham, at least three and a half hours away and possibly a lot worse around a 6 p.m. Memphis rush-hour traffic departure time (it was!)—so staying close to Birmingham but not in Birmingham turned out to be a good call. These kinds of issues become clearer to you if you build a detailed spreadsheet as recommended in chapter 5. Decisions made as you plan can make for a less stressful, more productive trip.

The takeaway: With a basic schematic of your trip done, you know where you will end up each evening. With those dates in hand and booked appointments where required, you can explore specific lodging possibilities. If you feel your plan is solid, make lodging reservations at specific properties. Often you can save a few dollars by booking a noncancellable room; that's not recommended if your plan is still coming together.

Request Tourism Information

The last item on the well-in-advance checklist is to seek out information on the places you will visit. State and local tourism bureaus offer free visitor guides, maps, and sometimes themed brochures on dining, lodging, attractions, events, or outdoor activities. In some cases, the themed brochures cover history and, to varying degrees, civil rights.

Much of this information is also available online and often can be downloaded or printed out. One other step to consider when you visit the tourism websites is to put yourself on their email lists. That way, you can stay current on what is going on in each city and tuned into what is happening at the time of your visit. You can always unsubscribe to these lists after your trip is over.

There is also a national consortium of civil rights locations, the United States Civil Rights Trail. Its own website provides the address and website information of its members. You would still have to do a lot of work to pull together your civil rights journey using the Civil Rights Trail website alone. This book makes structuring your plan much easier.

Planning Checklist: Within Two Months of Departure

- √ **Learn to use GPS software**
- √ **Download relevant audio**
- √ **Download relevant apps**
- √ **Organize trip elements**
- √ **Revisit key websites**
- √ **Prepare intellectually**

Trip Planning: Within Two Months of Departure

The hardest trip-planning work is done. Your route is finished, your day plans are done once you construct your detailed daily itinerary, reservations have been made at civil rights sites where appointments are necessary, and your lodging along the way is set.

Besides doing the normal things travelers do prior to heading out on a two-week car trip (stopping the mail and other deliveries; arranging for someone to care for your pets, plants, etc., automobile preps; and alerting friends and family to your itinerary), what else is there to do within two months of departure?

I'd recommend the six items on this second planning checklist.

Learn to Use Google Maps or Other GPS Software

You cannot make this trip efficiently without access to and familiarity with GPS. There's no prize for proving that statement wrong. Sure, there is a lot of interstate driving and maybe a paper map can help there. However, when you drive some of the two-lane state highways, you will be glad that GPS help is available. Further, when you choose to walk from one historic location to a nearby memorial marker in small cities like Selma or big municipalities like Atlanta and are unsure about whether you are supposed to turn left or right, you will be glad you have GPS software in your pocket.

The GPS package referenced in this book is Google Maps, the most widely used GPS app. It is free and works on both Android and iOS phones. Put the Google Maps app on your phone and learn how to use it before setting out on the trip.

Like any app connected to your mobile phone data plan, Google Maps cuts into your data limit when used online. Those with data plan caps may want to save a map via Google Maps for use offline. If you don't want to eat up precious megabytes, learn how to save maps via the app, which gives you access to a map of a city or part of a city as you tour.

These saved map downloads, however, use storage space on your phone. You may decide to download maps for the first day or two of your trip before you go, then delete those and add cities as you travel. There are many online tutorials about Google Maps and saving maps for later use. Check the Google website and YouTube.

Download Relevant Audio: Inspirational Music, Topical Podcasts, Famous Civil Rights Speeches

Have I mentioned that this will be long trip? Sorry to keep hammering that, but as you prepare, think about how you will fill time on the road. One way, of course, is to listen to speeches, music, and podcasts that relate back to the freedom movement.

Spotify, Pandora, Amazon Music, Apple Music, and other music streaming services have relevant civil rights–era playlists. Bring music that you find inspirational for a trip like this.

You will spend time in places with a lot of noise. Music and speeches on your mobile device and a good set of headphones or earbuds will come in handy at several points during your trip when you want to tune out the world. You will understand this advice better when you deal with noisy traffic as you walk across the Edmund Pettus Bridge in Selma.

Search for podcasts on the civil rights movement generally or on specific events. One example is the NPR true-crime podcast *White Lies*; it focuses on the murder of the Reverend James Reeb in Selma in 1965 and how the killers never paid for their crime. The Equal Justice Initiative (EJI) has a series of short podcasts on lynching victims and is a relevant listening experience prior to visiting the EJI facilities in Montgomery. Also recommended is *Seizing Freedom* hosted by Dr. Kidada Williams, or the *1619* podcast from the *New York Times* project by the same name.

Download Relevant Civil Rights-Related Tourism Apps

The states of Alabama and Arkansas and the city of Memphis have civil rights tourism apps. The National Civil Rights Museum in Memphis has an app that gives you a glimpse at their permanent exhibits, upcoming events, and the campus. The National Museum of African American History and Culture in the nation's capital also has an excellent app.

The Emmett Till Memory Project provides touring locations in both the Mississippi Delta and Chicago, the murdered teenager's home city and burial place. Georgia has an app presenting its historical markers. Apps come and go all the time. Search "civil rights" or "historical markers" where you find your apps to locate new ones. Other relevant apps not mentioned here are covered elsewhere in the book.

Organize Your Lodging Reservations

I had never booked so many different nights in so many different places in a two-week time frame. I found it helpful to have all the confirmation emails in one place, like an inbox subfolder. Print them all out beforehand if that's your thing, because you won't have easy access to a printer on the road. Add lodging specifics to the detailed planning template.

Doing this will be a good check that you have a confirmed reservation at every planned stop. Note the "cancel by" time and day for each in case unexpected delays (e.g., road closures, bad weather, or illness) cause you to have to adjust where you will stay on a given night. Keep your final template with everything in one place handy as you travel.

Revisit the Websites of the Places You Plan to Visit

This late check can both avoid disappointment and open up possible opportunities. On the downside, look for any changes in hours of operation that could alter your schedule. A museum could be hosting a special event, for example, that could move up their closing time. One check I did revealed that road work near one museum altered where visitors could park.

On the more positive side of a close-to-departure website check, you may find that a special exhibit will be open, or a lecture or special tour is available when you are visiting. Perhaps you will want to spend more time there than originally planned. Check if any extra fees are associated with the special events.

Also recommended is a call to confirm your reserved time and date at the appointment-only locations. Do this a day or two before the appointment as you travel from one place to the next. It is possible that something at the location has come up and an adjustment is needed in your visit's timing. Naturally, if it is *your* plan that has changed, please share that right away with the location. Many of the appointment-only destinations have modest staffs or rely on volunteers or both. Early notice of your change is always appreciated.

Prepare Yourself and Fellow Travelers Intellectually for the Trip

Do some reading on the people and events you will learn about along the way. Many excellent books on our civil rights history are available, and some of these authors are quoted throughout this text. The notes at the end of the book point you to many titles that will shed more insight on the people and events that made history.

If you are traveling in a group of any size, consider splitting up various civil rights topics across the group. Have one member of your traveling troupe do some reading on the Selma-to-Montgomery March, have another go to school on the Little Rock Nine, while another talks about the contributions of Rev. Fred Shuttlesworth from Birmingham, and so on. Perhaps on the long rides between cities, these docents on the bus could share what they learned about specific people and events that shaped the civil rights era.

Don't leave children or teens out of this idea. Use the resources found in Chapter 6 to select a few books for a young person to read. Have them give their fellow travelers a report on that person or event. It is a terrific way to engage them in a relevant topic and the trip in general.

A final thought: Realize going into this important journey that you are going to see example after example, day after day, of hatred, injustice, and brutality. It will take an emotional toll. Try your best to be prepared for that, too—but you will likely come up short. So take care of everything else that seems in your control in preparing for this journey into our civil rights history.

CHAPTER 5

Planning Your Trip: The Details

The planning checklists offered in the previous chapter present over a dozen items to do or think about before your journey to explore our civil rights history. One of the items on the to-do list two or more months out from departing is to build a day-by-day plan.

Whether you use the approach presented here or your own system for organizing a multicity driving trip with discovery experiences at each stop, think about your travel style or the travel style of the group traveling with you as you fill in how you will spend each day.

What is "travel style" anyway? In this case, it's how *you* like to do a road trip. If you are planning this trip for a group, think of the style that most of the group will be satisfied with and tolerate. In many respects, planning for a church group or group of coworkers taking a civil rights journey together is more challenging because you may have a wide range of tolerance levels on things like time spent in museums or what hour you check into your overnight stays.

Some questions to ask yourself and discuss with those you'll be doing this trip with are as follows:

- How much driving can you take in a typical day?
- Are you an up-and-out-early road warrior, or do you take a more leisurely approach to getting on the road in the morning?
- What type of lodging do you prefer? Five-star properties with lots of services? Chain motels? Local bed and breakfasts?
- Do you like to stay right in the heart of a city, or are close-to-the-highway options acceptable?

- What kind of places are must-sees? Major museums? Restored or preserved historical places? Markers where meaningful events occurred?
- Are there non–civil rights activities beyond eating and sleeping that you want to build into your schedule?

The answers to these questions help you plan the kind of itinerary that aligns with your driving tolerance, get you to the types of places that are of the highest interest to you, land you in accommodations that make you and your budget comfortable, and provide, if desired, some diversions from the day-after-day deep dive into America's civil rights history.

Some elements from this list are likely already baked into your own travel style. If you are used to staying at five-star hotels or at quaint B and Bs, you can find them on this trip. Major hotel/motel chains off a wide range of lodging properties. Your frequent-guest program account will certainly benefit from all the nights you spend on the road. No matter where you like to stay (in town versus on the highway), your preference should have no problem being accommodated.

Other travel-style issues are somewhat unique to an extended driving trip. Think through these items before setting a specific day-by-day plan:

- *Your typical driving tolerance:* Can it expand a bit for this trip to allow more time for visiting places of interest?
- *Your site-specific preferences across possible civil rights locations:* How long will your legs hold up in a museum? How far out of the way will you drive to see an historical marker?
- *If applicable, your desire to build non–civil rights activities into some of the days of your trip:* Can you forgo these diversions to keep the focus on the purpose of the trip?

Driving Tolerance Considerations

In our detailed trip plan, there were roughly fifteen hundred miles of total city-to-city travel, not including intracity driving nor instances of getting lost trying to find places not on Google Maps (remember, I didn't have this book). While some days had little or no driving, most included a significant number of miles. I was lucky to have a willing partner to share the driving. Having a second driver affects driving tolerance considerations.

Depending on the season, you are likely to have a mix of daytime and nighttime driving. If you don't like driving after sunset, do this trip in late spring or summer. Even then, unless you plan accordingly, some of your driving will be after dark. If you don't like night driving, construct your detailed itinerary (where you stay, when you stop touring, etc.) to avoid or minimize being on the road after sunset.

Let's talk about leaving your lodging in the morning and getting to your next destination in the evening. These choices affect driving demands and how much touring you can squeeze into a day.

True confession time: Before this trip, my wife and I would typically take a leisurely approach to clearing out of a hotel in the morning. We changed this aspect of our travel style for the civil rights trip. If our first stop was a museum that opened at 10 a.m., we would try to be there as close to that time as possible. When we visited Little Rock, we booked the 9 a.m. NPS ranger tour so that we would have more time for other touring that day.

Consider modifying some aspects of your usual travel style for this trip to maximize your time at sites of interest.

Touring Preferences

Each day presents no shortage of places to visit. Unless you spend very little time experiencing the location options presented, there are more of them than you could possibly see in the recommended time in each city. You will have to make some choices. Consider your priorities for each city:

- How do you view the role of the major museums on your trip? Are they as important to you toward the end of the trip as they were at the beginning? Can the time needed to tour a museum at the end of trip be reduced to fit more touring time elsewhere in that city?
- Would you prefer single-subject NPS sites, like the one in Little Rock, or interpretive centers, like the one at the Emmett Till murder trial site in Sumner, Mississippi?

- How do you rank in importance locations where historical events occurred or where civil rights icons lived that (a) look like they did decades ago, (b) are only memorialized by an historical marker, or (c) are not even memorialized with a marker?
- How far out of your way would you drive to see any of the three types of actual historic locations just mentioned? Said another way, would you drive twenty minutes outside of Philadelphia, Mississippi, to see the unmarked spot where the FBI found the burned-out station wagon of three murdered civil rights workers? Or would you make that twenty-minute drive to lay some flowers there?
- Whose gravesites would you want to visit? Or what about a distant, though important, church?

To help you plan, the book not only shares a diverse array of potential locations to visit but also relates the history associated with each person or place. Use these brief stories to design the journey to most benefit your interests. All the individual stories are woven into the tapestry of the long struggle for freedom. Shedding light on the historical relevance of each person or place is intended to help you finalize your itinerary.

Think of your typical touring day—10 a.m. to 6 p.m. for visiting places of interest—as your canvas. Paint your own masterpiece each day, filling up those eight hours with experiences that will best satisfy your interests and travel style.

For the major museums and other sites on the loop tour, I offer guidance on how much time to allot to each. You may rebel at the longer time recommendations at some places. If your legs turn to rubber (or cement) at the two-hour mark in a museum and the book recommends four hours, listen to your legs. Everyone's tolerance for standing and reading museum content boards differs.

Diversions

You go into this trip knowing how many miles you will be on the road and how many hours you will be on your feet. There is no way around it: this trip is physically demanding.

What you may not expect going into it is how emotionally draining it may be. Ugliness, hatred, and criminal behavior are part of our civil rights history in city after city. You will confront it day after day.

You may want to plan activities into the trip that temporarily take you away from the primary content. Obviously, if planned after your day of touring ends, these diversions will not cut into the main reason you have set out on this trip. This can be as simple as looking for a park to walk through near your hotel or going to a local movie theater. Consider some diversions that are locally distinctive to get you off your feet: a blues music venue, a Minor League Baseball game or other in-season sports event, a meal out at a local favorite haunt. If you are a fan of biking, many off-road trails run in and between the cities on your route. That was our diversion.

The major cities on your trip have other attractions, of course, besides those relating to civil rights. If you feel you need a day off at some point during your journey, build it into the plan and explore your options in the city where you plan to take time off. Tourist information bureaus can offer lots of ideas.

Construct a Detailed Itinerary

At this point, you know your trip's length and the cities you will visit, making sure you checked whether any sites will be closed when you will be in town. You have called your high-priority appointment-only locations to lock in reservations. You have thought about how you like to travel and your lodging preferences. Importantly, you have thought about how you view different types of civil rights experiences—from a quick stop-click-and-go visit at a roadside memorial marker to multihour visits at the top civil rights museums.

Let's now get specific about each day.

The basic three-column template introduced in chapter 4 serves as the foundation for this detailed plan. At this stage, focus on civil rights touring unless other activities will consume an entire day. You will revisit the plan again as you refine and finalize the details. Think of this as a first draft of your trip. You will certainly return to this plan as you make lodging reservations; then you can be more exact about your daily driving miles.

To that basic template with three columns, add a dozen more columns. Do this on a wide piece of paper or, better yet at this stage, on an electronic spreadsheet. Later, you may choose to add more columns with lodging specifics, contact names and numbers, or other notes. A spreadsheet makes it easy to make changes and add information.

Remember Nadine from Nashville from chapter 4? She was trying to figure out where Day 1 of her trip would be, deciding to begin her trip in Birmingham, as you'll recall. Let's illustrate how to construct a detailed template by doing that for the initial days of Nadine's loop trip.

Before explaining the new columns that are shown in a suggested expansion of the basic template, let's remember the three columns on the basic template: "Day Number," "Day of the Week," and "City Visited." To build a sample template for Nadine, we add these twelve columns:

- *Date:* Putting the specific dates you will be in which cities helps when you begin to make reservations or explore activities you might do after a day of touring.
- *Starting Point Today:* This is not where you will tour today but rather where your day begins. For our Nashville-based tourist, Nadine, Day 1 would start from her home, not in a Birmingham hotel. That makes a difference on how many miles need to be driven to start touring in Birmingham and for the total driving time on Day 1.
- *Start Time Today:* The time you will leave your starting point on a given day, not the time when you begin to visit museums and the like.
- *End Point Today:* This is where you will end the day and stay the night. For your first draft, you can use your destination city for your next day of touring. However, when you know where you will stay overnight, you can use the precise location of that lodging spot for a more accurate read of the driving required. Eventually, when you have this information, update your plan.
- *Stops Today:* This is a list of the specific places you want to see in each city. Add as many lines as you need to fit your ideal list;

you can always trim it back. Leave the top line in this column blank and fill in the lines below the empty first line. So, except for the very first line in the "City Visited Today" column, list all the planned stops for the day in the "Stops Today" column.

- *Driving Miles:* This estimate should be the total highway miles between today's starting point and the end point after making sure you route *through the city* you plan to visit. You don't have to include the miles you will drive *within the city* you will visit that day. Google Maps easily calculates your highway driving miles from a starting point to an intermediate stop (a destination city) to an end point (the night's lodging location). An upcoming example explains this further.
- *Time Needed for Four Trip Components and in Total:* Highway Driving, In-City Driving/Walking, Stops, Meals (and other non–civil rights stops), and the total of these four components. Here's a description of each one:
  - *Total Highway Driving Time*—the number of highway miles from the column to the left converted to time. Google Maps provides this time-required estimate too.
  - *In-City Driving Time:* This is the travel time needed between places you plan to visit within the city visited today. Incorporate walking time into the entry in this column too, unless you incorporate it into visiting a specific site like we do in our upcoming example with a visit to Kelly Ingram Park.
  - *Time for Civil Rights–Related Stops:* This is an estimate of the time at each place on your visitation list for the day. How long will you stay at that museum? How long will you spend at that historic park or neighborhood?
  - *Meals (and Other Non-Civil Rights Stops):* Limit this time entry to those activities that will cut into your touring day. In other words, if you have breakfast at the hotel before departing the hotel, don't count it; if you like having breakfast on the road, add it. If you take in a Minor League Baseball game after you arrive at your

lodging, don't count it. You don't need to add in time spent after you arrive at your final destination for the day.

    - *Total:* This is simply the sum of the other four columns. A spreadsheet like Excel can do this for you easily and accurately.

- *Arrive at Destination:* You should add the "Total" of the four "Time Needed For" columns to your "Starting Time Today" to calculate this field. (Again, Excel-type software does this for you.) Don't simply put in when you would like to arrive at the next lodging stop. Have your entries calculate when you will reach that stop. You may have gone past your wished-for arrival time and need to adjust your plan.

Let's fill in the first two days of Nadine's trip to illustrate this approach.

Nadine wants to begin her tour on Tuesday, so she opts to have her first stop be Birmingham instead of Memphis. Both cities are a three-hour drive from her home, but if she went to Memphis first, she would find the National Civil Rights Museum at the Lorraine Motel closed (but you already know that).

Because of her proximity to Birmingham, Nadine decides to leave Nashville Tuesday around 8 a.m. Here's her wish list and time estimates for the day:

- Drive directly to the Birmingham Civil Rights Institute (BCRI). Spend three hours there.

- She made an appointment at 2 p.m. for a Sixteenth Street Baptist Church tour; she reserves an hour for that.

- Walk Kelly Ingram Park and the area near the former Gaston Motel; allot an hour for that walk.

- Drive to the markers at the Birmingham jail where Dr. King wrote his famous 1963 letter and at Historic Bethel Baptist Church where Rev. Fred Shuttlesworth was pastor.

- Rather than stay in Birmingham, she opts to head to a hotel in Anniston after her touring in Birmingham. Her goal is to check in by 6:30 p.m. and rest up for her tour of Anniston on Wednesday.

Nadine begins to enter her wish list onto a spreadsheet to see how well it fits together. She notes the 8 a.m. departure from home and, using Google Maps, learns that from her home in Nashville to Birmingham to Anniston is 260 miles and four hours of driving.

Once she pulls into the parking lot at the BCRI, she won't need the car for the next five hours. However, to visit the Birmingham jail and Historic Bethel Baptist Church means about ten miles of driving. She estimates thirty minutes total in-city driving. Nadine enters that next on the Historic Bethel Baptist Church line and brings the half-hour figure up to the top line with other totals. At the church and the jail markers, Nadine estimates fifteen-minute visits for each.

All that gets entered into her spreadsheet:

- Four hours of highway driving: Nashville to Anniston with an intermediate stop in Birmingham
- A half hour of in-city driving within Birmingham to see the jail and the church
- Five and a half hours total at the five listed Birmingham stops
- An hour carved out for meals
- Total time needed from departure from Nashville to arrival at an Anniston hotel: eleven hours

Given her planned departure from home at 8 a.m. plus the eleven total hours from her listed itinerary, Nadine can see that she would be at her lodging near Anniston (still to be found and reserved) by 7 p.m. That's a little later than her ideal check-in time of 6:30 p.m. However, knowing she is bedding down right near where she needs to be the next morning and only about an hour and a half from Atlanta (albeit in a different time zone), she is fine with this approach.

Her first day of thirteen is planned:

Day #	Day of Week	Date	City Visted Today	Starting Point Today	Start Time Today	End Point Today	Planned Visits Today	H'way Driving Miles	Time Needed for: H'way Driving	In-City Driving + Walks	Stops + Visits	Meals Etc.	**Total Time Today**	Estimated Arrival at Overnight Destination
1	Tues.	6/1	Birmingham	Nashville	8:00 AM	Anniston		260	4:00	0:30	5:30	1:00	11:00	7:00 PM
							Birm. Civil Rights Institute				3:00			
							Sixteen Street Baptist				1:00			
							Kelly Ingram Park				1:00			
							Birmingham Jail Marker				0:15			
							Historic Bethel Baptist	10		0:30	0:15			

Laying your trip out like this takes time, but it helps immensely in avoiding surprises and disappointment on this consequential trip. Not only will you know what you are facing each day in terms of time behind the wheel, but you will know whether everything you want to see fits into whatever time block you find acceptable for sightseeing and discovery.

You also can use this approach to set yourself up well for subsequent days. Let's set up Day 2 for Nadine as an illustration.

After reading this book, Nadine knows that most of what she is interested in seeing in Anniston is in the heart of the city and walkable. However, a few locations are best reached by car, and she includes them on her Day 2 schedule.

Her time in Anniston falls as follows:

- Park near the NPS site at the Greyhound station where the Freedom Riders' bus was attacked. After that visit, walk to three other nearby locations. While the walk itself only takes about fifteen minutes, Nadine allots ninety minutes to walk to and visit all four places. She enters that hour and a half in the Stops column.
- Drive to four other Anniston locations, spending ten minutes at each, including the site of the future Freedom Riders Park. (Once that park is completed, visitors will need more than ten minutes here.) Nadine estimates thirty minutes of in-city driving.
- After filling in her spreadsheet with the Anniston sites, an hour for meals, and allotting for the ninety-one-mile and two-and-a-half-hour drive to Atlanta (including the hour lost to the time zone change), Nadine notices it will be early enough in Atlanta to do some touring on the same day she visits Anniston.
- So, on the evening of Day 2, Nadine blocks out two hours to walk around the civil rights–related places at the Atlanta University Complex (Spelman, Morehouse, Clark-Atlanta), padding a bit to accommodate getting to her hotel. Even with that time added plus the extra hour for moving from Central Time to Eastern Time, it looks like Nadine would be checking into her lodging for the night around 6 p.m.

Day #	Day of Week	Date	City Visted Today	Starting Point Today	Start Time Today	End Point Today	Planned Visits Today	H'way Driving Miles	Time Needed for:					Estimated Arrival at Overnight Destination
									H'way Driving	In-City Driving + Walks	Stops + Visits	Meals Etc.	**Total Time Today**	
1	Tues.	6/1	Birmingham	Nashville	8:00 AM	Anniston		260	4:00	0:30	5:30	1:00	11:00	7:00 PM
							Birm. Civil Rights Institute				3:00			
							Sixteen Street Baptist				1:00			
							Kelly Ingram Park				1:00			
							Birmingham Jail Marker				0:15			
							Historic Bethel Baptist	10		0:30	0:15			
2	Wed.	6/2	Anniston	Anniston	10:00 AM	Atlanta		91	2:30	0:30	4:10	1:00	8:10	6:10 PM
			Time Zone	Central to Eastern			Add 1 hour to drive time							
							Walk to:				1:30			
							*Former Greyhound Stn.							
							*Former Trailways Stn.							
							*Public Library Marker							
							*Willie Brewster Site							
							Drive to:	10		0:30				
							*Hospital Marker				0:10			
							*Southern Railways				0:10			
							*Freedom Riders Park				0:10			
							*Hwy. 202 Marker				0:10			
			Atlanta				Atlanta Univ. Complex				2:00			

Because Nadine has planned well, using the evening time to walk the campuses where so many historic African American figures studied and worked, she has opened up more touring time for the third day of her trip in Atlanta. She can do more on the one full day recommended for Georgia's capital city.

Some of the places in the example above may not be familiar to you yet. Every one of them is explained in later chapters. After you read the book, you can make your decisions like Nadine made hers. As you go through the process, your daily schedule unfolds.

The point of completing the first draft of a planning template is to make you aware of how all the pieces of a trip like this fit together. Completing the detailed template, and revising it as hotel reservations and any changes are made, gives you a chance to understand and refine your plan before you hit Freedom's Road.

CHAPTER 6

Preparing Children and Teens for the Trip

Earlier chapters discussed the importance of advance preparations for a successful civil rights trip across the South: planning each day's itinerary, making appointments where required, reserving lodging, and more. For an even more rewarding experience, prepare yourself by learning more about the people and events that sustained the freedom movement. Many books, videos, apps, and podcasts can help adults do this; many have been referenced throughout the book.

This chapter is about preparing children and teens for this trip, or even a one-day visit to a local museum. In either case, they need to be prepared beforehand about the harsh realities of the civil rights movement they will see.

Toward that goal, this chapter shares a range of resources to assist parents and others tasked with explaining the difficult aspects of the civil rights era to nonadults. Preparing them for the violence and other disturbing behavior they may see is also important.

The sampling of resources presented here is not a comprehensive guide but rather a helpful starting point. The variety of resources—museum-produced content, videos, books, and so on—should take your children beyond what they may be exposed to at school around Martin Luther King Jr. Day or even Black History Month. Your local library or museum as well as your child's school may also be helpful in this regard.

Talking to Children about Civil Rights

Getting a child or a teenager ready to join you on this journey takes more than sitting them down to watch a video or reading a book with them. Talk to them. Listen to them. Think of the concepts that were central to the drive for freedom. Let those central concepts drive your conversations. Talk to youngsters on a level they can understand.

Two core concepts can serve as an initial focal point of your chats: fairness and courage. Children understand the difference between fairness and unfairness. When someone won't share a toy with them, they don't think that's fair. When their older siblings stay up later than they do, they may complain to their parents that this is unfair. As trivial as those examples are, they provide a jumping-off point that a child can relate to from their own experiences.

Use their perceptions of what is unfair to them to connect to the issues central to the struggle for equality and fairness. Was it fair for Black children to be forced to go to schools that did not have the same resources as the schools white kids attended? Was it fair that Black people could not ride in any empty seat on a city bus or stay overnight at any hotel they could afford when they traveled?

Children also understand courage. They relate to and respect bravery. You know this if you've ever watched a superhero cartoon program or a Disney movie with your kids. Parents often tell their own children how brave they are. It could be for something as simple as going down a slide by themselves for the first time, or for older kids, sticking up for a friend who was being bullied.

Courage abounds across many events during the civil rights era, and they can serve as a platform for discussing the courage of activists of all ages. For younger children, it can be the bravery of young Ruby Bridges entering first grade at an all-white school in New Orleans in 1960. For teens, the actions of high school students in Little Rock in 1957 or during the Birmingham Campaign of 1963 provide impactful examples of courage. You won't lack for true-life examples of young people's courage during the civil rights era.

Whichever stories fit the ages of your young travelers, also look online for images that help your discussion. Let them see such heroic freedom fighters as

- Tiny Ruby Bridges walking with US marshals as she attended William Frantz Elementary School in New Orleans.

- Elizabeth Eckford heading to her first day at Little Rock Central High School surrounded by angry white students. 
- Young people braving snarling German shepherds and high-pressure fire hoses in Birmingham.
- Fifteen-year-old flag bearer Lewis Marshall marching from Selma to Montgomery and subsequently appearing on a 2005 stamp commemorating the Voting Rights Act of 1965.

Part of the preparation process for youngsters is, of course, discussing sensitive topics with them before they might be exposed to pictures and video in some museums. However, another aspect of preparation is to heighten a young person's anticipation of the trip and the places they will visit.

In a figurative sense, books can transport young visitors to places they will then see firsthand. Reading a book about Dr. King provides a terrific opportunity to let a child know what they will see at the Auburn Avenue house in which Dr. King grew up. A book on Rosa Parks can build anticipation for sitting on the same kind of bus that Mrs. Parks rode in when she refused to give up her seat. Giving children a preview in age-appropriate books of the people and places of the civil rights era would hopefully create not only the eagerness to go on this trip but also to learn more about the people and events they will encounter along the way.

Resources for Parents

Museum-Produced Content

Logical places to seek advice about preparing children and teens for this trip are the museums that you and they will likely visit. Four major museums in Memphis, Birmingham, Montgomery, and Jackson have content on their websites geared to educating youngsters before they arrive.

Beyond these four museums, others also take steps to help young visitors. For example, the Rosa Parks Museum in Montgomery has a Children's Wing as well as more simplified content for children in the main museum presented at their eye level. Check the websites of all museums—large and small—for appropriate information and guidance for nonadult visitors.

The National Park Service (NPS) locations often have content designed for young visitors. The *Children of Courage* exhibit in the NPS's Martin Luther King Jr. National Historical Park tells the story of the children of the movement. Ask the rangers for guidance on where you might find appropriate content for younger travelers in their facility.

Here's a peek at what can be found on the websites of four major museums.

National Civil Rights Museum at the Lorraine Motel (NCRM), Memphis

The museum offers a terrific eight-page full-color Family Guide on its website *https://www.civilrightsmuseum.org/visit*. It can be found toward the bottom of the Visit section. The guide outlines specific content in any of the museum's galleries that may be too violent or otherwise disturbing for some visitors. Parents can navigate around such material if they wish. In addition, advice is offered in having discussions with young visitors on topics like slavery, societal violence, discrimination, and more. This is a must-have guide for parents and other adults.

Under the Learn tab, find the Student Resources section. It contains an extensive bibliography, sixteen Story Time videos for children and other useful content. A similar section is offered to educators. One excellent item here is Learning Links for Exhibits that previews the content of each museum exhibit and suggests activities and discussion points for older students. The Educators section contains a thirty-minute video, *Understanding and Teaching Civil Rights*, presented by Dr. Hasan Jeffries of Ohio State University.

The museum recommends that the permanent exhibit areas be restricted to visitors twelve and older.

Birmingham Civil Rights Institute (BCRI), Birmingham

Over two dozen lesson plans are available for kindergarten through high school teachers. Find these under the Learn section on the BCRI website. Created by subject-matter experts, these lesson plans cover a broad range of topics. All are downloadable PDFs. The museum also has several programs for young people in the Birmingham area.

Mississippi Civil Rights Museum (MCRM), Jackson

Visitors should download the Field Trip guides that the museum has prepared for grades 3–6 and 7–12. Click on the Learn tab, then Field Trips to access them. The guides give young people a series of activities to do from gallery to gallery.

The MCRM is operated by the Mississippi Department of Archives and History (MDAH). On the MDAH website, educators and parents can find pages on a number of freedom movement topics, including "Civil Rights in Mississippi," "Freedom Summer," and "Foot Soldiers of the Civil Rights Movement."

Legacy Museum and the National Memorial for Peace and Justice, Montgomery

The strengths of both Equal Justice Initiative (EJI) locations are the honesty and frankness with which they cover the realities Black Americans faced. This benefit makes it more important here than perhaps anywhere else on the trip to judge whether to bring children with you when visiting. EJI, in fact, has this statement on its website: "When planning a visit with children, we encourage taking account the estimated time spent at each site. If you are concerned about preparing to engage with the subject matter, we recommend reviewing our website and exercising your discretion."

The EJI has published three excellent reports that would be appropriate for high schoolers and adults. Some of the photos used in these reports (e.g., segregated water fountains) might be useful in speaking with children. Others are too likely graphic for sensitive eyes. These reports, available on the EJI website, cover "Slavery in America," "Lynching in America," and "Segregation in America."

Other Resources

Not unexpectedly, the Public Broadcasting System (PBS) has a useful website containing over five thousand items dealing with the broadest definition of civil rights: women's rights, Native American rights, and so on. However, material relating to the civil rights era is abundant.

The website can be found at *https://vpm.pbslearningmedia.org/*. The site is straightforward to use and available filters direct you to content appropriate for specific grade levels and other variables.

To use this site,

- Go to the PBS Learning Media website landing page. In the search bar, type "civil rights movement." That broad search yields over five thousand possibilities; a narrower search (e.g., "Rosa Parks") produces fewer options.
- Use the search filters. Checking the desired Grade Level and Resource Type (video, audio, etc.) reduces the options delivered.

Another valuable resource is a website titled Civil Rights Teaching (*www.civilrightsteaching.org*). The site is a project of a Washington, DC–based nonprofit called Teaching for Change. This site provides a range of resources designed for teachers: lessons, handouts, and other elements for teaching about the role of everyday people in the civil rights movement. The materials on the site are aligned with a 2003 book, *Putting the Movement back into Civil Rights Teaching*. According to the website, a new edition of the book is forthcoming.

Apps and Puzzles for the Road Trip

Having things for young children to do on a car trip is never a bad idea. This is especially true when that car trip might exceed two thousand miles. On the Parent Map website (*https://www.parentmap.com/*), a search for "civil rights movement apps" will yield an article highlighting seven apps that help children learn about the era. Not mentioned in that list is the Black history app from Wyz Kid Labs. This app has videos, text, and quizzes to capture the attention of young travelers. If you search for "civil rights puzzles," you will find ample options that you can download and print out for use during the trip. These options may be free or carry a modest charge. Here are a few specific options:

- The Southern Poverty Law Center has a free twenty-eight-page PDF filled with puzzles, coloring pages, and educational content, available at *https://www.splcenter.org/sites/default/files/splc_civil_rights_activity_book_online.pdf*.
- The Teachers Pay Teachers website (*https://www.teacherspayteachers.com/*) describes itself as "the go-to place for educators to find the resources, knowledge, and inspiration they need to teach at their best." Among its three million free and paid resources, you can search for "civil rights resources" and "civil rights puzzles."
- Book publisher Houghton Mifflin Harcourt has several free puzzles and relevant teaching aids at *https://www.hmhco.com/blog/black-history-month-activities-lesson-plan-ideas-for-school*.
- At the Education.com website, there are some free civil rights crossword puzzles as well as civil rights workbooks and other materials available for purchase. In addition, parents can either download for free or purchase other types of social studies resources on topics like "Reading a Map" or "States and Capitals." Find these at *https://www.education.com/worksheets/social-studies/*.

Books for Children and Teens

A growing body of literature written on the civil rights movement is specifically for nonadults. Some of these books are historical fiction relating real events through the eyes of fictional youngsters. Other books, particularly those directed to teenagers, are nonfiction and provide a basic understanding of events like the desegregation of Little Rock Central High School, the Freedom Rides, and the Birmingham Campaign.

To find either type of youth-oriented literature on civil rights, ask your local librarian. They may have a "Best of Collection" list for their youth-directed civil rights titles. Use your library's search tool for topics of interest with keywords such as "juvenile literature" or "young adult literature" to describe the book.

The John F. Kennedy Library has a twenty-five-page annotated bibliography on its website titled "Literature on the Civil Rights Era for Young Readers." The list was compiled in 2013, so more recent works won't be included but the site gives a nice synopsis of the works covered. See *https://www.jfklibrary.org/sites/default/files/2018-06/Civil_Rights_Era_Bibliography.pdf*.

For more recent books on civil rights history for children and teens, check any of these websites:

- *https://www.commonsensemedia.org/lists/civil-rights-books*
- *https://www.the-best-childrens-books.org/civil-rights-kids.html*
- *https://socialjusticebooks.org/booklists/civil-rights-teaching/classroom/*
- *https://www.feministbooksforkids.com/books-about-civil-rights-movement/*

These sites and others make selecting an age-appropriate title on a person or topic of interest fairly simple. User reviews and overall ratings help in the selection process.

PART TWO

TRAVELING FREEDOM'S ROAD ON THE CIVIL RIGHTS LOOP

CHAPTER 7

Atlanta

"The city too busy to hate."

That's how William B. Hartsfield, the longest-serving mayor of Atlanta, used to refer to his city. During his twenty-five-year tenure from 1937 to 1962, that was his favorite way to position his city in those oft-turbulent years. There's perhaps a blend of public relations and image creation mixed with a bit of truth in Hartsfield's words.

While the city did not experience the assassinations of major civil rights leaders like Dr. King in Memphis or Medgar Evers in Jackson, it certainly was not void of civil rights activity and protests. Atlanta was more like the strategic hub of the movement. Prominent civil rights organizations like the Southern Christian Leadership Conference (SCLC) and the Student Nonviolent Coordinating Committee (SNCC) organized their work throughout the southeastern United States from their Atlanta-based headquarters. Dr. King had an Atlanta address all but five years of his life. Not surprisingly then, Dr. King is the focal point at most of the places recommended for a full day here.

Atlanta is an ideal starting point or ending stop for your two-week journey. International travelers can find flight options to the city's Hartsfield-Jackson International Airport (named after the aforementioned Mayor Hartsfield and Maynard Jackson, the first African American mayor of the city). Atlanta, as the easternmost city on our recommended loop of major civil rights locations, is also a likely starting or ending place for those driving in from the Northeast or Mid-Atlantic states, the Carolinas, or Florida, or flying in from distant parts of the country.

The Plan for Atlanta in 300 Words or Less

Plan one full day in Atlanta—more if you want to really go deep into the civil rights sites here or if you choose to visit any of several popular non–civil rights tourist spots in the city. The two civil rights movement must-see destinations in Atlanta are

- *The campus of the Martin Luther King Jr. Historical Park and Preservation District in the Sweet Auburn section of the city.* This includes the National Park Service (NPS) Visitors' Center; Dr. King's Birth Home; Ebenezer Baptist Church, where he preached and from which he was buried; and the King gravesite. There's more on famed Auburn Avenue than those four places. The chapter provides more details on other Sweet Auburn locations tied to civil rights history.
- *The campuses of Atlanta's historically Black colleges.* The students of Spelman, Morehouse, the Interdenominational Theological

Center, and other colleges were leaders of and participants in the protests here and elsewhere in the 1950s and 1960s. These campuses are not only close together but also just over three miles from the Auburn Avenue must-sees. This makes it possible to absorb a good part of Atlanta's civil rights history in one full but busy day.

There are also museums, churches, and other historic locations in Atlanta that you may want to see that aren't located within the above two areas. We note those as well in this chapter. However, first, let's get into the specifics on the two highest-priority areas.

The Top King-Related Places on Auburn Avenue

Martin Luther King Jr. National Historical Park, 450 Auburn Avenue NE

You begin where Dr. King began. Sweet Auburn was his neighborhood.

Start early! That's good advice any day on your trip but especially if you want to do the key Atlanta sites in a single day. Begin at the National Park Service's Martin Luther King Jr. National Historical Park Visitors' Center. There is plenty of free parking. Enter the lot from John Wesley Dobbs Avenue.

As soon as you walk into the NPS Visitors' Center, sign up for a King Home Tour at the main desk, assuming you have any interest in seeing the home where Dr. King grew up. Ranger-led tours are the only way one can see the inside of the King home; these tours fill up fast.

Don't be discouraged if you show up and all the tours are full. Check back with the rangers later to see if any spots have opened up; people and groups get tired or just change their mind. Spots can become available as the day goes on. If a home tour doesn't look like it is going to work out, a short film on the birth home offers a reasonable substitute.

While at the rangers' desk, make a note of what films are playing in the theater behind the main desk and their start times. Three films were available when I visited:

- *Children of Courage*—15 minutes. An introduction to the Auburn Avenue neighborhood of MLK's childhood and his formative years.
- *Birth Home Tour*—17 minutes. A good alternative to the ranger-led tours if they are full or if your time is limited. Like the tour, it shows the room young Martin shared with his brother A.D. and the room where all three King children were born. You'll hear about the three "S" philosophies that Daddy King and his wife instilled in their children about money—spending, saving, and sharing—as well as the importance of music, education, and family togetherness.
- *New Time, New Voice*—20 minutes. Julian Bond's narration covers MLK's adult life: earning a PhD at age twenty-six, leading the Montgomery Bus Boycott, his well-known "Letter from Birmingham Jail," earning the Nobel Peace Prize in 1964, and more.

Martin Luther King Jr. National Historical Park	
Location and Parking	450 Auburn Avenue NE, Atlanta, GA 30312—Free parking in the lot one enters from John Wesley Dobbs Avenue. From that lot, it is a short walk across Irwin Street to the Visitors' Center. Do not park on Irwin Street.
Public Transportation	The *Atlanta Streetcar* makes stops at the MLK National Historic Park (Stop 9) as well as at the National Center for Civil and Human Rights (Stop 3). The closest MARTA station (Peachtree Center) is about a mile away; that station is Stop 1 on the Streetcar route. Bus service to the park is provided by Routes 3 and 99. Check *MARTA's website* for details on public transit.
Days Closed	Federal holidays
Operating Days and Hours	Sunday to Saturday, 9 a.m. to 5 p.m.
Admission	Free
Website	*https://www.nps.gov/malu/index.htm*
Phone Number	404-331-5190 ext. 5046
Email Address	*MALU_Information@nps.gov*

At the rangers' desk, ask questions about this site or any other place in the MLK Preservation District. Know that some places in the Preservation District like the King Center are not run by the NPS, but the rangers may still know the answer.

Unless you immediately head to the theater or to the gift shop (of course, there's a gift shop), you will enter a large foyer. The large open space contains two items to note:

- The center of this space is an in-the-round display called *Children of Courage*. Directed toward younger visitors, it covers three topics: "Segregation" of the 1930s, the "Young Soldiers of Freedom" of the 1950s and 1960s, and "Today's Fight for Human Rights." Parents: Encourage your children to open the "discovery drawers" located in all three sections of this display. The objects in these drawers are meant to educate and inspire young visitors.
- The entry hall has a display case on the right wall that provides information on the evolution of this NPS site and the educational elements within.

The restrooms are toward the back of this foyer. Wheelchairs are available for visitors; inquire at the information desk. The Visitors' Center, the Birth Home, Fire Station No. 6, and Ebenezer Baptist Church are all wheelchair accessible.

The Main Exhibits

Six main galleries are on the left side of the Visitors' Center. These are semicircular alcoves devoted to the following topics:

- *Segregation*. A video presents some of the events that were precursors to the activism of the civil rights movement. The video ends with the challenges in desegregating Little Rock Central High School. A caution to those touring with children: graphic photos of lynching and the Emmett Till casket photo appear in the video.
- *The King Family*. This video covers key influences on Dr. King: the Auburn Avenue neighborhood, his family, and Gandhi. Take special note of the story of Daddy King choosing to leave a shoe store with Martin when the clerk asked him to go to the

back of the store to try on shoes. Also revealed is where Martin at age fifteen, just out of high school, received his call to pursue the ministry. No spoilers here, but it was a fact that I did not know prior to my visit. Look for it.

- *Call to Lead.* This alcove covers topics like Rosa Parks, the Montgomery Bus Boycott, activism at lunch counters, and the courage shown across the South by the Freedom Riders. Read the excerpt inside the kitchen window (it's easy to overlook); it shares how Dr. King experienced "the presence of the Divine" as never before in his parsonage home in Montgomery, an event he wrote about in *Stride toward Freedom: The Montgomery Story.*
- *Visiting the Mountain.* This section's video highlights Selma, Birmingham, and the March on Washington. Wall displays cover the Freedom Riders and Anniston (where one of the Freedom Riders' buses was set on fire), Birmingham and Dr. King's time in jail there, Mississippi's Fannie Lou Hamer, and the Cambridge, Maryland, protests.
- *Expanding the Dream.* Content within this alcove covers James Meredith's 1966 March against Fear; Meredith was the first Black person to attend the University of Mississippi. After Meredith was shot shortly after his march began, Dr. King continued the march to Jackson. Content boards cover Dr. King's tension-filled visit to Chicago in 1966, his stand on Vietnam, and the 1968 events in Memphis.
- *Overcoming Loss.* The focus here is Dr. King's assassination and funeral, with both video and still pictures.

Along the back wall of this horseshoe-shaped gallery is a 1955–1968 timeline focused on Dr. King. In the center are several life-sized statues of marchers on their journey up the "Freedom Road," a popular spot for photos and selfies.

To the right of the first three alcoves is the D.R.E.A.M. gallery. This space is devoted to special and changing exhibits. When I visited, *Memphis to Atlanta* was the special exhibit, covering Dr. King's assassination in Memphis on April 4, 1968. The centerpiece was the wooden wagon that two mules drew carrying Dr. King's body through Atlanta's streets on April 9, 1968. The wagon came from an Atlanta antique shop.

The display case on the right wall of the gallery has many mementos and artifacts, from young Martin's baseball mitt to the funeral program used at both Ebenezer Baptist Church and Morehouse College.

There's more to experience outside the visitors' center. The International Civil Rights Walk of Fame and a larger-than-life statue of Mahatma Gandhi are both to your left as you exit. You pass these tributes if you walk from the parking lot.

This promenade provides another learning opportunity for everyone, but particularly for young visitors. A wide range of individuals from civil rights activists, sports stars, politicians, entertainers, and individuals from other disciplines are honored on the walk. Parents might visit the *NPS website page* that lists the Walk of Fame honorees before their visit and challenge their children to learn about some of those whose shoe prints are found on this promenade prior to their visit. Then, during your visit, challenge the children to find that person's shoe print on the walk.

The Martin Luther King Jr. Center for Nonviolent Social Change (The King Center) and Freedom Hall, 449 Auburn Avenue NE

Across Auburn Avenue from the Visitors' Center are the King Center and Freedom Hall. The King Center is administered by the King estate and Freedom Hall by the NPS. Ebenezer Baptist Church's Heritage Sanctuary is right next door.

The King Center is the burial site for Dr. King and his wife, Coretta Scott King. It's a hallowed place, and an eternal flame and reflection pool add to the site's solemnity. Try to go when there's not a large crowd so that you can reflect on Dr. and Mrs. King's contributions in a quieter atmosphere. The King Center is closed on the same holidays as the NPS Visitors' Center plus Christmas Eve. It is open daily from 9 a.m. to 5 p.m. with a 6 p.m. closing time in the summer.

Freedom Hall on the King Center grounds is a special events facility. It also has an exhibit area, a bookstore, and resource center. The Grand Foyer displays art, while the second floor hosts special exhibits.

Historic Ebenezer Baptist Church Heritage Sanctuary, 407-413 Auburn Avenue NE

This church has witnessed so much African American and civil rights history. The initial Ebenezer congregation of thirteen members came together in 1886. The members met at a different location until membership growth created the need for a larger place to worship. The Ebenezer faithful began construction at 407-413 Auburn Avenue and finished the church in 1922 with Rev. A. D. Williams serving as pastor.

Rev. Williams died in 1931, and his copastor and son-in-law Rev. Martin Luther King Sr. (often called Daddy King) assumed the lead role. King Sr. remained pastor here for forty-four years. In 1960, King's son Martin joined him as copastor.

Part of the National Historical Park, the church is open to the public and there is no cost to visit. The sanctuary and fellowship hall have been restored to the look of the 1960s. Other aspects of the renovation have made the sanctuary cooler (air conditioning), safer (fire suppression), and more accessible (there is a chair lift to the sanctuary).

The new Ebenezer Baptist Church is across the street near the Visitors' Center. It is not open to the public except for services. Seating capacity there is three times the six hundred seats within the original Ebenezer Church.

As you stand in the sanctuary of Historic Ebenezer, reflect back to Dr. King's funeral here on April 9, 1968. You would be one of 750 or so mourners who crowded into this space. Outside, 200,000 strained to hear a taped replay of one of Dr. King's recent sermons, "The Drum Major Instinct."

He preached that sermon here on February 4, 1968, exactly two months before his murder. It's not one of his best-known orations, but Coretta Scott King wanted it played at the funeral service. *The Atlantic* called the sermon "haunting" and one in which Dr. King was "rehearsing his death, effectively spelling out the kind of eulogy he wanted delivered at his funeral."[11]

Google Dr. King's "Drum Major Instinct" sermon. The audio is on YouTube and on the King Papers website at Stanford University's Martin Luther King Jr. Research and Education Institute. Bring your headphones and listen to it (or at least the last five or so minutes) during your Ebenezer visit.

Martin Luther King Jr. Birth Home, 501 Auburn Avenue NE

This is the only NPS site on the Auburn Avenue campus where you need a ticket to enter. You get one at the rangers' desk; showing up at that desk as close to the 9 a.m. opening is strongly recommended. There is no advance registration in person or by phone for the Birth Home tours. The NPS website suggests visiting early in the week or on Sunday morning to improve your chances of landing a tour ticket.

The Birth Home tour is free and lasts thirty minutes. The first tour is at 10 a.m., and the final one each day begins at 4 p.m. Only fifteen people are allowed on each tour. (Large tour groups are limited to forty-five slots maximum, spread across three tours. If your group is larger than forty-five people, some will not make this tour.)

Anyone can, of course, view the outside of the two-story frame Queen Anne–style home at 501 Auburn Avenue. A white family owned the home until 1909 when the Reverend A. D. Williams, pastor of Ebenezer Baptist, bought it. The price: thirty-five hundred dollars.

The Williams family's only child to survive infancy, Christine, married Martin Luther King in 1926 and they moved in with her parents. Martin Jr. (whose original name was Michael) was born in the house. The tour—or the film on the Birth Home shown in the visitors' center— gives you a wonderful sense of the family life of young Martin and his two siblings. Martin Jr. lived here until age twelve.

How long should be blocked out for the four sites covered so far? Three hours are recommended, perhaps an hour more if you are able to tour the Birth Home and desire to see all three films at the Visitors' Center.

Elsewhere on and near Auburn Avenue

Once you finish at the must-see NPS sites and the King gravesite, take an hour and stroll around the Sweet Auburn neighborhood. Several locations in the area will likely interest a cultural heritage tourist.

We cover these from east to west in the neighborhood, starting with the historic firehouse at Boulevard and Auburn Avenue, just a few doors west of Dr. King's Birth Home. To keep you from constantly crossing Auburn Avenue, we'll go down the odd-numbered locations first (in other words, on the same side as the King Center and Fire Station Number 6). Once the odd-numbered side is covered, we cross Auburn Avenue and head back toward the NPS Visitors' Center.

Let's start with the Fire Station, one of the original eight stations built in Atlanta and now run by the NPS.

Fire Station Number 6, 39 Boulevard NE

This was an active station until 1991. The Park Service rangers will share a bit about the desegregation of the Atlanta Fire Department and tell you of MLK Jr.'s visits to the station as a boy.

The first sixteen Black firefighters were not hired by the city for any fire station until 1963, a year after Mayor Hartsfield of "too busy to hate" fame left office. All of them worked at Fire Station 16, not this one. Not long after that, however, Station Number 6 became the first integrated firehouse in the city.

Children and nostalgia buffs will enjoy seeing the vintage 1927 pumper hose truck at the station. There are informative exhibits as well as a bookstore here.

Wheat Street Baptist Church, 359 Auburn Avenue NE

This Gothic Revival church was pastored by Rev. William Holmes Borders from 1937 to 1988. Young MLK would leave his home church to hear Rev. Borders's sermons, widely known to be an outstanding preacher.

In 1943, Borders wrote a poem titled "I Am Somebody," which became a rallying cry decades later when the Reverend Jesse Jackson used it to inspire young Blacks.

Student Nonviolent Coordinating Committee (SNCC) activist Charles Cobb noted that Rev. Borders publicly denounced *Gone with the Wind* as giving "a racist, false, and romanticized view of slavery."[12] He also chastised his fellow Auburn Avenue pastor, King Sr., for letting the Ebenezer choir sing during the film's three-day Atlanta premiere.

As you continue down the odd-numbered side of Auburn, note the hard-to-miss, wall-sized tribute mural to John Lewis at 219 Auburn Avenue as you cross Jesse Hill Avenue.

Auburn Avenue Research Library, 191 Auburn Avenue NE

This special branch of the Atlanta Fulton Public Library has a reference collection and exhibits on African cultures in the Cary-McPheeters Gallery. Civil rights movement materials here would primarily interest scholars; there are no checkout privileges.

Atlanta Daily World, 145 Auburn Avenue NE

This newspaper was run by the conservative Scott family for eight decades (no direct relation to Coretta Scott King, who grew up outside of Marion, Alabama). Because the paper often editorialized against student activism in the late 1950s, local students started the competing *Atlanta Inquirer* in July 1960.

A tornado damaged the building in 2008, and the newspaper moved out. The Scott family announced its plans to sell the building, and a prospective buyer wanted to knock it down. Recognizing the structure's place in the neighborhood's history, residents rebelled, and the façade of the building was spared demolition. The blue hanging sign and some historical plaques on the brick wall keep the origins of the newspaper alive.

African-American Panoramic Experience Museum (APEX), 135 Auburn Avenue NE

This modest museum contains a gallery, a video theatre, and exhibit space. One permanent exhibit is a replica of the Yates & Milton Drugstore, a popular date spot at the time with its soda fountain.

More germane to the civil rights movement, at the drugstore in February 1960, three Morehouse College students (Lonnie King, Joseph Pierce, and Julian Bond) rallied students from Atlanta's other five historically Black institutions. They launched the Atlanta Student Movement, which played a role in challenging Jim Crow segregation in the South.

APEX's video on the Sweet Auburn neighborhood provides a look back in time for those who want a deeper understanding of the area's past. APEX is open Tuesday to Saturday, 11 a.m. to 3 p.m.

Now, cross over to the even-numbered side of Auburn Avenue and walk back toward the Visitors' Center where your day started—and where you likely parked your car.

Atlanta Life Insurance Company, 100 Auburn Avenue NE

Alonzo F. Herndon came to Atlanta at age twenty-four. After running three successful barbershops, he founded this company, which became one of the largest Black-owned insurers in the nation. Mr. Herndon became Atlanta's first Black millionaire. A historic marker here honors Mr. Herndon, providing more on his life and contributions.

Atlanta Life officials used their influence to support boycotts, sit-ins, and other civil rights efforts in Atlanta. They offered activists advice and helped with everything from launching the *Atlanta Inquirer* to providing bail money.

Big Bethel A.M.E. Church, 220 Auburn Avenue NE

On New Year's Day 1957, fresh from the bus boycott success in Montgomery, Martin Luther King Jr. led an afternoon rally here. The sanctuary was packed, the crowd spilling outside onto the sidewalks. Ten days later, six ministers (including Rev. Borders of Wheat Street Baptist Church) boarded an Atlanta city bus, taking the front seats. When they were arrested and placed in a paddy wagon, the driver oddly enough was a Black officer.

A point of interest: Morris Brown College was founded in the church basement in 1881. The school was the first in Georgia owned and operated by African Americans.

SCLC/W.O.M.E.N. Inc. (Women's Organizational Movement for Equality Now), 328 Auburn Avenue NE

Founded in 1979 by Evelyn Lowery, this organization promotes civil rights movement education. Toward that end, it runs tours to civil rights sites twice a year and places memorials honoring those who gave their lives to the movement, like the Viola Liuzzo marker between Selma and Montgomery. Directions to this marker appear in chapter 8.

Southern Christian Leadership Conference (SCLC) Former National Office, 334 Auburn Avenue NE

In 1965, the eastern part of this building became the headquarters of Martin Luther King Jr.'s SCLC. The SCLC moved out in 2006 and into its new headquarters at 320 Auburn Avenue, just a few doors away. You may wonder why a sign for the Prince Hall Masons of Georgia hangs on the building. They built it in 1940.

On the floor above Dr. King's office, Atlanta's first Black-owned radio station, WERD-AM, had its studios. Dr. King would bang on the ceiling when he wanted to broadcast to the WERD listeners. A microphone would be lowered out the station's window to a waiting Dr. King below, who would pull it in and go on the air.[13]

The **Behold** *Statue, 400 Auburn Avenue NE*

You almost can't miss the ten-foot bronze statue in front of the new Ebenezer Baptist Church. The statue, *Behold*, by sculptor Patrick Morelli, was dedicated to Dr. King. Coretta Scott King unveiled it in 1990.

Behold represents the African ritual of holding a newborn to the heavens and declaring, "Behold the only thing bigger than yourself." Not a bad thought to ponder as you end your tour of where Dr. King grew up, preached, influenced social change, and is now laid to rest.

The Atlanta University Center Consortium

The second recommended stop during one day in Atlanta are the three campuses of the Atlanta University Center Consortium (AUCC): Clark Atlanta University, Morehouse College, and Spelman College.

Students and faculty at these historically Black colleges and universities were instrumental during the civil rights era through their leadership of and participation in nonviolent efforts to effect change. From the parking lot at the MLK Jr. NPS Historical Park to the centrally located parking lot at Morehouse College is three miles.

The recommended walking route for the AUCC is two miles. Park at the Morehouse Parking Garage at the corner of Westview Drive and Greensferry Avenue. Parking costs $1 per hour; you probably will not need more than two hours for this walking tour.

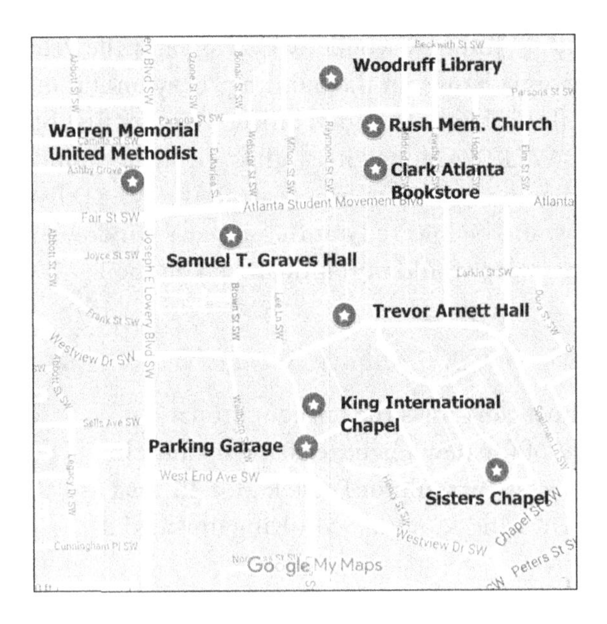

The first stop is the **Martin Luther King Jr. International Chapel at Morehouse College** (830 Westview Drive SW, across the street from the parking garage). Several noteworthy items here:

- The larger-than-life statue of Dr. King; he's pointing north, the general direction of your walk after leaving the chapel area.
- On the north side of the chapel and right behind the statue, Dr. King's "I Have a Dream" speech is engraved on a bronze plaque.
- On the west side of the chapel plaza is a tall white obelisk dedicated to Howard Thurman, one of Dr. King's mentors and friends. Thurman's book *Jesus and the Disinherited* (1949) and his discussions on Gandhi had a big impact on Dr. King, who carried Thurman's book during the Montgomery Bus Boycott. The Thurman obelisk becomes visible toward the end of the multicampus walk. Use it to navigate back to the parking deck. The Howard Thurman Historical Home in Daytona Beach, Florida, is covered later in the book.
- Inside the chapel is a large auditorium. On both sides of the auditorium are parallel inside hallways containing the International Hall of Honor, consisting of over two hundred original oil portraits of distinguished leaders in the civil and

human rights nonviolent movement globally.

Go around to the football-field side of the building (Wellborn Street). Note the side door on the lower level. Enter there, and someone in the Chapel Relations Office can direct you to the Hall of Honor and other highlights of the building. There are no regularly scheduled tours.

From the chapel plaza, walk north on Lee Lane for two tenths of a mile to **Samuel Graves Hall** on the west side of the Morehouse campus; it's the oldest Morehouse building. In front of Graves Hall is a statue of former Morehouse president and civil rights leader Benjamin E. Mays. Mays eulogized his friend Martin Luther King Jr. when his casket was in front of Harkness Hall. Mays and his wife, Sadie, now rest in a double crypt in the shadow of his statue.

Walk north to the Atlanta Student Movement Boulevard. Turn left, walk to the traffic light, and cross Joseph E. Lowery Boulevard SW. Just north of the light is **Warren Memorial United Methodist Church** at 181 Joseph Lowery Boulevard SW.

Here, in March 1960, over two thousand gathered for what started as a fairly combative meeting between those who supported a more cautious approach to effecting change (mostly the older-generation attendees) and the more impatient students from the

Not Up for More Walking?

If you toured the Auburn Avenue area in the morning, you've already done a fair amount of walking once you've arrived at Morehouse. After the Martin Luther King Jr. International Chapel, the other places mentioned here are designed as a walking tour.

However, if circumstances like weather, mobility, or just tired feet diminish your interest in a two-mile walk, here's a driving option to see a few places mentioned on the walking tour:

- Return to your car after visiting the International Chapel; drive to Warren Memorial Church, which has a parking lot. There is a marker on front lawn.
- Turn left onto Joseph E. Lowery Boulevard SW to head north, then right onto Parsons Street to drive past the Woodruff Library. (Rush Memorial Congregational Church is nearby but on the pedestrian-only James Brawley Boulevard).
- Turn right from Parsons onto Mildred Street to reach Atlanta Student Movement Boulevard. Turn right at ASM Boulevard and drive past the markers noted in this chapter near the Clark Atlanta Bookstore. That's it for the short driving tour.

nearby colleges. This was just over a month after four North Carolina A&T students made headlines with their lunch-counter sit-in in Greensboro, North Carolina.

Reverend King Sr. rose to make a proposal on desegregating local lunch counters and other businesses. To the ears of the students inside the church and outside listening on loudspeakers, Daddy King's timeline was too slow, and one of the students shouted, "Sellout!"

As the atmosphere turned even more boisterous, the moderator asked Martin Luther King Jr. to speak. He had just moved back to Atlanta on February 1, 1960. His views were not much different from his father's, but his way of speaking to the crowd calmed things down considerably. King spoke of "the cancerous disease of disunity" to get everyone's focus on the need for working together. Historian Tomiko Brown-Nagin has written that "after Dr. King's speech, the mood of those assembled at the church changed from defiance to resignation, and acceptance."[14]

Continue walking north from the church on Joseph Lowery. In five hundred feet, turn right on Parsons Street SW and proceed three tenths of a mile to **Rush Memorial Congregational Church** (150 James P. Brawley Drive SW; Brawley is a pedestrian-only street).

Convenient to all AUCC campuses, this church donated its space for planning a variety of civil rights movement initiatives by area college students, costing the church some members. The student organization went under the name Committee on Appeal for Human Rights (COAHR), and a plaque with information on COAHR is on a marker in front of the church.

Close to Rush Memorial is the **Robert W. Woodruff Library** (111 James P. Brawley Drive SW). Prior arrangements are necessary to use its extensive African American collection as well as materials on the civil rights movement. Learn about these materials and how to access them at *http://mcmlk.auctr.edu/*.

From the Rush Memorial Church, walk south on the pedestrian-only part of James P. Brawley Drive, back toward Morehouse and Spelman Colleges. On the left, you'll shortly reach the **Clark Atlanta University Bookstore** and Atlanta Student Movement (ASM) Boulevard. In front of the bookstore are two historical markers describing the Atlanta Student Movement and one memorializing "An Appeal for Human Rights" from March 1960.

Cross ASM Boulevard and keep to the right side of the walkway. In one hundred feet or so, note the sidewalk between the large buildings. Turn right and take that sidewalk into the quad that Clark Atlanta University shares with Morehouse. The south end of the quad was a gathering place and starting point for many civil rights demonstrations and marches. A small plaque in front of **Trevor Arnett Hall** commemorates the first sit-in.

Greensferry Avenue is right behind Arnett Hall. The garage where you parked is to the right. The Spelman College campus is to the left. *Spelman is a closed campus*: only students, faculty, and campus staff are allowed on campus unaccompanied by a guide. Guides are provided by the Admissions Office (404-270-5193).

One place you should see at Spelman is **Sisters Chapel**. Call Admissions to have someone meet you at the campus security station near Greensferry at an appointed time. Sisters Chapel is at the far end of the compact Spelman campus (350 Spelman Lane SW). Trevor Arnett Hall to Sisters Chapel is a seven-minute walk. While demonstrations were planned here and demonstrators were prayed for here, the reason Sisters Chapel is the recommended final stop of the AUCC area traces back to Dr. King, as so much has during this day in Atlanta.

On April 7 and 8, 1968, Martin Luther King Jr.'s body lay in state here. Why at Spelman and not on the campus of Morehouse, his alma mater? Morehouse didn't have a large enough chapel then to accommodate the eighty thousand mourners who came through to pay their respects to the murdered leader. The International Chapel where you began this part of your tour was not dedicated until 1978.

Like being in Historic Ebenezer Baptist Church or gazing at the *Behold* statue on Auburn Avenue, the Sisters Chapel is a fitting spot to reflect on what you have learned and experienced today in Atlanta—and to say a prayer of thanks to the leadership of Dr. King and how he and others pushed America to become a bit more like the nation the Founding Fathers envisioned.

Additional Civil Rights Locations in Atlanta

What's been covered so far will fill most of one day. Maybe you have some energy or daylight left after touring these recommended sites. Perhaps you want to add another day in Atlanta or some time before flying out of Atlanta when your entire loop tour is finished.

Whatever the case, other relevant civil rights sites in or near the city are worthy of your consideration. Here are seven additional options.

Sitting Down at Rich's Mural, 61 Forsyth Street NW (Corner of Spring Street and MLK Jr. Drive)

This mural is on the former site of Rich's Department Store, the target of many lunch-counter sit-ins. Today, it is the Sam Nunn Federal Building, and artist Mike Mandel's striking mural is in the main lobby. Made of one-inch-square colored porcelain and glass mosaic tiles and installed in early 2000, the artwork re-creates an Associated Press photo from the front page of the *Atlanta Constitution* on October 20, 1960.

The sit-in at Rich's may have had an important influence on the outcome of the 1960 John Kennedy versus Richard Nixon presidential election less than a month later. Let's back up to October 19, 1960, and let the story unfold from there:

Dr. King, Morehouse student Lonnie King, and Spelman students Marilyn Pryce and Ida Rose McCree sat in at the Magnolia Tea Room on the sixth floor of Rich's on October 19, 1960. All were arrested. Mayor Hartsfield ordered the students released from jail in Atlanta, but his plan to get Dr. King out hit a snag. It seems that Dr. King received a traffic citation in nearby DeKalb County the previous May when he and Mrs. King drove a friend to Emory University Hospital for cancer treatments. After moving his family from Montgomery to Atlanta in February, Dr. King neglected to get a Georgia driver's license.

Dr. King was headed for the Dekalb County jail unless he posted bail. He chose jail. Days passed, and around *3:30 a.m.* on October 26, Dr. King was pulled from his bed in the county jail and transported to the Georgia State Prison in Reidsville.

Reidsville is over three hours from Atlanta. There he was to serve four months for breaking the probation associated with failing to change his driver's license address fast enough following his return to Georgia. Complicating this harsh sentence at a prison a long way from home was the fact that Dr. King's wife was pregnant. John F. Kennedy, in a close race for the presidency, placed a call to the understandably concerned Coretta Scott King. The next day, Kennedy's campaign manager and brother, Robert, negotiated King's release and got the charges dropped.

That evening, Daddy King, who had always been a Republican, held a mass meeting to celebrate the release of his son Martin. There he pledged his support to the senator from Massachusetts, saying, "Because this man was willing to wipe the tears from my daughter's eyes, I've got a suitcase of votes and I'm going to take them to Mr. Kennedy and dump them in his lap."[15] Kennedy won a very close election and became the nation's thirty-fifth president.

As the crow flies, the Sam Nunn Federal Center is a little over a mile from Sweet Auburn and a half mile south of Centennial Olympic Park.

Booker T. Washington High School, 45 Whitehouse Drive SW

Martin Luther King spent his sophomore and junior years of high school here. King skipped his last year of high school and began his Morehouse career at age fifteen.

The high school was the first in all of Georgia built for African Americans. Singer-actress Lena Horne also graduated from the school. It's just under a mile from Morehouse College and easily added on to a stop at Atlanta's historically Black universities.

The school has a replica of the Booker T. Washington monument at Tuskegee University in Alabama, along with Washington's "Lifting the Veil of Ignorance" at the base. The school is on the National Register of Historic Places. A mile northeast of this high school is the home Dr. and Mrs. King purchased in 1965 to accommodate their growing family. The home is at 234 Sunset Avenue in the historic Vine City neighborhood. Now owned by the NPS, the home will be incorporated into the National Historical Park honoring Dr. King.

The Martin Luther King Statue at the Georgia State Capitol, 206 Washington Street SW

An eight-foot statue honors Dr. King on the northeast side of the state capitol grounds (near Martin Luther King Jr. Drive and Capitol Avenue). Dr. King stands tall on the same grounds as Confederate military men (like purported KKK leader General John Brown Gordon) and many politicians who opposed Dr. King's antisegregation views.

On the same side of the capitol and not far from the King statue is a monument titled *Expelled Because of Color*. It honors Black lawmakers, removed from the legislature in 1868. A white majority of legislators determined Black Georgians did not have the authority to hold office, apparently basing their opinion on the 1857 Dred Scot decision from the US Supreme Court.

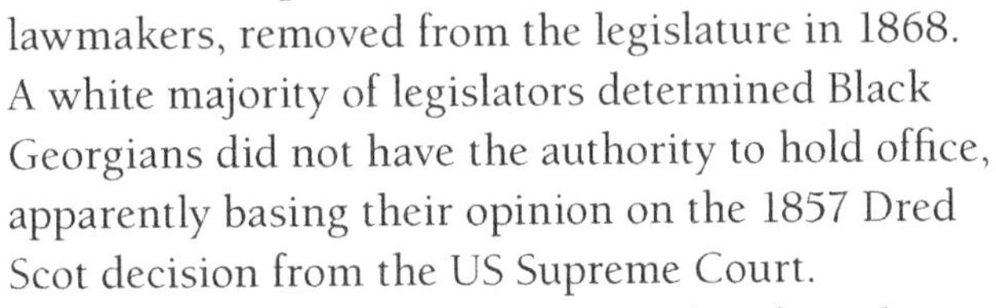

The Georgia capitol is six tenths of a mile southeast of the Sam Nunn Federal Building.

The Bridge Sculpture Honoring John Lewis, Freedom Park

This mixed-media sculpture is set in the John Lewis Plaza in Atlanta's Freedom Park. It's a half mile from the Carter Center and the Jimmy Carter Presidential Library and Museum.

The artist, Thornton Dial, arranged objects like tires, corrugated metal, and barrels to form a forty-two-foot-long bridgelike structure to represent Congressman Lewis's quest to advance civil and human rights. It also honors successful local efforts of nearby neighborhoods to stop the demolition of their homes for a planned highway.

The National Center for Human and Civil Rights, 100 Ivan Allen Jr. Boulevard NW

Absolutely stunning inside and out, the National Center for Human and Civil Rights tells the story of the American civil rights movement, tying it to the broader global effort to protect human rights. Permanent exhibits and special exhibits—one on Red Summer commemorated the one hundredth anniversary of the racial hatred that was present in dozens of American cities in 1919—capture a visitor's attention with many audiovisual elements.

The center is in downtown Atlanta, near the Georgia Aquarium and the World of Coca-Cola. Admission is $16 for adults, seniors, and children. The museum is open Thursday to Sunday from noon until 5 p.m.; on Saturday, the doors open at 10 a.m. Closed on Christmas and New Year's Day. Plan two hours for a visit.

The Site of the Hebrew Benevolent Congregation Temple Bombing, 1589 Peachtree Street NE

The Hebrew Benevolent Congregation grew out of the Hebrew Benevolent Society's mission to help Atlanta's Jewish poor. The Temple was the third home for its congregation. Rabbi Jacob Rothschild led the congregation from 1946 to 1973 and was a vocal supporter of social justice causes during the civil rights era. On October 12, 1958, white supremacists bombed the Temple in response to the Rabbi's support for civil rights. No one was ever convicted of the bombing. Rabbi Rothschild and Dr. King became friends in the ensuing years. The Rabbi organized a banquet to celebrate King's Nobel Peace Prize and delivered the eulogy for Dr. King at an ecumenical service for the assassinated leader in 1968.

The Temple is in Midtown Atlanta, about four typically traffic-filled miles north of the Martin Luther King Jr. National Historical Park.

South-View Cemetery, 1990 Jonesboro Road SE

Many notable African Americans are buried here: Alonzo Herndon (Atlanta Life Insurance); John Wesley Dobbs (gave Sweet Auburn its name); Martin Luther King Sr. and his wife, Alberta; Horace Bond (father of Julian Bond); William Holmes Borders (Wheat Street Baptist Church); and Ruby Doris Smith-Robinson (a person too few know but should). South-View is five and a half miles south of Sweet Auburn.

Unsung Hero—Ruby Doris Smith-Robinson

One civil rights activist whose name should be more widely known is that of Ruby Doris Smith-Robinson. Smith-Robinson's activism caused her to become a "guest" of the York County jail in Rock Hill, South Carolina; the Hinds County jail in Jackson, Mississippi; and at the infamous Parchman Penitentiary in Mississippi. In all, she spent over one hundred days in jail because of her activism, forty-five of those at Parchman.

In 1961, she participated in the Freedom Rides that restarted after the infamous bus attack in Anniston, Alabama, on May 14 of that year. Smith-Robinson was beaten in Montgomery and arrested in Jackson.

Ms. Smith-Robinson was an effective leader and administrator. She was the only woman elected executive secretary of the Student Nonviolent Coordinating Committee. She was only twenty-five years old when she died of cancer on October 7, 1967. To learn more about Smith-Robinson and her impact on SNCC, read her biography, *Soon We Will Not Cry*, by Cynthia Griggs Fleming.

Smith-Robinson is buried at South-View Cemetery. Whether you visit her grave there or not, ponder what is engraved on her tombstone: "If you think free, you are free."

CHAPTER 8

Montgomery and Tuskegee

Of all the cities on the tour, none has as many varied connections to the African American experience in the United States as Montgomery, Alabama. A hub of the mid-1800s southern slave trade, the initial capital of the Confederacy, and the site of both the successful yearlong bus boycott in the 1950s and a brutal attack on Freedom Riders in 1961, Montgomery was the endpoint of the march from Selma where Martin Luther King Jr.'s "How Long? Not Long" refrain on the state capitol steps, according to one historian, "represented the high-water mark of the nonviolent movement."[16]

Adding to the history Montgomery offers, visitors can find more in nearby Tuskegee. There, visitors can tour two National Historic Sites: one honoring the Tuskegee Airmen and the other for the Tuskegee Institute, founded by Booker T. Washington.

If you are driving from Atlanta, consider stopping at one or both Tuskegee National Park Service (NPS) sites on your way into Montgomery. Tuskegee is just under two hours into the two-and-a-half-hour trip. Keep in mind you will be going from Eastern to Central Time as you travel from Atlanta to Montgomery, so you gain an hour back. The NPS sites for the Tuskegee Airmen and the Tuskegee Institute close at 4:30 p.m. and are not open on Sunday.

Montgomery provides the chance to experience so much history. Here are five must-see spots around which our three days of touring are built:

- Dexter Avenue King Memorial Baptist Church.
- That church's parsonage, where the King family lived from 1954 to 1960.
- The Equal Justice Initiative's (EJI) Legacy Museum.

- The EJI's National Memorial for Peace and Justice (NMPJ).
- The Rosa Parks Museum.

Besides these, you have a choice of adding spots where history happened, such as:

- The Rosa Parks bus stop on Montgomery Street in front of the Rosa Parks Museum.
- The bus station (now a museum) where the Freedom Riders were met by an angry white mob, while police looked the other way.
- The state capitol steps where Dr. King delivered his moving remarks as the Selma-to-Montgomery March concluded.

A three-day stopover here is suggested, given the number of places of likely interest. That will be the most nights spent in one city, if you follow the recommended schedule. Be aware of closed-on days for the suggested must-see places, especially if you are here on a Sunday, Monday, or Tuesday. The next section helps you plan accordingly.

Putting a label on the three days can help us have a common shorthand. The labels relate back to the five locations just listed. The three days are

- The "EJI Day." This includes visits to the two Equal Justice Initiative sites. The EJI Day can be any day except Tuesday. (At press time, the EJI sites were also closed on Monday but expect to resume operating every day except Tuesday, post-COVID.)
- The "Dexter Church and Parsonage Day" (or "Dexter Day" for short). This day cannot be on a Sunday *or* Monday since they are closed both days, except for worship.
- The "Rosa Parks Museum Day." The Rosa Parks Museum gets a separate day because of Mrs. Parks's importance and the museum's strong content and use of technology. That visit will likely consume three hours; spend the rest of the day exploring other covered options.

Two points are worth noting about these three days. First, they can fall in any order that works with what is open on the days you visit Montgomery. Second, the locations that give these days their names are *not* necessarily the only ones that you will visit on that day. Add other experiences to each day to round out your time in Montgomery.

The map presents the five must-see locations in city plus selected other places mentioned in this chapter. If you are looking to get in some steps or don't want the hassle of moving your car, there are walking options in the vicinity of the Legacy Museum, the Rosa Parks Museum, and Dexter Avenue King Memorial Baptist Church. In other words, once you get to the Rosa Parks Museum, leave your car parked and walk to several other nearby places of interest. The walking distances to see other relevant locations near the five highly recommended places are moderate. We get specific when we present the walk-to options.

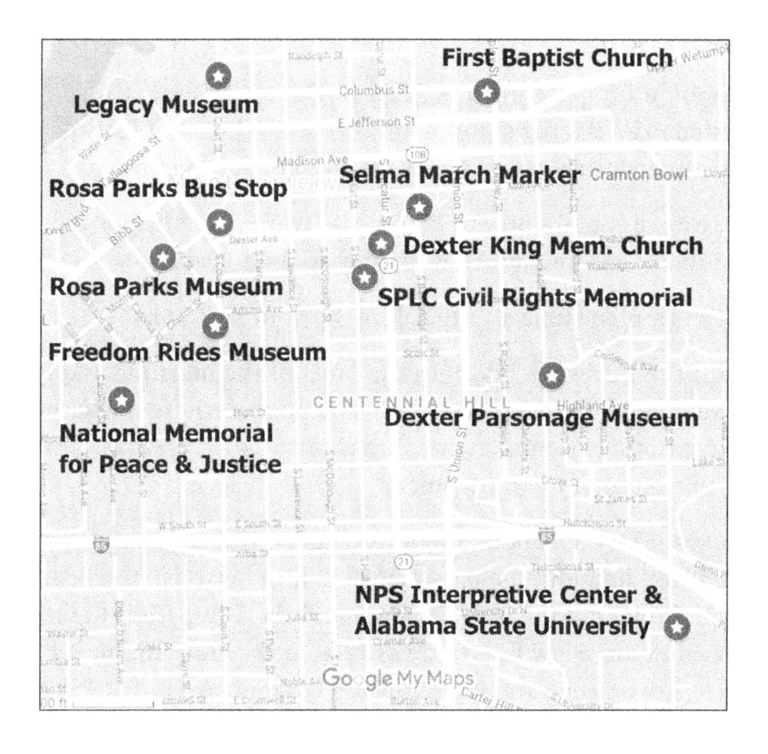

The Plan for Montgomery in 300 Words or Less

Let's start with the recommended and other excellent sites that are closed a day or two a week:

- Dexter Avenue King Memorial Baptist Church and Parsonage: closed Sunday and Monday.
- Legacy Museum and NMPJ: Closed Tuesday.
- Rosa Parks Museum (closed Sunday), Freedom Rides Museum (closed Sunday and Monday), and the two NPS Historical Sites in Tuskegee (closed Sunday).

The easiest way to avoid disappointment is for your three Montgomery and Tuskegee days to begin from Wednesday to Friday. This gives you at least two days when nothing recommended in this chapter is closed. What about other start-touring-on days?

If your touring in Montgomery begins any day from Saturday to Monday,

- Book tour appointments ASAP at Dexter Avenue King Memorial Baptist Church and Parsonage for that Saturday. No visits to either are available on Sunday or Monday.
- Reserve timed-entry tickets at the two EJI institutions for Sunday or Monday. They are closed on Tuesday.

Here is a plan subject to tweaking by your start day:

- *EJI Day.* Visit the NMPJ in the quiet of the morning and Legacy Museum before 3 p.m. In between, take a trip to Tuskegee—just not if it is Sunday or you visited Tuskegee as you drove from Atlanta to Montgomery.
- *Dexter Day.* Get both appointments on the same day: the church first and the parsonage later. In between, the Selma march memorials at the capitol and the SPLC Civil Rights Center are a few hundred yards from the church. The NPS facility on the campus of Alabama State University (ASU) is only a mile from the parsonage and there are several sites to visit at ASU.

- *Rosa Parks Museum Day*. Tour in the heart of the city, visiting the Rosa Parks Museum, the Freedom Rides Museum, or any of several other suggestions appearing later in the chapter.

The Equal Justice Initiative Cultural Sites Day

With so many relevant places to see here combined with all the varied closed-on days, this chapter departs from the structure used in chapter 7. In Atlanta, places were arranged within two neighborhoods: the Auburn Avenue area and the Atlanta University Consortium complex. That structure worked for Atlanta, but not here. In Montgomery we anchor a day with a must-see destination or two, then fill that day with other locales. With that approach in mind, here is a brief layout for the EJI Day.

- See the National Memorial for Peace and Justice in the morning. It opens at 9 a.m., and getting there when it is likely to be quieter may allow for a more reflective experience given the serious subject matter. Allow an hour for the NMPJ.
- Mid-morning, head to Tuskegee (unless it's Sunday). That drive takes about forty minutes. In Tuskegee, you'll have two options but likely only time for one; you need to make it back for your timed entry at the Legacy Museum.
- Leave Tuskegee around 1 p.m. and head to the Legacy Museum. Plan for up to three hours there; it closes at 5 p.m.

National Memorial for Peace and Justice, 417 Caroline Street

Words cannot fully capture how you will feel here. The experience is more than powerful, as to be expected when coming face-to-face with facts about the lynchings of more than forty-four hundred African Americans in the United States.

A dramatic sculpture by Ghanaian artist Kwame Akoto-Bamfoyou encountered shortly after entering sets the somber tone here: seven captured Africans bound by chains, including a mother and her infant, with facial expressions ranging from terror to defiance.

Set on six acres, the outdoor memorial is immense. While lynching primarily occurred in the South, it was not exclusive to that region. Victims' names appear county by county on over eight hundred rectangular steel monuments. When you enter the main structure, the monuments are at eye level. However, as you walk farther, the monuments are hung from the roof of the structure, getting higher and higher as you walk through. As your head tilts back and your neck strains to see them overhead, the thought may occur to you that, with your eyes skyward, you now appear identical to what those who witnessed lynchings looked like.

Elsewhere on the grounds, identical monuments to the ones you've just walked through lie side by side. These are waiting to be claimed by the many counties where African Americans were lynched. EJI's hope is for the counties they represent to install them locally. As the memorial's website states, "Over time, the national memorial will serve as a report on which parts of the country have confronted the truth of this terror and which have not."

Tickets can be reserved online, and there is a modest fee to visit. During the pandemic, EJI reduced its operating schedule and welcomed visitors into both facilities for free. While this is a self-guided experience, guides are stationed at different points to welcome visitors and answer questions. The site, though vast, is accessible to those with disabilities. Parking is available on the streets surrounding the NMPJ.

The National Memorial for Peace and Justice	
Location	417 Caroline Street, Montgomery, AL 36104
Days Closed	Tuesday
Operating Days and Hours	Wednesday to Monday: 9 a.m. to 5:30 p.m.
Admission	$5 and covers both EJI facilities
Website	*https://museumandmemorial.eji.org*
Phone Number	(334) 386-9100
Email Address	*ticketing@eji.org*

As you leave, drive down Caroline Street to Clayton Street. Turn left on Clayton and continue for two hundred yards to a traffic circle in the Five Points area. There you'll see one of the pieces of public art that Montgomery commissioned to mark the fiftieth anniversary of the Selma-to-Montgomery March. The work is titled *Marching On*.

The Legacy Museum: From Slavery to Mass Incarceration, 400 North Court Street

As its full name suggests, this EJI institution has a broader focus than the National Memorial for Peace and Justice. While the messages of both sites are clear, the NMPJ's bold minimalism with few words is absent here. The Legacy Museum is an intensive, information-rich seminar. A tremendous number of facts and examples on topics ranging from the transatlantic slave trade to the shortcomings in the nation's criminal justice system are presented in video and static formats in the new Legacy Pavilion building; the building houses the museum, a gift shop and Pannie-George's restaurant.

After passing through security with your timed-entry ticket, you see three screens dealing with the slave trade. These fill your time before you enter the main part of the museum. One of these presentations is *Montgomery: A City Shaped by Slavery*, the first of several artistic fast-illustration videos by Molly Crabapple. Her talent for storytelling through drawing is mesmerizing.

From 1840 to 1860, no slave market was more central or conspicuous than Montgomery's. In fact, the museum is just blocks from where a warehouse holding enslaved people once stood. By 1850, Montgomery had passed the Gulf Coast's New Orleans and Mississippi River port of Natchez in the number of enslaved people there.

Montgomery's slave market was situated in present-day Court Square, where a historical marker reminds passersby of the role this place had in the slave trade. Court Square is a ten-minute walk from the Legacy Museum and across the street from the Rosa Parks Bus Stop marker, where her historic bus ride began. That ride ended in front of the old Empire Theatre, now the site of the Rosa Parks Museum.

(We've digressed; there's so much in Montgomery. Back to the Legacy Museum.)

After the entry foyer, a darkened hallway leads to six separate cramped pens. At each one, an enslaved person in hologram form tells you their riveting story: for example, a mother searching for the children from whom she's been separated, a young woman asking if you've seen her sister, and two children calling out for their mother.

The Legacy Museum	
Location	400 North Court Street, Montgomery, AL 36104
Days Closed	Tuesday
Operating Days and Hours	Wednesday to Monday: 9 a.m. to 5:30 p.m.
Admission	$5 and covers both EJI facilities
Website	*https://museumandmemorial.eji.org*
Phone Number	(334) 386-9100
Email Address	*ticketing@eji.org*

The main exhibit hall of the museum tracks the story of slavery's evolution, Emancipation, Reconstruction, and the Jim Crow era. Among the creatively presented material and topics presented here are as follows:

- *Congress ends the importation of enslaved humans.* Congress banned bringing more enslaved people into the country in 1808. That year, Alabama had 40,000 people held in captivity, yet by 1860, the number grew almost eleven-fold to 435,000.
- *Slave auctions.* Spend time reading the upsetting "ad copy" describing humans available for purchase.
- *Convict leasing.* During the post-Reconstruction period, this practice resulted in Blacks, often convicted of bogus charges like vagrancy, to be rented out by the state. In 1898, 73 percent of Alabama's state revenue came from convict leasing. A sidebar on this horrific practice appears in Chapter 22 on Florida.
- *Lynching.* Large jars containing soil from lynching sites fill a wall. The names of the victims (when known) as well as where and when they were murdered are displayed on each jar. Why soil? Bryan Stevenson explained the reasoning in Susan Neiman's thought-provoking book *Learning from the Germans: Race and the Memory of Evil*: "The soil contains the sweat of

the people who were enslaved, the blood of the people who were lynched, the tears of the people who were humiliated by segregation."[17]

Among the many other displays and video screens that educate via data and examples are two on topics that merit additional reflection:

- *The Legalization of White Supremacy.* This display consistently attracted a crowd on the day I visited, and a lot of commentary from those assembled in front of it. Generating the crowd comments were small boards that displayed example after example of eye-popping laws that oppressed Black people. These laws weren't just from the South either.
- *Mass Incarceration.* The full name of the museum emphasizes EJI's interest in the issue. The topic, along with the criminal justice system more broadly, receives well-deserved attention. Here, facts make the point: the United States jails more of its citizens than any nation on earth. Moreover, the rate of growth of incarceration in the last fifty years is astonishingly high. In the early 1970s, two hundred thousand people were in US prisons; in 2020, the number exceeded 2.2 million.

One observation about some video displays: the sound on some is low, and there were no subtitles when I visited. My suggestion: get as close as possible to the video displays so the low sound problem is reduced, even if it means waiting for the crowd to dissipate. Perhaps the sound is low to enhance the seriousness of the subject matter covered. If that's the case, someone should let the docents who speak to visitors at certain displays know that, particularly when the docents are near low-volume video displays.

Planning Your Visit to the Two EJI sites

Reserve tickets to the Legacy Museum and the NMPJ as soon as you lock down your dates in Montgomery. A modest fee of five dollars covers admission to both sites. Reserve tickets online and note the following information:

- Large groups (twenty-five or more) should complete a form on the museum's website.

- No pictures are allowed inside the Legacy Museum.
- The museum is accessible to persons with disabilities.
- Free parking is available at the 400 Court Street location. A shuttle takes visitors from there to the NMPJ.

The two EJI locations require at least four hours total on the day you choose to see them. You don't have to see them on the same day. Because the Legacy Museum has timed-entry tickets, you must use that ticket at or near the time you select. However, the NMPJ ticket can be used on an adjacent day if that fits your schedule better.

The museum and NMPJ are a twenty-minute walk apart. EJI offers a shuttle running every fifteen minutes or so. Whatever you do, walk at least a bit in the area of the Legacy Museum after your visit. Two historical markers nearby relate to Rosa Parks and one to the slave market that flourished in the city, especially just prior to the Civil War. Because these are outside, there are no closing hours or closed days.

Here's the most efficient walk to these three markers from the Legacy Museum:

- The ***City of Montgomery v. Rosa Parks*** marker. The court where a thirty-minute trial was held on December 5, 1955, was at 200 North Perry Street. Mrs. Parks was found guilty of disorderly conduct, fined $14, lost her appeal, and in the process became one of the legendary figures of the civil rights movement.
- The **Rosa Parks Bus Stop** marker. This is where Mrs. Parks boarded the bus being driven by J. Fred Blake from Equality, Alabama (no joke).[18] The marker is along the circle opposite the Court Square Fountain.
- **Montgomery's Slave Market** marker. Find it at the corner of Montgomery Street and Commerce Street, about 180 degrees opposite from the Rosa Parks Bus Stop marker.

Tuskegee Historical Sites

If it's not Sunday, you might consider visiting nearby Tuskegee on the same day you visit the two EJI institutions. If you made a Tuskegee stop on the way from Atlanta to Montgomery, fill the mid-part of EJI Day with other options presented in this chapter.

Tuskegee is home to two National Park Service sites, one honoring the Tuskegee Airmen of World War II and the other covering the contributions of the Tuskegee Institute. By going to Tuskegee mid-morning and returning in the early afternoon, you hopefully are traveling outside of the busiest traffic times.

The two NPS sites are four miles apart. Both are open Monday through Saturday from 9 a.m. to 4:30 p.m. There are no admission fees at either one.

Tuskegee Airmen National Historic Site, 1616 Chappie James Avenue

Two large hangars make up this excellent NPS location. You'll see them as you walk down from the ample parking lot. Note: that long downhill walk could present a problem for some visitors. If mobility issues make parking closer to the hangars necessary, call (334) 724-0922, the NPS on-site management number, to inquire about parking possibilities that won't require the long downhill walk.

Hangar 1 is the one closest to the parking lot. Start here with a four-minute orientation film; see two restored vintage planes and learn about aspects of pilot training and support. However, be judicious about how much time you spend in this hangar. Hangar 2 has much more content and deserves most of your time. Hangar 1 focuses on topics like airplane maintenance, record-keeping, and building technical skills. You can try your hand at folding a parachute back into its pack. Good luck.

Hangar 2 is the main building and merits more time. There is a twenty-five-minute film, *Sacrifice and Triumph*. (The film may contain too much violence for younger children.) Spread around this hangar are also shorter films: *Segregation*, *More Than Just Pilots*, and *Life Overseas*. The museum also makes certain you know that, despite its name, this site is about more than the airmen. It took cooks, nurses, mechanics, and more to make the airmen successful. In fact, there were ten support personnel for every pilot.

One reason you will likely spend more time here than Hangar 1 is the many informative videos in the topical alcoves, which give you not only a choice of video content but benches so that you can get off your feet.

During World War II, over one thousand pilots served as Tuskegee Airmen (officially designated the 99th Fighter Squadron,

332nd Fighter Group); eighty-four were killed in service. Despite their service and sacrifice, they did not return to the same welcome that greeted other veterans when they came home from the war.

Be sure to read about one of the worst discrimination incidents in the military. It took place at Freeman Field in Seymour, Indiana. Faced with separate officer clubs at the field, the Black officers protested. Eventually, 101 officers were arrested. Learn the full story here.

Why Red Tails?

The name "Tuskegee Airmen" was not an official US Air Force designation. It actually came from a 1955 book by that title by Charles Francis. In fact, while named for their origins at the Tuskegee Institute, the pilots of the 332nd Fighter Group completed their final training in Walterboro, South Carolina, at Walterboro Army Airfield. At that airfield, visitors can see a Tuskegee Airmen Memorial on Aviation Way.

Another name that the group became known by was the "Red Tails" because of the distinctive, easily identifiable red color on the tail of the airplane. One of the restored Red Tail fighters resides inside Hangar 1. If you wonder why they chose red as the color for that part of the aircraft, the answer is simple: they had lots of red paint.

If you are trying to decide between the two NPS sites in Tuskegee, I suggest this one, primarily because the tie-ins to the civil rights era are stronger. My own visit to the Tuskegee Airmen NPS facility consumed two hours with all the videos and other excellent content offered here. That said, both Tuskegee NPS sites do an excellent job. Visit both if your schedule allows.

Tuskegee Institute National Historic Site, 1212 West Montgomery Road

This National Historic Site (NHS) honors two African Americans who made significant contributions in education, science, and politics, and generally advanced their race and humanity: Booker T. Washington and George Washington Carver. Both born enslaved, Washington founded Tuskegee Institute (now Tuskegee University, which surrounds this NHS), and Carver joined Washington there as head of the Agriculture Department in 1896. Carver taught there for forty-seven years.

In addition to Washington and Carver, a visit covers Dr. Robert Moton, who succeeded Washington as head of Tuskegee University and was a strong advocate for Black military veterans. Moton Field at the Tuskegee Airmen NHS is named after him.

The site has two main buildings: The Oaks, the home of Booker T. Washington, and the George Washington Carver Museum. Plan forty-five minutes at each facility. The two buildings are a five-minute walk one to the other. Both offer worthwhile guided tours, often led by Tuskegee University students.

Parking is available near both buildings. Park for free near The Oaks; there's a fee at the Kellogg Center's parking deck next to the Carver Museum.

The Carver Museum acts as the visitors' center, and I'd suggest starting there. No fees are associated with either part of this NHS.

Tuskegee History Center, 104 South Elm Street.

This museum is open from June to Labor Day, during February, and on a day in May to commemorate the Tuskegee Syphilis Study Presidential Apology. Hours and days of operation for 2022 were not certain; call the center (334-724-0800) to get that information.

The Tuskegee Civil Rights and Historical Trail—Various Locations

Over a dozen historical markers make up this trail, located throughout the city and on the Tuskegee University campus. Honored on the trail are individuals including Rosa Parks (born in Tuskegee) and events like the 1957 boycott of local merchants. Find *a map on the Historical Marker Database website*.

The Dexter Avenue Church and Parsonage Day

This day is anchored by two must-see locations associated with Dr. King's service at the then-named Dexter Avenue Baptist Church. The church and the parsonage are sacred and historic places, closely associated with Dr. Martin Luther King Jr. He led the 1955–56 Montgomery Bus Boycott as pastor of the church; the King family lived in the parsonage from 1954 to 1960. Plan on an hour or so at each of these places if an in-person visit inside is available; if that is not possible, a visit to these buildings is still highly recommended. It is a fifteen-minute walk or five-minute drive from one to the other.

In-person visits to the church and the parsonage stopped during the pandemic. Both facilities state they will offer virtual tours at least until their own in-person tours resume. However, no process for booking a virtual tour nor its cost was available as of September 2021.

Amid the uncertainty of resuming tours offered directly through the church's website (*https://www.dexterkingmemorial.org/tours/*) comes some good news. Legendary Tours—operated by Wanda Battle, who led the church tour I was fortunate to experience in 2018—is offering her amazing tour inside the church. For pricing and availability for this tour and a wide range of other culturally relevant tour experiences in Montgomery offered by Legendary Tours, call (334) 819-6044 or email them at *contact@wandahbattle.com*.

Whether in-person or virtually, visiting these two historic places needs to part of your civil rights journey. The descriptions that follow reflect my 2018 experiences as well as the hope that readers will get to step inside both and have a similarly unique encounter with the past. The schedule for and content of the in-person tours may change. Whatever the content, being inside both of these historic places is likely to be one of the high points of your travels on Freedom's Road.

These locations were open for visitor tours every day except Sunday and Monday prior to the pandemic. They are paired up to encourage you to visit them on the same day, ideally the church in the morning and the parsonage in the afternoon. Tour the area around the church in between. Eight options are within walking distance of the church. Five of them take you toward the Alabama state capitol, and three take you in the opposite direction. Follow the tip to park your car legally and free at the state capitol. Another set of site visit options are about a mile away from the parsonage: the NPS Montgomery Interpretive Center and some historic homes and markers at Alabama State University; these are covered at the end of this Dexter Day section.

Free Parking near the Alabama State Capitol

The Montgomery Visitors' Center has a wonderful benefit for tourists: a pass to park near the state capitol for free. To get it, head to 1 Court Square, close to the Rosa Park Bus Stop marker.

The folks who run the center are extremely helpful. Stop there before you begin your touring; definitely go early on the day you plan to visit the Dexter Avenue area. They have a limited number of the free capitol-area day parking passes. The center is open from 9:30 a.m. to 4:30 p.m. every day except Sunday.

If you can't get a pass from the visitors' center, there is metered parking near the capitol (two-hour limit). You don't have to feed the meters on the weekends. Free parking is also available at Cramton Bowl Stadium, about a half mile east of the capitol.

The Dexter Avenue King Memorial Baptist Church, 454 Dexter Avenue

Construction started on this National Historic Landmark church in 1883, and its first sanctuary service was held in 1889. Tours include Dr. King's office, an extensive wall mural, and the church sanctuary.

They begin on the hour on weekdays and Saturday at 10 a.m. There are no tours at noon. The last tour on weekdays is at 3 p.m. and at 2 p.m. on Saturday.

Church tours can be booked by filling out a reservation form on the church's website at *https://www.dexterkingmemorial.org/tours/book-tours/*. You may not get a confirmation back right away. If several days go by, call the church office at (334) 356-3494 for assistance. Note that *the church tour and the parsonage tour have different phone numbers*. You need to complete a separate online reservation form for each location.

The church tour's cost is $7.50 per person. If you haven't made an advance reservation, you might go to the *street-level* church door ten minutes before a scheduled tour. If the next tour is not fully booked, you could be in luck. Two people on my tour did that and it worked.

Our tour was conducted by Wanda Battle and she was phenomenal! Ms. Battle now operates Legendary Tours, providing visitor experiences at a variety of historic locations in the city in addition to this church.

A short video starts the tour and focuses largely on the bus boycott. After the video, you sit in Dr. King's office (no photos here) and hear anecdotes about Dr. King. A picture-taking session at the lectern from which Dr. King delivered his "How Long? Not Long!: speech follows. That speech at the nearby state capitol ended the Selma-to-Montgomery March on March 25, 1965. The actual lectern was used in the film *Selma*. On the film set, someone thinking it was just a movie prop and not a historical artifact signed the lectern. When you get behind it, be sure to look down to see who made that mistake. The tour continues in front of a large mural of heroes of the civil rights movement and finally upstairs to experience the historic church sanctuary, where pictures are allowed.

Being at the Dexter Avenue King Memorial Baptist Church is likely to be one of the most memorable hours you will spend on your journey. Being in Dr. King's office, standing behind that lectern, feeling the love and passion with which Wanda Battle conducts this tour, and seeing the church he served during the Montgomery Bus Boycott is a set of experiences one should not miss. Book this tour as soon as you nail down your schedule!

At the tour's end, Wanda asked everyone on the tour to join

hands and sing "We Shall Overcome" together. It's just another way this hour will stand out in your memory long after your civil rights journey ends. The history and evolution of "We Shall Overcome" represent stories in themselves. However, we'll save them until we get to Tennessee and South Carolina.

Dexter Avenue Baptist Church Parsonage, 309 South Jackson Street

The parsonage is in the Centennial Hill neighborhood of Montgomery, an influential Black enclave since the post–Civil War period. You can learn more about Centennial Hill at a marker located on the grounds of First Congregational Church at the corner of South Union Street and High Street, about three tenths of a mile from the parsonage.

Dr. King, Mrs. King, and two of their four children lived at the parsonage from 1954 to 1960. Visitors should stop first at the Interpretive Center next door. After paying a modest admission fee, visitors view a short orientation film that recalls the history of the church and the pastors who served it. One of those pastors, the one who preceded Dr. King, is Rev. Vernon Johns. The fearless Reverend Johns delivered a sermon that you will hear part of prior to the tour, where he preached that "it's okay to murder a Black man in Montgomery." A reenactment of the sermon by actor James Earl Jones is available on YouTube.

The guided visit to the parsonage follows. The home was placed on the National Register of Historic Places in 1982 and restored in 2003. The restoration reflects the home's appearance and includes many original furnishings from when the King family lived here.

In fact, you'll feel like you are back in another era (if you were ever there in the first place). Grandparents can show their grandchildren the kind of washing machines they had in their childhood homes, what a rotary dial phone was like, and what it meant to be on a "party line" or to use a manual typewriter. The wall decorations, the breadbox in the kitchen, and the knickknacks throughout are the touchstones of a bygone time.

Nostalgia is not why you are here, however. The history here hits you in the face when you first climb up the stairs to the home's wide front porch. There you'll see a clearly visible scar caused by a bomb blast in late January 1956, less than two months after the bus boycott began. No one was injured.

How Martin Luther King Jr. Came to Lead the Montgomery Bus Boycott

E. D. Nixon was a clever man. We suggest a stop at his former home on the day you head from Montgomery to Selma. For the moment, consider how Mr. Nixon "chose" Dr. King to lead the historic bus boycott.

After Rosa Parks was arrested in December 1955, local NAACP president E. D. Nixon called nineteen Black leaders in the city to arrange a group discussion on their next steps. The Reverend Ralph David Abernathy was Nixon's first call, and Rev. Abernathy told Nixon he would come to any meeting Mr. Nixon arranged. Dr. King was Nixon's third call. Dr. King wanted time to think about what he should do and asked Nixon to call him back. You can perhaps understand Dr. King's cautious initial reaction; after all, he had only been in Montgomery a short while.

Nixon continued his calls. Later, when he called Dr. King back as requested, King told Nixon he was on board for the meeting. "I'm glad of that, Reverend King," said Nixon, "because I talked to eighteen other people. I told them to meet at your church at 3 p.m."[19]

Napoleon Bonaparte is credited with introducing the idea that "Geography is destiny." In this case, the Little Corporal was right. The central location of King's church made it a logical choice for the gathering . . . and King the logical choice to lead the movement. As Rosa Parks wrote years later, "He was so new to Montgomery and to civil rights work that he hadn't been there long enough to make any strong friends or enemies."[20]

Inside the parsonage, you tour every room. While the entire home is a historic place, be sure to note the dining room table. Around that table, the Montgomery Bus Boycott was planned and managed.

If seeing that table doesn't give you a few goose bumps, being in the kitchen will. That is where the tour ends. In the kitchen, you hear an audio recording of Dr. King. In it, he talks about various threats to his life and, in particular, a threatening midnight phone call. After that call, King went to this kitchen to make himself a cup of coffee. He spoke of hearing a voice as he sat in the kitchen. The voice told him to "stand up for righteousness, justice, and truth. I will be with you." Check your arms for goose bumps.

The voice may have stopped Dr. King's fears, but not the threats. Several days after that midnight phone call, the bomb exploded that left the mark you saw on the front porch. King, only twenty-seven years old at the time, had been resisting the call to leadership given his age, but not after that.

On your tour, being in the room where it happened may produce a special feeling you will experience other times during this journey. You can have this unique sense of place in Dr. King's office at the church, in his kitchen, and, I suspect, standing in the living room of Medgar Evers's bullet-scarred home in Jackson.

Plan roughly one hour for an inside tour of the parsonage, less if you just view the outside of the home and the King-Johns Garden for Reflection behind the Interpretive Center.

More History Down the Street

A few doors from the parsonage at 333 South Jackson Street is the home of Mrs. Vera Harris. Mrs. Harris and her husband, Richard, were neighbors of the King family and civil rights luminaries in their own right. Mrs. Harris owned the Dean Drug Store with her pharmacist husband. Dean Drug Store was one of the alternative "bus stops" during the Montgomery Bus Boycott, a place where you could likely get a ride to wherever you needed to go and stay true to the boycott. Dr. Harris was one of several leaders who orchestrated taxi service for Blacks needing transportation during the boycott. Dr. Harris, a Tuskegee Airman, passed in 1976.

During the Freedom Rides, the Harris home housed dozens of Freedom Riders. A marker in front commemorates this and their other civil rights contributions.

Mrs. Harris was on her porch the day we visited the parsonage; my wife and I were able to say, "Hello." Mrs. Harris passed away in September 2019. Dr. Valda Montgomery, the Harrises' daughter, has written a book about growing up in the Centennial Hill neighborhood at such a historic time. The book is titled *Just a Neighbor.*

Indefatigable—Jo Ann Gibson Robinson

An educator and an activist, Jo Ann Robinson played an important but sometimes overlooked role in the success of the Montgomery Bus Boycott.

As president of the Women's Political Council, she pushed for better treatment of Black citizens on city buses.

In fact, six months before Rosa Parks was arrested, Ms. Robinson warned Montgomery's mayor that mistreatment of Black riders would result in a boycott of the bus system.

When Ms. Parks was arrested on Thursday, December 1, 1955, Ms. Robinson acted. She led a small group at Alabama State University, where she taught, to get the word out on an upcoming one-day boycott of city buses in response to the arrest. She and three others stayed up all night to mimeograph over fifty thousand handbills informing citizens of a one-day boycott the following Monday—no Facebook to spread the word back then!

Word fanned out over the weekend. Despite cold and rainy weather on December 5, 1955, supporters of the boycott stayed off the buses and walked. The planned one-day boycott was so successful that the tactic continued—for over a year. In November 1956, the US Supreme Court confirmed a lower court ruling that segregation on public transportation was unconstitutional. On December 20, 1956, the Montgomery Bus Boycott ended after 382 days: a major win in the nascent civil rights movement.

Though not one to seek the limelight, Jo Ann Robinson and her contributions did not go unnoticed by those who saw her tenacity up close. In his memoir of the bus boycott, Dr. King said of Ms. Robinson, "Apparently indefatigable, she, perhaps more than any other person, was active on every level of protest."[21]

Parsonage tours can be booked via a reservation form on the church's website at *https://www.dexterkingmemorial.org/tours/book-tours/*. Remember, complete separate online reservation forms for the church and the parsonage tours. If you do not hear back in few days, call the parsonage office at (334) 261-3270.

The parsonage tour schedule is Tuesday through Friday on the hour from 10 a.m. through 3 p.m., except for noontime and Saturday from 10 a.m. through 1 p.m., including noon. Walk-ins may be accommodated depending on prebookings.

Near Dexter Avenue King Memorial Baptist Church

The next eight touring options are within walking distance of the church. We divide them into two groups: the first five include the outdoor Civil Rights Memorial, a block from the church and four in the general direction of the nearby state capitol; the next three are just west of the church.

Visiting the group of five means a mile-and-a-half walk roundtrip. As you walk it, remember that several of these places commemorate the *fifty-plus-mile* march from Selma to where you stand—so recall the context and know you won't be walking that far.

All five locations offer an outdoor experience, so you can do them anytime and any day of the week. They make a perfect complement to your visit to the church because not only are they nearby but also they relate in some way to Dr. King.

The Civil Rights Memorial and Civil Rights Memorial Center, 403 Washington Avenue

These are part of the Southern Poverty Law Center, which is right across Washington Street (one block south of Dexter Avenue; metered parking). The Civil Rights Memorial pays tribute to many of the martyrs of the civil rights movement, names of people whose stories you learn about throughout the trip: Jimmie Lee Jackson, Willie Brewster, Viola Liuzzo, James Reeb, and others.

Maya Lin, the memorial's designer (who also did the Vietnam War Memorial in Washington, DC) drew her inspiration for this work from one of Dr. King's favorite Bible verses: "We will not be satisfied until justice rolls down like waters and righteousness like a mighty stream" (Amos 5:24). Dr. King quoted this verse when speaking at Holt Street Baptist Church, imploring those assembled there to action on the first night of the Montgomery Bus Boycott. As an outdoor memorial, it is always open and there is no fee. The plaza is wheelchair accessible.

The Civil Rights Memorial Center is an indoor space with a $2 admission charge for adults. Visitors can add their names to the Wall of Tolerance by pledging their commitment to human rights. The center is open Monday to Friday, 9 a.m. to 4:30 p.m., and Saturday 10 a.m. to 4 p.m.

Three Civil Rights Locations: Between the Dexter Avenue King Memorial Baptist Church and the State Capitol

The Foot Soldiers Crosswalk is right outside the church. As you use it to cross Dexter Avenue, you can see that people with all sorts of shoe sizes are remembered here for their work in the Freedom movement.

Once across Dexter, walk toward the capitol on the left side of the street. At the corner of Dexter and South Decatur, near a post office box, note the marble marker commemorating the Selma-to-Montgomery March. There is a similar one across the street. That one was placed there in 1942 by the United Daughters of the Confederacy memorializing the inauguration of Confederacy president Jefferson Davis. Two monuments: same marble, same shape, different messages.

Another Selma-to-Montgomery March marker stands to the left of the capitol steps on North Bainbridge Street. On March 25, 1961, thousands there listened to Dr. King deliver the "How Long? Not Long" speech.

First Baptist Church, 347 North Ripley Street

This historic church is a half-mile walk from the Selma-to-Montgomery marker at the capitol. The Reverend Ralph Abernathy was pastor here from 1952 to 1961. A marker in front of the church tells you several parts of this church's storied history—from its founding in the 1800s to a bombing attack in 1957 to a fifteen-hour standoff with an angry mob on the evening of May 21, 1961, the day after the violence against the arriving Freedom Riders at the local Greyhound station.

"Never Witnessed Anything Braver!"

The Freedom Riders arriving at Montgomery's Greyhound station on May 20, 1961, were viciously attacked by a violent mob. Several Riders ended up in the hospital. The next day, Dr. King, who had moved back to Atlanta the year before, returned to Montgomery for an afternoon meeting at the First Baptist Church.

Over a thousand supporters of the Riders gathered in the church. However, three times that many angry segregationists began assembling outside the church as night approached. They threw rocks, broke windows, and at times threatened to breach the doors of the church and burst inside. A car was set on fire.

Dr. King called Attorney General Robert Kennedy to let him know the US marshals outside were having trouble controlling the crowd and needed more help. He urged those in the church to "fear not. We've gone too far to turn back."[22]

For some reason, Dr. King decided to go outside and walk toward the mob. Rocks and taunts caused King's colleague, Bernard Lee, to get him back inside the sanctuary. One of the Freedom Riders, Bernard Lafayette, saw King's courage in going outside the relative safety of the church and into the clenched teeth of the ugliness outside. As a Freedom Rider, Lafayette understood courage but he "thought he had never witnessed anything braver" than King's actions that night.[23]

It was a long night for those in the church. Eventually, the National Guard stepped in and things settled down. Not all the Guardsmen were happy about this assignment. In fact, even though the mob had been gone for hours, the commander of the Guard wouldn't let anyone out of the hot church until dawn.

West of Dexter Avenue King Memorial Baptist Church

These three historic markers are also relatively close to the church, just in the opposite direction. Two honor individuals who played significant roles during the bus boycott. The third calls out the slave-trading past of Montgomery.

A seven-minute walk from the Dexter Avenue King Memorial Baptist Church will take you to all three markers.

The Fred Gray Historical Marker, 300 Dexter Avenue

Walk west just over a block from the church to this marker at the Alabama Judicial Building—a fitting spot for this marker honoring the service of attorney Fred Gray. He represented Rosa Parks, Martin Luther King Jr., and so many others in civil rights cases. He also was the plaintiffs' attorney in the infamous Tuskegee Institute syphilis study case.

The Montgomery's Slave Depot Marker, Monroe Street and Lawrence Street

From the Fred Gray marker, walk another block and a half to Lawrence and turn right. Head north one block to the intersection with Monroe Street to see the Equal Justice Initiative marker on Montgomery's slave depots. In 1859, Montgomery had as many slave depots as it did hotels and banks. Three out of the four major depots were between Lawrence and McDonough (the stretch you would walk to get to this marker).

The E. L. Posey Parking Lot Marker, On McDonough Street near the Corner of Monroe

Continue on Monroe to McDonough Street. On the left, find the final marker of this trio. At the Rosa Parks Museum, you will learn that private vehicles took over the job of transporting Black citizens during the bus boycott. The E. L. Posey parking lot was one of the main hubs for over two hundred sedans and station wagons. The fleet was dubbed "rolling churches" since so many of the vehicles were owned by African American churches.

Sites on the Alabama State University Campus

National Park Service Montgomery Interpretative Center, 1521 Harris Way

Less than a mile from the Dexter Avenue parsonage is the third and newest NPS center commemorating the patriotic and brave heroes of the 1965 Selma-to-Montgomery voting rights marches. The center is located on the campus of Alabama State University (ASU), right next to the school's football stadium. Stop at the security gate to enter the campus; a guard directs you to parking near the Interpretive Center

The building was designed by Chambless King Architects, who creatively dealt with the challenging wedged-shaped plot of land on which the center stands. Incorporated into the striking limestone façade is the iconic 1965 image of a long line of Selma marchers.

Once conditions allow, this NPS Interpretive Center, like the other NPS facilities in Lowndes County and in Selma that make up this National Historic Trail, will be open Monday to Saturday from 9 a.m. to 4:30 p.m. While the entire story of the events of the 1965 marches is told here, the final segment leading to the capitol is well covered, including the joyous Stars for Freedom rally held on the final night of the march at the City of St. Jude, about three miles from the Alabama capitol. There is parking near the center.

If you are able to book appointments at the two properties tied to Dr. King's service at the church on Dexter Avenue, time may be tight to see this NPS site on the same day. However, consider a drive over to the ASU campus after stopping at the Dexter Parsonage to visit the locations described next.

Historic Homes and Markers on the ASU Campus, Various Locations

As you drive onto the campus, two white houses stand out on the east side of the road. Take the short walk back to see them after you visit the NPS Interpretive Center. One is the former home of Dr. King's associate Rev. Ralph David Abernathy; the address is 1368 Harris Way. Next door is the birthplace of legendary singer and composer, Nat (King) Cole. Historic markers stand outside these two well-preserved homes.

Across the ASU campus, find a monument honoring Rosa Parks near the Tullibody Fine Arts Center at University Drive North and South Jackson Street. Cross University Drive North at the Rosa Parks monument and walk down Tullibody Drive a few hundred feet; in front of William Hooper Councill Hall stands a historical marker informing visitors that, in a room in the basement of Councill Hall, the Montgomery Bus Boycott was born through the actions of Jo Ann Robinson, then a faculty member at ASU.

As you walk back on Tullibody Drive, cross the street at the corner with University Drive North. In front of George Hubert Lockhart Hall, there is another marker; this one honors the Black members of the state legislature who served during Reconstruction. If you miss this marker, an identical one honoring these legislators stands on the west side of the Alabama state capitol.

Rosa Parks Museum Day

The Rosa Parks Museum should be part of your Montgomery visit. Not only does it tell the story of one of the major events and individuals of the civil rights era but does that with a highly creative reenactment that makes you feel you were present when Mrs. Parks refused to give up her seat. Make this museum the centerpiece of one of your three days here. We'll share some ideas on how to round out the day.

Rosa Parks Museum at Troy University, 252 Montgomery Street

The museum is at the site of the former Empire Theatre. Here, Rosa Parks refused to move to the back of the bus in 1955 when it stopped at the theater. A marker in front of the Rosa Parks Library and Museum commemorates her courageous action. Troy University initially planned to build a parking deck here, but so many people came to see the marker in front of the old theatre that they thought better of that plan. The museum opened on the forty-fifth anniversary of Mrs. Parks's arrest in 2000.

A life-sized bronze of a sitting Rosa Parks catches your eye as you soon as you enter the lobby. Other striking artwork enlivens the lobby and the entire museum. Check out any special exhibits as they often present thought-provoking artistic works in a wide range of media.

The museum consists of six sections plus a Children's Wing and special exhibit space. Educational touch screens and video displays are found throughout. Artifacts from the famous December 1, 1955, arrest (like her fingerprint records, police reports, and court documents) add realism for visitors. Plan on three hours here.

Your tour begins in the Orientation Room. A ten-minute film provides an excellent introduction to the antecedents of the bus boycott, the life of Mrs. Parks, and the successful boycott. You view the film in a group setting. More on that in a bit.

After the film ends, the doors open, and the whole group enters the Bus Room. Here, a very clever reenactment of Mrs. Parks's arrest is presented. The bus in the room is a restored Montgomery city bus from the 1950s. Where's the actual bus? It was found in a field years later, authenticated as the actual "Rosa Parks" bus, and restored. The reveal on where you can find it comes later in the book, but for now, here's a hint: it's over eight hundred miles from Montgomery.

This section of the museum contains the original arrest record from 1955. Depending on how large your Bus Room group is, you may want to hold back to read it. Maybe the next group entering the Bus Room will be smaller. Being away from a big group pays benefits when you get to parts of the museum where you are viewing artifacts up close and reading material on wall displays. Plus, by holding back a bit, you get to experience the reenactment again.

The third area features a faux façade of Holt Street Baptist Church, where the community met after the successful first day of the bus boycott, December 5, 1955. Should the boycott continue? Dr. King addressed the overflow crowd, and his talent for rhetorical brilliance was again on display. "There comes a time when people get tired of being trampled over by the iron feet of oppression," he preached. A vote was taken; the boycott continued. (Holt Street Baptist Church, south of downtown, is one of the stops suggested on your way out of Montgomery to visit Selma.)

The next section focuses on Dr. King with a lifelike model of him sitting in his kitchen. The tableau re-creates when he questioned whether he should be leading the boycott movement, given all the

Some Reenactment, Huh?

The reenactment of the arrest of Rosa Parks is amazing. My notes from my own visit read: "Find out who did this and how."

The first part is easier to convey. The reenactment and other aspects of the museum were done by Kansas City–based Eisterhold Inc., a firm that designs innovative interpretive exhibits. You can see more of their work at the African American Museum in Philadelphia, Pennsylvania (covered later in this book); the Harry S. Truman Presidential Library in Independence, Missouri (also covered); and the National Museum of the Marine Corps in Triangle, Virginia.

So, how did they do the reenactment that makes you feel part of that day in 1955? They almost make it sound easy on the company's *website*. **There, you can find out what creates the sensation of a moving bus and the historically accurate items they built into the street scene to give visitors the feeling of being in front of the Empire Theatre in 1955.**

threats he and his family were receiving.

Be sure to see a December 30, 1955, request to FBI director J. Edgar Hoover from Captain E. P. Brown of the Montgomery police. This was less than a month after the bus boycott began. Brown asked Hoover for "any available information on Martin Luther King, Jr." Hoover's short response was that he had nothing to offer, at least at that time. According to the Martin Luther King Jr. Research and Education Institute, the FBI began to surveil Dr. King during the Montgomery Bus Boycott.

In the fifth gallery you learn about the transportation workaround that the boycott organizers developed to get people to work, church, and elsewhere. A restored 1955 Chevy Bel Air Station Wagon dominates the space. It represents one of nineteen such wagons that helped the boycott succeed.

Those who donated time or treasure to the Montgomery Improvement Association, the organization behind the boycott, caught the attention of the police. The museum has a display of bank records of boycott supporters as well as police documents showing law enforcement's complicity in this invasion of privacy.

Appreciate all the artifacts that this museum has gathered for visitors.

The final area centers around the victory won by the boycott. The circuit court of the Middle District of Alabama ruled in *Browder v. Gayle* that bus segregation was unconstitutional under the Fourteenth Amendment. The state and the city appealed that ruling to the Supreme Court, but the high court affirmed the circuit court decision. The boycott ended on December 20, 1956. Two days later, a shotgun blast penetrated the front door of Dr. King's parsonage.

In the Children's Wing of the Rosa Parks Museum, visitors enter the Cleveland Avenue Time Machine, an exaggerated version of a 1950s-era Montgomery bus. Through the magic of technology and special effects (also created by Eisterhold of Kansas City), you are transported from 1955 Montgomery (where people are waiting to catch a bus) back to the nineteenth century. Scenes of the Jim Crow era and segregation and meeting historic people like Harriet Tubman, Dred Scott, and Homer Plessy educate those in the Time Machine. Soon, however, it returns you to 1955 Montgomery. The same people you saw about twenty minutes before are still waiting to board their bus.

Rosa Parks Museum	
Location	252 Montgomery Street, Montgomery, Alabama 36104
Days Closed	Sunday
Operating Days and Hours	Monday to Friday, 9 a.m. to 5 p.m.
	Saturday 9 am to 3 p.m.
Admission	Persons 12+: $7.50; children 4–12: $5.50; Children under 4: free; AARP and Military discounts with ID.
Website	*https://www.troy.edu/student-life-resources/arts-culture/rosa-parks-museum/index.html*
Phone Number	Museum Receptionist: (334) 241-8615; Group Tours: (334) 241-8661
Email Address	*rosaparks@troy.edu*

I would not confine a visit with children to the Children's Wing alone. In the main museum, the curators have placed little smiling bus icons at a child's eye level. These can be found in the different rooms, and they help younger visitors understand the boycott through more concise copy directed to them. Note the key role that children played during the boycott.

Reservations are required for groups of twenty or more persons to receive a guided tour; groups smaller than twenty cannot book a guided tour. Large tour groups also need to pay in advance to reserve a time slot. Payment for guided tours must be received three weeks prior to that scheduled tour. Call (334) 241-8616 to reserve a large group.

Convenient and free parking is available in any Troy University parking lot. There is one diagonally across Montgomery Street from the museum. Some of the places in the lot are designated "reserved" for nearby businesses. Avoid those spots.

Rosa Parks Museum Day—Three Other Possible Destinations

Three other locations within a short walk of the Rosa Parks Museum are a mural at the corner of Montgomery and Lee Streets; a federal building named after a judge whose decisions had a significant impact on civil rights progress; and the Freedom Rides Museum, a small facility with helpful outdoor panels that's your primary destination here. The other two spots are right on the way and worth your attention.

Leave your car at the free Troy University lot as the round trip from the Rosa Parks Museum would be about a half mile.

Besides these three options, you can round out your Rosa Parks Museum Day with anything that you don't want to squeeze into the other days (like a side trip to Tuskegee). Or read about three recommended stops as you depart Montgomery for Selma; they are in the Selma chapter but you may have time for them on Rosa Parks Museum Day. The choice is yours.

Here are the three options near the Rosa Parks Museum side of town:

A Mighty Walk from Selma, Corner of Montgomery and Lee Streets

Turn left leaving the Rosa Parks Museum; walk to Lee Street, the next corner. Turn right on Lee and the colorful mural *A Mighty Walk from Selma* by local artists Sunny Paulk and Corey Spearman is impossible to miss.

As you navigate around Montgomery, you might see another

mural by the same duo honoring native son Nat "King" Cole. That mural is located on the west-facing wall at 435 Maxwell Boulevard.

Frank M. Johnson Courthouse, 15 Lee Street

Continue to walk away from the mural on Lee for about 150 yards. You may see an American flag blowing in the wind at a tall building on the right side of the road. This is the Frank M. Johnson Courthouse. No need to go inside necessarily (there is a marker on the side of the courthouse), but the person whose name is on the building is significant in civil rights history.

Frank Minis Johnson sat on the circuit court of the Middle District of Alabama in the mid-1950s. He and Judge Richard Reeves constituted the majority in the *Browder v. Gayle* decision that ruled segregation on city buses was a violation of the Fourteenth Amendment. Judge Frank Johnson also ruled in 1965 that the Selma-to-Montgomery March could proceed after Governor George Wallace had blocked it on the grounds of public safety. These were two important civil rights–era rulings.

Freedom Rides Museum, 210 South Court Street

Right around the corner on Court Street from the courthouse (Lee Street becomes South Court Street) is this museum on the former site of Montgomery's Greyhound bus station. Here, an angry and violent mob attacked Freedom Riders arriving from Birmingham on May 20, 1961. Among those injured by the attackers was John Lewis.

The inside of the museum is open from 11 a.m. to 4 p.m., Tuesday to Friday (10 a.m. on Saturday); the outside information

boards are available all the time. Adult admission is $5. Students, seniors, groups of ten or more, and military pay less. Children under six are free. One to two hours here is recommended.

"One More Swing and You're Dead!"

Floyd Mann was Alabama's public safety director during the 1961 Freedom Rides. Those responsibilities and some healthy skepticism about the trustworthiness of Montgomery's police commissioner put him in the center of the action at the city's Greyhound bus station on May 20, 1961. Mann had been promised by the commissioner that local police would take over for Mann's state troopers when the bus carrying the Freedom Riders from Birmingham reached Montgomery's city limits. Mann didn't buy it.

As the bus approached the station, local police protection was nowhere to be seen. Future congressman John Lewis, a Freedom Rider on that bus, recalled the atmosphere in May 1961 in a 2004 interview with author Ann Bausum. Said Lewis, "It was so quiet, it was so eerie, it was almost frightening" as the bus rolled into the station.[24]

Suddenly the mob appeared and attacked. Floyd Mann fought his way into the crate-throwing and bat-wielding thugs. John Lewis was knocked unconscious. Mann reached Lewis and fired his handgun in the air, causing some in the mob to back off, yet one Klansman kept swinging a baseball bat. Mann put his cocked gun to the guy's head, warning him, "One more swing and you're dead!" Mann called in more troopers and soon the mob dispersed. Some semblance of order was restored.

In 1989, Floyd Mann and John Lewis met again at the dedication of the Civil Rights Memorial in Montgomery. Lewis told Mann, "Thank you for saving my life."

CHAPTER 9

Selma and Marion

"Selma."

Just saying the name "Selma" conjures up such vivid images, especially for those of a certain age. The Edmund Pettus Bridge. Young James Armstrong, a foot soldier from Birmingham, carrying the American flag near the front of the marchers. Mounted police wielding billy clubs, mowing down peaceful marchers on a Sunday morning. Undeterred, courageous marchers starting over on their five-day trek to the state capitol fourteen days later.

"Selma."

Its name stands among a handful of towns where turning points in American history happened: Lexington, Concord, Yorktown, Gettysburg, and Selma. Small towns all, where history came to visit.

What happened on the Edmund Pettus Bridge in Selma on March 7, 1965, is fairly well known. While one may not recognize that specific date, few wouldn't know what is being referenced when someone brings up Bloody Sunday in Selma. This stop is probably one of the most anticipated on your journey.

Because of the pivotal role Selma played in US civil rights history, you are probably familiar with what happened here in March 1965. If you toured any major civil rights museum prior to arriving in Selma, you were undoubtedly exposed to a significant amount of content about Selma. So rather than cover already familiar ground, perhaps a focus on the events that led up to the Selma-to-Montgomery March would help. In the process, you'll see why historic Selma is paired with less well-known Marion for this day of your journey.

Marion, Alabama, is the county seat for Perry County. It was February 1965, a month before anything happened in Selma. A young staff member of Dr. King's Southern Christian Leadership Conference (SCLC), Rev. James Orange, is locked up in the Perry County jail in Marion.

Why was the minister in jail? Rev. Orange was facing the trumped-up charge of contributing to the delinquency of a minor. A conviction on that charge would mean prison. The local Black community, in support of Rev. Orange, organized a protest march in Marion on the night of February 18, 1965.

A civil rights protest after sunset was not common in places like Marion. Frye Gaillard pointed out that "night marches were rare in the civil rights movement, for the cloak of darkness often brought out the worst. The night was a time that belonged to the Klan."[25]

Marchers protesting Rev. Orange's situation streamed out of Zion Methodist Church. Not long after leaving the church, the marchers were met by the police, who began to assault them. To avoid the police attack, eighty-two-year-old Cager Lee and his daughter sought safety in Mack's Cafe (no longer there) near the Methodist church.

Troopers went into the café and began to beat the elderly gentleman. When his grandson Jimmie Lee Jackson tried to stop the beating, a trooper shot the unarmed Jackson. Jimmie Lee Jackson died eight days later. Ideas surfaced about how to respond to this egregious shooting. One was to bring Mr. Jackson's body to Montgomery and lay it on the capitol steps. While that specific idea lost traction, the idea for a march to the capitol "swept like wildfire through the 'Black Belt'" of Alabama.[26]

Three marches set out from Selma between March 7 and March 21. The first was on Bloody Sunday on March 7, and the third march set out two weeks later, eventually making it all the way to Montgomery. But what about the one in between? What happened to that one?

The day after Bloody Sunday, Dr. King filed a motion before Montgomery-based U.S. District Judge Frank M. Johnson Jr. petitioning the court to block the state from interfering with a second march. A court hearing on that motion was scheduled for Thursday, March 11. The judge issued a restraining order prohibiting any marches until he ruled on that day.

Not everyone wanted to wait for a judge's ruling. Preferring to march on Tuesday, March 9, the more activist-minded elements with the movement did not want to hang back for a few days. Thinking better of defying a federal judge, King was in a difficult spot.

The solution was to march on that Tuesday, cross the Edmund Pettus Bridge, but then stop. King knelt to pray when the march reached the foot of the bridge where troopers were again blocking the highway. He would march no further on March 9.

A compromise had been struck for an abbreviated march in exchange for no police action. However, few marchers knew about this. So when King stopped and led the marchers back across the bridge, there was confusion and even anger in some quarters. The term "Turnaround Tuesday" joined "Bloody Sunday" in the civil rights lexicon.

Young John Lewis, who had been savagely beaten and hospitalized on Bloody Sunday, felt there was no reason to be upset at Dr. King, unlike some other SNCC leaders. Showing the good judgment that was a hallmark of his distinguished career, John Lewis noted, "SCLC is not the enemy. George Wallace and segregation are the enemy."[27] On March 11, Judge Johnson heard arguments. On the March 17, he approved the march.

The historic march headed out on March 21. Jimmie Lee Jackson's eighty-two-year-old grandfather was there.

The Plan for Selma and Marion in 300 Words or Less

Today's route will take you from Montgomery to Selma on historic US Highway 80, the same road used for the 1965 march. Before reaching Selma (an hour's drive), I recommend a few stops.

First, you're not quite finished with Montgomery and its environs. I suggest three stops in Montgomery before getting on US 80:

- Holt Street Baptist Church
- The home of E. D. Nixon
- The City of St. Jude

Once on Highway 80, consider two recommended stops:

- The National Park Service Interpretive Center in Lowndes County
- A memorial to civil rights martyr Viola Liuzzo near Mile Marker 111

In Selma, you can walk across the Edmund Pettus Bridge, stop by two historic churches, see several markers and memorials, and visit the National Voting Rights Museum and perhaps the NPS Interpretive Center in town.

Marion is about a half hour northwest of Selma. It's where the nighttime march from the Zion Methodist Church to the Perry County jail (both still there) triggered events that ultimately led to the Selma March. There, you can also see memorials to Jimmie Lee Jackson and Rev. James Orange. Coretta Scott (King) was born about ten miles north of Marion. Details on seeing a hometown tribute to her appear later.

The final destination for this day is lodging that will put you in the position of seeing Philadelphia, Mississippi, the following day. Meridian, Mississippi, is one option, and a couple of places there are noted either for later in the day you visit Selma or for early the morning you depart for Philadelphia.

Leaving Montgomery: Three More Stops

Three days in Montgomery didn't exhaust the city's entire role in the civil rights story. Before getting on Highway 80 to Selma, consider three stops on your way out of town. They would be easy stops exiting the city if you are staying downtown. All three are south of the downtown area and less than two miles apart.

Holt Street Baptist Church, 903 South Holt Street

On the first day of the Montgomery Bus Boycott, leaders called for a 7 p.m. meeting at this now (sadly) deteriorating church. By 5 p.m., every seat was taken. Even Dr. King had to park four blocks away.

Hundreds had to listen outside as Dr. King urged those assembled "to work and fight until justice runs down like water and righteousness like a mighty stream" (Amos 5:24). We know Dr. King's words that evening because someone, sensing history was being made in this church, recorded the young pastor's remarks.

Not even fifteen seconds into the speech, Dr. King immediately grabbed the crowd's attention saying, "We are here for serious business." He then proceeded to deliver an inspiring talk that historian Taylor Branch noted was not only "full of theology but also full of the Constitution."[28] You can read the speech on the *website* of the King Institute at Stanford University.

There is a historical marker in front of the church.

The Home of E. D. Nixon, 647 Clinton Avenue

E. D. Nixon was a fighter for equal rights before the Montgomery Bus Boycott. He served as local president of the Brotherhood of Sleeping Car Porters and, as head of the Montgomery National Association for the Advancement of Colored People (NAACP), organized the first meeting of ministers and community leaders at Dr. King's church after Rosa Parks's arrest. A marker here sheds more light on what Mr. Nixon meant to the movement.

The City of St. Jude, 2048 West Fairview Avenue

This was the fourth and final "campsite" for the Selma-to-Montgomery March. You can imagine the excitement here on the night of March 24, 1965, as the marchers bedded down only three miles from the capitol. Adding to the sense of exhilaration was the lineup of entertainers who would perform that night: Bob Dylan, Joan Baez, Harry Belafonte, Tony Bennett, Peter, Paul, and Mary, and many others.

Here, there are three memorials. Two would be quick stop-click-and-go types of visits, and one would require about forty-five minutes:

- *Quick stops:* Remember the shiny sculpture of the Selma marchers at the corner of Monroe and Montgomery Streets in Montgomery? The one close to the National Memorial for Peace and Justice? The metal piece from which that was cut is at the corner of West Fairview and Oak Street. Besides this public art, there is an Alabama historic marker near the main entrance to the City of St. Jude on West Fairview (halfway between Oak Street and Hill Street).

- *Longer visit:* The City of St. Jude runs an Interpretive Center, housed in the original St. Jude social center. There is a collection of more than one hundred photos and other items documenting the Selma-to-Montgomery March. Every wall has a theme devoted to various aspects of the march. The center is open on weekdays from 9 a.m. to 4 p.m. and by appointment on weekends (334-265-6791).

On the Road to Selma

There are two recommended stops along Alabama Highway 80, besides snapping a photo of one of the iconic "Selma to Montgomery Historic Route" signs.

The Viola Liuzzo Memorial at Mile Marker 111, Highway 80, Lowndesboro

Viola Liuzzo, a white woman and mother of five, was from Detroit, Michigan. She came to Selma after seeing images of the Bloody Sunday attack. On the evening of March 25, as she was transporting a young Black civil rights protester back to Selma, she was murdered by Klansmen who overtook her car.

Search Google Maps for "Viola Liuzzo Memorial." If you are traveling west on Highway 80, do a legal U-turn after Mile Marker 111 to head east to the Liuzzo Memorial. Google Maps instructs you to go almost five miles to do the U-turn. There are several before that.

Whenever you begin to head east, stay in the right lane so that you can turn right into the entrance for Wright Chapel A.M.E. Zion Church. Walk over to the memorial.

Who Killed Viola Liuzzo?

One of the four Klansmen arrested for the 1965 murder of Viola Liuzzo was Gary Thomas Rowe. Rowe was acting as a paid FBI informant at the time of the killing. When Rowe was not indicted like the other three, his role as an informant became apparent.

Rowe had his own baggage on matters related to race. Testifying at a US Senate hearing in 1975, his identity hidden having entered the US Witness Protection Program, he admitted to wielding a baseball bat at the Freedom Riders on their arrival in Montgomery in 1961 and other atrocities during the time he served as informant.

As historian Diane McWhorter pointed out, the Klansmen on trial for the killing fingered him for pulling the trigger. "At the very least," noted McWhorter, "this violent racist on the payroll of the U.S. government had done absolutely nothing to prevent Liuzzo's cold-blooded execution."[29]

Besides this memorial to Mrs. Liuzzo, there is one in Detroit. At a playground named in her honor at 20087 Winthrop Street, there is a statue of her created by twenty-three-year-old Detroit sculptor Austen Brantley.

National Park Service Lowndes Interpretive Center, 7002 Highway 80, Hayneville

In 1965, white landowners evicted sharecropper tenants from their homes and land in retaliation for the push for Black voting rights in Alabama. To provide somewhere for those displaced families to live, a tent city was established here and provided shelter for two and a half years. Today, the NPS Visitors' Center is on the same land, and a path leads you to the former tent city site.

The center is roughly five miles past the Liuzzo memorial. You need to do a legal U-turn after seeing the Liuzzo memorial to head west to stop at this excellent and free NPS location. Normally, this center is closed on Sunday but open other days from 9 a.m. to 4:30 p.m. During the pandemic, the center's schedule was cut back.

The Lowndes Interpretative Center is more comprehensive and better managed than the one in Selma based on my experience at both. *Don't pass this by, thinking you will see the same content in Selma.* Allocate an hour and a half here, less if you don't view the orientation film. Here are three reasons my own experience was better here that at the NPS center in Selma:

- The Lowndes staff was more helpful and knowledgeable.
- The twenty-five-minute-long orientation film (*Fifty-Four Miles to Freedom*) worked here. It did not work in Selma and, even worse, no one in Selma seemed to care that it was not working.
- Lowndes has better information on other civil rights sites and general tourism in the area. The book shop is better stocked with more variety.

Stop at both centers, as my experience may have not been representative. However, if time is tight, this is the one I'd recommend. (The NPS site in Hayneville may be easier for those in wheelchairs to navigate as well, since it is on one floor.)

The Lowndes Interpretative Center has six exhibit rooms:

- *A Change Is Gonna Come*
- *The Making of the Movement*
- *Bloody Sunday*
- *Marching toward Freedom*
- *Tent City*
- *Towards Equality*

Multiple story boards, video screens, and interactive quizzes enhance a visitor's learning experience. Among the artifacts you will see is an original copy of *LIFE* magazine from March 19, 1965. (If you remember the role *LIFE* magazine played in presenting the visual story of America every week, please explain this to those who think of Life only as a popular cereal that Mikey came to like. Oh, wait a minute. . . . That explanation might not work either!)

Finally, as you watch the video presentation in the *Towards Equality* section on the Voting Rights Act of 1965, you'll see many political and news personalities comment on the importance of the law. People like newscasters Brian Williams and Ann Curry are identified by name on-screen. However, one congresswoman, now a high-profile member of Congress, was identified only by the general subtitle "Speaker #2." See if you can spot who it is.

Selma

Selma is a modest-sized city, and the locations likely of interest here are only a short distance from the town side of the Edmund Pettus Bridge. Detailed information is coming up, but in brief, here are the nine places suggested for Selma:

- As you arrive in town, drive across the **Edmund Pettus Bridge** to J. L. Chestnut Jr. Boulevard, about a half mile from the bridge. Turn right there.
- Drive four tenths of a mile to Martin Luther King Street. **First Baptist Church** is at 709 Martin Luther King Street. Park and read the historical display.
- Drive down MLK Street one and a half blocks to **Brown Chapel A.M.E. Church** on the left.
- If you want to walk the route of the Selma march in 1965, leave your car here and follow the next set of directions on foot.
- If you don't want to do a two-mile round-trip walk, hop back in the car and follow the next set of directions, parking near the NPS Visitors' Center.
- Continue down Martin Luther King Street for two tenths of a mile until you get to the **Old Depot Museum**. A monument to the Reverend James Reeb is in front.
- The Old Depot Museum is at MLK Street and Water Avenue. Proceed down Water Avenue, back toward the bridge and US Highway 80 (three tenths of a mile).
- At the bridge, the **NPS Selma Interpretive Center** is on the right-hand corner. Wait to visit this NPS location after you return from crossing the bridge. If you drove, park on Water near the Interpretive Center.

- Across from the NPS Center, there is a historical marker to see. Cross the bridge.
- The **Selma Civil Rights Park** is on the other side of the bridge. Here are several monuments that we describe later.
- Across from the park is the **National Voting Rights Museum**. If you choose to visit it, *carefully* cross Highway 80. (Vehicles approach and cross that bridge at high rates of speed.)
- Return to your car by walking back across the Bridge, perhaps stopping in the NPS Center if time allows.

Same stops . . . one-by-one . . . same order as above.

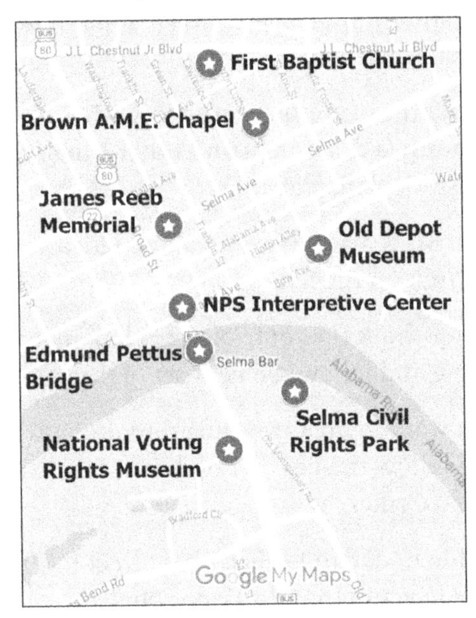

First Baptist Church, 709 Martin Luther King Street

This church was the first in Selma to open its doors to the Dallas County Voters League (DCVL). The DCVL was formed in the 1920s and revitalized in the 1950s by local leaders to advocate for voting rights. In the 1960s, the church hosted mass meetings and nonviolent teaching sessions run by SNCC. In late 1964, planning meetings at the church led to demonstrations early in 1965, all of which culminated in the Selma-to-Montgomery March. After the

Selma march, First Baptist continued to headquarter SNCC and served as a distribution center for food and clothing for those in need.

Tours inside the church are by appointment only. Contact Louretta Wimberly at (334) 875-5894. Email: *lcwimberly@bellsouth.net.*

Selma has two churches named "First Baptist Church." The other is on Lauderdale Street in Selma and is not the right one for your tour.

Malcolm X Supports Dr. King at Brown Chapel A.M.E. Church

In January 1965, Dr. Martin Luther King Jr. was awarded the Nobel Peace Prize. On February 1, he led a march in Selma protesting voting registration impediments and was arrested. After a few hours in jail, he was released but was quickly rearrested when he did not obey police orders to leave the scene.

King was in jail on February 4, 1965, when Malcolm X came to Selma to support him. Dr. King's lieutenants were concerned about having the fiery Malcolm in town, even after he assured Coretta Scott King that he would not complicate things for her imprisoned spouse.

On February 4, Malcolm X spoke at Brown Chapel A.M.E. Church. Frye Gaillard quotes Malcolm X telling that crowd, "I think the people in this part of the world would do well to listen to Dr. Martin Luther King."[30] Historian Peniel Joseph noted Malcolm's remarks "reaffirmed Coretta Scott King's private regard for him, one that she recalled her husband shared."[31]

Ten days after his appearance in Selma, Malcolm X's house was set on fire. Five days later, he was assassinated in the Audubon Ballroom in Harlem by three gunmen. All three were convicted of his murder in 1966. The convictions of Muhammad A. Aziz and Khalil Islam were thrown out in November 2021. The exoneration came after an investigation found that the prosecutors, the FBI, and the New York Police Department withheld key evidence that would have likely led to an acquittal for the two men. Each man spent over two decades in prison.

Brown Chapel A.M.E. Church, 410 Martin Luther King Street

This was the origin point for the Selma-to-Montgomery March. The church served as the headquarters for Dr. King's Southern Christian Leadership Conference (SCLC) in this region of Alabama. Two structures in front of the church grab your attention: a monument honoring Dr. King and a Civil Rights Freedom Wall engraved with a lengthy list of honorees.

The phone number of the church is (334) 874-7897, but tours are arranged by contacting Joyce O'Neal at (334) 875-3112 or (334) 505-9779.

James Reeb Memorial at the Old Depot Museum, 4 Martin Luther King Street

James Reeb was a Unitarian minister from Boston. Like many other members of the faith community across the country, he responded to Dr. King's call for the clergy to come to Selma after the Bloody Sunday police attack.

On the evening of Turnaround Tuesday, Reeb and two other white ministers ate dinner at Walker's Café. After finishing, they began to walk back toward Brown Chapel A.M.E. Church. Near the corner of Washington Street and Selma Avenue, they passed the Silver Moon Café, in its day a Klan gathering spot. The three ministers were soon surrounded, and Rev. Reeb's skull was bashed in with a blow from a baseball bat. He died two days later on March 11, 1965. The excellent National Public Radio podcast *White Lies* can shed more light on Reverend Reeb, his murder, and how it forever went unpunished.[32]

A marble James Reeb memorial is in front of the Old Depot Museum. The museum has a Civil Rights Room, its most heavily trafficked place. The museum is open from 9 a.m. to 4 p.m., Monday through Friday, and costs $7 for adults, $2 for students.

The Silver Moon Café is gone, but near the corner of Washington and Selma is a second memorial to James Reeb. Depending on the amount of green overgrowth, you may also be able to see the *Selma Voting Rights* mural on the side of an abandoned white brick building next to the James Reeb bronze relief.

National Park Service Selma Interpretive Center, 2 Broad Street

This center is at the town end of the Edmund Pettus Bridge. Unless you need a rest stop before walking across the bridge, I'd defer going into this NPS site until after you cross. Set in a former bank building, it has high ceilings and mostly modest-sized exhibit rooms. You'll find less content here compared to the NPS Center in Lowndes County. A half hour here is sufficient—unless the film is running properly, and you didn't see it in the Lowndes Interpretive Center.

The first floor has the rangers' desk, the gift shop, and a few displays behind the rangers' desk. The second floor has several life-sized statues of police and marchers and several information banners. One of those banners provides some good information on where you are likely to be headed next: Marion. The third floor is where the film should be showing but was not working during my visit. The restrooms are also on this floor. Elevators are available.

There is on-street parking near the center. Hours of operation are identical to the much more comprehensive NPS site in Lowndes County (Monday to Saturday, 9 a.m. to 4:30 p.m.).

The Edmund Pettus Bridge

Walking across this iconic and historic bridge is likely one of the bucket-list items on your civil rights itinerary, perhaps on your entire lifetime travel wish list. The structure is important symbolically because of the events in March 1965 and the legislative changes in voting rights that occurred as a result of the bravery exhibited here and elsewhere in the country.

If I could change one thing about my own trip, before crossing the bridge, I should have sat down on the town side of the bridge for a bit before crossing and listened to a speech of Dr. King or some relevant music—on some noise-cancelling headphones. When you walk the bridge, you will be struck by the noise from and the speed of the passing vehicles. Blocking out the world a bit as you walk the roughly quarter-mile span gives the place the reverence the 1965 marchers endowed in it.

Who Was Edmund Pettus Anyway?

Born in 1821 in north central Alabama, Edmund Winston Pettus was a delegate to the secession convention of 1861 in Mississippi, where his older brother John was governor. In the Civil War, Pettus served as an officer in the Confederate Army, rising to the rank of brigadier general.

After the war, he returned to Alabama, practicing law in Selma. In 1877, Pettus was named the Grand Dragon of the Ku Klux Klan in Alabama. His KKK role raised his statewide visibility to the point where in 1896, at age seventy-five, he beat an incumbent US senator to take over his seat. Six years later, he was reelected to the Senate.

When the bridge was completed in 1940, Edmund Pettus's name was chosen to adorn the distinctive steel beams across the structure. The irony of having a bridge named after a Confederate brigadier general and a grand dragon of the Klan become such a powerful symbol of the civil rights movement—emblematic of real courage and true patriotism—should be apparent.

There have been and are currently attempts to change the name of the bridge. That would require the approval of the Alabama legislature. An online petition garnered over 185,000 signatures to name the bridge in honor of the late congressman John Lewis.

National Voting Rights Museum and Institute, 6 US Highway 80 East

From the street, this museum does not look like much. However, I learned more here than I did at the Selma NPS Interpretive Center. I especially appreciated how this museum called attention to brave individuals who were not garnering the headlines back in the 1960s—the foot soldiers of the movement. Their footprints are everywhere through the museum, recognizing their hard work in support for those who walked in front of the march.

Inside, tour nine galleries and ten exhibit rooms devoted to the events and people who were woven into the fabric of the country's civil rights movement. Included among the people covered are infamous local Selma sheriff Jim Clark and much less well-known John Ballard, a nineteen-year-old Harvard student who drove down to Selma to take part in the march. John Ballard's story is in the Church Gallery.

On the downside, music plays here relentlessly. Those noise-cancelling headphones that you used at the other side of the Edmund Pettus Bridge may come in handy here too. It is challenging at times to discern the logic of the content flow from one room to the next. That might be a function of the sprawling nature of this large, one-story building, as though it had been a furniture store in the past.

The museum is open on Monday through Thursday from 10 a.m. to 4 p.m., other days by appointment. Adult admission is $6.50, with a $2 discount for students and those ages fifty-five and up. A combination ticket is offered with their partner museum on Slavery and the Civil War on Water Street. Tours can be booked through Ophelia Survia at (334) 526-4340.

The Selma Civil Rights Park, US Highway 80 across from the National Voting Rights Museum

Several monuments and markers are in the park opposite from the National Voting Rights Museum. The honorees include Amelia Boynton Robinson, Marie Foster, Rev. Hosea Williams, Congressman John Lewis, and Drs. Joseph Lowery and Evelyn Gibson Lowery. There is also a mural on the building that borders the park.

If you need a place to sit and reflect on your day here in Selma, the park offers a covered bench. A narrow sidewalk on this side of the bridge can take you back to the other side and your parked car.

Marion

Marion, Alabama, is twenty-eight miles northwest of Selma. While it may be tempting to head west on Highway 80 from Selma toward the Mississippi border to be in a position to see Philadelphia the following day, a detour to Marion is recommended. Traveling to and walking around Marion (much smaller than Selma) will add less than two hours to your day.

A visit here gives you more context for the historic march from Selma to the state capitol. The five recommended places to see are a short walk from the Perry County Courthouse, complete with its *Johnny Reb* Confederate statue on the lawn. Let's cover these five locations first and then mention two others that are outside of town, but which may be of interest.

Jimmie Lee Jackson Historical Marker, Southeast Corner of Perry County Courthouse Square

Park near the Pickens Street and Jefferson Street corner of the courthouse square and you can't miss this marker, which memorializes the slain twenty-six-year-old army veteran whose February 1965 death sparked the Selma-to-Montgomery March a month later. The marker was installed in 2015 on the fiftieth anniversary of the passage of the Voting Rights Act of 1965.

Zion United Methodist Church, 301 Pickens Street

Walk across Pickens Street to the church at 301 Pickens Street. On February 18, 1965, C. T. Vivian from Dr. King's SCLC delivered a moving sermon to activists gathered here to protest the arrest and jailing of the Reverend James Orange. Protesters moved out of the church and into the streets, where they were met by local police reinforced with Alabama state troopers. Two memorials are on the church's front lawn:

- The Civil Rights Freedom Wall listing about one hundred freedom fighters

- A storyboard titled *A Seed Is Planted*, explaining Marion's role in the movement

Site of Jimmy Lee Jackson's Shooting, 226 Jefferson Street

The location of the former Mack's Café, where Mr. Jackson was shot (and now the site of a funeral home) has another memorial sign to the civil rights martyr. Go behind Zion United Methodist Church to see this memorial.

Perry County Jail, 202 Pickens Street

Walk north two blocks on Pickens Street, on the same side as the church. This county jail held the Reverend James Orange on the night Jimmie Lee Jackson was killed. A memorial marker and a storyboard honoring Rev. Orange are outside the jail.

The Albert Turner Sr. Courthouse Annex

Right next to the Perry County jail, this building and the marker outside pay tribute to civil rights activist Albert Turner. An ally of Dr. King, Turner also led those at the Zion United Methodist Church on the night of February 18, 1965, on the march up Pickens Street to protest the charges against Rev. James Orange.

You may want to see two sites outside of Marion either as you come into town from Selma or head out and travel west.

Jimmy Lee Jackson Gravesite, Heard Cemetery, State Highway 14

Mr. Jackson's final resting place in the Heard Cemetery is about four miles northeast of Marion. If you travel from Selma to Marion on Alabama Highway 14, you come to the cemetery a few minutes after passing the town of Sprott. To find the Jackson tombstone, use these GPS coordinates: 32.658131, -87.273057.

Coretta Scott King's Childhood Church and Home, County Road 29, Perry County

Coretta Scott grew up fifteen minutes outside of Marion. Her childhood home and her church (Mt. Tabor A.M.E. Zion Church) are on County Road 29 just under ten miles from Marion. The family home has no clear marking and is not open to the public. The home is about 150 yards north of the church where Coretta Scott and Martin Luther King Jr. were married on June 18, 1953. The ceremony was performed by Martin Luther King Sr. Outside the church, there is an eight-foot statue honoring Mrs. King.

To find the church, use these GPS coordinates 32.744695, -87.365533. Or put "Calvary Baptist Church, Co Rd 29, Marion, AL 36756" into Google Maps and go just under another mile north of that church.

Whether your final stop is the Jackson gravesite, Coretta Scott King's childhood church, or the town of Marion, head west toward Mississippi. We return to Alabama later to visit Birmingham and Anniston.

Tomorrow's destination is Philadelphia, Mississippi. In 1964, three civil rights workers—Michael Schwerner, James Chaney, and Andrew Goodman—were sent to investigate a suspicious fire at a local church. While heading back to Meridian, they were arrested and jailed, and after being released that same night, killed by a group of Klansmen. Visiting sites related to this horrendous triple murder are the focus for tomorrow—and the next chapter.

The shortest route to Philadelphia from Marion is on rural roads, not interstate highways. A better choice may be to head west from where today's Alabama touring will end, get on Interstate 20, and spend the night in Meridian, Mississippi. You will find a wider array of lodging choices there compared to the more direct but more rural routes to Philadelphia.

There are two civil rights–related options to consider if you are overnighting in Meridian.

The James Chaney Gravesite, 5052 Fish Lodge Road, Meridian

James Chaney is buried in the small cemetery at Rest Haven Church (5052 Fish Lodge Road), located five miles south of exit 152 on I-20. Rita Schwerner, the widow of Mickey Schwerner, wanted her husband and his good friend and coworker James to be buried together. In the Mississippi of 1964, such an interracial burial idea was not going to happen.

The Meridian Civil Rights Trail, Various Locations

This is a two-hour self-guided tour to a dozen and a half sites in and around Meridian. At each stop, visitors encounter a marker with a QR code. Using that code on a smartphone allows access to a short video about that location, so your phone needs to include a QR reading camera or app.

Seven of the locations are walkable from the intersection of Fifth Street and Twenty-Fifth Street, the heart of the historic African American business district. However, the rest of the locations require a car ride. Look at the descriptions of the eighteen locations at the Visit Meridian website (www.visitmeridian.com) and customize those sites of greatest interest to you.

On the chance that time doesn't permit you to get to James Chaney's gravesite in Meridian, let me share what's on his tombstone:

> THERE ARE THOSE WHO ARE ALIVE
> YET WILL NEVER LIVE.
>
> THERE ARE THOSE WHO ARE DEAD
> YET WILL LIVE FOREVER.
>
> GREAT DEEDS INSPIRE AND
> ENCOURAGE THE LIVING.

Something to think about every day but particularly as you prepare to head to Philadelphia, Mississippi, tomorrow: the site of one of the most important events in US civil rights history.

CHAPTER 10

Philadelphia

If you are traveling on the recommended loop, you spent the previous day in Selma and Marion. Philadelphia may feel a bit like those places. All three are fairly small southern towns (under fifteen square miles) facing population declines in the past decade and still displaying various Confederate iconography.

Those are the similarities the three share today, but Philadelphia wasn't much different from the other two in the 1960s either. Like Selma and Marion in the 1960s, Philadelphia was a hostile place for Black citizens and outsiders. A reporter for *LIFE* magazine wrote of Philadelphia in the 1960s: "This is a strange, tight little town. Its fear and hatred of things that come from the outside is nearly pathological. As the stranger walks its streets, hostile eyes track him as a swivel gun tracks a target."[33]

Back then, both Philadelphia and Selma had violent segregationists serving as county sheriffs, each creating an antagonistic atmosphere for African Americans, but even that term seems too kind a description, given the history you are visiting in these cities. Selma in the mid-1960s had Dallas County sheriff Jim Clark. Clark wore a button proclaiming "NEVER" on his uniform to let folks know what he thought of integration. He often used a cattle prod against civil rights demonstrators.

Philadelphia and Neshoba County, Mississippi, of that period had corrupt lawmen like Sheriff Lawrence Andrew Rainey and his deputy sheriff Cecil Ray Price. Rainey and Price figure prominently in the murders that cause Philadelphia to be on your civil rights journey. These two men (and sixteen others) were tried in 1967 for conspiring in a plot to murder the three young civil rights workers. Price was convicted of conspiracy and sentenced to six years in prison. Rainey was not convicted.

The murder of James Chaney, Michael Schwerner, and Andrew Goodman occurred in the summer of 1964. Chaney, a Black man and a native of Meridian, was twenty-one years old; Schwerner and Goodman, both white, were twenty-four and twenty, respectively.

The summer of 1964 was Freedom Summer in Mississippi, so designated and organized by the Council of Federated Organizations (COFO). COFO was a coalition of the Mississippi branches of the four major civil rights organizations of the time: the Student Nonviolent Coordinating Committee (SNCC), the Congress of Racial Equality (CORE), the National Association for the Advancement of Colored People (NAACP), and the Southern Christian Leadership Conference (SCLC). Most of the impetus, leadership, and financing for the Summer Project came from SNCC. Bob Moses, SNCC field secretary and codirector of COFO, not only directed the summer project but also infused it with his passion for grassroots activism.

Freedom Summer followed a violent year in the South. In April 1963, police dogs attacked civil rights workers in Greenwood, Mississippi. In June 1963, civil rights activist Fannie Lou Hamer and others were arrested and severely beaten while in jail in Winona, Mississippi. That same week, Mississippi NAACP field secretary Medgar Evers was gunned down in the driveway of his home in Jackson. Three months later, a bomb went off at the Sixteenth Street Baptist Church in Birmingham, Alabama, killing four young girls. Two young Black males were shot to death on the same day as the church bombing. In November 1963, President John F. Kennedy was assassinated in Dallas.

Just about a month before hundreds of college students gathered at the Western College for Women in Oxford, Ohio, for their Freedom Summer training, two Black hitchhikers, Henry Hezekiah Dee and Charles Eddie Moore, were kidnapped, beaten, and murdered by KKK members in Meadville, Mississippi. Their badly decomposed bodies were found by chance in July 1964 during the search for Chaney, Goodman, and Schwerner.

Yet pushing potential danger to some remote corner of their minds, hundreds of well-intentioned, optimistic college students from across the nation still came to Oxford, Ohio, in June 1964 to be trained to help Black citizens register to vote in Mississippi, and to teach children in so-called Freedom Schools across that state.

On the first night of training, Bob Moses addressed the assembled volunteers. Consistent with his typical gentle style, he spoke to the group "so quietly the students had to strain to hear him,"[34] yet his words were powerful and blunt. "Don't come to Mississippi this summer to save the Mississippi Negro. Only come if you understand, really understand, that his freedom and yours are one."[35]

The training for the Freedom Summer volunteers went beyond just dealing with voter registration in Mississippi. They also needed to be prepared to withstand the abuse they would likely encounter from local whites. If they were naive about what they would face in Mississippi when they came to Ohio, their naivete likely dissolved quickly. In *Freedom Summer*, Bruce Watson likened the SNCC trainers in Oxford to "sergeants in boot camp . . . duty bound to turn innocent idealists into anxious, even terrified realists."[36]

One of the volunteers in Oxford was a twenty-year-old student from Queens College in New York. Inspired by a speech he heard Fannie Lou Hamer deliver at his school, the young man decided to go to Mississippi that summer. When his father asked why he had to go there, the son replied, "Because this is the most important thing going on in our country!"[37]

Andrew Goodman would begin his training in Oxford on June 13, 1964. Initially assigned to work setting up a cooperative in Canton, Mississippi, his assignment changed, and Goodman was asked to report instead to the COFO office in Meridian. A fire had been set at Mount Zion United Methodist Church in the Longdale community near Philadelphia on June 16. The congregation had agreed to host one of the Freedom Summer schools. The Meridian COFO office would investigate the fire and explore options for the school.

Andrew Goodman wrote to his parents of his safe arrival in Meridian, noting that it was "a wonderful town . . . wish you were here." On Sunday morning, June 21, 1964, he and his two more experienced COFO colleagues would head to Neshoba County to investigate the burning of the church in Longdale. It would be the last day all three men would be seen alive.

Robert Moses: An Inspiring Leader, Inspired by Others

Bob Moses's reputation preceded him to Oxford. A product of Harlem with degrees from Hamilton College and Harvard University, Moses began to work for one of CORE's founders, Bayard Rustin, in 1959. In the summer of 1960, he worked at the SCLC in Atlanta. The next year, Moses was tapped by the NAACP to begin a voter registration effort in McComb, Mississippi, and after 1961, he traveled all over Mississippi setting up similar voter registration drives.

Inspired by Amzie Moore of Cleveland, Mississippi, to start an organization to coordinate the activities of SNCC, CORE, the NAACP, and others, Moses became the program coordinator for the Council of Federated Organizations (COFO). This position gave him high visibility within the civil rights movement. In fact, he testified before Congress in support of the Civil Rights Act of 1964. His visibility was equally high to those hostile to progress in social justice. In 1963, Moses and two companions were shot at point-blank range as they drove in Greenwood, Mississippi.

Who inspired Robert Moses? In *Radical Equations*, Moses wrote how the student lunch-counter sit-ins in the spring of 1960 "woke me up." He was a teacher at a private school in the Bronx, New York, and wrote that he witnessed "almost every day on the front pages of the *New York Times* young committed Black faces seated at lunch counters or picketing, directly and with great dignity, challenging white supremacy in the South. They looked like I felt."[38]

Robert Parris Moses died on July 25, 2021.

The Plan for Philadelphia in 300 Words or Less

Visiting Philadelphia connects with places associated with the murders of James Chaney, Michael Schwerner, and Andrew Goodman. There are no museums here. There are no memorials at two significant places in that tragedy:

- Where their burned-out station wagon was dragged from the Bogue Chitto Swamp.
- Where their three bodies shared a temporary grave in an earthen dam meant to conceal their fate from the world forever.

With no museums or interpretive centers, this day will be spent primarily traveling from one historic marker or unmarked place to the next. The thought might cross your mind to skip coming here. That would be a mistake. Museums certainly have a role in everyone's civil rights journey, but so does being where history happened. For me, seeing the church bell that survived the church fire in Longdale was as impactful as any moment in a museum.

The suggested plan in Philadelphia is to experience two aspects of the city's civil rights history:

- The five places related to the murder of the three slain civil rights workers: (1) the church they visited on June 21; (2) the county jail where they were held after their arrest that day; (3) the marker near the road on which they were killed; (4) the swamp where their smoldering station wagon was found three days after they went missing; and (5) the private property where their bodies were discovered after a two-month search.
- The Carver Avenue neighborhood: the center of much civil rights activism in the 1960s.

If the Meridian area is your starting point, allow about three to four hours for driving to and around Philadelphia to see all the recommended sites. This is one of the shorter days in a loop tour city, which affords travelers the chance for a later departure from their lodging the morning they head to Philadelphia or an early start the same afternoon to their next stop.

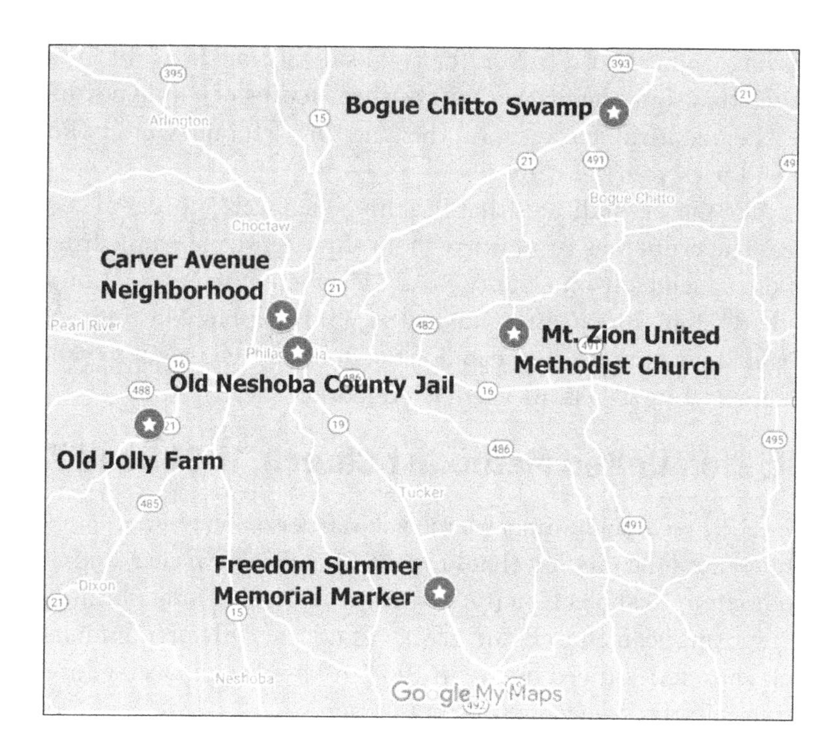

Freedom Summer Memorial Marker, State Road 19 and County Road 515

The five locations noted are presented in the chronological order in which they happened, from the fire in Longdale to the recovery of the young men's bodies. In directing you around these five places, we switch to a logical driving order, presenting them—plus the Carver Avenue neighborhood—in a fashion that makes the best use of your time.

As you drive from Meridian, the first place to stop is a marker close to the location of the murders. From Meridian to this marker on State Road 19 is about twenty-nine miles. State Road 19 is the same road the three civil rights workers took from Meridian the morning of June 21, 1964.

Put "Freedom Summer Memorial Marker" into Google Maps; Google has it marked. It's the best way to know how close you are to the marker. Otherwise, watch closely after being on State Road 19 for twenty-seven miles or so. Look for a ridiculously small green sign denoting County Road 517 on the right side of State Road 19. When you see that sign, the marker will be three tenths of a mile north of 517. The historical marker is on the left. Turn left onto County Road 515 and park your car carefully.

The marker indicates that the three men were murdered "near here." The crime was committed about three tenths of a mile from the marker, specifically on County Road 515 where it intersects County Road 284. Put "1000 County Road 284, Philadelphia, MS" into Google Maps to make sure you don't go too far if you want to venture to that exact intersection. There is no marker there.

Mt. Zion United Methodist Church, 11191 Road 747

The Freedom Summer Memorial Marker on State Road 19 references the mission that brought Chaney, Schwerner, and Goodman to Neshoba County: investigating the burning of this African American church. Mt. Zion was not the only predominantly Black church destroyed by fire in 1964 in Mississippi; over a dozen churches in the state were subject to arson.

The church is twenty to twenty-five minutes northeast of the Freedom Summer Memorial Marker. Google Maps will likely give you a couple of routing options to reach the address above. If you take the option on State Road 16E, you are traveling some of the same roads the three civil rights workers used after leaving the church on that fateful Sunday. When you pass the Longdale Hunting Club, you are a minute from the church.

At the church, note the following:

- *The church bell:* It was the only surviving item from the 1964 fire, a symbol of the endurance of the quest for freedom that drove the movement and the tenacity of those who believed in that idea of equality.
- The "tombstone-style" memorial to the three men in front of the church.
- The Mississippi Department of Archives and History (MDAH) marker down the driveway to the right.
- Another memorial stone right in front of the MDAH marker.

- The cornerstone on the church noting that the church was built in 1893, rebuilt in 1965 after the fire set by the KKK, and then rebuilt again in 1971 following another fire. The cornerstone also lists the names of trustees and others at the church, including members of the Cole family. That family was attacked the night Klan members burned the church to the ground in 1964.
- A plaque inside the church dedicated to the three civil rights martyrs, quoting in part from the Bible: "Out of One Blood God Hath Made All Men" (Acts 17:26).
- The cemetery next to the church that contains the graves of J. R. (Bud) Cole and his wife, Beatrice. Mr. Cole was beaten on the night of the fire in 1964, causing him severe leg and back injuries. For the balance of his life, he had to wear a brace. Also buried here is Lillie Jones, a fundraiser for the movement whom you read more about when we cover the Carver Avenue neighborhood.

The church holds a memorial service each year for Chaney, Schwerner, and Goodman around the anniversary of their murders. At a recent service, Philadelphia mayor James Young described the church as hallowed ground for the civil rights movement. Mayor Young was the city's first Black mayor when elected in 2009.

The Bogue Chitto Swamp, Highway 21, Neshoba County

A person identified by the FBI as "T. Hudson" was a little "later than usual" leaving for work in the wee hours of Monday, June 22, 1964. According to the FBI files on the murder of the three civil rights workers (code named MIBURN by the FBI), Hudson lived near the border of Neshoba and Kemper Counties, just north of this destination. As he drove toward Philadelphia, Hudson noticed a "big fire alongside Highway 21 in the Bogue Chitto swamp" around 2 a.m. He continued to his job, only reporting what he saw after the burned-out Ford station wagon owned by CORE was discovered.

Around 5 p.m. that same Monday afternoon, some folks fishing on the bridge over the Bogue Chitto Creek on Highway 21 decided they

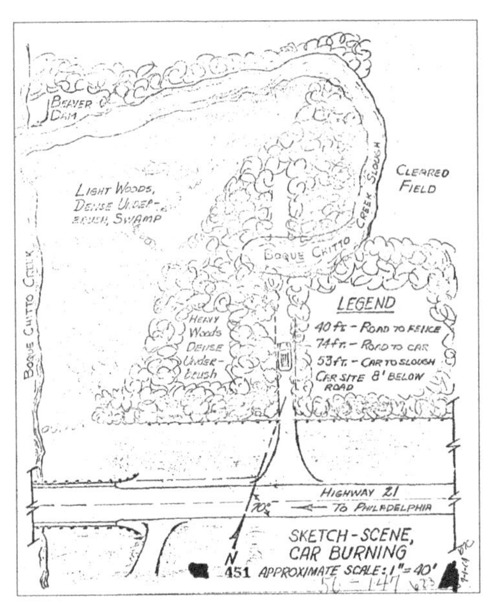

might have better luck near the beaver dam farther away from the highway. As they headed toward the dam, they noticed a car in the brush just off the highway. Subsequently, they told the FBI that the "motor was still smoking" but barely warm; the car "smelled like whiskey or alcohol of some form." They looked the car over briefly, hid three hubcaps and the side mirror from the car in some nearby blackberry bushes, and proceeded to the river to fish for two more hours.

The next day, in the early afternoon, the FBI was at the site of the burned-out station wagon. The MIBURN files report that the victims' automobile was 112 feet east of the east end of the concrete bridge over the Bogue Chitto Creek. The rear of the car was 74 feet from Highway 21.

No marker indicates this spot. If you want to visit it, do the following to spend a safe few minutes here:

- Put these coordinates into Google Maps or your GPS device: 32.881708, -88.938019.
- If you are coming here from Mt. Zion United Methodist Church, you will at some point get onto Highway 21. The most direct route from the church has you turn right onto Highway 21 from State Road 491. From there, you have 1.1 miles to the bridge over the Bogue Chitto Creek. (Note: There are two bridges over two different but quite proximate creeks. Owl Creek is the first creek; Bogue Chitto Creek and its bridge are just feet past Owl Creek.)
- If you are traveling north on Highway 21 (away from Philadelphia), don't pull onto the side of the road across from the destination as you drive north. Go about four tenths of a mile

past the destination and turn around where there is a safe place to head back the other way. As you approach the bridge over the Bogue Chitto Creek, slow down, put your right turn signal on, and carefully pull off the road just before the guard rails begin. It's easier there than on the opposite side of the road.

A logical question to ask is: "Where is that burned-out blue Ford station wagon today?" One might expect it would be in a museum to prevent the memory of what happened to these three men from ever fading. Award-winning investigative journalist Jerry Mitchell's book *Race against Time* provides a not totally unexpected answer. When Mitchell went looking for the trial exhibits from the 1967 federal trial of eighteen Klansmen, he found those exhibits were gone and that the Ford station wagon had been destroyed.[39]

The Old Neshoba County Jail Site, 422 East Myrtle Street

After meeting with members of Mt. Zion United Methodist Church on June 21, 1964, Chaney, Schwerner, and Goodman headed back to Meridian with Chaney behind the wheel. CORE and other civil rights groups discouraged their workers from driving after dark, and the three men had no intention of ignoring that advice. The blue COFO station wagon traveled on Route 16, east of Philadelphia. The vehicle was seen there with the trio fixing a flat tire as two lawmen looked on.

FBI records indicate that Deputy Sheriff Cecil Price arrested James Chaney for speeding prior to 4 p.m., indicating the trio left Longdale in plenty of time to make it back to Meridian prior to nightfall. Price also held James Chaney's two white colleagues "for investigation."[40]

The three men were transported separately to the jail that used to be at this East Myrtle Street location, Chaney in one patrolman's car and Schwerner and Goodman in the other. Price followed the two patrol cars into Philadelphia. The three men were held here in segregated cells until released about 10:20 p.m. that same Sunday night.

After their release, the three men headed to Meridian. The warnings that civil rights workers heard about driving in Mississippi after dark turned out to be prescient.

As the historic marker here at the former jail notes, two years after the murders, Dr. Martin Luther King Jr. and Rev. Ralph Abernathy led a voter registration march in Philadelphia. That march stopped at this location before reaching the Neshoba County Courthouse, just one-tenth of a mile away at 401 East Beacon.

In 2005, that courthouse was the site of the trial of Edgar Ray Killen, a Klansman charged with orchestrating the interception and murder of the three civil rights workers. Killen at age eighty was convicted of manslaughter, forty-one years to the day of his crime. He was sentenced to sixty years and died at Parchman Penitentiary in January 2018.

The Carver Avenue Neighborhood

Only a mile away from the site of the old Neshoba County jail is Carver Avenue, named after George Washington Carver. This neighborhood served as the center of civil rights–era organizing activities. A short walk on Carver Avenue may resurrect some of the same feelings you experienced walking historic Auburn Avenue. The walk up Carter Avenue is less than two hundred yards.

Your first stop should be the **Mt. Nebo Missionary Baptist Church** at 257 Carver Avenue. The church was the first in Neshoba County to allow CORE organizers space for their mass meetings. Dr. King held a memorial here following the 1966 march mentioned in conjunction with the old Neshoba County jail. The three slain civil rights workers are remembered here on a monument in front of the church. Unless something is going on at the church, park your car here or on the street next to the church.

From the church, walk south on Carver; the address numbers will get lower. At 250 Carver Avenue is a building that served the community from birth to death, being everything from a day care center to a memorial chapel in its time. In the 1950s, it was a **funeral home managed by Charles Evers**, the brother of Medgar Evers. (Medgar Evers was murdered in his driveway in Jackson, Mississippi, in June 1963.) Charles Evers also owned a hotel near his funeral home that housed COFO workers.

At 245 Carver Avenue, you'll see **McClellan Café & Grocery**. Stop in and meet owners Beverly McClellan Gill and her husband, Randy. Beverly is the daughter of Amos McClellan, the owner of the café when it was a favorite meeting place for activists in the 1960s. You'll enjoy the coffee and the conversation there as movement workers did decades ago.

Continue up the street to the corner of Carver and Atkins. On the right side of the street at what was 242-44 Carver, you would have seen the **COFO office for Neshoba County**. The sign that used to be in front of COFO headquarters with linked Black and white hands is now housed in the Old Capitol Museum in Jackson.

Finally, look across the street and use your imagination. At 241 Carver stood the **home of Lillie Jones**. Ms. Jones would sit on her porch encouraging COFO workers coming and going from the COFO building while keeping her eye out for any potentially unfriendly cars coming up the street. As you stand at Carver and Atkins, you can see that she had a good view down Carver. Ms. Jones, a driving force behind the memorial to the three slain civil rights workers you saw in front of the Mt. Nebo Church, is buried in the Mt. Zion United Methodist cemetery.

It's time to head back to your car—or for another cup of coffee at McClellan's.

The Old Jolly Farm, off Highway 21

Here the bodies of James Chaney, Michael Schwerner, and Andrew Goodman were discovered on August 4, 1964, forty-four days after they went missing. Like the site where their blue Ford station wagon was pulled from the brush near the Bogue Chitto Creek, no marker here memorializes what happened. This makes it the second important spot in the murder of Chaney, Schwerner, and Goodman that has not been memorialized in the nearly sixty years that have passed.

Wondering why these places that played a central role in historic crimes—that held the nation's attention for a month and a half—have not merited a historical marker is natural. Perhaps the absence of markers emerges from a concern that they might suffer the same vandalizing as historical markers related to the Emmett Till murder in the Mississippi Delta. One Till-related sign on a farm road over two miles off a rural highway has been shot up and replaced so often that a new bulletproof sign was put in place in October 2019.

Is it better to leave a historic spot void of any memorial just because that memorial might be vandalized? Bryan Stevenson of Montgomery's Equal Justice Initiative supplied an answer when asked about the repeated damage done to Emmett Till–related markers by author Susan Neiman: "It's so much healthier to have a marker that is desecrated than to have no marker that no one needs to desecrate. . . . It expresses something about who we are. That even creates a little bit of change to some people in Mississippi."[41]

While the location where the scorched wagon was found on the other side of Philadelphia and this location southwest of the city share being on Highway 21 and the reality that neither has been memorialized properly, those traveling Freedom's Road need to know one important difference. The Old Jolly Farm, the place where the men's bodies were removed from an earthen dam, is private property.

Thus, while you can drive along the stretch of Highway 21 that borders the property, trespassing onto the property is *definitely not recommended*. Google Maps pinpoints the location when you search "Location of Bodies of 1964 Freedom Summer Civil Rights Workers Found." Drop a bouquet on the right shoulder opposite County Road 1333, if that's your style.

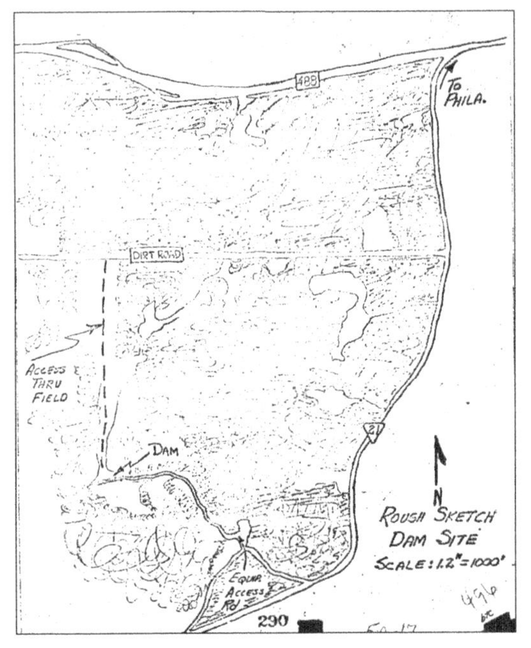

The location on Google Maps is consistent with what the *New York Times* reported to its readers in 1964: that the earthen dam was "several hundred yards off State Highway 21, near the Neshoba County Fairgrounds." The fairgrounds are about two miles down Highway 21. How did the FBI ever find this location?

On a journey in and around Philadelphia, you can see the thick walls of tall trees often blocking any view of what lies beyond from the road. If you take a wrong turn or just feel adventurous, you will end up on winding, dusty gravel roads that often just end, connecting to nothing: so many out-of-sight places to get rid of a body or three.

Why even search here? This spot is over twenty miles from where the station wagon was pulled from the Bogue Chitto Swamp muck. What led the FBI to search this spot? The answer comes from Bruce Watson's book *Freedom Summer.*[42] A couple of possibilities led to dead ends. In one case, the FBI drove a Black man all over Philadelphia trying to find the spot he was taken by five armed men after he was released from "official custody." His offense was allegedly asking a white woman for a date. After two days, he led the FBI to a place that failed to reveal any clues on the whereabouts of the three missing civil rights workers.

A second dead end resulted when comedian Dick Gregory's offer of a twenty-five-thousand-dollar reward for information on the missing three men yielded a letter "rife with backwoods grammar."[43] Investigators traced the letter's author to a Mississippi native living in the nation's capital. The FBI called him "a nuisance" and kept searching.

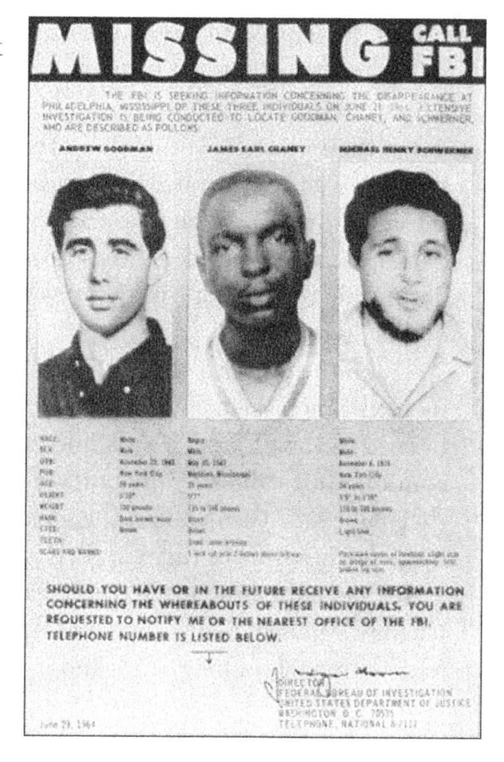

The missing poster with the three men had been staring the country in the face for weeks. The calendar had turned from June to July and now was about to flip to August. The men were still missing. The FBI was frustrated.

The lead FBI agent during the investigation was Joseph Sullivan. He had been meeting with a possible source, a highway patrolman from Meridian, since late June. Most of those conversations were unproductive. On July 30, Sullivan took the informant to a steak dinner at a Holiday Inn. Sullivan never admitted to any payoff for the information, but the source told Sullivan where the bodies were buried. The next day around Philadelphia, the FBI began spreading rumors, questioning suspects, and offering rewards for information to stir suspicion among the conspirators.

On Saturday, August 1, the FBI headed to the Old Jolly Farm. Thwarted by the dense thicket in their land-based search for a large earthen dam, they called in air support: a helicopter from the Meridian Naval Air Station. The copter found the dam, which bulged from the earth "like the back of a half-submerged whale."[44] It measured 20 feet high, 547 feet long, and 83 feet thick.[45] With the initial aid of a steam shovel and, eventually, the more delicate intervention of FBI-manned trowels after the smell of decaying flesh filled the air, a black Wellington boot became visible. Shortly after 5 p.m., the three men were no longer missing.

Your day in Philadelphia is finished. No matter where you are heading next, Philadelphia has given you much to think about for the rest of the day—and beyond.

On the negative side, think about the hate that led so-called Christian men to beat up innocent churchgoers and then to burn down their church. Think about the corrupt lawmen who thought they were above the laws they had sworn to enforce. Think about the cowardice of a mob who had to act not only under the cover of darkness but also under the code of silence to carry out an act so despicable that not one of them would likely have done such a thing on his own.

On the positive side, think of the fearlessness of three young men willing to visit a rural, Black church only days after it was burned to the ground. Think about their selflessness in leaving their comfort zones and literally putting their lives on the line for what they believed. Think about the ideals of freedom and equality that brought the three of them to Mississippi in 1964.

I was finishing my second year of high school when James Chaney, Michael Schwerner, and Andrew Goodman went missing. It had an impact on me then—and it still does.

Preparing to Be a Freedom Summer Volunteer

Turn the clock back and imagine that you've applied to volunteer in Mississippi during Freedom Summer. How would they ask you to prepare? What would they ask you to bring with you to Oxford, Ohio?

Howard Ball's *Murder in Mississippi*[46] provides a rundown of some of the musts for the young Freedom Summer volunteers. For starters, they were to read three books before they arrived in Ohio:

- *Souls of Black Folk* by W. E. B. DuBois
- *The Mind of the South* by W. J. Cash
- *The Other America* by Michael Harrington

The list of items they were to bring with them for the summer included the following:

- Power-of-attorney documents
- One hundred and fifty dollars for transportation and living expenses "for the entire summer"
- Contacts of individuals or groups back home who could post bail for them

Lastly, the handbook listed a variety of warnings:

- No one should go anywhere alone, certainly not in an automobile and certainly not at night.
- Know locations of sanctuaries and safe homes in the county.
- When getting out of a car at night, make sure the car's inside light is out.
- If it can be avoided, try not to sleep near open windows.
- Try to avoid bizarre or provocative clothing and beards. Be neat.
- No interracial groups traveling, day or night, unless absolutely necessary. And if that happened, whoever is in the minority must be hidden, covered by blankets, lying on the floorboards.

Despite all of that, hundreds of young people, Black and white, showed up in Oxford, Ohio, to become Freedom Summer volunteers.

CHAPTER 11

Jackson

What southern city initially comes to mind when the topic is civil rights–targeted bombings? I imagine it is Birmingham—and for good reason. The city earned the nickname "Bombingham" because of all the racially motivated bomb attacks there.

What about a place remembered for harassing Freedom Riders? Anniston, Alabama, where a bus carrying the 1961 Freedom Riders was set on fire.

How about successful boycotts? Perhaps Montgomery in conjunction with the bus boycott there.

Lunch-counter sit-ins? Greensboro, North Carolina; after all, the sit-in at Woolworth's there in 1960 set off a tsunami of similar protests across the South.

Finally, what city is most associated with the assassination of a major civil rights leader? My guess is that Memphis is the first to come to mind for most people.

Well, Jackson, Mississippi, had all of these: bombings, boycotts, Freedom Rider arrests, sit-ins, and a targeted assassination. On top of these, Jackson, as Mississippi's capital, had the notorious distinction of being the home of the state's Sovereignty Commission. That agency, overseen by the governor and operating from 1956 to 1977, had the authority to investigate citizens and exercise a wide range of police powers to suppress civil rights activities. The time you spend here can increase your understanding of all of these issues and events as you learn the role Jackson played in furthering the movement.

Calvin Trillin is an award-winning author, much of whose writing has appeared in the *New Yorker*. In the 1960s, he reported often on the civil rights movement. In August 1964, Mr. Trillin composed an article for the magazine that captured the oppressive atmosphere that Black citizens of Jackson experienced in the 1960s.

Trillin characterized the Jackson of that era as a city where "the community bulletin board of a local radio station occasionally includes, among reports of rummage sales and church suppers, the announcement that Americans for the Preservation of the White Race will hold its weekly meeting that evening and 'that all interested white people are invited to attend.'" He also noted that the inventory of a local bookstore would "begin with the writings of the John Birch Society and move to the right."[47]

Many places, of course, were hostile to Black citizens in the 1960s. By the time you get to Jackson, you will have already visited a few. However, the Jackson of the 1960s takes a backseat to no other city in terms of racial discrimination and violence.

Before recommending how you might spend your Jackson time, let's review some of the main civil rights actions that took place here. Many paralleled those that occurred elsewhere: boycotts, lunch-counter sit-ins, and the like. However, the events in Jackson often did not rise to the same level of national awareness as similar activities in other southern cities. For example,

- In March 1961, nine Tougaloo College students conducted a read-in at a whites-only public library. For simply trying to enter the library, they spent a night in jail, were fined one hundred dollars, and spent a year on probation.
- Two months later, Freedom Riders arrived here intending Jackson to be a stop on their way to their ultimate destination: New Orleans. Local police had other ideas, and many Riders ended up in the maximum-security Parchman State Penitentiary—a place to consider for a quick stop on your travels in the Mississippi Delta.
- From 1961 to 1963, boycotts and demonstrations pushed for an end to discriminatory practices in hiring, voting, and public accommodations.
- In May 1963, two African American women and an African American man sat down at a local F. W. Woolworth's lunch counter to protest the store's segregated seating policy. They were joined by five others. A white mob attacked the group with fists, obscenities, and any condiment they could

find. Despite the assault, the police arrested the nonviolent protesters.

- Two tension-filled weeks after the Woolworth's lunch-counter sit-in, the most infamous event in the civil rights story of Jackson occurred. Medgar Evers, the National Association for the Advancement of Colored People's (NAACP) field secretary, was gunned down in his driveway. His home is a must-see on your visit to Jackson.
- James Meredith's March against Fear ended here in June 1966. An estimated fifteen thousand joined Mr. Meredith, who had been shot and wounded in Hernando, Mississippi, on the second day of the march.
- In September 1967, the Ku Klux Klan bombed the Beth Israel synagogue. Two months later, the home of its rabbi, Perry Nussbaum, was also bombed. Rabbi Nussbaum and his congregation supported the civil rights movement.

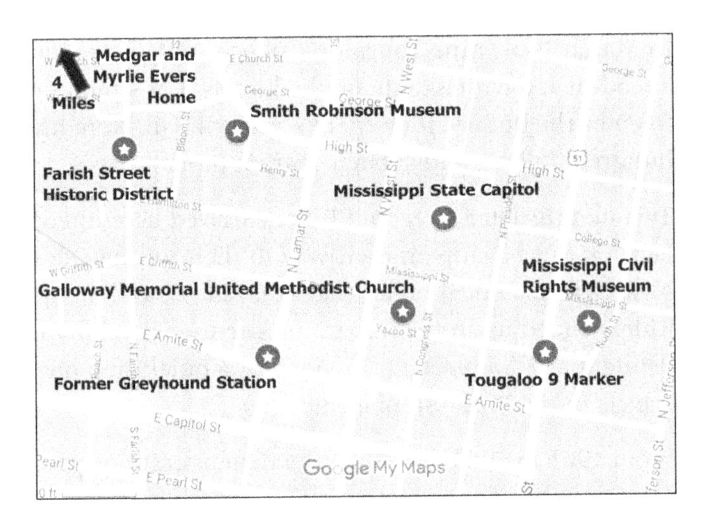

The Plan for Jackson in 300 Words or Less

You can visit all the places associated with the above events. In some cases, sadly, the building involved in the actual event has either been repurposed or is gone. However, markers commemorate these events.

Despite the failure to preserve many landmark buildings from the city's civil rights history, the destination atop the list of places associated with Jackson's civil rights past remains almost unchanged since minutes after midnight on June 12, 1963: the home of Medgar and Myrlie Evers. That home must be on your Jackson itinerary.

Also plan time at these other recommended stops:

- The Mississippi Civil Rights Museum (MCRM): Combine with a visit to the Evers home as the two places are fifteen minutes apart. Block out at three to four hours for this engaging museum.
- Walk or drive to see as many historic places around the city as your time here allows. A half dozen relevant sites, including the state capitol, are within a mile walk of the MCRM. Other sites require getting back in your car to reach. We'll divide all walk-to and drive-to places into a few neighborhoods—the Farish Street Historic District, the Jackson State University area, and so on—so that you can decide which ones you try to see.

Two days are suggested for Jackson just to be sure you see the Everses' home, the MCRM, and other locations that appeal to you.

The Medgar and Myrlie Evers Home, 2332 Margaret W. Alexander Drive

June 11, 1963, was a consequential day in our civil rights history. On that day, Alabama governor George Wallace stood in the door of Foster Auditorium at the University of Alabama to block the school's integration. President John F. Kennedy went on national TV that evening to tell the country that "this nation, for all its boasts, will not be fully free until all its citizens are free." Returning from an NAACP meeting that same night, Medgar Evers was assassinated in the driveway of his own home. Mr. Evers was a World War II veteran, the NAACP field secretary for Mississippi, and the father of three.

In June 2020, the modest ranch-style home was acquired by the

A Tip on Overnighting in Jackson

Consider staying north of Jackson if you opt for two nights there. The Ridgeland, Mississippi, area has many lodging options. This will cut a little bit out of your travel to the Delta on the morning you depart the Jackson area. Saving fifteen or so minutes may be nice benefit on what could be a long day in the Delta and on to Little Rock.

Ridgeland is only fifteen to twenty minutes from the two highly recommended places to see in Jackson: the Medgar and Myrlie Evers Home and the Mississippi Civil Rights Museum. Plus, Ridgeland provides easy access to the scenic and historic Natchez Trace Parkway if you like to walk, run, or ride a bike.

That said, the idea of spending the night before your Mississippi Delta day in Greenwood, Mississippi, is explored later in the chapter. Greenwood has its own civil rights history, and it is only a short drive from Greenwood to Money, an important stop in the Emmett Till murder case.

National Park Service from Tougaloo College, which had maintained the home for nearly a quarter century. Later in 2020, it earned the National Monument designation.

During 2021, the NPS began to prepare the home and property for public access. These activities included assessing the home's condition, authenticating its furnishings, and conducting public meetings to establish the theme of monument's public face. According to NPS park superintendent Keena Graham, since this preparation would be extending into 2022, not only was the inside of the home closed to the public at press time, inside access will remain unlikely into 2022.

While the NPS works to ready the home and property for the public, visitors are encouraged to make a respectful visit to the outside of the home. There, one can read content boards that inform on the events of June 1963 and the contributions of Medgar and Myrlie Evers. A Mississippi Freedom Trail marker is also in front of the home.

Once reopened, visitors will see greater use of technology, new information boards, and a more structured experience overall. The permanent marks made by the bullets from the powerful rifle used by Mr. Evers's assassin will still be evident in the living room and the kitchen, serving as a reminder of the destructiveness of hate.

Plans call for the facility to remain free to the public but no final decision on operating days and hours has been made. As before, however, an appointment will be needed to visit due to the size of the home and its neighborhood setting. Check *https://www.nps.gov/memy/index.htm* for updates and for educational programming that will serve as a soft reopening for the facility.

After visiting the Evers Home National Monument, drive over to the Medgar Evers Library and Statue. It is less than a mile away, located at 4215 Medgar Evers Boulevard. The life-size bronze of Mr. Evers is impressive. Also close to the Evers home is Freedom Corner. Here, at the intersection of Medgar Evers Boulevard and Martin Luther King Jr. Drive is a memorial to the two leaders and another popular photo spot. A little hard to spot, it is across from the gas station on Medgar Evers Boulevard.

To learn more about the consequential life of Medgar Evers, his courtship of Myrlie, his work for civil rights, his murder, and the trials (yes, trials) of his murderer, read *Ghosts of Mississippi: The Murder of Medgar Evers, The Trials of Byron De La Beckwith, and the Haunting of the New South* by Maryanne Vollers.

The Mississippi Civil Rights Museum, 222 North Street

Less than five miles from the Medgar and Myrlie Evers home is this major civil rights museum. It opened in December 2017, becoming the first state museum in the country devoted to civil rights. Reaction to it has been generally positive, though the thought of the state itself benefiting from civil rights tourism angered some, given Mississippi's dark past. On the positive side, *New York Times* reviewer Holland Cotter recognized that "the museum refuses to sugarcoat history" and that it "privileges truth-telling, [and] messy facts over clean-cut aesthetics."[48]

Despite praise like this, when the idea for the museum was initially raised in 2011, movement veterans Revs. James Lawson Jr. and C. T. Vivian as well as Diane Nash and others questioned why Jackson and Mississippi should reap financial benefits from the growing interest in civil rights tourism.[49]

This issue is challenging. The museum, however, seems true to its stated goal of promoting understanding of the movement "by highlighting the strength and sacrifices of its peoples."

Museum Overview

This facility is incredibly comprehensive and wonderfully interactive, with eight first-floor galleries and special exhibition space on the second floor. Photographs, text boards, artifacts, and many audiovisual elements make for an immersive and stimulating presentation gallery after gallery. This museum is likely to be one of your journey's highlights. What made this one stand out for me were the large number of African American senior citizens going through the museum. Many likely lived through some of the history covered here. Their presence made for an especially moving experience I don't recall having as powerfully in other civil rights–related venues. Some of these seniors were using their canes, walkers, or wheelchairs as they viewed the exhibits. For the most part, the path width through the galleries accommodated these visitors well—good planning ahead by the museum's designers.

Mississippi Civil Rights Museum	
Location	222 North Street, Jackson, Mississippi 39201
Days Closed	Monday
Operating Days and Hours	Tuesday to Saturday, 9 a.m. to 5 p.m.
	Sunday, 11 a.m. to 5 p.m.
Admission	Adults: $15 Youth (ages 4-18): $8 Senior (ages 60+) or military: $13 Children under 3 years: Free These ticket prices include admission to the adjacent Museum of Mississippi History. Admission to both museums is free on Sunday.
Website	*http://mcrm.mdah.ms.gov/*
Phone Number	(601) 576-6800
Email Address	*info@mscivilrightsmuseum.com*

Block out at least three hours for your visit, especially if a special exhibit interests you. A special exhibit of African American quilts took over the second floor during my visit.

There is free on-street parking near the museum. However, the museum does have a parking garage that is accessed from Jefferson Street between Amite and Mississippi Street.

What You'll See

Visitors proceed through eight galleries, seven of these surrounding a central sitting area that makes up Gallery 3, titled *This Little Light of Mine*. Here, you not only can take a seat, but you get to hear (repeatedly!) the song that gives this gallery its name. The focal point of Gallery 3 is a dramatic sculpture that glows brighter and the music swells as more people gather in the space. The constant music, sometimes very loud, may become annoying. Noise-cancelling headphones may be a good idea here too, as sound can also be an issue in other galleries.

Each gallery focuses on a specific time frame, and each includes a helpful timeline of events in Mississippi and the United States.

Gallery One: Mississippi's Freedom Struggle

This introductory gallery provides visitors with the context for the civil rights movement. Visitors are inspired by the thoughts of brave men, women, and children who put their lives on the line to push for equality and freedom.

One story to watch for in the first gallery has a surprising historical twist. It is the odd connection between a family member of Confederate president Jefferson Davis and the founding of the country's first community made up of formerly enslaved people. Joseph Davis (brother of Jefferson Davis) sold his Davis Bend Plantation to his former enslaved laborer Benjamin Montgomery after the Civil War. A host of problems at the plantation eventually caused Benjamin's son Isaiah to move the community off that plantation. Isaiah Montgomery established an all-Black community in the Mississippi Delta called Mound Bayou, a historic town discussed further in the chapter on Mississippi Delta sites.

Gallery Two: Mississippi in Black and White

This gallery covers the years 1865 to 1941 with a nice mix of text displays, historical artifacts, and still images. Particularly clever is the use of spinning boards with a question on one side and the answer revealed on the reverse. Also instructive was the material on the role of church, work, and family. The five pillars naming the state's lynching victims from 1887 to 1928 are a focal point of this gallery.

Two important topics are recommended for particular attention:

- *The Great Mississippi River Flood of 1927.* This was the most destructive river flood in US history. Among the many horrible aspects of this event was the particular cruelty shown to Black sharecroppers. Fearing that once they were off the land they farmed for the landowners, the sharecroppers would never return, many were not allowed to escape the flood's impact. William Percy, the son of then–US senator LeRoy Percy, wanted to evacuate the Black sharecroppers. White landowners asked Senator Percy to stop his son from bringing in vessels to evacuate the sharecroppers, fearing that the African Americans would become part of the Great Migration to the North. The senator agreed, and the sharecroppers were left stranded.
- *Facts on Black Voter Registration.* Just two years after the Civil War ended, two out of three Black voting-age citizens were registered to vote. After Reconstruction, and specifically by 1892, that percentage had fallen sharply to 5.7 percent. Even worse, by *1955*, it was down to 4.4 percent. Like the Legacy Museum in Montgomery, this museum uses data to drive home reality.

Gallery Three: This Little Light of Mine

As noted earlier, this central gallery makes a good resting spot. It's a creative idea with some downsides due to the volume of the music when a large group is gathered.

Gallery Four: A Closed Society

The time frame shifts here to the period from 1941 to 1960. Among the topics presented is the impact Black Mississippians who served in World War II had in fueling the civil rights movement.

A particularly interesting section is on the accepting attitudes of Europeans toward American Blacks; a small audio room is devoted to this topic. Separate theaters educate visitors on two significant events of the 1950s: the landmark *Brown v. Board of Education* decision and Emmett Till's murder, the latter film narrated by Oprah Winfrey.

The gallery has a lot of extraneous noise. Some of it comes from a video of Mississippi US senator James Eastland from June 29, 1945, on the Senate floor saying, "The Negro was an utter and dismal failure in combat in Europe." Even if the noise itself doesn't bother you, put on your headphones to avoid hearing Eastland.

Gallery Five: Tremor in the Iceberg

This gallery takes visitors to the early 1960s. The title of this cleverly named exhibit comes from civil rights activist Bob Moses. He described the early 1960s as the "tremor in the middle of the iceberg." Use the interactive touch-screen exhibit to read personal stories of participants in the 1961 Freedom Rides.

The gallery has many artifacts from the early 1960s: from simple jailhouse flip-flops to a spent teargas canister from the 1962 integration battle at the University of Mississippi to enroll James Meredith. *Tremor in the Iceberg* rightly gives much attention to the life and sacrifice of Medgar Evers. The museum is also the conservator for the rifle that Byron De La Beckwith used to assassinate Mr. Evers; it is displayed within the gallery.

Gallery Six: I Question America

In a museum with so many important exhibits, this gallery has one of my favorite elements: the re-created country church with another film narrated by Oprah Winfrey. The gallery's focus is on 1963 and 1964, so here you learn about the Freedom Summer volunteers and the murders of volunteers James Chaney, Andrew Goodman, and Michael Schwerner. Plus, visitors learn about the role that COFO played in the state; see the clasped Black and white hands sign from the COFO office in Philadelphia, Mississippi; and meet courageous and passionate civil rights icon Fannie Lou Hamer. This gallery caused my own visit to go right up against closing time.

Gallery Seven: Black Empowerment

In 1965, the US Congress passed the Voting Rights Act, ushering in a rise in Black empowerment. However, this section covering 1965 to the mid-1970s is not solely focused on Black successes. Tragedies like the murder of Vernon F. Dahmer Sr. of Hattiesburg, the shooting at Jackson State University, and the shots fired at James Meredith in Hernando on the second day of his 1966 March against Fear are also presented.

Gallery Eight: Where Do We Go from Here?

In the final gallery, the museum encourages visitors to stop and reflect on what they have seen and heard. For inspiration, read the words on the picture wall of Mississippians from all walks of life. The presentation balances a sense of optimism given the progress these Mississippians see with a sense of reality that challenges remain. Share your thoughts here as well.

The State Capitol Building and the Neighboring Area

Several spots that are relatively close to the Mississippi Civil Rights Museum merit your time. Leave your car at the museum unless you simply want to drive past the four destinations listed below. In total, they require roughly a one-mile walk (one way), shorter if you return to your car before going to the Smith Robinson Museum.

I recommend going inside the state capitol, which you may recall I didn't do with Alabama's capitol. Mississippi's is beautiful inside. Go up to the top floor for an experience that relates to your civil rights journey; I'll explain in a moment.

Here are the four walkable spots from the Mississippi Civil Rights Museum.

Former Site of Jackson Municipal Library, 301 North State

Head west out of the MCRM on Mississippi Street. Take a left on North State. Walk south. Look for the marker across from the present library, named in honor of Black writer Eudora Welty. Here the Tougaloo

Nine staged their read-in at the former whites-only library in March 1961. They spent thirty-two hours in jail for breaching the peace.

Historic Galloway United Methodist Church, 305 North Congress Street

At North State and Yazoo, walk two blocks west to North Congress Street to this church. In 1963, the church board voted to exclude Blacks, contrary to the policy of the national United Methodist Church (UMC). When the church denied Blacks entrance, the pastor and the associate minister resigned. In 1966, the board reversed itself and admitted Blacks to worship here. About one third of its members left the church when Blacks were admitted.

Mississippi State Capitol—Enter on the Lower Level, Mississippi Street Side

Walk toward the capitol on Congress. Cross Mississippi Street and head toward an entry door under the driveway arches. A guard there should allow you to enter, so you can avoid having to walk around the building.

Frankly, it may seem odd to find the Mississippi state capitol in a civil rights travel book. I have two reasons for suggesting you go in:

- *It's absolutely stunning.* Marvel that it was built for just over a million dollars, from back taxes owed to the state by the Illinois Central Gulf Railroad.

- *You need to visit the photo gallery of the state's legislative bodies on the top floor.* In particular, pay attention to the racial composition of the legislature in the 1950s and 1960s. The absence of Black faces in a state with over one third of its population being Black provides a vivid visual teaching moment about discrimination on par with any text display one might see in a museum. And remember Mississippi's Sovereignty Commission, essentially a state-run spy agency? That top floor of the capitol served as its operations hub when it was surveilling civil rights activists and doing all it could to disrupt their activities. Eventually the commission moved to West Street.

Smith Robinson Museum and Cultural Center, 528 Bloom Street

This building played a big role in Jackson's Black history. It was Jackson's first public school for Blacks and is listed on the National Register of Historic Places. Author Richard Wright (*Native Son*, *Black Boy*, and more) attended school here in the 1920s. Among the exhibits here is one describing the historic Farish Street District from 1910 to 1970. Since so much of that neighborhood has not been preserved, this exhibit helps you understand the Black and civil rights history created there.

The museum is open Monday to Friday from 9 a.m. to 5 p.m., and 10 a.m. to 1 p.m. on Saturday. Closed on Sunday. Admission: $4.50 for adults, $3 for seniors, and $1.50 for children under eighteen. Block out an hour if you visit.

Head back to your car but follow a different route back to pass by two noteworthy locations:

- Walk back on High Street. You're on the opposite side of the capitol now. Just past the north entrance drive for cars, you will see a "**Capitol Rally**" **marker**. It memorializes the end of James Meredith's March against Fear rally that occurred here on June 26, 1966.
- Keep walking on High Street; turn right when you get to North State Street. In one block, you'll pass the **First Baptist Sanctuary** at 431 North State. Medgar Evers attempted to integrate this church the year he was murdered. It took until 1973 for two Black ministers to become the first to worship with this congregation since the Civil War. Three years later, the first Black member was allowed to join.

You should recognize where you are now: a block from the Tougaloo Nine marker. Turn left onto Mississippi Street, and there's the Civil Rights Museum.

The Farish Street District

Like Sweet Auburn in Atlanta, Farish Street was the center of African American business and culture in Jackson in the 1960s. As such, its restaurants, churches, and other facilities were places where national and local civil rights leaders would organize and socialize. To see the area in its heyday, go to *https://olemiss.edu/projects/sfa/farish-street-project/.*

Being there today is distressing. In late 2018, the city announced plans to restore some of the luster to the area. Despite its current state, a visit to Farish Street takes you to a district that played an important role in the civil rights era. However, depending on how quickly that luster is restored, if ever, some visitors may be squeamish about a short walk on this street. If that is the case, drive down one side, turn around legally, and come back down the opposite direction.

As in the description of the Sweet Auburn neighborhood in Atlanta, I walk you down the odd-numbered side of North Farish Street and then back to your car on the opposite side of the street. The whole trip is not even a half mile.

Collins Funeral Home, 415 North Farish Street

Park your car and start here. After Medgar Evers's funeral at the Masonic Temple near Jackson State University, thousands of mourners marched two miles to this funeral home. Here, Evers's body was prepared for the trip to his burial place in Arlington National Cemetery. A memorial service was also held here.

Big Apple Inn, 509 North Farish Street

This is the last remaining restaurant on Farish from the civil rights era. The Big Apple Inn began in 1939 across the street. Previous owner Juan Mora moved the business to the current location in 1952. Civil rights–era connections:

- Medgar Evers had an office above the restaurant. Activists would come by to meet with him and get their next set of instructions.
- Current owner, Geno Lee, is the son of a Freedom Rider. The specialty of the house is the pig's ear sandwich. At under $2, give it a try.

Farish Street Baptist Church, 619 North Farish Street

The congregation here hosted mass meetings and voter registration workshops in the 1960s. During the boycott of Jackson's downtown businesses for discriminating against Blacks, the church was used for strategy sessions supporting the boycott. In May 1963, students gathered here to learn about nonviolent protest. They left the church and marched down Farish toward Capitol Street. There, several hundred marchers were arrested, loaded into city garbage trucks, and taken to the livestock buildings at the Fairgrounds, which you may have seen in the vicinity of the Civil Rights Museum. It wasn't the first or last time that civil rights demonstrators ended up being detained by law enforcement at the Fairgrounds.

Time to cross Farish and head back on the even-numbered side. As you do that, you will note many of the boarded-up storefronts; some have connections to civil rights activism. To learn more about these and other sites in Jackson not covered in this chapter, pick up a copy of the Visit Jackson tourism brochure titled *Jackson Civil Rights Movement Driving Tour.*

Former Site of Steven's Kitchen, 604 North Farish Street

Another eatery where you wish the walls could talk. Marianne Vollers, in her book on the murder of the civil rights leader Medgar Evers, wrote that Steven's Kitchen was "where everybody who was anybody in civil rights could be found at lunchtime."[50] The place has clearly been closed for quite awhile. The electric sign hanging precariously above the entrance in 2018 may not be there when you visit. Look closely at the left side of the building to see the "Welcome to Steven's" cornerstone.

Historic Central United Methodist Church, 512 North Farish Street

Like Farish Street Baptist Church, this congregation welcomed mass meetings in support of voter registration, the boycott of downtown merchants, and Freedom Summer 1964 activities.

Before you hop in your car or leave the street, I'll mention one other spot you may want to visit: a shoe repair place. Odd to include in a book of civil rights travel? Maybe. However, this could be another unique in-person experience like meeting Wanda Battle in Montgomery or Beverly McClellan Gill and her husband, Randy, in Philadelphia.

Dennis Brothers Shoe Repair is at 325 North Farish. You can see the Alamo Theatre sign from where you likely parked your car. The shoe repair place is just past the theatre. Go in and see if Tony Brothers is there. He can tell you more about the history of the Farish Street Business District than your short walk up and down Farish Street ever could.

Additional Options in or near Jackson

The Plan for Jackson recommended two nights in this city. On an east-to-west itinerary that began in Atlanta, Jackson's the midway point, so a second night here might give you a welcomed breather. Moreover, the Natchez Trace Trail, north of the city, is a terrific spot for a walk or bike ride.

On our east-to-west itinerary, you arrive in Jackson from Philadelphia. Because Philadelphia has no museums and no long location visits, you could arrive in Jackson by mid-afternoon. While that's not likely sufficient time to visit the Mississippi Civil Rights Museum, it could be ample time to see the Medgar Evers home, the state capitol, or the Farish Street District.

Besides making use of the remaining daylight after you arrive in Jackson to visit those locations, others may interest you that fall into the always-open category. For example, civil rights history ties can be found at Jackson State University west of downtown and Tougaloo College north of downtown. In addition, sites are related to Jackson's lunch-counter sit-ins, Freedom Rides, and more are memorialized with outdoor historical markers; in most cases, though, the actual building is long gone.

Let's segment these additional options into four distinct geographies: south of the Capitol, near Jackson State, north of the Farish Street District, and far from downtown.

Civil Rights Destinations South of the State Capitol

The following four places are too spread out to add to the walking tour we recommended in conjunction with a visit to the Mississippi Civil Rights Museum and the state capitol, yet they are somewhat close together for travelers in a car. If you started from the capitol or the MCRM, you would see all of these in about two miles of driving if you followed this order.

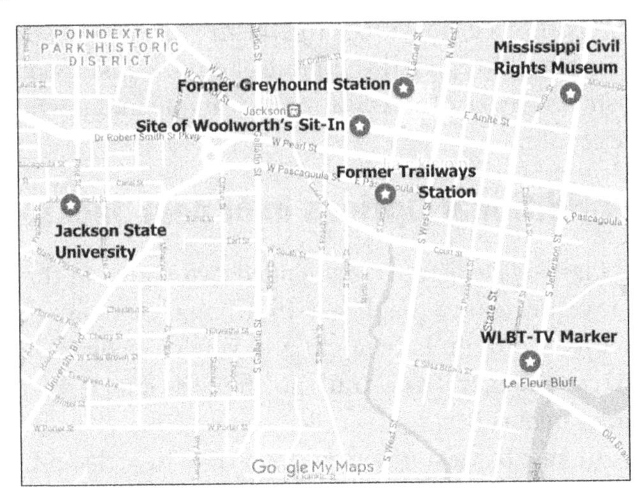

Former Greyhound Bus Station, 219 North Lamar Street

In front of the architectural firm now at this address, you will find a marker memorializing the 1961 arrests of over three hundred Freedom Riders protesting the segregation in interstate bus travel. The building is beautifully restored; visit at night when its art deco–style lights are on.

Former Site of F. W. Woolworth Store, 124 East Capitol

Many ugly incidents occurred at lunch-counter sit-ins. The sit-in that happened here on May 28, 1963, had to be among the worst. As police watched and the FBI stood down, local high school students and store customers verbally insulted the sit-in protesters and pelted them with mustard, ketchup, water, and more. The sit-in protesters went to jail. Their assailants did not.

The date of this lunch-counter sit-in in Jackson may strike readers as odd. Didn't the sit-in movement take off in 1960 after

Greensboro? Author M. J. O'Brien explains: "Only in Mississippi could a sit-in of this magnitude occur in 1963—nearly three years after many other southern cities had conceded the point—and break into a full-scale riot."[51] The marker commemorating the incident is at the far end of the current structure, near the Wasabi Grill.

Across South Farish Street at 100 West Capitol is the McCoy Federal Building, the first federal building in the United States named after an African American. Dr. A. H. McCoy was a tireless advocate for equal rights.

Former Trailways Bus Station, 201 East Pascagoula Street

Now the Davis Planetarium, this location was the site of the arrest of twenty-seven Freedom Riders on May 25, 1961, when they "breached the peace" in attempting to use whites-only facilities at the bus station. On the way to or from this location on East Pascagoula, you will pass an official-looking building with a giant spindle in front. That's the Hinds County Courthouse (407 East Pascagoula Street), where two of the trials of Byron De La Beckwith, Medgar Evers's killer, occurred.

WLBT-TV, 715 South Jefferson Street

The station was one of two TV outlets to ever have its license revoked by the Federal Communications Commission (FCC). This NBC affiliate regularly cut out news coverage from the network during the civil rights era citing "technical problems." In 1971, the FCC stripped the station of its license. A Mississippi Freedom Trail marker is here.

Civil Rights Destinations at Jackson State University

I'd suggest three places on the Jackson State University (JSU) campus, all within just over a half mile from one another. Due to the traffic patterns around the school, driving to the third one would force you to drive around the entire JSU campus, so drive to the first two and then walk to the third. All three are on J. R. Lynch Street.

The COFO Civil Rights Education Center, 1017 J. R. Lynch Street

Established in 1961, the Council of Federated Organizations (COFO) acted as an umbrella organization for disparate and sometimes feuding civil rights organizations (SNCC, CORE, the SCLC, the NAACP, and some local organizations). From this building, important civil rights initiatives were formed, like the 1963 Freedom Vote, the Mississippi Freedom Democratic Party, and the 1964 Freedom Summer Project. Two historic markers are here—one next to the building and one in the traffic island on Lynch Street. The center is open Monday through Friday, 9 a.m. to 4 p.m., and Saturday by appointment. Call (601) 979-3935 or email *COFO.Center@jsums.edu.*

Masonic Temple, 1072 J. R. Lynch Street

The temple's large auditorium hosted many civil rights functions, from mass meetings to funerals. Perhaps the most famous event here was the funeral service for Medgar Evers. Afterward, mourners marched from the Masonic Temple to Collins Funeral Home in the Farish Street District. The marker at this site is about seven hundred feet from the COFO Center.

Jackson State Tragedy Marker, 1600 J. R. Lynch Street

The university is a historically Black campus, and its students were active in civil rights work in the 1960s. The marker near the west entrance to the school and across from the Rose Embly McCoy Auditorium commemorates a tragedy that happened in 1970. Eleven days after the National Guard killed four students at Kent State University in Ohio in May 1970, police came to this campus to break up students who had gathered near the ROTC building. Gunshots were fired into the crowd, and a JSU student and a high school student were killed; eleven others were wounded. The marker is on Lynch Street west of South Prentiss Street. Walk to this marker on J. R. Lynch Street from the Masonic Temple rather than driving around the campus.

Civil Rights Destinations North of the Farish Street District

These three places could be added onto a visit to Farish Street, all north of the district. Each location relates to a civil rights hero. Two may be familiar to you, but the third may not.

Elmwood Cemetery: Aaron Henry Gravesite, Erie Street near Woodlawn Street

A pharmacist by training, an activist by choice, Aaron Henry had an impact on civil rights across four decades, serving as the president of the Mississippi NAACP from 1960 to 1992. To find his grave, enter opposite 701 Erie Street. The grave is near the fifth raised brick tomb on the left side of the cut-through road just before the road bends left. Look beyond the second and third cedar trees near headstones for the Michael family.

Former New Jerusalem Baptist Church, 226 Whitfield Street

On June 11, 1963, Medgar Evers drove here from the Masonic Temple where he picked up the mimeo paper (remember mimeo paper?) needed for a legal brief he had to print. The brief was the response to an injunction against local civil rights demonstrations. That June evening, there was a mass meeting at this church to discuss the successful picketing that occurred that day, successful because none of the ten young people wearing NAACP T-shirts were arrested. This was Evers's last visit here as he was shot and killed in his own driveway shortly after midnight that evening.

Benjamin Brown Park, 1320 North Mill Street

Benjamin Brown was shot in the back on the JSU campus when a confrontation occurred between students and police on the night of May 10, 1967. Brown was involved in civil rights work; that night he left a restaurant in the former COFO headquarters and was shot. He died the following day, his twenty-second birthday.

The park is one minute away down Whitfield Street from the former New Jerusalem Baptist Church. If you are traveling with children or grandchildren, there is playground equipment on the Fairbanks Street side of the park.

Civil Rights Destinations Far from Downtown

The last two possibilities are several miles north of the downtown area. Both are closer to Ridgeland than to downtown Jackson.

Temple Beth Israel, 5315 Old Canton Road

This synagogue and the home of its rabbi, Perry Nussbaum, were both bombed in 1967. The explosion at Temple Beth Israel targeted the rabbi's office and caused significant damage but no injuries. Rabbi Nussbaum visited Freedom Riders in Parchman Penitentiary and wrote their parents to share how their offspring were doing in the maximum-security facility.

Woodworth Chapel, Tougaloo College, 6500 Tougaloo Boulevard

Tougaloo students and faculty played a major role in the Jackson civil rights movement. The campus hosted countless planning sessions, speakers, and other events in support of the freedom movement. Recall the Tougaloo Nine marker on North Street near the Mississippi Civil Rights Museum, honoring the students' read-in at the local public library. Tougaloo students were also arrested at the Woolworth's sit-in mentioned earlier.

A Mississippi Freedom Trail marker is near the Woodworth Chapel. Enter the campus on West County Line Road and navigate to the intersection of Tougaloo Boulevard and Berkshire Street. Park on the roads near the chapel.

An Alternative to Two Nights in Jackson

After you leave Jackson, next up is likely the Mississippi Delta, primarily to visit sites connected to the murder of Emmett Till. After seeing those locations, your driving is not over. Little Rock, your next likely destination, is up to three hours from your last Delta stop. Getting close to Little Rock is smart so that you can be in a position to spend a day there and move on.

There is a lot of driving associated with a Jackson-to-the-Delta-to-Little-Rock day. Yet, it is not impossible to do. Tiring, yes; impossible, no.

An alternative is to stay in or near Jackson for one night and then spend the following night in Greenwood, Mississippi, about one hundred miles away. The advantage of staying in Greenwood is that you will be closer to the Delta's Emmett Till locations, giving you less driving to do on the day you head to Little Rock.

Importantly, in deciding between one or two nights in Jackson, don't shortchange that city. The Mississippi Civil Rights Museum and the Medgar Evers home are must-sees, and many other possibilities are here too. However, with good planning and by taking advantage of the benefits of Daylight Savings Time, one night here may be sufficient.

If you decide to overnight in Greenwood, you have a couple of options on how to get there. The fastest way is to do most of the drive on Interstate 55. That takes about an hour and a half.

An alternate, noninterstate route—via US-49, US-49W, and US-82—takes about an hour more. However, this route brings you through three places with connections to civil rights history: Yazoo City, Belzoni, and Indianola. Indianola is thirty-two miles west of Greenwood.

Since you might be staying in or near Greenwood, this chapter concludes by sharing three specific facts about Greenwood:

- How to find the park where Stokely Carmichael first publicly used the phrase "Black Power"
- Some Greenwood connections to the Emmett Till case
- A story about a trip to Greenwood by Harry Belafonte and Sidney Poitier (we explain who these folks are to those too young to know)

Unita Blackwell
From Sharecropper's Daughter to Presidential Adviser

One of the wonderful aspects of diving into civil rights history is discovering historic individuals whom you may have never read about. Unita Blackwell exemplifies the kinds of heroes and heroines you meet when you dig deeper to learn about less well-known civil rights icons.

Born during the Great Depression in the tiny Mississippi Delta town of Lula, Unita Blackwell is a prime example of how the Freedom movement changed the trajectory of a person's life and, in the process, created a legend. Born in a sharecropper's shack, Ms. Blackwell dropped out of school after the eighth grade, and picked cotton until age thirty-one. Her prospects seemed slim.

Then, Freedom Summer 1964 happened. Civil rights workers came to Mayersville, and Unita Blackwell's life was transformed. As she wrote in her memoir, *Barefootin': Life Lessons on the Road to Freedom*, "Overnight, I went from field hand to full-time freedom fighter."[52]

She marched, pushed to integrate schools, agitated for

continued

continued from previous page

voting rights, filed lawsuits, and more. By her own estimate, she was jailed at least seventy times, often on contrived charges. After one march on the state capitol in Jackson, she was held with over a thousand demonstrators in a livestock pen for eleven days. They were forced to sleep on concrete floors; the women were sprayed with disinfectant and subjected to strip searches.

Her election as mayor of Mayersville in 1976 gave her the opportunity to better the lives of the people in her town. Serving as mayor for a quarter of a century, she paved the streets, installed streetlights and sewers, improved public safety, and fought for better housing. She was the first African American woman to be elected mayor of any city or town in Mississippi.

Her horizons and impact, however, went beyond her town's limits. As the US-China relationship was changing in the early 1970s, she founded the U.S. China Peoples Friendship Association and traveled to China over a dozen times. Ms. Blackwell was an adviser to every US president from Lyndon Johnson to Bill Clinton, except for George H. W. Bush.

Unita Blackwell passed on May 13, 2019 at age eighty-six.

You probably won't detour to Mayersville, ninety miles northwest of Jackson. However, if you are ever near this small Mississippi River town, a marker honoring Unita Blackwell stands opposite the Issaquena County Courthouse.

Yazoo City (46 Miles North of Jackson)

Heading north on US Highway 49 places you east of Yazoo City. Here, there was a confrontation between Martin Luther King Jr. and associates of Stokely Carmichael a few days after Carmichael first used the phrase "Black Power" in Greenwood on June 17, 1966. More on that speech when we get to Greenwood. Here's the Yazoo City part of that story.

Many civil rights leaders were in Yazoo City when James Meredith's March against Fear arrived here as it headed toward Jackson. In *Freedom Bound: A History of the Civil Rights Movement*, Robert Weisbrot describes the dust-up that deepened the split between King's SCLC and Carmichael's SNCC.[53]

Dr. King spoke at a rally at Roy Campanella Park in Yazoo City on June 22, 1966. After the rally, King chastised a SNCC worker about the use of "Black Power" at the Greenwood rally. King viewed the phrase as "an emotional concept," having "connotations of violence and separatism." The next morning, staff members of the two organizations met in Yazoo City to try to smooth things over, but as Weisbrot noted, "The phrase Black Power was out there and couldn't be dialed back."[54]

The only marker remotely related to any of this is eleven miles east of Yazoo City in Benton. Meredith's march camped there at Oak Grove A.M.E. Church on Highway 16, and a marker adorns the church lawn.

Belzoni (27 Miles North of Yazoo City)

The Reverend George Lee was born in 1902 to a white father and Black mother. In the 1930s, he became pastor to a Baptist congregation in Belzoni. There, he and his colleague, Gus Counts, organized the local branch of the NAACP. Lee became the first Black in Humphreys County since Reconstruction to register to vote. A little over three months *before* Emmett Till's death, Rev. Lee was assassinated. The details are in a sidebar on page 183.

Reverend Lee's Mississippi Freedom Trail marker is at the intersection of Church and First Streets, next to the Greengrove Baptist Church at 603 Church Street. The marker is only two minutes off Highway 49 West.

Indianola (24 miles Northwest of Belzoni)

Robert Patterson, founder of the White Citizens' Council (WCC), was from Indianola. After its formation in 1954, this white supremacist organization quickly grew to eighty thousand members in Mississippi and three hundred thousand across the South. Years after the murder of Rev. Lee in Belzoni, the FBI implicated two members of the WCC in his murder. Given Indianola's connections with the WCC, it's not surprising that violence directed toward Blacks was common here.

Three specific incidents that occurred within two months of each other illustrate what Indianola was like in the mid-1960s. All three have markers memorializing the following people and events.

The Freedom School in Indianola was set on fire on March 5, 1965. The building, a former Baptist church, was also headquarters for local civil rights activities. The fire destroyed the building. A marker is located on Jefferson Street near the Community Garden. Enter "611 Jefferson Street, Indianola" into your mapping app to find the marker. It's a mile off Highway 49 West.

On May 1, 1965, Irene Magruder's home was destroyed by a Molotov cocktail. Mrs. Magruder's residence was a boardinghouse for civil rights workers registering Black voters in Sunflower County. For ten dollars a week, the workers received room and board. There is a commemorative marker at the site of the house at the corner of Byas Street and Front Street Extension, a half mile away from the Freedom School marker.

Also on May 1, 1965, the Giles Penny Saver Store was firebombed as well. No store exists today, but there is a marker at 801 Church Avenue, just a short drive from the Magruder marker. Owner Oscar Giles often called instances of racial discrimination to the attention of the US Department of Justice. However, not trusting the post office in Indianola, he would drive forty miles to Mound Bayou to mail those letters.

Greenwood (31 Miles East of Indianola)

One way or another, you are likely to pass through Greenwood. If you want to visit one of the critical parts of what occurred to Emmett Till in Money, Greenwood is in your path.

Greenwood has connections to the Till case; to the launch of the White Citizens' Council, which sprouted up across the state after the US Supreme Court's *Brown v. Board of Education* desegregation decision; and to the origin of the phrase "Black Power." None of these may be a reason to stop here. However, you should be aware of some Greenwood facts and places, even if you just pass through.

The primary civil rights–related site to see in Greenwood is Broad Street Park, where the phrase "Black Power" began to gain currency in the movement and where its use exacerbated existing divisions between SNCC and the SCLC.

Reverend George Lee

Late on May 7, 1955, the Reverend George Lee was returning to his home near Belzoni when a convertible pulled behind him and fired a shot that flattened his tires. The car then pulled alongside, and a shotgun blast blew away Lee's left jaw, subsequently sending his car crashing into a nearby house. The crash destroyed the home's front porch.

Lee staggered from the wreckage but died in the backseat of a cab on the way to the hospital. The coroner ruled that blood loss from two dozen buckshot rounds was the cause of death.

The Jackson *Clarion-Ledger*'s headline the next day read, "Negro Leader Dies in Odd Accident."[55] The Belzoni sheriff claimed that the metal fragments in his jaw were likely tooth fillings. No one ever was ever arrested for this shooting.

In a decision that was a precursor to one made later that same year by Emmett Till's mom, Mamie, Rev. Lee's widow, Rosebud, opted for an open-casket service so that others could see the injuries her husband suffered. *Jet* magazine published a picture of Lee's open casket in its May 26, 1955, issue.

Broad Street Park, Corner of Broad Street and Avenue M

The park covers two blocks. Be sure to visit this corner to see the historical marker memorializing the June 1966 "Black Power" event. If you have little ones in the car, there's a small children's playground near the marker at Broad and Avenue M.

Stokely Carmichael (who changed his name to Kwame Ture) became SNCC chairman in May 1966. On June 16, 1966, Carmichael had just been released from jail. He told those gathered in the park that this was his twenty-seventh arrest. Carmichael proclaimed to the large crowd, "I ain't going to jail no more. . . . We been saying freedom for six years—and we ain't got nothin'. What we gonna start saying now is 'Black Power.'"

When the crowd roared back, "Black Power!" Willie Ricks (who previously used that phrase to whip audiences into a frenzy) jumped to the platform. "What do you want?" he shouted. The crowd came back in unison: "BLACK POWER!"[56]

At least four Emmett Till case connections exist with Greenwood. None are memorialized:

- Emmett Till spent the night prior to his kidnapping in Greenwood with his cousins and their friends.
- Greenwood and Money are both in Leflore County. Since Till was kidnapped in the county, the kidnapping charge against J. W. Milam and Roy Bryant was brought before a grand jury in Greenwood. They failed to indict the two men on the charge.
- The Century Burial Association here was called to the Tallahatchie River to get Till's body. When the request came to Century undertaker Chester Miller to prepare the body for transport to Chicago, Miller passed the job onto an undertaker in Tutwiler, Mississippi. Century Burial is still in business, located at 801 Walthall Street here. No markers tie it to the Till case.
- Roy and Carolyn Bryant were married at Greenwood's Second Baptist Church in 1951. They divorced in 1979.

Some sources cite Greenwood as the place where the infamous White Citizens' Council was founded in mid-1954; others view Indianola as the place where this segregationist society began.[57] Both cities have apparently decided that no marker is needed to spar over this distinction.

Many high-profile Black entertainers lent their time, talent, contacts, and money to the civil rights movement. One story of the experience that Grammy Award–winner Harry Belafonte and Academy Award–winner Sidney Poitier had in Greenwood is worth telling. Both have been icons for over sixty years.

Ghost Stories in Greenwood

Fundraising is important to any movement, and the civil rights movement was no exception. Singer Harry Belafonte was a significant help in this area, and in 1964, he had one hundred thousand dollars ready to bring to Mississippi to help with Freedom Summer.

Mr. Belafonte told the *Clarion Ledger* (October 2, 2012) that, back then, he would often telephone his best friend, actor Sidney Poitier, asking him what he was doing for the weekend. The call typically signaled the promise of a trip, perhaps to the Bahamas or some other fun locale. But Mr. Belafonte had other plans when he rang Poitier in the summer of 1964.

"Where are we going?" Mr. Poitier asked. "Greenwood, Mississippi," Mr. Belafonte replied.

There was a long pause. The singer explained that the pair needed to deliver one hundred thousand dollars in cash to the Freedom Summer workers. "I'll go," Poitier replied.

The pair landed at a Greenwood airport after dark on August 16 and attended a rally in the local Elks Hall. Klansmen harassed the convoy driving the men to the Elks Hall. Poitier called it a "nerve-wracking experience." That night, the two stars stayed in a house guarded by men with shotguns. Too frightened to sleep, they did calisthenics and told ghost stories to keep calm.[58]

That Elks Hall is located at 106 East Scott Street. A marker appears here from the Mississippi Blues Commission as the hall also used to host music legends like B. B. King and James Brown. The location's role in the civil rights movement is briefly mentioned on the marker.

Not far from the Elks Hall on East Scott are two churches that played key roles in the voter registration efforts of the 1960s. Both churches are still there: Wesley United Methodist Church, 800 Howard Street, and Turner Chapel: 717 Walthall Street (down the street from the Century Burial Association).

CHAPTER 12

The Mississippi Delta

This day may feel different from the rest. It did for me, not just because of the miles traveled. It felt different because of what happened here in 1955 and what didn't happen here in 1955. A fourteen-year-old, visiting from Chicago, was brutally murdered. His body was weighted down by a cotton gin fan and tossed in a river. His killers went unpunished.

It felt different because of the landscape and a sense of isolation. We traveled to and through the Delta on a Saturday in early June. The dominant color was brown. Field after field that perhaps later that summer would show some other colors were just varying shades of brown. People and cars seemed to be in hibernation. We knew Money and Glendora were tiny towns but thought things might be different in Sumner, county seat of Tallahatchie County. They weren't. Except for a teenager on a cell phone, we saw no one walking around Sumner.

If this absence-of-life feeling happens to you, use it to reflect on why you have come here: Emmett Till.

Today's primary focus is on Emmett Till's abduction and murder, the recovery of his body, and the trial of his killers. Unlike Montgomery or Jackson, there is no major museum here. There's no National Park Service site. Instead, this day is centered on three small Mississippi towns where significant events in the Emmett Till saga occurred.

In comparison to some other days, the travel on this day is simple. Money, Glendora, and Sumner are small. Once you get to each one, you'll barely need street addresses. What you'll want to see in each town is, for the most part, close together—pretty simple.

What isn't simple here is the history. Misinformation and many unknowns remain associated with the Emmett Till case. The twists and turns rival those of the Tallahatchie River and are often just as muddy. This chapter presents a healthy dose of history as it navigates you to the locations where significant events happened, or may have happened, in some instances.

Besides making sure you make it successfully to Money, Glendora, and Sumner, the chapter points out other historic sites in the Mississippi Delta. Some relate to Emmett Till; others tie to major figures in the civil rights movement—including Fannie Lou Hamer, Amzie Moore, and Aaron Henry—or other aspects of African American history.

Who Was Emmett Till?

Emmett Till, a fourteen-year-old from Chicago, wanted to spend some time in Mississippi with his cousins and his uncle, Mose

Wright, a local preacher. After nearly missing the train that would take him to Mississippi, he was picked up by relatives at the train stop in Grenada, Mississippi, on August 21, 1955. A week later, in the early morning hours of August 28, Emmett was kidnapped from his uncle's home near Money by at least two men. Three days later, his savagely beaten body with a gunshot wound in the head was found floating in the Tallahatchie River by a seventeen-year-old checking his fishing lines. Questions:

- What happened during that week that caused Emmett to be snatched from his uncle's home around 2:30 a.m. on August 28?
- Who were the men who took him, and where did they go?
- Were these men charged with a crime or crimes? If so, what were the charges?
- Was justice done?
- What heroic decision did Emmett's mother, Mamie Till Bradley, make regarding her son's body that "galvanized a generation," according to activist and sociologist Dr. Joyce Ladner?[59]

Your travels today may help answer some of these questions. Some answers remain hard to pin down, even after so many intervening years. Much uncertainty surrounded the case in 1955 and, while significant new information has come out over time, parts of the case are still cloudy. The US Department of Justice reopened its investigation of the murder in July 2018; media reports in July 2021 suggest that the investigation remains open, sixty-six years after the crime.

The Plan for Visiting the Emmett Till Sites in 300 Words or Less

Get a good night's sleep. You will have lots of driving today, on everything from interstates to all-gravel farm roads. If you leave Jackson in the morning, visit the recommended sites in the three towns below, and drive on to the Little Rock area in the evening, that could be a ten-hour day. If you have stayed in Greenwood (see chapter 11), you will have gained almost two more hours for touring on this day.

In three towns, most of the Emmett Till story unfolded:

- *Money*, where Bryant's Grocery & Meat Market (the place where Emmett Till allegedly whistled at the owner's wife) and the home of his uncle Mose (where his kidnapping occurred) were.
- *Glendora and the nearby river sites*, where the murderers lived and possibly where the body was discovered in the Tallahatchie River.
- *Sumner*, where his killers were found not guilty of his murder at the Tallahatchie County Courthouse.

There are other significant places to visit, mostly west of these three towns, and they are covered later in the chapter. For example, Mound Bayou (forty-five minutes from Sumner) not only figured into the Till trial but also holds another important place in Black history. The town was founded as an autonomous, self-reliant, all-Black community in 1887. Ruleville, a half-hour west of Money, was the home of Fannie Lou Hamer, and the town honors this amazing woman in several ways. Any added stops mean more time and miles. We cover the possibilities; you can make the call on how to structure your trip.

While planning out every day is smart, doing so thoroughly is particularly wise when you visit the Delta and head on to your next stop.

Money

Bryant's Grocery & Meat Market, Money Road

Writing in 1956 in "Time Bomb: Mississippi Exposed and the Full Story of Emmett Till," Olive Arnold Adams called Money "a wide place in the road." At the time, Money had a post office, a gas station, and three stores around a school and a gin—a collection that "would have hardly qualified in your mind as a town."[60]

Money is even less today. If ever a town was misnamed, this is it.

Money is twenty minutes north of Greenwood. Coming from the south, the first building that's likely to catch your eye is the restored gas station. It's Ben Roy's Service Station looking like it did (or much better perhaps) than it did in the mid-1950s, thanks to a $206,000 grant from the Mississippi Department of Archives and History. However, one of those three stores from the mid-1950s—Bryant's Grocery & Meat Market—lies in ruins right next door to Ben Roy's.

Both places are now owned by members of the same family, all descendants of Emmett Till trial juror Ray Tribble. To fully understand why the gas station looks like it does while the historically more relevant grocery store is wrapped in vines and plastic fencing, read Dave Tell's *Remembering Emmett Till*.[61] The grocery store ruins are where the series of events that the producers of the award-winning fourteen-part documentary *Eyes on the Prize* selected to mark where the civil rights movement began. But for a moment, we need to turn the clock back to August 1955 to put some context around the significance of the crumbling shell of Bryant's Grocery you'll see.

Wednesday, August 24, 1955, had been a day of picking cotton for Emmett Till, his three cousins (the sons of Uncle Mose Wright), and Emmett's Chicago pal, Wheeler Parker. That night, Mose Wright was holding church services at his East Money Church of God in Christ. Rather than compel the young people to attend church that night, Rev. Wright lent them his 1941 Ford, telling them not to go any farther than a nearby country store. After all, Maurice Wright, the preacher's sixteen-year-old son, was going to be the driver, and he had yet to get his license.

Eventually, six boys, including Emmett Till, and one girl piled into the Ford. They disregarded the reverend's command that they stay close to the church and instead headed to Bryant's Grocery in Money, less than four miles up Whaley Road from the church.

On the front porch at Bryant's, Emmett was the center of attention, telling stories about life in Chicago and, according to some reports, bragging that the picture of a white girl in his wallet was his girlfriend. While Emmett's mother had warned him about the differences between Mississippi and Chicago, right now those cautions did not seem top of mind to the teen. Years later, his mother, Mamie Till Bradley, suggested that the wallet picture may have been one of actress Hedy Lamarr, the kind of picture that came in many new wallets in the 1950s.[62]

Emmett eventually went into the store to purchase some bubble gum or candy. What precisely happened in the store between Emmett and the twenty-one-year-old store owner's wife, Carolyn Bryant, is not known.

- Did he touch the woman's hand as he paid for his purchase rather than just placing his coins on the counter, as was protocol in the Jim Crow South?
- Did he take up a challenge of one of the cousins to ask the woman for a date? Or brag that he had been "with a white woman" before?
- Did he whistle at her as he left the store? Some media outlets labeled the subsequent murder trial as the "Wolf Whistle Trial" due to claims Emmett whistled at Mrs. Bryant. Mamie Till Bradley explained later than the noise that sounded like a whistle may have simply been an attempt by Emmett to compensate for a speech impediment he developed after suffering from polio.

Whatever happened in Bryant's Grocery led to Emmett's abduction in the wee hours of Sunday, August 28, 1955, and his murder sometime after that.

Finding Bryant's Grocery & Meat Market should be easy. Google Maps saves it as a historic landmark (search "Bryant's Grocery & Meat Market, Money, Mississippi"). Sadly, there is not much to see here. The storefront and front porch collapsed years ago. The boarded brick building, while still standing, is covered in green overgrowth and posted "private property." There is a two-sided Mississippi Freedom Trail marker right in front.

While there's not much to see here, there's certainly much on which to reflect as you stand near the structure's remains. Whatever happened inside Bryant's store should have never triggered the reactions of Roy Bryant and J. W. Milam. What happened in Sumner when the jury acquitted these (later) self-admitted killers sparked instant national and international outrage, affecting millions and, according to many, providing a catalyst for a movement that would bring significant changes to the United States.

Emmett Till's murder had an immediate impact in the African American community. One Black woman in Alabama wrote a letter to a friend shortly after Till's murder:

> "I am sure you read of the lynch-murder of young Emmett Till of Chicago. This case could be multiplied many times in the South."[63]

On November 27, 1955, about two months after the not-guilty verdict in the Till case came down, the same Alabama woman was part of an overflow crowd in the Dexter Avenue Baptist Church in

Montgomery. There she heard Dr. Martin Luther King Jr. introduce a guest from the Mississippi Delta. Dr. T. R. M. Howard of Mound Bayou, Mississippi, gave a fiery and moving speech on several race-related murders in the Delta, including Emmett Till's. Dr. Howard's impassioned speech preoccupied the mind of this woman. Four days later, while riding home from work on a Montgomery city bus, she was asked to give up her seat for a white passenger. She refused. The woman—Rosa Parks—later said that she was thinking of Emmett Till as she stayed in her seat on that bus on December 1, 1955.[64]

The tragedy of Emmett Till didn't just move Mrs. Parks; it's not surprising that it "galvanized a generation," as activist Joyce Ladner has remarked.[65]

Think about how old those who sat in at lunch counters in the 1960s in Greensboro, North Carolina; Rock Hill, South Carolina; Hampton, Virginia; and other cities were when Emmett Till was killed. Think about how old many of the Freedom Riders who boarded interstate buses in 1961 were when Emmett Till's murderers were acquitted. They were about the same age as the fourteen-year-old Till was in 1955. While Mrs. Parks acted months later, the "Emmett Till generation," still in junior high and high school, would have their own moment in the movement just a few years hence.

Site of the Former East Money Church of God in Christ, Whaley Road

One relatively quick diversion to consider before departing Money adds about twenty minutes to your day. There are no markers at the three places on this side trip. The choice to go or not is yours.

Just two tenths of a mile north of Bryant's Grocery is Whaley Road. Whaley is where Emmett Till and his cousins and friends likely traveled to go to and from Bryant's Grocery; it's the most direct route. The road leads to three places related to the Till case that were there when Emmett visited Money, though not there today:

- East Money Church of God in Christ, Mose Wright's church: This was where cousin Maurice Wright dropped his parents off for Wednesday-evening church services before gathering his two brothers, cousin Emmett, and the others for their trip to Bryant's on August 28, 1955.

- The cemetery at the church where Emmett's body was nearly buried without his mother's permission, a significant turning point in the overall story.
- The G. C. Frederick Plantation on which Rev. Wright had his house, the latter being site of Emmett Till's August 28, 1955, kidnapping.

This diversion is seven miles round trip. Traveling Whaley Road may make you wonder whether Emmett and his pals had any concerns about Emmett's encounter with Carolyn Bryant, or were they more worried about whether Rev. Wright might learn they ignored his wish that they go no farther than the nearby country store?

Follow these directions to get to where East Money Church of God in Christ and its small cemetery used to be:

- From Bryant's Grocery on Money Road (Highway 518), go 0.2 miles north to Whaley Road and turn right.
- Continue on Whaley for 3.2 miles; the Yalobusha River is on your left and rich farmland on your right.
- Turn right onto County Road 88; about four hundred to five hundred feet after the turn, you should see the ruins of the church; depending on the degree of overgrowth, you might also be able to see the cemetery.
- Head back the way you came to continue to Glendora.

Where's the plantation of G. C. Frederick, the land on which Mose Wright had his sharecropper home? At the murder trial, Mose Wright was asked this question. He replied that it was three miles east of Money. In other words, it was somewhere on the south side of Whaley Road.

Glendora and the Tallahatchie River Sites

Glendora is a tiny (150 people or so) and quite poor village, twenty miles north of Bryant's Grocery. It's about twenty-five minutes to Glendora. To find the first recommended stop, the Clinton Melton memorial marker, enter "832 Sturdivant Road, Glendora, MS" into your map app or GPS program.

There are two important connections to the Emmett Till story in Glendora. First, it was the home of the older of his murderers, J. W. Milam. According to a paid-for confession published after the trial in January 1956, Milam told *Look* magazine that Glendora was where he and his half-brother Roy Bryant beat and tortured Emmett. Later facts revealed this to be false. They weren't the only inaccuracies in *Look*'s early version of checkbook journalism.

Second, as bad as the magazine's reporting was, another journalist's efforts proved instrumental in bringing important facts about the murder to light. James L. Hicks, one of the leading investigative reporters of his generation, covered the Till trial for dozens of African American newspapers. Some of his best and most dangerous work was done here in Glendora. A marker in the village calls attention to reporter Hicks's work. We cover his role when we get to that marker.

Glendora is very compact; there are four markers here to see. Three of them relate to the Till tragedy directly and the fourth one indirectly. The last one is the first one you'll see, so we start there.

Clinton Melton Marker, Sturdivant Road and Burrough Street (Also Referred To as Main Street)

As soon as you cross the railroad tracks and enter Glendora, you see this purple-colored marker. All the markers here are the same color.

Clinton Melton, his wife, Beulah, and their children lived in Glendora. Melton worked as a service station attendant. Shortly after the Emmett Till trial (December 3, 1955), Elmer Otis Kimball, a cotton gin operator, asked Melton to gas up his car. Kimball became enraged during that interaction and threatened to come back to the station and kill Melton.

Kimball was driving the automobile of J. W. Milam, who had just been acquitted of killing Emmett Till. Kimball returned to the station with a shotgun and, with no provocation, shot and killed Melton. The incident happened in full view of the gas station owner and other witnesses. Kimball was charged with murder.

At the trial, the prosecution called three witnesses:

- The white filling station owner, who testified that the victim Melton did not have a gun and did not provoke the attack.

- A Black man who testified that shooter Kimball said he was going to kill Melton and would kill him (the witness) too if he got in the way.
- A third man who was ten feet away but did not see a gun in Melton's hand.

The defense argued that Kimball was defending himself and called, among others, the sheriff, deputy sheriff, and chief of police. None of them were eyewitnesses. Kimball claimed Melton cursed at him during an argument.

An all-white jury acquitted Kimball after deliberating for four hours. Four hours, as you'll learn more when reading about Sumner, the site of the Till trial, was significantly longer than the Till jury took.

As if the killing of Clinton Melton weren't difficult enough on his family, more tragedy struck just before Kimball's trial began. Mr. Melton's widow, Beulah, was apparently forced off the road near Glendora and she drowned in the Black Bayou, leaving the couple's children orphaned. The official reason given for the accident was faulty driving.

King's Place Marker, Main Street

Drive slowly down Main Street and be sure to stay on the same side of the railroad tracks as the Clinton Melton marker. It will take a minute to drive from that marker to this one. As you come down Main Street, a large white building at first will look like it's in the middle of the road. The road splits here; slow down before the split. In a lot across the street and to the left is the King's Place marker.

King's Place was a juke joint with music, dancing, food, and drink. Reporter James L. Hicks received a tip during the Till trial that a young boy named "Too Tight" was in the truck carrying Emmett Till the night of the murder. As important as that information was, the next statement from the tipster was also shocking. Too Tight had disappeared; no one knew where he was.

The advice to Hicks was to go to Glendora "to a place called King's . . . the only colored dance hall in town."[66] There he should find "the right people" who could tell Hicks more about Too Tight, like his real name and possible whereabouts. Just before the tipster left, Hicks wrote that she warned him not to "get caught down there after dark."

Hicks's account can be read in full in Christopher Metress's compilation of original reporting of the Till case.[67] At King's Place, James Hicks learned that this possible witness (and possible accessory) to the murder was in jail under a false name and trumped-up charges—and that jail was in Charleston, Mississippi, nearly an hour away from the courthouse in Sumner. Plus, Too Tight wasn't the only local in the Charleston jail. Another man, Henry Lee Loggins, the common-law husband of the woman relating all of this to Hicks at King's Place, was locked up there as well.

One last fact that Hicks gleaned from this visit to King's Place: both of the missing and likely jailed individuals worked for J. W. Milam, one of the men on trial for killing Emmett Till.

J. W. Milam's House and the Glendora Gin Markers

Main Street ends about where the King's Place marker is. Remember the split in the road at that white building? Take the road to the right side of that building (Thomas Street) to reach the final two markers and the Emmett Till Historic Intrepid Center (ETHIC). There may be a directional sign pointing you to ETHIC. After 250 yards on Thomas Street, park near the markers and make a decision on visiting ETHIC.

Both markers contain information of dubious accuracy. The first marker is the Milan's House marker; it's on the left side of the road. There's no reason to dispute the Milam's House marker claim that the killer lived here. It's well established that he was from Glendora. (He had a store adjacent to King's Place.)

The inaccuracy on this marker is the claim that Milam and Bryant beat Emmett Till in a shed on this property. The Emmett Till Memory Project website labels this claim and the purported "confession" generally as "pure hooey." Investigative work by James L. Hicks and other reporters led to the discovery that Emmett was actually brutalized in a seed barn on a property managed by Milam's brother, Leslie Milam. A witness at the trial, William Reed, who lived near the plantation managed by Leslie Milam, testified that he heard screams coming from a seed barn on that property.

William Reed also testified that, before the screams began, he saw a person he believed to be Emmett Till in the back of truck (along with two other Black men) and four white men in the cab of that truck. He identified J. W. Milam as one of the men at the barn. According to the Emmett Till Memory Project website, in a deathbed confession discovered by the FBI, Leslie Milam admitted to his own involvement in murdering Emmett Till.

Where was this barn, the one on the farm managed by Leslie Milam, the barn where Emmett was beaten? Near Drew, Mississippi, a half hour away from Glendora. More importantly, Drew is in Sunflower County. If the kidnapping was in Money, which is in Leflore County, and the brutalization of Emmett Till took place in Sunflower County, why was the trial in Sumner, which is in Tallahatchie County?

One reason was that Tallahatchie County sheriff Henry Clarence (H. C.) Strider claimed jurisdiction when the body was recovered. Leflore County could charge Bryant and Milam with kidnapping since that happened in Money (Leflore County), and they did. Yet a Leflore County grand jury did not return an indictment, so the two half-brothers not only went free on the murder charge but on kidnapping as well.

No one knew at the time where the murder took place nor where exactly the body went in the river. However, Sheriff Strider, a "tobacco-chewing, cigar-smoking former football player with a bad heart and gruff demeanor,"[68] asserted that the case belonged to Tallahatchie County. The local newspaper from Greenwood reported on August 31, 1955, that Till's body was pulled from the river near Philipp, Mississippi, which borders Leflore County. Sheriff Strider made the point that the body must have gone into the Tallahatchie in his county because the body "couldn't have floated up the river."[69]

The Leflore County district attorney, Stanny Sanders, agreed with Strider. Any murder charges would have to come from Tallahatchie County. For what it's worth, in 2006, an FBI report suggested that the body was pulled from the Tallahatchie River at a point where it dips into Leflore County.

With his jurisdiction claim unchallenged, Sheriff Strider moved to bury the body quickly, with no need for an autopsy of the teenager's bloated body. Strider pushed for burial in the cemetery at Mose Wright's church back in Money. Emmett's local relatives did not challenge the sheriff. However, Emmett's mom, Mamie Till Bradley, did. We pick up that thread in the story shortly.

But, finally, the Glendora Gin marker, right in front of ETHIC. The marker makes two claims. One is clearly true: the old gin you see houses the Emmett Till Historic Intrepid Center. The other is less certain: namely, that the cotton gin fan strung around Emmett Till's neck with barbed wire came from this building.

No facts support this claim. Where that cotton gin fan came from has never been established. What is known is that the fan entered as evidence during the trial of the killers went missing sometime after 1973 during an ultimately unsuccessful renovation of the Tallahatchie County Courthouse in Sumner.[70]

Claiming that your building is the source of that infamous cotton gin fan does make for a good hook if you want people to visit your museum. In the discredited "confession" published by *Look* magazine, the killers claim that they got the heavy cotton gin fan from the Progressive Ginning Company located 3.4 miles east of Boyle, Mississippi. That puts the gin fan's origin about 10 miles from the seed barn on the plantation near Drew where Emmett was beaten.

Where Milam and Bryant snatched the seventy-pound cotton gin fan may never be known, nor may be where that fan is today.

The Emmett Till Historic Intrepid Center, 33 Thomas Street

The building itself lets you know that you are not at a branch of the Smithsonian. This is a local effort to share a version of the Emmett Till story and Glendora's connections to the murder. There are well-curated galleries on Emmett Till at major museums in Jackson and Memphis. Therefore, given the in-depth coverage you can experience elsewhere on your tour and the heavy travel demands on this particular day, you might pass on spending time at ETHIC. That said, the admission price of $5 is modest, and you are likely to appreciate the passion of the guides who take visitors through the museum. The mayor of Glendora, Johnny B. Thomas, is the museum's founder.

Mayor Thomas himself has an interesting connection to the Emmett Till case. Remember how reporter James Hicks met a woman who gave him information at King's Place about a man named Too Tight? Remember that the woman told Mr. Hicks that Too Tight was in jail? She also told Hicks "they came for him Monday a week ago." That Monday was September 19, 1955, the day the murder trial began.

The man she lived with also was picked up with Too Tight on the same Monday. Hicks asked for that man's name. The reply: "Henry Lee Loggins."

Mayor Thomas was the second child of twelve born to Henry Lee Loggins and the woman James Hicks spoke with at King's Place. Her name: Adeline Hill.

Henry Lee Loggins worked as an overseer for J. W. Milam on his farm. Loggins and Leroy "Too Tight" Collins have been accused by some as having participated in aspects of Emmett Till's murder. After death threats on his life and his family, Henry Lee Loggins decided to leave Glendora and go into hiding to protect the family. The ETHIC website states, "Mr. Thomas made it his life-long quest to clear his father's name."

Emmett Till Historic Intrepid Center	
Location	33 Thomas Street, Glendora, Mississippi 38928
Days Closed	Sunday and Monday
Operating Days and Hours	Tuesday to Friday, 10 a.m. to 5 p.m.
	Saturday, 10 a.m. to 2 p.m.
Admission	$5 per person; $3 for students 18 and under
Website	*www.glendorams.com*
Phone Number	(662) 375-7333 or (662) 757-0032
Email Address	*glendora1900@yahoo.com*

One final observation before moving on to the two river markers that designate locations that possibly played a role in the Emmett Till case. Some, including Henry Lee Loggins when he was alive, maintain that Emmett's body was tossed into the Black Bayou, specifically over a now-unused bridge. While that bridge is an often-used backdrop for TV crews doing stories on Emmett Till, the Black Bayou Bridge has not been unequivocally designated as the place from which Emmett's horribly beaten body was thrown into the water. However, it is a possibility. The Little Tallahatchie River that flows under the Black Bayou Bridge connects to the Tallahatchie River right where some claim Emmett Till's body was recovered.

The Black Bayou Bridge is a half mile from ETHIC. If you go back on Thomas Street to where it intersects with Burrough (Main) Street and Gipson (formerly Second) Street, take a hard left onto

Gipson Street and follow it as far as you can. At some point, you must get out and walk through brush and who knows what else to get to the bridge.

If you don't want to make that trek (I did not), you can see one of Mayor Thomas's videos to the Black Bayou Bridge on YouTube. On YouTube, search "Black Bayou Bridge/Glendora." Even if you think you want to brave the overgrowth leading to the bridge, watching the video might change your mind—especially if you're not used to summer in the South.

The Tallahatchie River Site Markers

Whether you decided to hike to the Black Bayou Bridge or not, navigate back to Main Street to get to the two river site markers. On Google Maps, enter "Emmett Till River Marker 1," and the app takes you there. Don't use Google Maps? Do the following to find this first marker:

- Once back on Burrough (Main) Street, head back in the direction toward where you came into the village.
- The name of Burrough Street changes to Swan Lake Road as you pass to the right of the Clinton Melton marker, also passing the road in which you came into Glendora (Black Bayou Road).
- Stay on Swan Lake Road for 2.4 miles to Sharkey Road.
- Turn right onto Sharkey Road. The first river sign marker is on the right.

This sign (hereafter, River Marker 1) points you in the direction of the second river sign, which Google Maps labels as "Emmett Till River Marker 2." We shorten this to River Marker 2 or Graball Landing. The location of the Graball Landing sign has been cited as the spot where Emmett's body was recovered from the Tallahatchie River. River Marker 1 says that the body was discovered "on a piece of land" and "dumped as a warning to the Black community."

The discovered-on-land claim runs counter to the trial record. Robert Hodges, the seventeen-year-old fisherman who first saw the body, testified at the trial in Sumner where he saw the body. Hodges told the court the body "was hung up on a snag in the bottom of the river."[71]

The Emmett Till Memory Project (ETMP) website, an important source of research-based information on Emmett Till, and others dispute what River Marker 1 says about the body's location. The ETMP also questions whether the body was dumped "as a warning to the Black community."

One fact on this first River Marker is certainly true: Emmett was identified by a ring on his finger, a very distinctive ring. Emmett's dad was Louis Till. Emmett's parents permanently separated in 1942, the year after Emmett was born. Louis Till joined the army during World War II and sent his wife and son twenty-two dollars each month for child support.[72] Midway through 1945, the payments stopped. Louis Till had been court-martialed and executed for "willful misconduct." The army sent his belongings back to his family, including a silver ring with the initials "L.T.," a ring that one day Emmett would receive from his mom.

When Emmett's body was discovered, there was a bullet wound near his right ear, his face was beaten so horribly that Sheriff Strider of Tallahatchie County speculated that "an axe was used,"[73] and the body was quite bloated. Identification of the body presented a challenge. A ring was spotted on the victim, and Chester Miller, a Black undertaker at the scene, was asked to remove the ring. Miller delegated the job to his assistant.

When the ring was removed, the engraved initials "L.T." were revealed. While that ring eventually should have made it a certainty that this was the body of Emmett Till, it was argued in court and in some media coverage at the time that the body spotted in the river on August 31, 1955, was *not* that of Emmett Till. This was a significant aspect of Milam's and Bryant's defense. The defense team theorized that, if it wasn't certain that this body was Emmett Till's, the jury couldn't be sure Emmett was dead.

As you know, the jury acquitted the defendants. In June 2005, the FBI exhumed the body from the Burr Oak Cemetery outside of Chicago. Less than three months later, after performing DNA testing, the FBI confirmed that the body was indeed Emmett Till.

Now, head down the river on the all-gravel and aptly named River Road.

River Marker 1 points you to the right, suggesting the next stop is 2.6 miles away. River Marker 2 is actually 2.3 miles away, so watch your odometer and don't drive past it. The marker is on the right side of the road.

The reason I share this detail on distance is that, when I visited the area, River Marker 2 was gone. The Emmett Till Memory Project app navigated me back to where the sign should have been. After getting out of the car and looking around in the weeds growing near the road, I saw the sawed-off posts that held up the former sign.

On June 21, 2018, a new marker replaced the previous bullet-ridden sign. After about a month went by, the replacement marker had been vandalized by gunshots once again. Supposedly, the newest and fourth sign here, installed in October 2019, is bulletproof. Crafted and donated by Lite Brite Neon of Brooklyn, New York, the sign weighs nearly five hundred pounds; the likelihood that someone is going to carry it away is remote. If further vandalism attempts are made, a security camera is now part of the site and designed to capture visual evidence on the culprits.

The new sign now not only relates the possibility that Emmett Till's body was pulled from the river near here, but it also shares some of the history of Graball Landing, once a steamboat landing prior to the Civil War.

Questions remain. Basically, is this really where Emmett Till's body was recovered? As with other aspects of the tragedy, the facts are as unclear as the muddy Tallahatchie that flows a few hundred feet from this marker. Some analysts assert that Emmett's battered body was recovered about five or six miles farther downstream. Wherever Emmett Till's battered corpse was found in 1955, this isolated spot between the cotton fields on one side and the Tallahatchie on the other gives you a good place for reflection. Think about all the hate and violence that the fourteen-year-old encountered in less than ten days in Mississippi—and then think about the hate and small-mindedness that necessitated a bullet-resistant sign with its own security system to be placed here—six decades later.

Where Was the Body of Emmett Till Recovered?

No one knows with certainty where Emmett Till's body was recovered. The Emmett Till Memory Project website and Dave Tell's book *Remembering Emmett Till* make that clear. Both sources also point out where it certainly was *not* recovered—namely, near River Marker 2 or Graball Landing. Both note that the FBI concluded in 2006 that the body was not discovered here. Instead, the FBI speculated that the site was likely five miles downriver, at a point where the Tallahatchie dips into neighboring Leflore County.

Contemporaneous press reports of the discovery of the body as well as testimony given at the trial support the FBI's opinion.

- On August 31, 1955, the *Greenwood Commonwealth* reported "the body was in shallow water near the bank . . . and was found at Pecan Point near Phillipp [*sic*]."[74]
- On September 1, 1955, the Memphis *Commercial Appeal* reported the body was found twelve miles north of Money. That's pretty consistent with the distance from Money to Philipp.[75]
- Testimony at the trial from B. L. Mims supports somewhere near Pecan Point as the recovery location as well. Mims, the landlord where the family of young fisherman Robert Hodges lived, was also at the scene since it was "near his home," in the words of the prosecutor questioning Mims. When asked where his home was, Mims replied, "About five miles north of Philipp."[76] Using Google Maps, the geodesic—as-the-crow-flies—distance between Philipp and Pecan Point is 4.7 miles.
- Mose Wright confirmed Philipp as where he saw his nephew's body after being called to the scene by the sheriff.[77]
- Finally, Timothy Tyson in *The Blood of Emmett Till* wrote that law enforcement officers "made their way to a landing at Pecan Point . . . where they met Robert Hodges and his father."[78]

continued

continued from previous page

Pecan Point is five or so miles downriver from River Marker 2 / Graball Landing. There's no marker there, and the river is just as muddy there as where River Marker 2 is. We traveled a few miles down River Road past the Graball Landing location to see if it leads to Pecan Point. However, when the road didn't get much better or less dusty, we turned around and headed to Sumner.

Sumner

Head back to Sharkey Road, where River Marker 1 is. From there, Sumner is twenty minutes away. The ten-mile trip takes you past Webb, Mississippi, the birthplace of Emmett's mother, Mamie. She moved to Argo, Illinois, at age two.

Let's bookend two events in the Emmett Till story. First, there's August 31, 1955, the day his body was recovered. Next, September 19, 1955, the starting date of the trial of his murderers. That's a short time span to prepare for a murder trial, unless you have a good idea of how the verdict will go. In that narrow window of time, Mamie Till Bradley made one of the boldest, most courageous, and most consequential decisions of the civil rights movement.

Remember the church cemetery in Money? There, Tallahatchie sheriff H. C. Strider wanted to expedite the burial of Till's body. The gravediggers had finished their work when Crosby Smith arrived at the cemetery. Smith, Mose Wright's brother-in-law, told the gravediggers, "The body ain't going in the ground."[79]

Mamie Till Bradley wanted her son's body brought back to Chicago. The Black undertaker from Greenwood, Chester Miller, overseeing the burial knew this meant trouble. Stopping the burial would run counter to the sheriff's wishes. Word would certainly get back to Sheriff Strider, and undertaker Miller knew the risks of defying the sheriff.

Mose Wright called Chester Nelson, a white undertaker in Tutwiler, Mississippi, and asked him to prepare the body for a train ride to Chicago. Nelson owned two funeral homes: one serving whites, the other serving Blacks. It was the Jim Crow South: separate water fountains, separate schools, separate undertakers. Undertaker

Nelson took the young man's body with the condition that the seal on the casket would not be broken. Nelson felt that no one needed to see the gruesome condition of the young man's body.

Mamie Till Bradley didn't agree. Along with a thousand others, she met the train carrying her son in a pine box casket at Chicago's Twelfth Street Station on Friday, September 2, 1955. Even at the station, she was pushing funeral director A. A. Rayner to open the casket. Rayner had agreed with the terms laid out by undertaker Nelson: namely, that the casket remain sealed. He reminded Mrs. Bradley that her own relatives in Mississippi had signed papers agreeing to keep the casket sealed. But Mamie Till Bradley hadn't signed any papers.

Years later, she wrote, "I told him that if I had to take a hammer and open that box myself, it was going to be opened."[80] At the Rayner Funeral Home, two of Mrs. Bradley's friends steadied her as the casket was opened. Starting with the feet and working her way up, she thought "the body didn't even appear human."[81]

"Let the people see what they did to my boy," she declared according to the *Chicago Sun Times*. Emmett's casket would be open for the funeral. On September 3, the first night for public viewing, thousands stood in line to pay their respects. The lines continued daily through September 6 when the funeral was held at the Roberts Temple Church of God in Christ (4021 South State Street), now a Chicago city landmark.

With Mrs. Bradley's permission, two photographers, David Jackson of *Jet* and Ernest Withers of *Ebony*, took pictures of the body as it lay in the glass-sealed casket. In its September 15, 1955, issue, *Jet* published the photos. Their impact was immediate and long-lasting.

John Johnson, the magazine's publisher, noted the issue "sold out immediately and did as much as any other event to traumatize Black America and prepare the way for the Freedom Movement of the sixties."[82]

In her 1968 autobiography, *Coming of Age in Mississippi*, Anne Moody recalled how Emmett Till affected her. "Before Emmett Till's murder, I had known the fear of hunger, hell, and the Devil. But now there was a new fear known to me—the fear of being killed just because I was black."[83] Anne Moody was fourteen years old when Emmett was murdered, the same age.

Hall of Fame basketball star Kareem Abdul-Jabbar (then Lew Alcindor, growing up in New York City) reflected on seeing the photo published in *Jet* when he was eight years old: "It made me sick." "It [the murder] shocked me; I began thinking of myself as a black person for the first time, not just a person. . . . All of a sudden, the color of my skin represented danger."[84]

For decades afterward, the impact of the Till murder in general and the open-casket photos in particular would be significant. Many have testified to what both meant to their social consciousness and activism. Perhaps no better statement sums up the impact than Chris Crowe's:

> "Before the Emmett Till case, no single event had ever generated enough support, enough publicity, or enough outrage to unify a large-scale effort to oppose segregation. The unification began when *Jet* magazine published its article about Emmett's murder along with the photo of Emmett in his casket."[85]

Several events can lay claim to being a catalyst to the civil rights movement of mid-twentieth-century America. The murder of Emmett Till would be high on that list. As you drive into Sumner, remember how three decisions driven by the love of a courageous mother may have lit the spark that ignited a movement. Mamie Till Bradley wanted her son buried in Chicago, insisted on seeing him, and finally—having witnessed what "they did to my boy"—she shared with the world the result of what intolerance and hatred look like in the United States.

Sumner is one of two county seats for Tallahatchie County. Sumner covers the west part of the county and Charleston, the east part. Charleston's center is your classic courthouse-square design: courthouse in the middle with a variety of businesses on the surrounding sides. Sumner also follows this classic southern courthouse square design with a tall statue of a Confederate soldier on the courthouse lawn.

The town wasn't incorporated until 1900, thirty-five years after the Civil War, and the courthouse wasn't built for a couple of years after that. Despite being a twentieth-century town, that Confederate statue was placed in front of the courthouse in 1913.

Get close enough to see the inscription on this statue and see its dedication to "the cause that never yet has failed." Blacks who wanted to hear what was going on inside the courthouse during the trial of Emmett Till's killers sat near this monument to the Lost Cause.

The two reasons to go to Sumner are

- To see the courthouse where J. W. Milam and Roy Bryant were tried and ultimately acquitted for the murder of Emmett Till.
- To spend time at the Emmett Till Interpretive Center (ETIC) and tour inside the courthouse.

Tallahatchie County Courthouse, 401 West Court Street

Built in 1902, the courthouse was designated as a state landmark in 2007 by the Mississippi Department of Archives and History (MDAH). The MDAH has a historical marker on the grounds of the building, noting that it was the site of the Milam/Bryant trial in September 1955.

Also in 2007, the Tallahatchie Board of Supervisors appointed the Emmett Till Memorial Commission (ETMC) to explore how to commemorate Till and encourage reconciliation in the area. In addition, the ETMC undertook to restore the county courthouse to its appearance at the time of the trial and adapt it as the site of an interpretive center to commemorate Emmett Till. The restoration of the courthouse was overseen by Belinda Stewart Architects of Eupora, Mississippi. The firm received several well-deserved awards for their work on the project, including the Mississippi Heritage Trust Award for Preservation in 2016.

So what happened here in 1955? Four days after *Jet* published the photo of Emmett's mutilated body and not even two weeks after the defendants were indicted, the trial began; it was September 19, 1955. On September 22, the jury returned a not-guilty verdict. The all-male, all-white jury deliberated for sixty-seven minutes, and it may have been shorter had they not decided they needed a soda break. After they were in the jury room for just eight minutes, they sent out a request for Coca-Cola.[86]

During the trial, seating inside the courtroom was at a premium. As many as 350 spectators crammed into the second-floor courtroom, designed for about 280. The overflow crowd numbering as high as 1,000 waited on the courthouse lawn to receive regular updates. Blacks and whites were separated in the courtroom and on the lawn. Why would this be any different than the rest of Mississippi in 1955?

Much hostility was directed toward the Black people who came to the trial. In fact, James Hicks later reported, "a cross was burned fifty yards from the courthouse during the trial."[87] Murray Kempton reported in the *New York Post* that the town of Sumner saw on the courthouse lawn what it perceived to be "the invasion of spectacles that were not just unfamiliar but shocking to its sense of fitness." Kempton noted that Black and white reporters were talking to each other and exchanging notes; that was not the Mississippi the local whites knew. Local Blacks, rather than being out in the fields working, "watched from the base of the Confederate monument which is the only seat available to them."[88]

If Sumner locals found these things "shocking," then one act of extreme courage and defiance during the trial must have absolutely stunned them. Black men in Mississippi typically didn't make accusations against white men in the mid-1950s, yet that's exactly what Emmett's uncle, Mose Wright, did in the courtroom on the first day of the trial.

Despite being warned against testifying by one of the defense attorneys the day before the trial started, Mose Wright made his way to the witness chair as the first prosecution witness. After testifying that Roy Bryant had identified himself by name when he pounded on the door of his home about 2:30 a.m. on August 28, Wright stated he recognized the other man as J. W. Milam.

The prosecutor said to the witness, "I want you to point out Mr. Milam if you see him here."

The slight, diminutive Wright lifted all of his five feet, three inches out of the witness chair. He pointed "a knobby finger at J. W. Milam," reported Sam Johnston on the front page of the *Greenwood Commonwealth*.[89]

Wright proclaimed, "There he is."

Ernest Withers, one of the photographers who snapped photos of Emmett Till's battered face and body in Chicago, was covering the trial. Withers surreptitiously took an iconic shot of Mose Wright standing, pointing at Milam, and performing what many might have viewed as a suicidal act. (We meet up with photographer Withers again in Memphis.)

Mose Wright did not go into hiding after his testimony. While his wife, Elizabeth, departed for Chicago even before Emmett's body was found, Mose Wright was at the courthouse during the rest of the trial. *The Nation* reported that Wright "walked through the Negro section of the lawn with his hands in his pockets and his chin held up in the air of a man who has done what there was to do."[90]

The trial ended on September 23, 1955. The jury began its deliberations just after 2:30 p.m. James Kilgallen reported that "the large crowd in the courtroom—apparently anticipating a fairly quick verdict—remained in their seats."[91] While the jury was quick, they certainly were not compliant with Judge Curtis Swango's directive to put their verdict in writing. When they returned with the speedy verdict but no paperwork, Judge Swango made them go back and do it as ordered.

Mamie Till Bradley was not there to hear the verdict. Accompanied by Congressman Charles Diggs of Michigan, she made her way out of the courtroom right after the trial, through the crowds on the lawn, to their car. They headed to Memphis to catch a flight back to Chicago.

Mamie Till Bradley knew how this would turn out. As they drove, the verdict came on the radio. In the memoir written (as Mamie Till-Mobley) with Christopher Benson, she recalled, "You could hear the celebration in the background," believing the broadcast may have been coming from the courthouse square. "It was like the Fourth of July."[92]

The Emmett Till Interpretive Center (ETIC), 158 North Court Street

Emmett Till
INTERPRETIVE CENTER

Located directly across from the courthouse, the ETIC not only tells the story of the Emmett Till tragedy but seeks pathways to racial healing. Book a tour of the renovated courthouse where the trial of Milam and Bryant was held through ETIC's website or by phone; be sure to specify how many will be in your party. Walk-ins are welcome, but advance reservations are recommended. The center is open weekdays from 10 a.m. to 5:30 p.m.

Emmett Till Interpretive Center	
Location	158 North Court Street, Sumner, Mississippi 38957
Days Closed	Saturday and Sunday unless an appointment is made in advance.
Operating Days and Hours	Open Monday to Friday, 10 a.m. to 5:30 p.m., and by appointment.
Admission	No charge for visiting the Interpretive Center nor the courtroom. Donations are encouraged, especially for groups and anyone desiring a tour.
Website	*http://www.emmett-till.org/*
Phone Number	(662) 483-1231
Email Address	*info@emmett-till.org*

Mississippi Delta—Additional Options

Up to now, Emmett Till–related locations have been this chapter's focus. Having visited Money, Glendora, and Sumner, travelers now have a choice. Head to Little Rock (if you are traveling from east to west on the loop tour) or spend more time exploring the Delta. Little Rock is just under three hours away. Additional touring of relevant towns in the Delta is likely to add a day to your itinerary. However, you can see several important places in civil rights history, some of which tie into the Emmett Till story.

These additional options are laid out assuming that your starting point is Sumner. The map here pinpoints eight towns. Not all of these may pique your interest. After explaining the historic significance of each one and what you can see there, decide if you want to do a quick stop at a few, add a day to the itinerary to see them all, or just head to Little Rock.

The route begins in Sumner. After a stop in Tutwiler, where Emmett Till's body was prepared to be taken back to Chicago, head south toward Ruleville, then west to Cleveland, and north to put you in position for a good night's sleep (there are chain motels in Clarksdale) and a possible drive to Little Rock in the morning.

Traveling to all the towns mapped except for Marks requires two hours of driving, stops not included. Marks is excluded from that driving time tally since it would take twenty-five minutes to drive there from Clarksdale. While certainly historically important, you can judge whether the reason to visit Marks is sufficiently memorialized to make a stop.

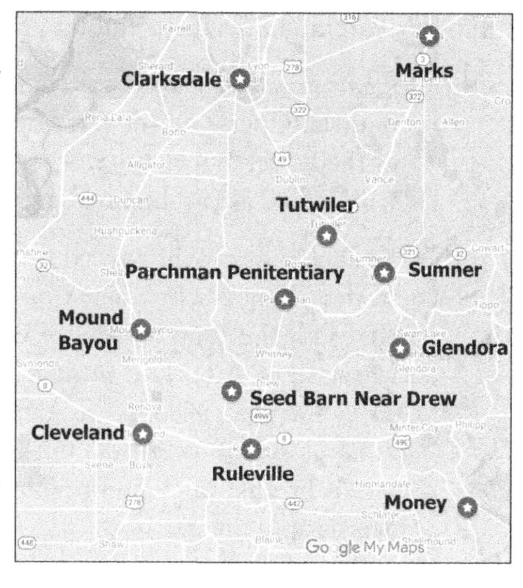

Here are all eight locales, including Marks, in a recommended drive order.

Tutwiler (5 Miles Northwest of Sumner)

Remember Chester Miller? He was the Black undertaker who did not want Emmett Till's body in his funeral home in Greenwood when Mamie Till Bradley ordered the body to come back to Chicago. Miller contacted Chester Nelson, a white undertaker in Tutwiler. Nelson, the mayor of Tutwiler, owned two funeral homes—one for whites and one for Blacks. Nelson agreed to prepare the body for the train ride north, as long as the casket's seal remained intact.

There is an Emmett Till Memorial Commission marker in front of the crumbling ruins of the former Tutwiler Funeral Home; the marker is near the corner of Hancock Avenue and Market Street, not far from the Tutwiler City Hall and Police Station. (Use this intersection in Google Maps, not "Tutwiler Funeral Home." If you do stop here, spin around the corner on Market to Front Street. Drive along Front Street to see murals paying tribute to the town's blues heritage, including a portrait of Sonny Boy Williamson and even a map to his gravesite.

Parchman State Penitentiary (9 Miles South of Tutwiler)

Parchman is the oldest and largest penitentiary in Mississippi, the only maximum-security prison in the state. What started as just four stockades in 1901 grew to cover twenty-eight square miles.

Given its maximum-security status, you might assume that among those claiming a bed here would be some of those found guilty of violent crimes against civil rights heroes. You'd be right. Some former Parchman residents fall into this category:

- *Edgar Ray Killen*, who was finally convicted—of manslaughter—on the forty-first anniversary of the murder of the three civil rights workers in Philadelphia, Mississippi. Killen died at Parchman at age ninety-two in early 2018.
- *Samuel Bowers*, who served time in federal prison for his role in the Chaney-Schwerner-Goodman killings, was tried five times for the 1966 murder of Vernon Dahmer of Hattiesburg, Mississippi. After four hung juries, Bowers was found guilty in 1998 and sentenced to life. He died here in 2006. In eight years at Parchman, Bowers had but one visitor, a person claiming to be his brother but who provided a fake address in a fictitious Mississippi town.

However, while the state penitentiary has held some bad criminals, it's highlighted here because of its connection to the Freedom Riders of 1961. Hoping to intimidate and eventually deter the young Freedom Riders, the state began sending them to Parchman. Governor Ross Barnett instructed the guards there "to break their spirit, not their bones."[93] At one point, as many as three hundred Freedom Riders were housed at Parchman.

Among them were now-familiar names like John Lewis, James Farmer (CORE cofounder), and Stokely Carmichael. A less familiar name who spent time here is Carol Ruth Silver. Ms. Silver, a white woman, was raised in a Jewish household in central Massachusetts. She had just finished her undergraduate degree at the University of Chicago when she became a Freedom Rider. To say the least, Parchman was way out of the mainstream in her life experiences up to that point. Learn about her time in Parchman in her book, *Freedom Rider Diary: Smuggled Notes from Parchman Prison*. It's worth your attention.

There is a Mississippi Blues Trail marker across from the main gate of the prison on US 49W (just after Mississippi Highway 32). There is no mention of any civil rights connections to the prison on the marker. Warning: Don't pull in in front of the large prison gate. Park across the highway, on the same side as the Blues Trail sign and heed the advice on the marker: "Don't linger."

The Seed Barn near Drew (13 Miles Southwest of Parchman)

Of all the eight extra Delta sites, this one is most connected to Emmett Till, and perhaps the hardest to find.

It's the site of the former Sturdivant Plantation, which was managed by J. W. Milam's brother Leslie when Emmett Till was killed. Here, early in the morning of August 28, 1955, Emmett Till was brutalized. Farmworker Frank Young saw a green and white Chevrolet pickup drive onto this Sunflower County property. According to Mr. Young, he saw four white men in the truck's cab and Emmett Till along with two Black men in the back.

The truck stopped near a small seed barn. The occupants in the truck went in. Young and others, including trial witnesses Willie Reed and Amanda Bradley, heard loud screams coming from the barn.

There is *no marker here* nor any indication of the infamous nature of this spot. Dave Tell's *Remembering Emmett Till* has an entire chapter on why there is no memorial to what occurred here.

Using the location provided by the Emmett Till Memory Project, here is how to find the seed barn. The easiest way is to enter these coordinates into Google Maps or your mapping software: 33.799455, -90.583231. Another way is to follow these directions from Parchman (thirteen miles; twenty minutes):

- Go south on US 49W for 8.5 miles.
- Turn right onto South Front Street and travel about 0.3 miles.
- Turn left onto South Main Street and another quick left onto South Boulevard for 0.8 miles.
- Continue onto Drew Ruleville Road for 2.2 miles. Slow down after you cross Radio Station Road. Take your next slight right.
- After that slight right, the former location of the seed barn is about a quarter of a mile up that road on the left. If you get to Bethel Church on Drew Ruleville Road, you have gone almost a mile too far.

A couple of questions may cross your mind as you read the directions to the former Sturdivant Plantation or while you drive to it.

First, how far is this from where Emmett Till was kidnapped, and how far was it from Glendora where J. W. Milam lived? The plantation is about thirty miles from Glendora and nearly forty miles from Preacher Wright's home where Emmett was staying. The killers, and their unindicted accomplices whom Frank Young saw, had plenty of time to think about the crime they were about to commit.

Second, "How can this spot be unmarked?" In Philadelphia, Mississippi, there was no marker near the property where the three civil rights workers' bodies were unearthed. In Money, a marker is in place at Bryant's Grocery, but it is in miserable condition, while the restored Ben Roy's Service Station less than seventy feet away looks better than it did sixty-five-plus years ago. Perhaps what Sherron Wright, the great-niece of Moses Wright, said of the current owners of the former grocery store explains why these important historic sites are not properly memorialized: "They just want history to die. They just want history erased."[94]

Even though you don't memorialize the past with a marker, the past remains. Some may want to hide the past, but the past does not evaporate just because it is ignored or disrespected.

Ruleville (8 Miles South of the Seed Barn Near Drew)

Fannie Lou Hamer, a monumental figure in the struggle for civil rights, voting rights, and women's rights, is properly showcased in museums across the country. Hear her moving speech at the 1964 Democratic Convention when you visit the National Civil Rights Museum in Memphis, or pull it up on YouTube. She was the cofounder of the Mississippi Freedom Democratic Party (MFDP) as well as the cofounder of the National Women's Political Caucus.

Here, in her hometown, she is honored with a memorial garden containing a statue and her tombstone; the local post office is named in her honor.

The statue, her gravesite, and a historical marker are in the **Fannie Lou Hamer Park** at 929 Byron Street in Ruleville. Her headstone is engraved with one of her famous quotes: "I am sick and tired of being sick and tired." The post office is at 115 North Chester Avenue.

Also in Ruleville is William Chapel Missionary Baptist Church, the venue for many civil rights gatherings. Fannie Lou Hamer attended a mass meeting here and committed herself to registering to vote. Though it took her three tries to register due to the obstacles put in place to discourage Black voter registration, her steely will prevailed; her first vote was for herself as an MFDP candidate for Congress in 1964. The Mississippi Freedom Trail marker for the church is on O. B. Avenue, near where it meets Elisha and Everette Langdon Street.

Cleveland (11 Miles West of Ruleville)

Like Ruleville, this is the hometown of another civil rights–era icon, Amzie Moore. Mr. Moore has been described as "bear-like" and as a "godfather to squads of young activists who eventually broke the back of Mississippi's Jim Crow."[95] He was an army veteran, a successful businessman, and the president of the Cleveland, Mississippi, branch of the NAACP.

The house he built at 614 South Christman Street sheltered Martin Luther King Jr., Andrew Young, John Lewis, and hosts of other young activists who traveled the dirt roads of the Delta educating folks about voter registration. Two markers grace the lawn at the house, which serves as a museum and interpretive center. Visits inside are possible on Tuesday, Thursday, Friday, and Saturday from 10 a.m. to 2 p.m. The home's restoration is the work of Belinda Stewart Architects of Eupora, Mississippi, the same firm that restored the courthouse in Sumner.

Moore, who claimed that Moses Wright called him shortly after his nephew Emmett Till was kidnapped,[96] is buried in Cleveland's **Westlawn Memorial Gardens** at 400-498 Mullins Road, a little over a mile south of the house.

Mound Bayou (11 Miles North of Cleveland)

This historically significant town has important ties not only to notable people in the civil rights movement but also to the Emmett Till case.

- Mound Bayou was founded in 1887 as an independent community for Blacks by former slaves under the leadership of Isaiah Montgomery.
- Dr. T. R. M. Howard served as the chief surgeon at the local Taborian Hospital and brought the city back economically

in the 1940s. Dr. Howard became one of the wealthiest men in Mississippi. He founded the Regional Council of Negro Leadership (RCNL), which held annual conferences on civil rights topics as early as 1952. Top entertainment talent, like Mahalia Jackson, performed at these meetings, and the top legal minds of the period gave updates on various court challenges. At the 1954 meeting, which took place ten days before the *Brown v. Board of Education* decision, eight thousand attended to hear Thurgood Marshall speak.

- Medgar and Myrlie Evers moved to Mound Bayou in 1951. Mr. Evers sold insurance for Dr. Howard's Magnolia Mutual Life Insurance Company. Howard introduced Evers to civil rights activism through the RCNL. Together, Howard and Evers organized a boycott against service stations that refused to provide restrooms for Blacks.
- During the Till trial, Black reporters and witnesses stayed in Dr. Howard's Mound Bayou home. Also, Mamie Till Bradley and Representative Charles Diggs of Michigan were guests of Dr. Howard, who provided his guests with an armed escort to and from the courthouse in Sumner.
- African American farmworker Frank Young showed up at Dr. Howard's gate at midnight on the eve of the Till murder trial. The guards did not want to wake the doctor, but Young, who had walked and hitchhiked for eighty miles to bring Howard some news, was not going to speak with anyone else. The news: he and others had "ear-witnessed" the brutalization of Emmett Till, a crime that was committed in Sunflower County, not Tallahatchie County.

Mound Bayou today is in decline. The Taborian Hospital is shuttered. The home of Isaiah Montgomery, even though it's on the National Registry of Historic Places, is abandoned. Mound Bayou citizens lost their appeal to the state supreme court to keep its high school open.

Three places of note, all within a half mile of each other:

- *The Dr. T. R. M. Howard marker:* It's across from the corner of Edwards and Roosevelt and in front of the site of the former

Taborian Hospital. Attempts are under way to restore the hospital building into an urgent care center.

- *Isaiah T. Montgomery House:* In disrepair, it's located at 302 West Main Street South. A sign in front describes the vision of the Mississippi Department of Archives and History for the home of the city's founder.
- *City Hall:* A visit here (106 Green Street West) will reward you with three signboards presenting the community's history as well as artwork on the outside of the building depicting famous African Americans.

Clarksdale (28 Miles Northeast of Mound Bayou)

Compared to any other place you may have been in the Delta since leaving Greenwood, Clarksdale is big, with about sixteen thousand residents.

If you opted for this add-a-day extension exploring other towns in the Delta, you might consider lodging here, as there are multiple options. Little Rock is another two and a half hours from here, though there are also lodging options once you get on Interstate 40 well east of Little Rock.

Clarksdale was where a long boycott began in December 1961 and went on for two years, *twice as long as the bus boycott in Montgomery, Alabama.* The trigger was a ban on two Black marching bands from participating in the local Christmas parade. Clarksdale businesses were boycotted by the Black community, which rallied behind the slogan, "If we can't parade downtown, why should we trade downtown?"

The leader of the boycott was Aaron Henry. Along with Dr. T. R. M. Howard and Medgar Evers, Mr. Henry was a driving force behind the gas station boycott in Mississippi in the 1950s. A World War II veteran and owner of a local pharmacy, Mr. Henry was also the head of the NAACP in Mississippi and a cofounder of the Mississippi Freedom Democratic Party. He served in the state legislature from 1982 to 1996. The Mississippi Freedom Trail marker honoring Aaron Henry for his decades of civil rights work is opposite 212 Martin Luther King Boulevard, not far from Haven United Methodist Church on Yazoo Avenue. The vacant lot where

the marker is placed was the location of Mr. Henry's Fourth Street Drug Store. The store was bombed in March 1963, and the Henrys' home was set on fire shortly after the bombing. Fund-raising is under way to build the Northern Mississippi Civil Rights Museum on this lot.

Haven United Methodist Church hosted NAACP meetings. Mr. Henry and his wife, Noelle, worshipped here; there is a marker in front of the church (Yazoo Avenue and Martin Luther King Boulevard).

Singer-songwriter Sam Cooke ("You Send Me," "A Change Is Gonna Come," "Cupid," "Wonderful World," and more) was born in Clarksdale in 1931. A marker honoring him is in front of the New Roxy Theater at 357 Issaquena Avenue, just a few hundred feet from the Aaron Henry marker. Read more about Sam Cooke and his composition that became a civil rights anthem, "A Change Is Gonna Come," in the chapter on Louisiana.

Not interested in adding a day? If you head to Little Rock after departing Sumner, along the way you could visit two of the towns named above. Both Tutwiler (location of the Till funeral home) and Clarksdale can be quick stops as you travel to Little Rock.

Marks (18 Miles East of Clarksdale)

Martin Luther King Jr. began to raise the idea of a Poor People's Campaign a year and a half before his assassination. He favored a multiracial march of poor people to Washington in early 1968.

Dr. King toured several cities to raise support for the campaign. On March 18, 1968, he went to Marks and witnessed something that brought him to tears. Dr. King saw schoolchildren eating a lunch consisting only of a slice of apple and some crackers.

Though Dr. King did not live to see the campaign begin, he wanted rural Marks included as one of the originating communities. As a result, Marks joined a group of other larger and well-known cities from which the Poor People's March to Washington would begin. Others included Selma, Los Angeles, Seattle, and San Francisco. However, Marks became the focus of much media attention when a mule train departed there on May 13, 1968. The marker commemorating the Marks mule train is at 1098 Martin Luther King Jr. Drive here in front of the Citgo station. **Alice's Soul Food** restaurant near Main Street and Second Avenue also has a wall mural depicting the mule train.

I leave it to you to decide whether a side trip to Marks fits your travel schedule.

Clarksdale and the Emmett Till Trial

Just from the length of the downtown merchant boycott and the violence brought against Aaron Henry's home and business, one can tell that Clarksdale was a tough town for African Americans in the 1960s. The town wasn't any better the previous decade during the trial of Emmett Till's killers.

At the trial of Milam and Bryant, prosecution and defense lawyers both addressed Mrs. Mamie Till Bradley as "Mamie" when she was on the witness stand. Both sides knew they would pay a price with the all-male, all-white jury should they refer to the victim's mother with the more respectful "Mrs. Bradley." (In contrast, the accused's wife, Carolyn Bryant, was always referred to as "Mrs. Bryant.")

Writing in *The Nation* in October 1955, Dan Wakefield pointed out that a Clarksdale radio station wasn't as careful about this. The station referred to Emmett's mother as "Mrs. Bradley" on a news broadcast reporting on the trial. The station "spent the next hour answering calls of protest."[97]

CHAPTER 13

Little Rock

Do I really need to go to Little Rock? That thought crossed my mind as I planned my own trip. Why consider skipping Little Rock?

For one, my previous day's touring would end in Sumner. From Sumner to Little Rock is nearly a three-hour drive. On the other hand, the distance from Sumner to Memphis, the next stop if Little Rock was skipped, is under one hundred miles, less than two hours away.

Second, I knew that our day in the Delta would be a long one, and that one long day in the Delta meant a late arrival in the Little Rock area.

Finally, on top of the distance considerations and worries about the likely taxing nature of the prior day, my thought process was clouded by the misguided going-in belief that the Little Rock story was pretty simple. Wasn't it as straightforward as the unanimous *Brown v. Board of Education* decision in 1954 doing away with the "separate but equal" standard, established by the Supreme Court's 1896 decision in *Plessy v. Ferguson* that and forced integration to begin? Didn't the effort to integrate succeed after some initial resistance and the perseverance of nine courageous young people?

Yes, on a simplistic level, that was all true—except that is not the whole story by any stretch. The full story of Little Rock in 1957 is one with heroes and villains, a story with drama not only in the streets but also in classrooms and courtrooms.

We decided to go to Little Rock. The drive was long, but the payoff was big. This stop would contrast with some others because, in Little Rock, perseverance and justice ultimately triumphed. Consider the sixty-seven-minute not-guilty verdict in Sumner or the delayed and insufficient justice for the murder of the three civil rights workers in Philadelphia, Mississippi. Little Rock provides visitors a different, more satisfying outcome, though it didn't happen easily or quickly.

There was so much more to integrating Little Rock Central High School (LRCHS) in 1957 that I didn't know. For example, I didn't know how these nine brave young people came to be selected. I had no idea of the restrictions that were placed on them as they attended. They couldn't play high school sports, for example. Not only that but they also couldn't even attend the school's sports events! Plus, they had to forgo one of the more anticipated rites of being a high school student: they could not go to a school prom.

Two more quick confessions of how going to Little Rock chipped away at my own ignorance. I was not aware of the details behind the three attempts the Little Rock Nine made to get in the door and stay there. I also didn't know that Dr. Martin Luther King attended the graduation ceremony of Ernest Green, the first Black student to complete high school at LRCHS.

The Little Rock Nine—and Why Nine?

The Little Rock Nine consisted of six young women and three young men. As the school year began in 1957, three were sophomores, five were juniors, and one was a senior. Because Daisy Bates was so involved with them as they went through their ordeal that fall, some believe that Mrs. Bates selected them. That's not the case. They were picked from a long list of potential enrollees submitted by principals at the city's Black schools.

The lists, totaling about eighty students, were submitted to School Superintendent Virgil Blossom. That was too many, according to the superintendent. The National Park Service (NPS) site sheds a lot of light on his process of whittling down the number. The restrictions he imposed on candidates caused many to drop out. Exemplary grades and attendance were expected.

The process cut the number down to seventeen potential students. When the local paper published the names, addresses, and phone numbers of these seventeen, the harassment began. That caused seven students to pull out. On the morning of September 4, 1957, ten students went to

continued

continued from the previous page

Little Rock Central to start the school year.

The mob and the National Guard (then under state control) kept all ten out of the building. The mob scene of this first day was enough for the parents of one student, Jane Hill. Their daughter wasn't going back to Little Rock Central. Now it was the Little Rock Nine.

During your visit, you will learn more about each one. All of them have had successful careers in fields from communications to technology, from government service to investment banking, from education to social justice activism. All nine of them were college graduates, and five received advanced degrees. Two of them served in the Armed Forces. One of them, Melba Pattillo Beals, wrote a memoir of her Little Rock experiences titled *Warriors Don't Cry*.

The Little Rock Nine

Melba Pattillo Beals
Elizabeth Ann Eckford
Ernest Green
Gloria Ray Karlmark
Carlotta Walls LaNier
Terrence James Roberts
Jefferson Allison Thomas
Minnijean Brown Trickey
Thelma Mothershed Wair

Why did they put themselves through such a trying and dangerous ordeal?

Perhaps some light is shed on this question by what Little Rock Nine member Terrence Roberts wrote in *Remember Little Rock*:

> "We were aware that hundreds of people before us had given their lives for the cause for equality. Saying no to this opportunity would have been the same as spitting on their graves."[98]

If you are still wavering about whether to include a stop in Little Rock, here are a few things you can experience during your visit:

- You may feel transported back in time here. Seeing the Gothic Revival–style Little Rock Central High School is likely to make you feel, "They don't build them like that anymore." The fortresslike building, the reflecting pool in front, and the four impressive statues at the front entrance (representing ambition, personality, opportunity, and preparation) are just magnificent and such a contrast to the ugliness that happened on the street in front of them in 1957.

- The neighborhood proximate to the school and a restored gas station (part of the National Park Service complex) take you back to the 1950s, if you were ever there. The gas station is where reporters covering the fall 1957 events would wait for the pay phone to free up so they could file their news reports in the pre–cell service and pre-WiFi days. Finally, you will feel you have stepped back in time should you make an appointment to see the home of Daisy and L. C. Bates. The Bateses' home was the command center for the integration effort.

- You'll meet heroes and villains. We just mentioned Daisy Bates. Her name is not as well known as Rosa Parks or Dr. King or others, but you will get to know her during your visit. Mrs. Bates clearly was a hero in this story. She was head of the Arkansas NAACP chapter and liaised between local city and school administrators and the Nine during the crisis. Importantly, she provided comfort and guidance to the Nine, all heroes, as they faced physical and emotional abuse from various villains. Some of those villains are nameless, like the angry mob outside the school or some of the students inside the school who harassed the Nine. Other villains are certainly known, like Arkansas governor Orville Faubus.

- The integration of LRCHS didn't just happen on a single day in September 1957. The Nine entered the school on three different days that month. The final one occurred on September 25, 1957, after President Dwight Eisenhower ordered the 101st Airborne Division to the city to ensure the Nine not only were able to enter the building but also were protected inside (to a degree). Even on that day, a bomb threat cleared the school. The crisis didn't end in September 1957 or even after the school year ended. Governor Faubus closed all Little Rock's public high schools for the entire following school year.

Being in Little Rock helped me see the progression of successful activism in the mid-1950s more clearly. Rosa Parks refused to vacate her bus seat in December 1955; this led to the successful bus boycott through 1956 and the emergence of Dr. King. In 1957, the courage and determination of nine young people under the guidance of Daisy Bates put a third link in the chain of change that became the civil rights movement.

The perseverance of the Little Rock Nine would soon arouse other young people to sit in at lunch counters, ride interstate buses as Freedom Riders, spend Freedom Summer in Mississippi to spur voter registration, and create Freedom Schools for children to make up for the shortcomings of local public education.

Little Rock is an important part of the chain of change that was the civil rights movement. As such, it merits a day as you plan your journey.

The Plan for Little Rock in 300 Words or Less

There are two must-see locations:

- *The Little Rock Central High School National Historic Site run by the National Park Service.* It's open seven days a week, making Little Rock a place you could stop even on Sunday.
- *The Daisy Bates House.* It is a National Historic Landmark. An appointment must be made to see the inside; a stop-click-and-go visit is another option.

While the drive to Little Rock is long, there is not a lot of driving to do once you arrive. The two locations just mentioned are less than two miles apart. Later in the chapter, two other nearby sites worth considering are presented: the *Testament* statue honoring the Nine at the state capitol and the Arkansas Civil Rights Heritage Trail. Several sites in Little Rock relate to the broader topic of Black history. Content on visiting these locations during your time in the city closes out this chapter.

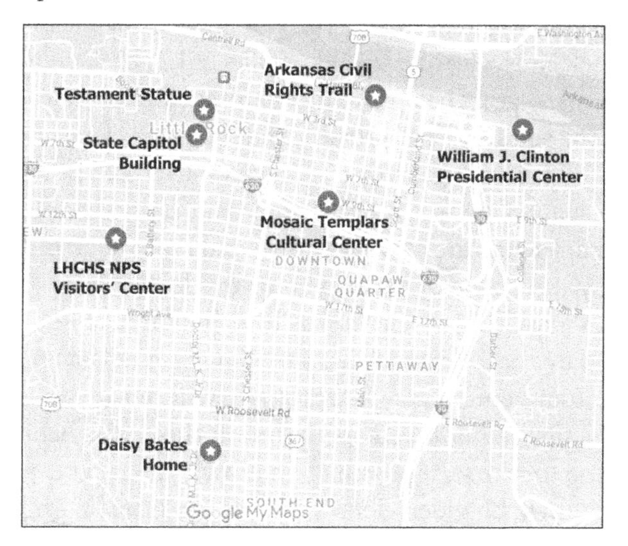

Little Rock Central High School National Historic Site Visitors' Center, 2120 West Daisy L. Gatson Bates Drive

The visitors' center is open from 9 a.m. to 4:30 p.m. every day of the year except Thanksgiving, Christmas Day, and New Year's Day. No fee is charged to visit the center nor for the ranger tours offered here. Ample parking is available at the center. It is kitty-corner from the high school, which is still an active school. Do not park in front of the school.

The facility is very well run and thoughtfully organized, much like the NPS site in Lowndes County, Alabama. Like the Lowndes site, it is modest in size, all on one floor. There is a theater with an orientation film. A gift shop and bookstore round out the similarities between the two NPS facilities.

Multimedia resources enlighten visitors. Video monitors, some offering interactive features, relate information on topics like "Living with Jim Crow" and the Supreme Court's *Brown* decision. Other monitors share black-and-white TV news clips from 1957 such as announcements from Governor Faubus, the three attempts of the Little Rock Nine to enter the school, and the arrival of the 101st Airborne Division that helped pave the way for the Nine to enter LRCHS on September 25, 1957.

Especially enlightening were the oral histories by members of the Little Rock Nine. Hearing them as adults reflect back on their experiences many years before is a memorable experience. The video monitors at the site are also captioned, and the video elements are all supplemented by listening devices with relevant audio. The ample video and audio resources are supported by informative storyboards that give visitors a complete picture of what occurred in Little Rock in 1957 and in the ensuing years. Spend one to two hours inside the center.

Besides exploring inside the visitors' center, take one of the tours offered by the rangers at this site. These tours last an hour. Some of the tour content may be repetitive with what you gleaned from the visitors' center if you spent time at the center before your tour. Take the tour first, if possible. That way, you can be a bit more selective about which video elements you spend time with back in the visitors' center after the tour.

"America at War with Itself": Television and the Little Rock Central Crisis

Take yourself out of the wall-to-wall world of nonstop cable and internet news availability. Imagine yourself back in the late 1950s. That's key to understanding the role television played in telling Americans about Little Rock in the fall of '57. In 1957, four out of five homes in the United States had a television set. Forget cable or streaming. Network news was just a fifteen-minute telecast. The first half-hour network nightly newscast was still six years away.

Despite the minimal amount of time devoted to broadcasting the news, special reports put the angry mobs and the armed soldiers in Little Rock into Americans' living

rooms. The TV network coverage of the Little Rock Central events had a major impact. In his 1993 book *The Fifties*, Pulitzer Prize–winning author David Halberstam recalled the medium's role:

> "The most indelible images of America that fall [of 1957] came from Little Rock, scenes captured by still photographers and, far more significantly, by movie cameramen working for network television news shows. The first and most jarring of these images was of angry mobs of white rednecks, pure hatred contorting their faces, as they assaulted the nine young Black students who dared to integrate Little Rock Central High.
>
> "The second and almost equally chilling image came a few weeks later, showing the same Black children entering the same school under the protection of elite US Army paratroopers. The anger and hatred that had been smoldering just beneath the surface in the South since the enactment of *Brown v. Board of Education* had finally exploded, and now because of television, the whole nation and soon the whole world could watch America at war with itself."[99]

Historian Doris Kearns (later Goodwin) was a high school student in New York in 1957. After watching the confrontations in Little Rock on television, Kearns wrote a letter to President Dwight D. Eisenhower urging him to intervene. Goodwin recalled the impact watching the TV coverage had on her:

> "Aside from the death of James Dean and the struggle to keep the Dodgers in Brooklyn, no public event had so fully engaged my private emotions. To challenge the president of the country, to berate angrily a governor I had never heard of from a place I did not know, was for me an immense expansion of political consciousness. It was a turning point or, at least, the start of a turning point."[100]

The images of hate presented to the country and the world would have an impact again when shared from Anniston in 1961, Birmingham in 1963, Philadelphia in 1964, Selma in 1965, and Memphis in 1968.

Two types of tours are offered at the visitors' center. Both are given at 9 a.m. and 1 p.m. The major difference between the two types are tours is whether visitors can go inside LRCHS or not.

"School-Included" Tours: These are offered on select weekdays. The key is whether school is in session or not, so these tours are not available on federal holidays, during LRCHS spring and winter breaks, and on certain other dates during the school year. The dates when "school-included" tours are not available can be found on the LRCHS NPS website (*https://www.nps.gov/chsc/planyourvisit/guidedtours.htm*).

- Those with mobility issues should know that the tour inside the school may involve ascending two flights of stairs to enter the school, a walk into the auditorium, and possibly walking down two flights of stairs to the cafeteria. An ADA-accessible entrance is available, and an elevator can be taken between floors. If accessibility accommodations are needed, let the park know when reserving your visit.
- The NPS also makes it clear that only tour attendees *with a ranger* can enter the high school. Do not enter the school on your own.

"Streetscape" Tours: Offered on select weekends, these are guided walking tours from the visitors' center to (but not inside) Little Rock Central High School. Along the way, rangers share the story of the Little Rock Nine and the events that led to the school's desegregation.

All tours should be reserved in advance to avoid disappointment. The number to call is (501) 374-1957. The NPS asks for tours to be reserved *and confirmed* at least forty-eight hours in advance. They recommend reserving a tour a month in advance. Have this information ready:

- The name of the individual or group requesting and the number of people seeking a tour
- The phone number of the cell phone you will have on the day of the tour
- An email address to receive the tour confirmation
- Any special or ADA accessibility needs

The tours have size limitations, especially those going inside the school. Calling early is wise.

Besides the visitors' center and the restored Magnolia Gas Station, visit the Central High Commemorative Garden, directly across Daisy Bates Drive from the visitors' center. The arch in the garden should be viewed up close as it tells the story of Little Rock Central High School, from its segregation days through the integration challenges to today. Your ranger-led tour may end here; it's a fitting place to conclude your visit to this NPS Historical Site. Not only can you think about what you learned here but also what happened here more than sixty years ago.

The garden contains nine trees and nine benches—for obvious reasons. Sit on one of the benches and consider what it must have been like as a Black Little Rock teenager just trying to get an education. Think about what it must have felt like to face phone threats at home, angry adults on the streets, and abusive fellow students in the school hallways. Reflect on how the hopes of each one of the Nine triumphed over their fears. You can even be thankful for the change they made in their school, their community, and the nation. These nine young people are true heroes.

"Dear God: Please Walk with Ernie in the Graduation Line at Central"

That's what classmate Melba Pattillo wrote in her diary as Ernest Green's graduation approached in late May 1958. Ernest, the only senior among the Nine, had his own concerns about participating in the graduation ceremonies in the school's football stadium. He expressed those worries to Mrs. Bates.

He had reason to worry. In the weeks leading up to the two graduation ceremonies on May 25 and May 27, there was a rock fight outside the school, firecrackers were exploded in the school, and Little Rock Nine member Terrence Roberts was struck by a rock as he walked on campus. Black students were regularly the target of rotten eggs and rocks as they entered or left the school.

continued

continued from the previous page

Mrs. Bates traveled to Washington, DC, to arrange protection for Ernest. The FBI became involved, checking windows of houses near the stadium for sniper positions. The National Guard was positioned under the stands in the stadium, and Little Rock police were stationed throughout the crowd.

At the ceremony on May 25, over six hundred seniors heard a minister's sermon; there was one incident. A white graduating senior was arrested when he spat in the face of a young girl attending as a guest of Ernest Green.

Two days later, diplomas were handed out. When Ernest's name was called, there were some whistles and insults but no other incidents. For the most part, though, the crowd that had been cheering as other names were called went silent when they called, "Ernest Green." Melba Pattillo Beals wrote in her memoir, *Warriors Don't Cry*, that she listened to the ceremony on the radio with her mother and grandmother. She recalled how upset her mom was when no one cheered as Ernest received his diploma. Melba's grandmother had a different take: "Who cares if they applaud, they didn't shoot him."[101]

Ernest's family sat proudly in the stands at the event. With them at the event was Dr. Martin Luther King Jr., who attended the graduation virtually unnoticed—but it was only 1958.

The Daisy Bates Home, 1207 West 28th Street

Daisy Bates was a force for change and no latecomer to the quest for freedom. She and her husband L.C. were in the fight a long time.

You likely noticed that the street in front of Little Rock Central High School is now Daisy L. Gatson Bates Drive. While you can learn more about Mrs. Bates at the NPS Visitors' Center and during a tour there, all that she did can get a bit lost in the many focal points of the Little Rock Central High School desegregation story: the Little Rock

Nine, Governor Faubus, the threatening mob, the violence against Black journalists, the involvement of the National Guard and then the 101st Airborne, and so on.

Daisy Bates: Public Advocate, Private Confidante

Daisy Bates and her husband, Lucious Christopher (or L.C., as he was known) Bates, were instrumental in the struggle for equality long before the 1957 events at Little Rock Central High School. They founded the *Arkansas State Press* in 1941, a weekly paper that served the Black community.

The paper's unwavering support of integration cost it and Mr. and Mrs. Bates dearly. At one point, they had to close the paper after white advertisers withdrew support under pressure from racists. The Bateses' home was vandalized. Once, a rock came through their window along with a KKK-signed note attached, saying, "The next will be dynamite."[102] Someone later made good on that threat; the home was bombed when Little Rock public schools were closed during the 1958–1959 school year.

As president of the Arkansas chapter of the NAACP, Mrs. Bates met with city officials and interfaced with the legal team from the national NAACP throughout the battle to get the high school integrated. Forecasting how challenging things would be the morning of the first attempt to have the Nine enter LRCHS on September 4, 1957, Mrs. Bates arranged for a group of white and Black ministers to escort the students into school that morning.

After the clash that day, the Bateses' house was the place for the nine students and their parents to meet. Daisy Bates's role vis-à-vis the Little Rock Nine was substantial, ranging from public advocate to private confidante. In her home, Mrs. Bates would host not only the Nine but also other dignitaries like Dr. Martin Luther King Jr., future Supreme Court Justice Thurgood Marshall, and actors Ossie Davis and wife, Ruby Dee.

Come to her modest two-bedroom home and learn more about the critical role she played. You need an appointment to enter the house. To reserve a time to visit, call (501) 375-1957 or contact the foundation that operates the home at *info@batesmuseumfoundation.org*. The entryway is ADA-compliant, and a marker is installed in front of the home should you not be able to arrange a visit inside. The home was listed on the National Register of Historic Places in 2001.

Other Little Rock Destinations

Besides the two recommended stops, other locations related to the city's civil rights history could be considered. Two that are relatively close to the LRCHS NPS Visitors' Center are the *Testament* statue honoring the Little Rock Nine on the grounds of the state capitol (about a mile and a half from the visitors' center) and the Arkansas Civil Rights Heritage Trail on West Markham Street (a mile from the capitol).

Furthermore, two additional ideas are offered for your Little Rock agenda:

- *The sites covered on the Arkansas Civil Rights History app*: the three dozen locations deal with the civil rights era and others with the broader subject of Black history.
- *The William J. Clinton Presidential Library*: Though certainly going well beyond the bounds of the civil rights era, the Clinton Library has an important piece of Little Rock civil rights history within.

The Testament Statue, Arkansas State Capitol Grounds

This tribute to the nine teenagers who courageously faced the hostile environment outside and inside the LRCHS from September 1957 and throughout the school year is located on the north side of the state capitol. It faces the governor of Arkansas's second-floor office window.

To find the statue, put "1524 West Fourth Street" in your mapping app. That will track you to a hard-to-miss seven-story redbrick building and importantly to the correct side of the capitol. The bronze sculpture (officially named *Testament: The Little Rock Nine Monument*) is on a strip of land near the state capitol and West Fourth Street. On-street parking should be available right next to the statue; however, there is a paid parking lot at the corner of West Fourth and Woodland Streets, should your visit coincide with some major event at the capitol.

The statue is the work of artists John and Cathy Deering and Steve Scallion. The life-sized representations of each of the students, schoolbooks in hand, were cast by the Shidoni Foundry of Santa Fe, New Mexico. Besides the bronze statues, quotes from each one of the Little Rock Nine add their voices to this tribute.

The name of the work was chosen not only to honor the witness these nine young people gave to equal rights but also, according to John Deering, to motivate observers to become virtual witnesses, imagining themselves amid the chaotic mix of angry segregationists, inquiring journalists, and armed troops who made up the atmosphere outside the high school.

The Arkansas Civil Rights Heritage Trail, 300 West Markham Street

The Arkansas Civil Rights Heritage Trail began in 2011 paying tribute to those who fought for racial justice. The markers that year, much to my surprise, honored the Freedom Riders who came to Little Rock from St. Louis in July 1961 as well as the Philander Smith College students who sat in at local lunch counters between 1960 and 1962.

Don't confuse my surprise with an implication that these activists were not worthy of markers to commemorate their brave actions. I just expected those involved with the desegregation of Little Rock Central High School to have been the first. The Little Rock Nine, Daisy and L. C. Bates, and others who pushed for desegregation in 1957 were honored in 2012.

The impetus behind the trail is the Anderson Institute on Race and Ethnicity at the University of Arkansas at Little Rock. New twelve-inch markers are added to the trail each year. In November 2019, a marker memorializing the Elaine 12 became part of the trail.

The Elaine 12 were Black sharecroppers in Phillips County, Arkansas, who were wrongfully convicted of murder and sentenced to death by an all-white jury following the Elaine Massacre in 1919. They were exonerated in 1923. Chapter 20 has information on visiting a memorial on the Elaine Massacre and on other civil rights and African American history sites in Arkansas beyond Little Rock.

The Arkansas Civil Rights Heritage Trail begins at 300 West Markham Street, directly in front of the Old State House Convention Center. There is a short biography of each person honored on the trail on the Anderson Institute on Race and Ethnicity's website (*http://arkansascivilrightsheritage.org/*).

Mosaic Templars Cultural Center, 501 West 9th Street

The Arkansas Civil Rights History app lists three dozen historical sites, all in Little Rock. At least one-third of them relate to the desegregation battle of 1957; the remaining sites have greater relevance to the larger subject of Black history, including the historic West Ninth Street Black business district, the site of the 1927 lynching of John Carter, and significant Black churches and schools.

One location on the app is the **Mosaic Templars Cultural Center**. The Mosaic Templars of America was an 1870s business providing insurance and other services to African Americans. The organization expanded in time, evolving to include a fraternal aspect.

The Mosaic Templars Cultural Center is at 501 West Ninth Street. There is no charge to visit; it is open Tuesday to Saturday, 9 to 5 p.m. The center and its museum focus on Black achievement during the period from 1865 to 1950. A genealogy research room, special exhibits, and local art displays can be part of a visitor's experience.

William J. Clinton Presidential Center, 1200 President Clinton Avenue

The Clinton Center is the second presidential center in one of the cities on our tour. The Carter Center in Atlanta is the other. We didn't bring up the Carter Center in the Atlanta chapter, though it is a popular place to visit. So why are we bringing up the Clinton Center here?

Bill Clinton is connected to the Little Rock civil rights story. As governor of Arkansas, Clinton invited the Nine to return to Little Rock in 1987 to mark the thirtieth anniversary of their historic bravery. In 1999, the last full year of Clinton's second term as president, the Little Rock Nine joined him at the White House. Congress had awarded each of the Nine the Congressional Gold Medal, the highest honor an American citizen can receive. President Clinton personally presented the medals.

More to the point regarding why a person interested in civil rights history might want to visit the Clinton Center. One of the Nine turned over their precious Congressional Gold Medal to the Center. If you go there, you can see it, but they will not tell you which one of the Nine gave up their medal so that the public could see it. At least they wouldn't tell my tour group!

Admission: $10 for adults under 62; seniors, college students, and retired military $8; $6 for those between 6 and 17. Children, active-duty military, and school groups with reservations are free. Open: Wednesday to Saturday, 10 a.m. to 4 p.m., and Sunday, 1 to 5 p.m.

CHAPTER 14

Memphis

The two-hour drive from Little Rock to Memphis will be one of the shorter intercity drives during your tour. However, you leap ahead in civil rights history as you travel from Little Rock to Memphis. The desegregation of Little Rock Central High School occurred in 1957, close to the early days of the modern US civil rights era. The tragic event that brings you to Memphis happened in 1968. While not the end of the quest for equal rights by any means, an assassin ended Martin Luther King Jr.'s life here that year.

Dr. King and others were planning the Poor People's Campaign in the spring of 1968. That campaign was focused on economic justice. The plight of Memphis sanitation workers was a fitting way for Dr. King to spotlight the injustices faced by these municipal workers. Economic rights and civil rights were entwined in Dr. King's mind, so he came to Memphis.

Memphis had a new mayor on New Year's Day 1968, well, sort of new. Henry Loeb was the Memphis mayor from 1960 to 1963. Now he was back, bringing his "avowed segregationist" views to the job.[103] Prior to his first mayoral stint, Loeb served as public works commissioner, and the sanitation division was one of his departments.

Sanitation equipment in Memphis was often in disrepair, putting the workers in danger. Sanitation workers received neither sick pay nor overtime pay despite frequent lengthy shifts. As bad as those two facts were, the workers were prohibited from seeking public shelter from torrential rainstorms when they occurred in Memphis. Apparently, the sight of sanitation workers shielding themselves from a downpour offended some folks in white neighborhoods.

On the morning of February 1, 1968, sanitation workers Echol

Cole, age thirty-six, and Robert Walker, age thirty, headed for work. They would not return home again. That afternoon, it began to rain as they headed to the Shelby Drive dump. With no rain gear, Cole and Walker sought shelter from the storm in the compactor compartment of the truck. When the compactor's motor shorted as the truck headed down Colonial Street, the two men were crushed to death. This type of malfunction had occurred before, once resulting in two previous fatalities.

The sanitation workers went on strike on February 12. Two weeks later, the strikers marched from **Clayborn Temple** to the steps of City Hall, and they repeated this fourteen-block march for sixty-five days. They carried picket signs proclaiming, "I Am a Man," iconic signs captured in well-known photos by Ernest Withers.

The issues here were a mixture of economic injustice and racial condescension, just what Dr. King wanted to call attention to via the Poor People's Campaign. On March 18, 1968, Dr. King flew to Memphis and spoke to a large crowd at the **Mason Temple**. No marches occurred on this visit, but he promised to come back to lead one on March 22. A major late-winter snowstorm dumped sixteen inches on Memphis that day, cancelling the plans for that march.

The first Memphis sanitation strike march that Dr. King led occurred on March 28. It did not go well. As the protest proceeded along Beale Street, some young Blacks began breaking store windows. The police intervened, moving in with tear gas and nightsticks. Rocks flew from the young people toward the police. The police responded. By the end of the day, sixteen-year-old Larry Payne had been shot and killed by police and at least sixty-four others were injured.

When the atmosphere during the march began to sour, Dr. King's aides felt it was time to get him to safety. That move caused the local papers to mock King's exit from the scene. The Memphis *Commercial Appeal* carried an editorial cartoon poking fun at his "retreat" with the caption "Chicken a la King." The paper editorialized that King had "wrecked his reputation as a leader as he took off at high speed when violence occurred."[104]

The criticism of the March 28 protest by the Memphis papers and others was still on Dr. King's mind on April 3 when, with a very sore throat, he spoke at the **Mason Temple**. He noted that he "read the articles," telling his audience the papers glossed over that "one thousand, three hundred sanitation workers are on strike, and that Memphis is not being fair to them."[105]

Dr. King's forty-three-minute speech that night is known by how he ended it: the "I've Been to the Mountaintop" speech—his last. "Mine eyes have seen the glory of the coming of the Lord!" were his final public words, words that some believe signaled Dr. King foreseeing his own death. You can read or listen to the speech at *https://www.americanrhetoric.com/speeches/mlkivebeentothemountaintop.htm*.

That night, Martin Luther King Jr. would return to **Room 306 at the Lorraine Motel**. Just west of the Lorraine Motel was **Bessie Brewer's boardinghouse on South Main Street**. James Earl Ray had checked into one of its second-floor rooms. The window in the shared bathroom of the second floor of the boardinghouse had a clear view of the Lorraine and the balcony outside of Room 306.

At 6:01 p.m. on April 4, 1968, a bullet killed Dr. King as he stood with friends on the balcony outside his room. A white and red wreath marks the spot outside Room 306 where Dr. King lay. You will see this and so much more when you come to Memphis. Every bolded location above should be part of your Memphis itinerary, and we explain how to do it all in the rest of this chapter.

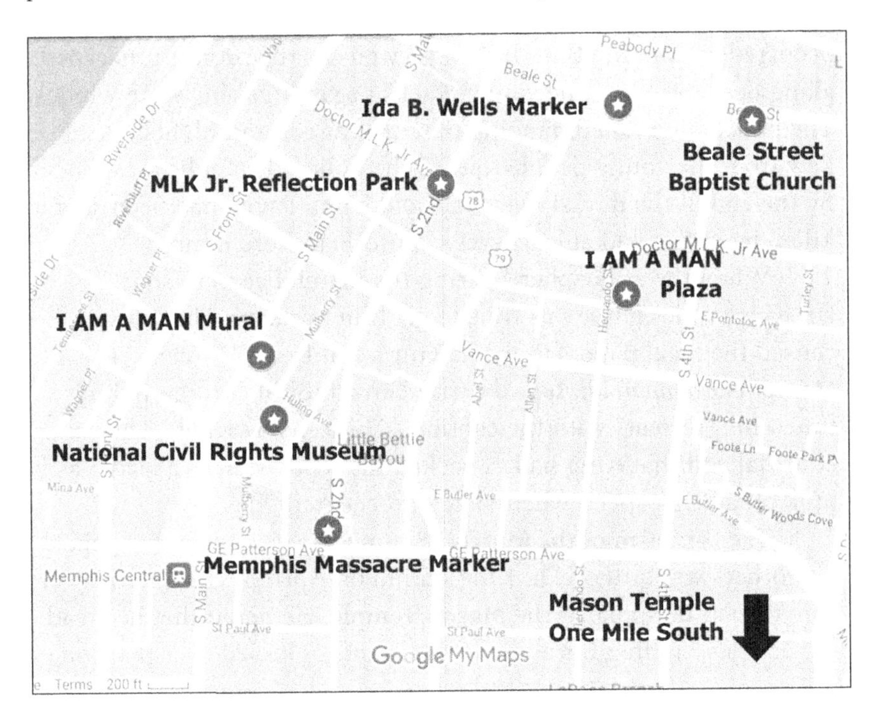

The Plan for Memphis in 300 Words or Less

Dr. King's assassination is the reason you want to come to Memphis. Most of the locations recommended here connect to the events leading up to April 4, 1968. However, it is fitting that your visit here begin where the story of early 1968 begins, at a marker on Colonial Road honoring sanitation workers Echol Cole and Robert Walker. The marker is one block south of where their garbage truck malfunctioned and crushed them. It's twenty-five minutes east of the National Civil Rights Museum (NCRM).

That museum is your major stop in Memphis. Allocate four hours for it. In addition, the Clayborn Temple (and the adjacent I Am a Man Plaza) and Mason Temple are recommended stops. The Clayborn Temple is less than a mile from the NCRM. Between the NCRM and the Clayborn Temple, we lay out a driving route for you that includes two relevant plazas, a historical marker, another church, and a collection of photographs of major southern civil rights scenes taken by a man later revealed to be an FBI informant.

If you made it over to the Cole and Walker marker on Colonial Road on your arrival in Memphis (as recommended), Mason Temple will be your last stop before you head south into northern Mississippi and eventually to Birmingham, Alabama.

The Echol Cole and Robert Walker Memorial Marker, Colonial Road and Sea Isle Road

The title on the marker is "Tragic Accident Sparks Sanitation Strike." With all the known problems that Memphis sanitation trucks had prior to February 1968, the word "accident" seems so wrong. "Tragic Preventable Accident" or "Tragic Accident Waiting to Happen" seems more fitting. This is not the only historical marker on the entire journey that is likely to rile you.

The marker is on the east side of Colonial Road where it intersects Sea Isle Road. If you put the address "1405 Colonial Road, Memphis" into Google Maps, you will find the marker across the street from that address. Park on Sea Isle Road.

This location is twenty to twenty-five minutes southeast of where you will spend the bulk of your Memphis touring. The other Memphis locations are relatively close together, near the Mississippi River.

If you are coming from Little Rock, try to see this marker as you drive into Memphis. You might even consider spending the night before your full Memphis day at a hotel on Interstate 240. There you'll find many hotels, each not that far from this marker. Depending on when you visit, you may find the I-240 hotels less expensive than those closer to downtown. You can head to the NCRM as your first stop the following morning.

The National Civil Rights Museum at the Lorraine Motel, 450 Mulberry Street

If you combined one of the sacred places of the civil rights movement with an incredibly comprehensive museum on that movement and its antecedents, you would have the National Civil Rights Museum (NCRM). The Lorraine Motel is where Dr. King and other civil rights leaders as well as major Black entertainers often stayed. Two major hit songs from the mid-1960s, "In the Midnight Hour" and "Knock on Wood," were composed at the Lorraine.

Dr. King was staying in Room 306. Visitors can see that room, looking much like it did in 1968, during their visit to the NCRM. It was never rented out after April 4.

The NCRM consists of two proximate and large buildings:

- The Lorraine Building is the main building, with two dozen permanent exhibits. Start here.
- The Legacy Building is across from the Lorraine. Its exhibits are incorporated into the boardinghouse from which James Earl Ray fired the shot that killed Dr. King.

As you tour the main building, keep in mind that, after seeing its two dozen exhibits and many of its nearly four dozen films, the equally intriguing exhibits in the Legacy Building still await you. The museum's website suggests that guests allow at least two hours for a quality experience. I'd block four hours.

Tickets can be purchased online as well as in person. There is ample parking in a free lot south of and adjacent to the Lorraine Building. Enter the visitor lot by turning north on Mulberry Street from G. E. Patterson Avenue. If you are traveling with a tour group by bus, your bus driver should look for a spot on St. Martin Street to the east of the visitor parking lot.

The museum does an excellent job preparing parents, teachers, and other adults who bring young people to the NCRM. If you are visiting with children, read the *Family Guide* on the museum's website. The guide identifies specific content in various galleries that might be disturbing to young visitors.

Parents should also appreciate a section of the Family Guide that gives some advice on speaking with children about the photos, films, and even audio they may experience in this and other civil rights museums. That said, the museum recommends that their exhibits only be viewed by children twelve and older.

Educators bringing their students to the museum might review a comprehensive *Learning Links document* provided by the museum. Besides an excellent preview of what the museum offers, Learning Links shares questions to think about and activities to do when preparing for a visit. One of my favorites was the link to the literacy tests from five southern states. Black citizens had to take tests like these to register to vote before such tests were outlawed. These old literacy tests are an eye-opening way to prepare for your overall civil rights journey.

National Civil Rights Museum at the Lorraine Motel	
Location	450 Mulberry Street, Memphis, Tennessee 38103
Days Closed	Tuesday
Operating Days and Hours	Open 9 a.m. to 5 p.m. every day except Tuesday; 6 p.m. closing during the summer
Admission	Adults: $18; seniors 55+ and students: $16; children 5–17: $15. Children 4 and under and active military: Free.
Website	*www.civilrightsmuseum.org*
Phone Number	(901) 521-9699
Email Address	*guestservices@civilrightsmuseum.org*

The Lorraine Building

After taking the obligatory picture of the red and white wreath and the two classic cars below Room 306, enter the Lorraine. The admissions desk is to the right. Guest services are to the left, as are restrooms and an elevator.

The first room you enter is the *State of Tennessee Gallery*, the home of the museum's temporary exhibits. To check out ahead of your visit what the temporary exhibit is, go to the "Exhibitions" tab on the museum's website and click on "Changing Gallery Exhibitions."

To give you a sense of the range and quality of the temporary exhibits, here are the two on display during my visit:

- *The Voices of the Movement.* An interactive exhibit with two parts, one focused on the 1963 March on Washington ("His Dream, Our Voices"), and the other ("Moments in Civil Rights History"), which highlights over four dozen historic episodes giving voice to the nation's civil rights journey. This exhibit is a collaborative effort between the Equal Justice Initiative and NBC Universal Comcast.

- *MLK50: A Legacy Remembered.* An outstanding and information-rich exhibit focusing on Dr. King's activism and achievements. Particular attention is paid to his last two days in Memphis with a detailed hour-by-hour timeline of his activities on April 3 and 4, 1968. Curated by Dr. Noelle Trent, director of interpretation, collection, and education, and Ryan Jones, the museum's educator, the exhibit concludes by presenting how Dr. King's contributions have been memorialized, including the fact that 955 communities (and that was as of 2007) had named a street after Dr. King. Chicago was the first to do this, in 1968.

While there may be exceptions from time to time, these temporary exhibits are included in the price of admission to the museum. Often there are restrictions on taking photos in the major temporary exhibits like *MLK50*. However, photos are permitted in the main Lorraine Galleries.

The Lorraine Galleries

Twenty-four permanent galleries are installed on the two floors of the Lorraine Building. Keep that in mind as you work your way through the major chapters of African American history in this building, and that you have another part of the museum across Mulberry Street to visit. Pace yourself. The first permanent gallery in the Lorraine is the circular *Slavery in America: 1619–1861*, and it begins a chronological journey that ends with a walk past Room 306.

Every gallery is worth your time. Some topics will be more familiar to you, especially if you have been to other museums before here. For example, you may know more about the 1955–56 Montgomery Bus Boycott and Rosa Parks; however, the gallery on Dr. King's Campaign in Albany, Georgia (which some point to as a disappointment), may give you new insights into the Albany movement. Take each room as an opportunity to round out and expand your knowledge of civil rights history.

After a a few tips on the first gallery, we'll highlight some others.

The first gallery is *Slavery and the Culture of Resistance*. It really sets up a visitor for how excellent this museum is. On entering, your eyes are drawn to a life-sized statue of an auctioneer seeking bids on an enslaved mother with babe in arms standing next to him. As arresting as this image is, the biggest impact may occur when you step into an alcove to the right as you face the slave auctioneer.

In this small space, your senses combine to leave an admittedly partial yet still powerful impression of what the Middle Passage across the Atlantic must have been like. Your eyes see the riveting sculpture of many enslaved people on the floor in front of you, sitting in a tight row with their knees to their chests and three feet, three inches of clearance from floor to the overhead plank. Walk into the alcove with three or four people. You will feel instantly cramped, yet you are standing up. The depictions on the wall of how the enslaved were laid out in the keel of a ship only adds to your discomfort.

If all that doesn't make an impression on you, listen. Your ears will pick up the pumped-in sounds of whips cracking and human screams. As your feet move, you hear the wooden floor creak. It's all quite a powerful way to simulate just a small part of the indignity of what human beings did to each other.

The resistance aspect of the gallery's title comes, in part, via information about slaves like Ibrahima abd-Al Rahman or Joseph Cinqué and others. Al-Rahman was born a prince in what today is Guinea in West Africa. Captured and enslaved in 1788, Al-Rahman began forty years in bondage on a Mississippi tobacco plantation. His written appeals for freedom reached the sultan of Morocco, who interceded with the administration of John Quincy Adams for Rahman's release from bondage. Once free, Al-Rahman raised funds to buy freedom for his wife and two of their nine children. Al-Rahman returned to West Africa prior to his death.

Cinqué was born in Sierra Leone and captured by slave traders in 1839. He led a rebellion on the Spanish ship *La Amistad*. The ship eventually landed in the United States, and the mutineers were arrested for murder. The case eventually made it to the Supreme Court. Thanks to the efforts of then–former president John Quincy Adams, Cinque and his companions were acquitted and allowed to return to Africa.

The gallery makes it clear that resistance didn't just come from former princes and mutineers. As one of the wallboards in the gallery says, "Blacks defied oppression with words and weapons, everyday actions, and impassioned agitation." Read the display of quotations from twelve generations of African Americans. There is a lot to absorb in this room's wall display, impressive video screens, and content kiosks. Many rebellions by the enslaved in the United States are covered in later chapters.

This gallery also serves as a holding area as you wait to see a twelve-minute orientation film titled *Fight for Equality*. That's your next stop. There is a countdown clock near the doors to Gallery 2's theater; museum attendants provide periodic updates on when the next showing begins.

A tip: Do not go in to see the film until you have finished seeing all the *Slavery* exhibit area. At the film's end, you exit the theatre to a different gallery, *Combatting Jim Crow*, so you may not be able to easily return to the first gallery once the film is done. Exhaust your curiosity in Gallery 1 before moving on.

Unsung Hero: Irene Morgan

In the gallery on the Freedom Rides, NCRM visitors learn about Irene Morgan, a Baltimore defense contractor and a hero in the struggle for equality. After visiting her mother in Virginia, she was returning home by bus in July 1944. Somewhere in Middlesex County, Virginia, the bus driver told her and her African American seatmate to move out of the "white" section of the bus and back to the "colored" section. The seatmate complied, but Ms. Morgan refused.

When Morgan would not move, the bus driver brought a sheriff on board. He presented Ms. Morgan with an arrest warrant. That didn't change her mind. She ripped up the warrant and tossed it out of the bus window.

When the sheriff grabbed her in an attempt to get out of her seat, her foot ended up in his groin. A different sheriff was sent to handle the situation. Assisted by a deputy, the two men eventually arrested Ms. Morgan, charging her with resisting arrest and violating Virginia's Jim Crow transit law.

In October 1944, Ms. Morgan agreed to pay a one-hundred-dollar fine for resisting arrest but refused to plead to the segregation violation. The NAACP took up her case, assigning future Supreme Court Justice Thurgood Marshall to the defense team. After the highest court in Virginia ruled her in violation of the law, the case went to the US Supreme Court. In *Morgan v. Virginia*, the US Supreme Court found the Virginia law restricting interstate travel unconstitutional in 1946.

A decade and a half later, the Freedom Riders risked their lives to get this ruling enforced in the South. As for Ms. Morgan, she was not finished making headlines. After moving to New York, she received her bachelor's degree when she was sixty-eight years old. Five years later, she earned a master's degree in urban studies from Queens College. In 2001, President Bill Clinton awarded her the Presidential Citizens Medal.

Gallery Topic	Selected Gallery Highlights
Combatting Jim Crow: 1896–1954	Listen to the disturbing recollections of individuals from the Jim Crow era.
Brown v. Board of Education: 1954	Always a headscratcher for me is seeing what cruelty so-called Christians did to people and property during the civil rights era, especially violence to churches. Be sure to see the late 1950s cartoon warning of the dangers of "race mixing" from the Christian Education Association of Union, New Jersey.
Montgomery Bus Boycott: 195–56	Hopping on the replica bus with Mrs. Parks provides a great teaching moment for children. Be sure to check out the face on the bus driver. Read over the day-by-day timeline of the yearlong boycott to appreciate the community's persistence. Listen to the audio here of Dr. King's remarks on the first night of the Montgomery Bus Boycott at Holt Street Baptist Church (mentioned in chapter 1).
Student Sit-Ins: 1960	Watch the training that sit-in protesters received. Use the touchscreen to get a sense of how geographically widespread sit-ins and other protests were.
Freedom Rides: 1961	A replica of the burned-out Greyhound bus from Anniston, Alabama, is the compelling visual here, but listen to the audio accounts of Freedom Riders Bernard Lafayette, James Peck, and Catherine Burks-Brooks. Learn about *Morgan v. Virginia*, in which the US Supreme Court in 1946 (!) ruled that segregation in interstate bus travel was unconstitutional.
Albany, Georgia Campaign: 1961–1963	This gallery focuses on a less well-known initiative of Dr. King. See what happened to Black attorney C. R. King when he went to visit jailed protesters. Learn the origins of the movement's anthem, "We Shall Overcome"
Mississippi Summer: 1964	Check the August 1964 calendar to understand the scope of the beatings, killings, and arson that occurred in Mississippi during this month. Listen to the ever-moving Fannie Lou Hamer speak during the Democratic National Convention.
Join the Movement	Stop at the interactive Smart Table to take a stand on issues like nonviolence, poverty, war, and integration.
Memphis Sanitation Strike: 1968	See the videos featuring key local leaders during the strike, particularly the Reverend James Lawson and union organizer Thomas Oliver (T. O.) Jones
Mountaintop Theatre	Experience Dr. King's powerful final speech delivered at Mason Temple on April 3, 1968

The National Civil Rights Museum deserves a guaranteed place on your itinerary, so rather than a summary of all the remaining galleries, here to the left are some don't-miss aspects of selected galleries. Some of these like the Smart Table technology in the *Join the Movement* area (Gallery 18) are hard to ignore; others might be missed if you are not looking for them, like a calendar from August 1964 in *Mississippi Summer Project: 1964* (Gallery 13).

After reviewing just these few suggestions, you might be convinced that at least four hours are needed here.

The Legacy Building

This building is directly across from the Lorraine Building on closed-to-cars Mulberry Street. Enter through a tunnel, passing an exhibit on the Poor People's Campaign as you get to an elevator to take you to the second floor. The second floor is the starting point of your visit to the Legacy Building. Restrooms are located behind the elevators on the first floor.

On the elevator ride to the second floor, radio bulletins from April 4, 1968, playing on the elevator's speaker set the mood. These bulletins aired just after 6:01 p.m. on that fateful day, minutes after the killer's shot was fired. Once off the elevator, videos of some of the early reports of the shooting from NBC News play.

The second floor is the former boardinghouse where James Earl Ray stayed. The re-created bathroom from which he fired his rifle is on the east-facing side of the floor. Don't start there but rather at the "Final Days" timeline providing the movements of both Dr. King and the killer.

Between April 4 and June 8, 1968, Ray was on the run. The two-sided *Search for the Killer* display and the adjacent evidence case would be the logical next places to spend time to follow the story. The actual evidence from Ray's trial (still the property of the state of Tennessee) is noted with green tags, while replica evidence is tagged in red.

In the southwest corner of the floor, the museum deals with the *Lingering Questions* about whether Ray was a lone assassin or part of a conspiracy. The question *Did Someone Else Do It?* is posed. Speculation on other possibilities besides Ray is covered: organized crime, the military, rivals in the civil rights movement, and the police. The final exhibit on the second floor is on the *Meaning of Assassination*.

Visitors return to the first floor to conclude your time here. There, those who have been honored by the museum as fighters for human rights have their portraits on the *Freedom Award Wall*. Spend your last ten minutes or so viewing a film highlighting the freedom movement in Russia, China, South Africa, as well as the United States on the three-sided screen. Another museum store is on the first floor of the Legacy Building in case you missed the one on the second floor of the Lorraine Building.

The Memphis Massacre: 1866

A short walk from the National Civil Rights Museum is a marker memorializing an often-overlooked event in not only Black history but also American post–Civil War history. For three days in May 1866, white mobs—unimpeded by and, in some instances, aided by local police—brought terror to African Americans in the city. Forty-six Blacks were murdered, several Black women were raped, and every Black school and church in the city was burned down. No one was prosecuted for these crimes.

A marker to keep the events of May 1866 in Memphis's collective memory is in Army Navy Park near the corner of G. E. Patterson Avenue and South Second Street. It is a five-minute walk from the NCRM. Before you leave the parking lot of the National Civil Rights Museum, consider walking south down either Mulberry Street or St. Martin Street toward G. E. Patterson Avenue.

Erected in 2016 on the 150th anniversary of the violence, the marker has stirred local passions. The marker is titled "1866 Memphis Massacre." The historical commissions of the state of Tennessee and Shelby County did not want the word "massacre" on the marker. The Memphis branch of the NAACP felt strongly that "massacre" was the accurate way to describe what happened, and they and the National Park Service persevered over the two historical commissions. The marker is in the Army Navy Park because the mobs initially targeted Black soldiers from the victorious Union Army. The city approved the marker's location.

After the National Civil Rights Museum

Memphis has eight other locations of interest, none of which require a significant time investment. You can spend the morning and even part of the early afternoon at the NCRM and still see all these other places in the same afternoon.

All but one of the eight recommended destinations in Memphis would require less than two miles of driving from the NCRM. (If you leave your car in the visitors' parking lot at the NCRM and walked to all seven and back to your vehicle, it is about two miles of walking.) Some are historic markers or memorial plazas where a short stop or just a drive-by might suffice. Others may be of enough interest to warrant a longer visit.

We cover the next seven destinations in driving or walking order. The eighth location is Mason Temple and it is not on the map shown earlier because it is a mile and a half from the Clayborn Temple. However, it is on the route you are likely to take as you head out of Memphis if Birmingham is your next stop. (Note: the Ernest Withers Collection Museum is not mapped because its location is only one hundred yards from the Ida B. Wells marker.)

The I Am a Man Mural, 398 South Main Street

This stunning mural is close (about a tenth of a mile) to the NCRM. Walking to it from the museum is smart as on-street parking nearby is challenging. The mural's vibrant colors make for a great picture-taking opportunity.

If your feet absolutely refuse any more walking, you will drive by it as you head out of the museum's parking lot and head up South Main Street to the next destination, the MLK Reflection Park.

MLK Reflection Park, King Boulevard and South Second Street

The Dr. Martin Luther King Jr. Reflection Park is at the northwest corner of Dr. Martin Luther King Jr. Boulevard and South Second Street. The park was dedicated in 2018 during the MLK50 remembrance. Its main feature is the corten steel sculpture *I Have Been to the Mountaintop*. The work was created in 1977 by Chicago sculptor Richard Hunt and originally placed on Main

Street in Memphis north of Poplar. This permanent location in the MLK Reflection Park gives Hunt's dramatic sculpture much greater exposure than its original location. There is a public parking lot on the south side of Dr. Martin Luther King Jr. Boulevard.

In the park, you can also see photos from the Ernest Withers Collection. More on Ernest Withers when we cover the sixth recommended destination.

The Ida B. Wells Marker, 211 Beale Street

In the shadow of cocktail bar Wet Willie's is a historic marker honoring a major figure in the fight for racial justice. Born enslaved during the Civil War, Ida B. Wells (later Ida B. Wells-Barnett) was a crusading and influential journalist in Memphis in the late 1800s. She became an equal partner in the *Memphis Free Speech and Headlight*, a newspaper that would provide a springboard for her bold and powerful voice.

Her fearless reporting of lynching incidents across the South made her a target of hate. Her printing presses in Memphis were destroyed by a white mob, and Wells moved to Chicago where she continued her activism for civil rights, woman's suffrage, and other social justice causes.

Ida B. Wells: "Brave Woman!"

"Brave woman!" is what Frederick Douglass called Ida B. Wells in a letter he wrote to her in 1895, commending her research and writing on the topic of the lynching of African Americans. In 1892, her reporting and opinion pieces on lynching incensed whites in Memphis.

When the offices of her Memphis newspaper were burned to the ground, she moved to Chicago, where she continued her crusading ways. In 1893, the World's Columbian Exposition came to Chicago. Blacks were excluded from this major event in the city, but Ms. Wells, Mr. Douglass, and other Black leaders protested. This raised her profile in her new hometown, where her activism supported school integration and women's suffrage.

Born in 1862 in Holly Springs, Mississippi, she was emancipated from slavery in theory by the 1863 Emancipation Proclamation and in fact by the Union's victory two years later. Ms. Wells was one of eight children. At the age of sixteen, she lost both her parents. She resisted the separation of her surviving siblings after her parents died; with the help of her grandmother, she kept most of them together when she moved to Memphis.

There she took a job as a teacher but soon gravitated to journalism, eventually becoming a co-owner of the *Memphis Free Speech and Headlight* newspaper. Her investigative reporting was carried by many Black-owned papers across the country. When a white mob destroyed her newspaper office and presses, she continued promoting racial justice in Chicago.

In Chicago, you can visit several locations honoring her. The home she shared with her husband and fellow journalist Ferdinand Lee Barnett is at 3624 South Doctor Martin Luther King Jr. Drive. Nearby, at Thirty-Seventh Street and King Drive, you will find a tribute in the form of a large stone marker. If you depart Chicago using what used to be called the Congress Parkway, you are actually on Ida B. Wells Drive.

In Holly Springs, Mississippi, the Bolling-Gatewood House where she once lived is now the Ida B. Wells Museum (220 Randolph Street North). There is also a marker in Holly Springs honoring Ms. Wells at the northeast corner of the Marshall County Courthouse lawn.

You may never go to either Chicago or Holly Springs, but another spot where you can learn more about this major early fighter for civil rights is at the National Memorial for Peace and Justice in Montgomery, where a reflection space is dedicated to Ms. Wells for her work exposing the horrors of lynching.

Withers Collection Museum and Gallery, 333 Beale Street

Ernest Withers snapped some of the iconic photographs of the civil rights era. At the Emmett Till murder trial, he defied the no-photos order of the judge to capture Emmett's uncle, Mose Wright, standing and pointing at one of the defendants to indicate who took his nephew from his home in the wee hours of the morning of August 28, 1955.

A year later, he photographed Dr. Martin Luther King Jr. getting on a Montgomery bus following the successful boycott there. In 1968, he was in position to get the photo most associated with sanitation strike in Memphis: the shot of hundreds of workers standing shoulder to shoulder holding the "I AM A MAN" signs.

Withers died in 2007. Three years later, it was revealed that he served as an informant for the FBI as early as 1958. You can read more about Withers and the FBI-related revelation in Preston Lauterbach's *Bluff City: The Secret Life of Photographer Ernest Withers* or Marc Perrusquia's *A Spy in Canaan: How the FBI Used a Famous Photographer to Infiltrate the Civil Rights Movement.*

The Withers Collection Museum and Gallery hours vary by season. Call (901) 523-2344 for current information. Admission ranges from $7 to $10.

Beale Street Baptist Church, 379 Beale Street

Only 450 feet farther east on Beale Street is the first church built for Black worshipers in Memphis. Beale Street Baptist was home for Ida B. Wells's newspaper. Unless you are in town on a Sunday when services are held and the church is open, you should call the church office at (901) 522-9073 to see if they can arrange a tour.

Clayborn Temple and the I AM A MAN Plaza, 294 Hernando Street

Clayborn Temple was the starting point for the daily marches that the sanitation workers made for sixty-five days during the 1968 strike. Signs on and around the outside of the church provide background on the church's origins as Second Presbyterian Church. In 1949, the church was sold and renamed Clayborn Temple to honor an African Methodist Episcopal bishop.

After closing in 1999, the church fell into disrepair. Restoration efforts are under way. The space can be booked for special events, but at this writing, no tours inside are offered.

Right next to the magnificent Clayborn Temple is the stunning I AM A MAN plaza. This was opened (like the MLK Reflection Park) to commemorate the fiftieth anniversary of Dr. King's assassination. The words from Dr. King's "Mountaintop" speech are laser cut into the twelve-foot letters. Visitors see themselves in the reflective, mirror-polished stainless-steel letters.

The sculpture is striking any time of day but particularly when lights illuminate the entire plaza. Be sure to check the wall containing the names of over one thousand strikers. Parking is available on Hernando Street.

Mason Temple Church of God in Christ, 930 Mason Street

At the I AM A MAN Plaza, you see the words of Dr. King's "Mountaintop" speech. If you drive five minutes south of that plaza, you see where those words were delivered. This global headquarters of the Church of God in Christ is open weekdays until 4 p.m. On the night of April 3, 1968, a severe storm rocked Memphis. Dr. King was nursing a sore throat following an exhausting day. He stayed back in his room at the Lorraine Motel, asking Rev. Ralph David Abernathy to take his place at the Mason Temple.

When Rev. Abernathy entered the church, he saw two thousand to three thousand souls who braved the bad weather. When "a discernible disappointment rippled through the room,"[106] Abernathy knew they weren't here to hear him. Rev. Abernathy called his friend back at the Lorraine and convinced him to join him at Mason Temple. At 9:30 p.m., Dr. King stepped to the podium.

While Mason Temple is the last recommended stop in Memphis, one more place for visitors to consider is the **Four Way**, a soul food restaurant with its own ties to civil rights history. Normally, where you eat and where you stay are off limits for this book. However, an exception is made when an establishment has a connection to why you are on Freedom's Road in the first place.

"The Four Way's place in history is sealed to Martin Luther King Jr., the man who loved [owner] Irene Cleve's fried catfish, fried chicken, and her peach cobbler," wrote the Memphis *Commercial Appeal* in April 2018.[107] Back in the 1960s, movement leaders would meet in a room in the back where you needed to ring a bell to be admitted. Today, if you visit the Four Way, you can see the door that led to that "room where it happened," but now it leads to an expanded kitchen.

The place has changed owners a few times since the era of Dr. King, but diners still give the Four Way high marks. The restaurant is at 988 Mississippi Boulevard in Memphis, less than a mile from Mason Temple. It is open Thursday to Sunday 11 a.m. to 4 p.m. but the restaurant is only open on Sunday for the first three Sundays of each month.

> **"We had waited, agonizing through the nights and days without sleep, startled by nearly any sound, unable to eat, simply staring at our meals.**
>
> **Suddenly, in a few seconds of radio time it was over. My first son, whose birth had brought me so much joy that I jumped up in a hall outside the room where he was born and touched the ceiling—the child, the scholar, the preacher, the boy singing and smiling, the son—**
>
> **ALL OF IT WAS GONE."**
>
> **REVEREND MARTIN LUTHER KING SR.**

CHAPTER 15

Birmingham

At the Mississippi Civil Rights Museum in Jackson, I wrote down a quote. I didn't know then what I would do with it, but that became clear to me after I visited Birmingham. Admittedly, the quote comes not only from a different state but a different era. I suppose there are even other contexts besides Birmingham where the words written in a May 1889 edition of the Vicksburg *Commercial Herald* in Mississippi would fit. Sadly though, the threat fits the anti-integration venom that permeated Birmingham in the early 1960s.

> Don't monkey with white supremacy; it is loaded with determination, gunpowder and dynamite.

In the category of horrific violence leveled against those fighting for freedom, Birmingham takes a backseat to no one.

In April 1963, the world witnessed attack dogs in Birmingham jumping at teenage protesters and water cannons strong enough to rip the bark from trees being directed at children. Bombs targeted churches, hotels, and homes. On September 15, 1963, four little girls were killed in the widely known segregationist bombing of the Sixteenth Street Baptist Church. On the very same day, two young Black teens were shot and killed, a tragedy often overlooked considering the day's other events, but one discussed later in this chapter.

When you left Little Rock to visit Memphis, you jumped ahead in civil rights history by over a decade. Here, we back up five years along the civil rights timeline. The events that made the biggest headlines in Birmingham occurred mainly in 1963.

Consider the context in which the campaign for change in Birmingham really accelerated in 1963. The *Brown v. Board of Education* decision in 1954 eliminated "separate but equal" in law, but widespread resistance to school integration still occurred across the South. The 1955–56 Montgomery Bus Boycott brought changes to municipal public transportation. The lunch-counter sit-ins in 1960 and the Freedom Rides in 1961 brought some progress across the South but not without serious pushback and pain.

These actions were focused on specific aspects of society where segregation existed: education, public accommodations, and equal access. The so-called Birmingham Campaign of 1962–63 tried to change an entire city, a terribly segregated one at that. Dr. King, recruited to the Birmingham Campaign by local pastor Rev. Fred Shuttlesworth (discussed later in this chapter), wrote this of Birmingham in his famous "Letter from Birmingham Jail": "Birmingham is probably the most thoroughly segregated city in the United States."[108]

The 1960 Census revealed a 60/40 white/Black split in Birmingham's population. Despite two in five residents being Black, the entire police force was white—not a single Black officer in a city with over 135,000 Black citizens. It wasn't for the lack of trying. Diane McWhorter in *Carry Me Home* noted that Jonathan McPherson was the first Black person to pass the civil service exam, the exam required to join the Birmingham police department.[109] Somehow his name kept vanishing off the list of eligible police recruits. In 1966, the city finally hired its first Black policeman, but it wasn't McPherson. By then, he had moved outside the city limits.

The year 1963 ushered in a new governor for the state of Alabama, a person who was back at the capitol in a manner of speaking. As a teenager, he had served there as a legislative page. Frye Gaillard reported that, as a teen, the new governor stood on the brass star marking the spot where Jefferson Davis took the oath of office to become the president of the Confederate States of America. "I knew then that I would become governor," George Wallace said later.[110]

On January 14, 1963, George Wallace was back on the Alabama capitol's steps being sworn in as the state's forty-fifth governor. He boldly declared, "Segregation now . . . segregation tomorrow . . . segregation forever!" in his blunt inaugural address. Less than six months later, Wallace would try to put his words into practice when he stood in the door of Foster Auditorium on the University of Alabama campus to block the integration of the school. He failed.

In the same year and amid much racial tension, Birmingham was in political turmoil. The incumbent mayor, Arthur Haynes, attempted to block a mayoral election from occurring in March. He felt he had been elected to serve as mayor until 1965. However, the state's Supreme Court ruled otherwise; the election for a new mayor could proceed. (Haynes and his son would eventually serve as defense counsel for one of the men who bombed the Sixteenth Street Baptist Church.)

Alabama's lieutenant governor Albert Boutwell and Birmingham's commissioner of public safety Theophilus Eugene "Bull" Connor were the two top vote recipients in the mayoral election of March 5, but neither garnered enough support to avoid a runoff. That occurred on April 2, and Boutwell won. However, Bull Connor did not slip from the limelight. He went on to earn a reputation for malevolence nationally and internationally as a result of his words and actions during the events you learn about during your Birmingham visit.

While the white power structure had its challenges in determining who would run the city, Blacks clearly would not. Seeking to improve employment and educational opportunities, some Black citizens began a boycott of downtown businesses in 1962 that had an impact. In early April 1963, more confrontational and more obvious protests like lunch-counter sit-ins and marches began. For example,

- April 6: The Reverend Fred Shuttlesworth led a march from the A. G. Gaston Motel toward City Hall. Less than a half mile into the march, the police halted the march and arrested thirty-two participants.

- April 7: The Reverend A. D. King (Martin's brother) and two other clergymen led a march from St. Paul United Methodist Church. Police used dogs to disperse Black onlookers.

- April 10: Attempted sit-ins were thwarted by closed lunch counters, yet police still arrested twenty-seven protesters.

The night of April 10, Dr. King spoke at a mass meeting at St. James A.M.E. Church. Perhaps sensing possible skepticism of his outsider status, he told the crowd, "We are not here to do something for you but to do something with you."[111]

Learning of Dr. King's remarks, Bull Connor dispatched two city attorneys that very night to the home of a judge who had a reputation for passing out injunctions like candy on Halloween. The two attorneys left the judge's residence with an injunction prohibiting Dr. King, his brother A. D. King, the Reverends Fred Shuttlesworth and Ralph Abernathy, as well as over 130 named persons including the ever-handy "John Doe" from any "plans or projects commonly called 'sit-in' demonstrations, 'kneel in' demonstrations, mass street parades," and so on.

The officer charged with serving the order found Dr. King and his friends in the restaurant of the A. G. Gaston Motel sipping coffee at 1:15 a.m., surrounded by the media. The press had been alerted by the civil rights leaders, providing another example of how adept Dr. King and his colleagues were at skillful media relations.

The injunction significantly raised the stakes. Not only would marching without a permit be a violation, but doing so in the face of a court order also meant a contempt charge. The fines could be high, and the jail sentences could be long.

In a more formal press conference on April 11, Dr. King made it clear the movement was not going to abide by a decree viewed as "unjust, undemocratic, and unconstitutional." Supporters on the balconies of the Gaston Motel cheered and Dr. King let everyone know that he was prepared to go to jail "as long as necessary."

That night, Bull Connor seemed to want to grant Dr. King his wish. The city informed the movement's local bail bondsmen that they viewed King's SCLC as having too few assets to cover future bonds, so no more bail bonds could be posted. No bail meant that protesters who ended up in jail would likely be there a long time.

Friday, April 12, was Good Friday. Just before 3 p.m., Dr. King and Rev. Abernathy led fifty marchers in two columns out of Zion Hill Baptist Church with Kelly Ingram Park as the intended destination. As they marched along the perimeter of the park, Bull Connor had seen enough. "Stop them there!" he ordered.

King and Abernathy were pushed into a police wagon. Confusion reigned for a while as the police couldn't distinguish marchers from supportive spectators. Years later, Dr. King's associate Andrew Young reflected on what King's decision to defy the injunction and march in Birmingham meant. In the award-winning television series *Eyes on the Prize: America's Civil Rights Years (1954–1965)*, Young observed that Dr. King's choice here was "the beginning of his true leadership."[112]

From his Birmingham jail cell, Dr. King would write his famous letter, initially using the margins of the newspaper that carried a letter from eight local white ministers critical of King's actions.

With Dr. King in jail, the SCLC sent Rev. James Bevel to Birmingham to try to keep the campaign (named Project C, with the "C" standing for Confrontation) moving ahead. Bevel saw that, with King out of the picture for the moment, local hearts had refilled with fear. At a meeting of seven hundred people on April 16, Bevel could not even find ten who were ready to march. On April 17, Andrew Young fared worse, getting only seven willing to march. Things did not improve immediately either when King and Abernathy were released on April 20.

Rev. Bevel had an idea on how to find willing marchers—a controversial one at that. If adults were hesitant to go into the streets, he would persuade students to get involved. He would do this through appeals to student leaders in high schools and to a group who had the ears of teens: Black disc jockeys. On Monday, April 29, students at several Black high schools were given leaflets asking them to leave class on May 2 and meet at the Sixteenth Street Baptist Church at noon. On the morning of May 2, local disc jockeys were also encouraging their young listeners with statements like, "Kids, there's going to be a party in the park."[113]

Despite warnings that leaving school would mean expulsion, many students did anyway—or skipped school altogether that day and headed to Sixteenth Street Baptist. Just after 1 p.m., clapping students burst from the church singing "We Shall Overcome" and "Ain't Gonna Let Nobody Turn Me Around." By the end of the day, Birmingham jails had six hundred new, very young residents. The idea of a protest march with teens and even children had, as you might expect, produced a broad range of denouncers, from Malcolm X to US Attorney General Robert Kennedy.

The following day, May 3, over one thousand students heard Martin Luther King Jr. at Sixteenth Street Baptist. Around 1 p.m. again, young people filed out of the church, this time chanting, "Freedom!" Robert Weisbrot wrote, "The children filled the streets with a joy that was untouched by the danger."[114] When a group of marchers drew closer to Seventeenth and Fifth, Bull Connor warned them to stop or the fire hoses would be turned on them.

At first, the firemen used nozzle settings that resulted in "misting their human targets as if they were prize flowers."[115] As demonstrators turned from the spray, the pressure coming from the hoses intensified, ripping clothing and lacerating skin. The water pressure bloodied noses and knocked marchers off their feet.

"Bring the dogs!" bellowed Connor. The K-9 Corps of German shepherds, trained to chase burglars, were ordered, "Clear the park out!" The black-and-white images of the charging dogs and blasts from the fire hoses were carried in newspapers across the nation and around the world. The *New York Times* called the police and fire department's actions "a national disgrace."[116]

Project C certainly had achieved its goal of confrontation. The movement could not have found a better villain than Bull Connor. As Jonathan Rieder observes in *Gospel of Freedom*, "Bull Connor had become the star of the spectacle the movement needed to dramatize oppression and galvanize the nation. His fire hoses and snarling dogs were now props in the movement's theatre."[117] After President John F. Kennedy viewed television coverage of the uniformed and canine brutality in Birmingham on May 2, the president said, "The civil rights movement should thank God for Bull Connor. He's helped it as much as Abraham Lincoln."

Those who witnessed the action up close agreed with the president. In the offices of a Black insurance agency whose windows were broken by the pressure from the fire hoses, a distraught Lola Hendricks who was working when Connor ordered the hoses on was consoled by her boss: "Don't cry. That's what they want you to do. This may be the best thing that ever happened to the Movement."[118]

Historian Taylor Branch sees the significance of Birmingham the same way as Lola Hendricks's boss. Branch called the Birmingham Campaign the "turning point" of Dr. King's career as well as "a turning point in American history that pushed the civil rights movement into momentum that lasted."[119]

Demonstrations continued until May 8. That day's edition of the *New York Times* reported that the jails were so crowded that it took four hours just to distribute breakfast.[120] Downtown business activity ground to a standstill.

On May 8, the city's business leaders said it was time to meet the protesters' demands. Two days later, Dr. King and Rev. Shuttlesworth told the media that an agreement had been reached with the city to desegregate lunch counters, restrooms, and other such public places; to hire Blacks in retail sales jobs; and to release those in jail on bond or their own recognizance. That fall, the city's schools were desegregated.

The day after the agreement designed to transform Birmingham was announced, a bomb blew up part of the Gaston Motel, missing Dr. King, who had departed only hours earlier. Dr. King's brother's home was bombed the same day.

Changing the laws of any jurisdiction is not easy. The Birmingham Campaign and the children's march proved that. However, changing people's hearts is much harder still, as even the most recent years in US history remind us.

Four months after the Gaston Motel bombing, at 10:22 a.m. on Sunday, September 15, at least fifteen sticks of dynamite hidden under the steps of the Sixteenth Street Baptist Church exploded. The blast took the lives of Addie Mae Collins, Carol Denise McNair, Carole Robertson, and Cynthia Wesley. The girls were ages eleven to fourteen.

Your visit to Birmingham will contrast sharply the cowardly act of detonating such a powerful bomb at a church on a Sunday morning with the fearless bravery shown by the Black youth of Birmingham during the campaign only months earlier.

The Plan for Birmingham in 300 Words or Less

As in Memphis, almost all the places to visit in Birmingham are close together. Park your car in the lot at the Birmingham Civil Rights Institute (BCRI), where you should plan two to three hours. Book a tour at the Sixteenth Street Baptist Church, directly across the street from the BCRI. Individuals and groups of ten or more can make one-hour-tour appointments on the church's website.

Across from the BCRI is Kelly Ingram Park. You can tour the park using a mobile phone resource. Walk to the location of the Gaston Motel. Depending on when you visit, this could either be the current or the future site of a new National Park Service (NPS)

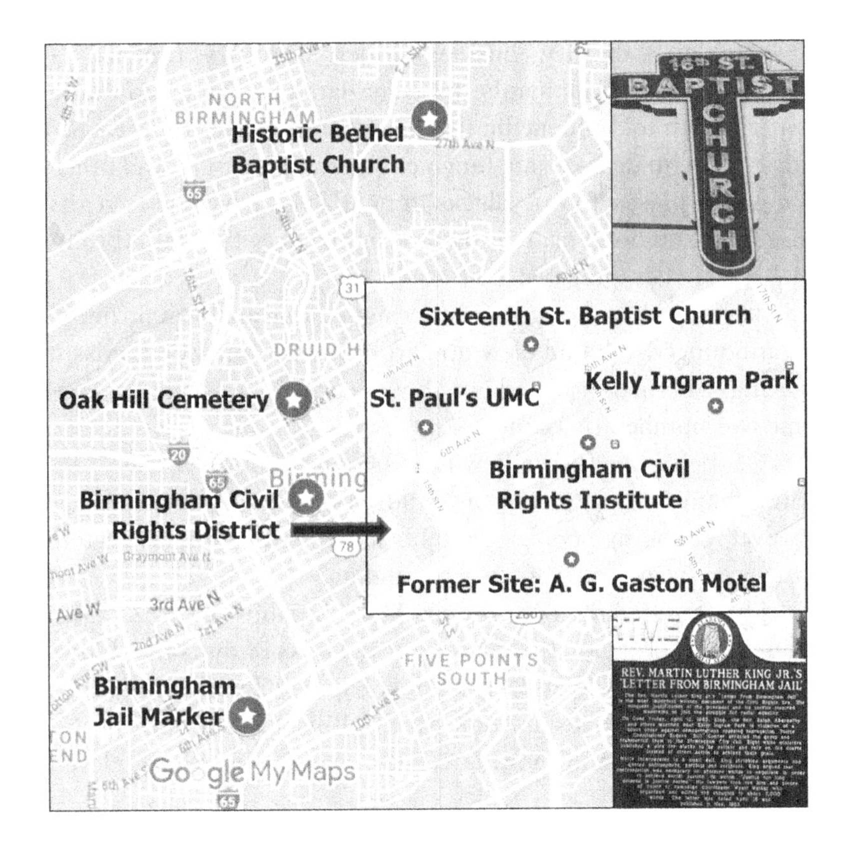

Visitors' Center. By the spring of 2021, the NPS had completed the work on the exterior, and the interior renovation was under way.

Block out about two hours for the stops near the BCRI. Once back to your car, I suggest two other destinations, unfortunately in opposite directions from the BCRI:

- The Birmingham jail, where Dr. King wrote his famous letter.
- Historic Bethel Baptist Church, the church pastored by Rev. Shuttlesworth. You may pass Oak Hill Cemetery on your way, and this chapter describes how to find Rev. Shuttlesworth's grave, should you want to pay your respects to a man John Lewis called the "last of a kind."

Though these two recommended stops are in different sections of the city, the drives to visit them both are short. You should still be en route to your next destination before dinnertime.

Birmingham Destinations

Memphis-to-Birmingham is about a three-and-a-half-hour drive. Consider your options for your overnight stay prior to visiting Birmingham:

- Stay outside of Birmingham along Interstate 22 to avoid a long drive from Memphis. Plan to rise and shine early, though.
- Stay in the heart of Birmingham so that you can begin your day early. Note, however, that the BCRI opens at 10 a.m. Tuesday to Saturday. The Sixteenth Street Baptist Church tours also do not begin until 10 a.m., also Tuesday to Saturday. You could start with Kelly Ingram Park, as that doesn't close.
- Push yourself to get to an Anniston hotel. Come back to tour Birmingham the next morning. This gives you two consecutive nights in or near Anniston.

If you are within an hour of Birmingham, you will be able to see the recommended locations in a day, as long as it is not Monday. Keep in mind that the BCRI and Sixteenth Street Baptist Church are not open on Monday; the church also does not offer tours on Sunday.

Sixteenth Street Baptist Church, 1530 Sixth Avenue North

First, the address looks like a mistake, but it is not. The church is at the corner of Sixth Avenue North and Sixteenth Street.

The church holds a dual significant place in civil rights and American history. From here, many of the protest marches of April and May 1963 originated. The church was also the site of the bombing that took the lives of Addie Mae Collins, Carol Denise McNair, Carole Robertson, and Cynthia Wesley on September 15, 1963. The first Black church in the city and in its present location since 1880, Sixteenth Street Baptist was designated as a National Historic Landmark in 2006. It is also under consideration as a World Heritage Site.

The church offers tours to individuals and groups. Book in advance. If you arrive without a reservation, try going to the side door to see if you can join one of the hourly tours that take place from 10 a.m. to 3 p.m. each day.

Tours last an hour and are available Tuesday through Saturday. Adults: $10; students: $5. No fee for children under six years old. Book via *the church website*. No backpacks or tote bags are allowed in the church building.

There is an exhibit in the church's basement; after that, visitors are escorted up to the sanctuary. Many noted Black American voices have graced this sanctuary: W. E. B. DuBois, Mary McLeod Bethune, Paul Robeson, Ralph Bunche, and Martin Luther King, Jr., among them. On September 18, 1963, at Birmingham's Sixth Avenue Baptist Church, Dr. King eulogized the young victims of the bombing. Only three weeks earlier, Dr. King had delivered his "I Have a Dream" speech during the March on Washington.

All the stained glass in the church is beautiful, but the window donated by the people of Wales after the bombing is just stunning and its message so relevant.

Birmingham Civil Rights Institute (BCRI), 520 Sixteenth Street

Your thought as you come to this museum might be how perfectly located it is relative to Birmingham's civil rights history. Not only is it across the street from the Sixteenth Street Baptist Church, but the BCRI is also directly across from Kelly Ingram Park and just a short distance from the site of the A. G. Gaston Motel, where so much strategizing for the protests of early 1963 took place. So much history so close together.

To my surprise, I learned later that some people wanted the BCRI to be located closer to the city's business district. One white councilman even suggested that the site be near the affluent, almost exclusively white suburb of Mountain Brook. As if that wasn't tone deaf enough, the councilman also wanted to replace the term "civil rights" in the institute's name with "human rights."[121]

One might think this museum could be a letdown after visiting the National Civil Rights Museum in Memphis. Far from it. Not only does it do a wonderful job reporting on the general civil rights movement, but it also performs excellently in helping visitors understand the history of Birmingham itself and its African American citizens.

The short introductory film *Going Up to Birmingham* teaches a lot in twelve minutes. Did you know that Birmingham was founded after the Civil War in 1871? Or that the nearby iron mines provided a source of stolen dynamite used in the attacks that gave the city the nickname "Bombingham"?

Volunteers greet visitors upon entering the building and thank them for coming as they finish touring the museum. Many of these volunteers came through the Legacy Youth Leadership program, geared to involve high school students in the institute and eventually lead to the role of docent, guiding tour groups through the museum.

While I was touring, I shared an alcove with a docent and a young person in training to become one. These docent trainers are demanding. I overheard that trainer, who, while supportive and encouraging, would not settle for anything but perfection. "Let's try it again. We're going to do this until you get it right," he said. The BCRI is not a place where everyone gets a trophy. Visitors benefit from that kind of attitude.

Birmingham Civil Rights Institute	
Location	520 Sixteenth Street North, Birmingham, AL 35203
Days Closed	Closed on Sunday and Monday
Operating Days and Hours	Tuesday to Saturday, 10 a.m. to 3 p.m.
Admission	Adults: $15; seniors, college students, and grades 4–12: $13; children grades 3 and below: free.
Website	*www.bcri.org*
Phone Number	(866) 328-9696
Email Address	*bcri@bcri.org*

Discounts are available for the military as well as AAA and Smithsonian members (the BCRI is a Smithsonian affiliate). There is street parking around the BCRI and free parking for cars and buses behind the building. Enter the parking lot via Fifteenth Street North.

Before sharing some of the highlights of the BCRI, here's a helpful BCRI policy: Visitors can leave the museum and come back on the same day. This allows you to walk across the street to make your tour time at the Sixteenth Street Baptist Church or explore Kelly Ingram Park and get some fresh air. Since policies can change, ask whether this visitor-friendly policy is still in effect when you enter.

Like other major museums, the BCRI does a solid job with video, audio, and content boards on the main chapters of civil rights history: *Brown v. Board of Education*, Little Rock, the Montgomery Bus Boycott, Selma, and more. At the institute, however, you receive more content on and a deeper understanding of the Birmingham-specific events.

These galleries did an especially strong job and merit your attention:

- *African American Life in a Segregated World:* The first area after the introductory film includes a display of everyday objects that show how whites distorted Blacks' images. Stereotypes in entertainment and advertising appear in a wide variety of artifacts.

- *The Confrontation Section:* Be sure to watch the video of the city in the 1940s through the early 1960s when fifty racially motivated bombings went unsolved. It sets the stage for the protests in 1963.

- *Who Speaks for Birmingham?* This eleven-minute segment is from a documentary prepared for *CBS Reports* by journalist Howard K. Smith in May 1961. In it, Smith calls Birmingham "the most segregated city in the South." CBS fired Smith for his report. Watch all eleven minutes of this amazing piece of video.

- *The video playing in Harold's TV Shop:* This video plays on three old TV sets and provides first-person accounts and actual news footage of the Project C marches. A lot is going on in this area, so a tip: stand under the speaker in the ceiling in the entryway to *Harold's TV Shop* on the right side to hear the audio better.

- *A High Price* In this gallery, which focuses on the Sixteenth Street Baptist Church bombing, visitors also see photos of Virgil Ware and Johnnie Robinson, the two teenagers who were killed in separate shooting incidents on the same day. Their deaths are often overlooked.
- *The replica of the Birmingham jail cell with the original cell bars:* Audio of Dr. King's letter plays while the text appears on the wall.
- *Justice Delayed:* This display near the end of the museum shows the difficulty of building a case against the bombers and how persistence paid off eventually. You learn how the case was closed, reopened, and successfully prosecuted by Doug Jones (former US senator from Alabama). The legal details are actually quite fascinating and one of the unique aspects of this museum.

September 15, 1963—Death Toll: 6

The explosion at the Sixteenth Street Baptist Church and the deaths of Addie Mae Collins, Carol Denise McNair, Carole Robertson, and Cynthia Wesley dominated the news across the country as well as in Birmingham. Overshadowed by that tragedy were the shooting deaths of two youngsters in different sections of Birmingham later that same Sunday.

Virgil Ware accompanied his older brother when they went to pick up a bicycle in the Sandusky area, northwest of the city. The bike would help them cover their newspaper route faster. Virgil, who his brothers and sisters nicknamed "Peanut," hopped on the handlebars as his brother began to pedal them home.

Two white Eagle Scouts, Michael Lee Farley and Larry Joe Sims, had visited the headquarters of the National States Rights Party that Sunday before heading out on Michael's scooter. The Scouts passed the paperboys riding their bike. Sims fired a pistol, hitting young Virgil, who tumbled off the handlebars and died.

continued

continued from previous page

The following day, Farley and Sims were arrested, charged with first-degree murder. At trial, Sims was convicted of second-degree manslaughter; Farley pled guilty to the same charge. They were both sentenced to seven months in jail, but Judge Wallace Gibson then altered the penalty, giving them two years' probation instead.[122]

Yet Virgil Ware's death that day in mid-September wasn't the only one that would go unpunished. Sixteen-year-old Johnnie Robinson had heard about the bombing at Sixteenth Street Baptist. He and other outraged Black youth were demonstrating in the 800 block of Twenty-Sixth Street North when they were confronted by white teens driving by in cars draped with Confederate flags and hurling racial comments like "Go back to Africa." Reports suggest that rocks were hurled, hitting one of the cars. Soon the police came, scattering the young Blacks, including Robinson. As he ran down an alley, Johnny Robinson was shot in the back by police officer Jack Parker.

Two grand juries refused to bring Officer Parker to trial, and no one was ever prosecuted for Robinson's death.

Today, Virgil Ware and Johnny Robinson are both honored in Birmingham's Gallery of Distinguished Citizens. The gallery is located on the second floor of Birmingham City Hall, 710 North Twentieth Street.

The BCRI also has special exhibits. Past special exhibits include *The Music of the Movement*, one on A.G. Gaston, and another titled *Black Citizenship in the Age of Jim Crow*. Check the website in advance to learn what special exhibit will be up when you visit.

Teachers of grades K through 12 (and parents too) can take advantage of over two dozen curriculum guides on a wide range of civil rights topics, related to Birmingham and to the movement more generally. Access these under the Learn tab on the BCRI's website.

While the museum deserves many kudos, two issues could interfere with your experience if left unaddressed:

- While there is an abundance of fascinating audio content, some places get quite noisy. The concrete floors in some areas don't help.
- The Richard Arrington Jr. Resource Gallery gives visitors and students access to multimedia materials through computer terminals, including an oral history archive. Named after the city's first Black mayor, it is a fantastic resource—if the computer terminals are working. During my visit, several were not operating. After trying three of them, I moved on, to my disappointment.

Before you leave, go to the area near the parking lot side of the rotunda. There is a large cast-iron bell there that was part of the Sixteenth Street Baptist Church. That bell sat atop the steps at the Lincoln Memorial in the nation's capital on the fiftieth anniversary of Dr. King's "I Have a Dream" speech. The bell is near the museum's second-floor restrooms. Restrooms are also available on the first floor.

The museum is fully accessible to all visitors. Special needs are met with designated parking spaces and a ground-level entrance adjacent to the museum parking lot. Ramps and elevators serve the entrance and lobby. A limited number of wheelchairs are available at the security station near the parking lot entrance.

Kelly Ingram Park, Sixth Avenue North and Sixteenth Street

The sculptures in Kelly Ingram Park capture the personalities and perils that made up the events of April, May, and September 1963. One of the first sculptures you see after crossing Sixteenth Street and enter the park is Elizabeth MacQueen's *Four Spirits*. Her work captures the innocence of the four victims:

- Cynthia Wesley sits on one end of the bench with a Bible in her lap.
- Young Carol Denise McNair releases doves into the air.
- Addie Mae Collins ties a sash around her friend's dress.
- Carole Robertson, standing a short way from the other three, appears as if she is beckoning the others to their ushering duties the morning of September 15, 1963.

Just up the path from *Four Spirits* is a seven-foot statue of Dr. King. Sculpted by an Italian artist from one of Coretta Scott King's favorite photos of her husband, many of Dr. King's friends do not find the likeness true to the great leader. You be the judge.

After these two serene works, the sculptures in Kelly Ingram Park get more graphic, depicting events that happened in early 1963: the snarling German shepherds, the high-pressure water cannons, and children in jail cells.

Your tour here can be self-guided using markers in the park, or you can access a free dial-in tour on your mobile phone at (205) 307-5455. Plan for your Kelly Ingram Park stop to take thirty to sixty minutes.

The Former Site of the A. G. Gaston Motel, 1510 Fifth Avenue North

The Birmingham Civil Rights National Monument was created in January 2017 by a proclamation from President Barack Obama, just days before leaving office. This new in-development National Monument consists of the Sixteenth Street Baptist Church, the BCRI, Kelly Ingram Park, the Fourth Avenue Historic District, and the site of the Gaston Motel. In all, it will encompass four city blocks.

The Gaston Motel was owned by prominent African American businessman Arthur George (A. G.) Gaston. Built in 1954 when the city enforced the segregation of public accommodations, the Gaston provided restaurant services and modern lodging accommodations for African American travelers. Like the Lorraine Motel in Memphis, the Gaston Motel was popular with civil rights leaders and African American entertainers. Dr. King's decision to defy the court's injunction against further marches without a permit was made and announced here.

Vacant since the mid-1990s and in disrepair, the National Park Service and the city are restoring the property for a visitors' center. A Historic Structures Report is guiding the restoration work to return the motel to its late 1950s look. The switch was flipped on the iconic A. G. Gaston Motel sign in March 2021. Take a short walk to see the restoration in progress.

As you walk back to the BCRI parking lot, notice the large brick church on the corner of Fifteenth Street North and Sixth Avenue North. It is St. Paul United Methodist Church and one of the oldest Black houses of worship in the city. St. Paul's hosted meetings and training in nonviolence for the young people who participated in the demonstrations of April and May 1963, earning the church a spot on the Civil Rights Heritage Trail in Birmingham. The Reverend Dr. Joseph Lowery, another SCLC founder, was one of its pastors during the civil rights era.

Tours of the church are by appointment only; the number to call is (205) 252-3236. In 2019, St. Paul's was awarded a five-hundred-thousand-dollar NPS grant to preserve and restore the historic church. These funds may create opportunities to eventually see the church on a regular schedule.

Birmingham Jail Marker, 425 Sixth Avenue South

At this point, your time in this part of the city is over. As you depart the parking lot at the BCRI, you have a choice to make:

- You can drive about two and a half miles south of the BCRI and visit the Birmingham jail—or more precisely, the marker outside of the building in which Dr. King wrote his famous letter.

- You can drive about six miles north to see the marker outside of the church pastored by Rev. Fred Shuttlesworth, Historic Bethel Baptist.

- You can head to Anniston if that is your next destination on the loop tour.

Whether from the BCRI area or from either the jail or Historic Bethel Baptist, Anniston is an hour away.

Recall that Dr. King was arrested on Good Friday, April 12, 1963. Sitting alone in his cell, he read a statement in the paper from eight self-assessed moderate southern clergymen. They branded the protests King was leading as "unwise and untimely." Those criticisms were leveled *before* the children's march.

King wrote a rebuttal, one that Jonathan Rieder argued "would take its place among the masterpieces of American moral argument alongside Thoreau and Lincoln."[123] Given the stature of Dr. King's letter today, I would have thought it became widely known at the time he wrote it. That was not the case.

Jonathan Rieder's book *Gospel of Freedom* points out how long it took for the "Letter from Birmingham Jail" to crack the nation's consciousness. The missive was largely ignored after King's release from jail on April 20. By early June, it began gaining some attention in small-circulation liberal and religious publications such as *Liberation* and the *Christian Century*. It would take until late summer 1963 before the *Atlantic Monthly* reprinted the letter in its August 1963 issue under the headline "The Negro Is Your Brother."[124]

Getting to this marker can be confusing. Pay attention to what road is labeled "Avenue" and what is labeled "Street."

The address of "425 Sixth *Avenue* South" is the address of the entire Police Department complex here; it is somewhat spread out. The road Sixth *Street* South winds all the way around the complex. As a result, Sixth Street South has two openings onto Sixth Avenue South. However, only the first one you encounter, on the east side of the complex, is marked (like this wasn't difficult enough).

The marker is on the west side of the multistory Birmingham Police Department. Turn at the second Sixth Street South entrance. If you miss that turn, turn off Sixth Avenue South at Beta Street, right after the ideal Sixth Street South entrance. On Beta Street, you will see the tall Birmingham Police Department name on the side of the light stone building. The marker is in front of that side of the building.

This may sound harder than it will be. Because it is such a historic place, make the effort to find it. See both sides of the marker; quotes from the "Letter" appear on the reverse side.

Historic Bethel Baptist Church, 3233 Twenty-Ninth Avenue North

Historic Bethel Baptist Church was an important part of the Birmingham Campaign and the civil rights movement generally. The church served as headquarters for the Alabama Christian Movement for Human Rights (ACMHR). That organization was formed in 1956, when Alabama's attorney general (later governor) John Patterson banned the NAACP from operating within the state. The ACMHR and the church rose to prominence under the leadership of Rev. Fred Shuttlesworth.

Segregationists targeted the church on at least three separate occasions. On Christmas Day 1956, a bomb destroyed the parsonage. Rev. Shuttlesworth, pastor at the time, was home but miraculously was not harmed. In June 1958, a bomb at the church was removed before it exploded. In December 1962, another bomb inflicted damage to the church.

Rev. Shuttlesworth left Birmingham in 1961 and moved to Cincinnati, Ohio, but he stayed involved in the Birmingham civil rights movement. After the 1962 bomb attack, his successor, the Reverend Vincent Provitt, suggested that a sign be placed in the window of the parsonage to alert terrorists that Rev. Shuttlesworth was no longer living there.

"BETHEL WAS THE MOVEMENT AND THE MOVEMENT WAS THE CHURCH."

A new Bethel Baptist Church (at 3200 Twenty-Eighth Avenue North) is just around the corner from the historic church. Be sure to map yourself to the correct address. Tours and the marker honoring the work of the congregation and Rev. Shuttlesworth are at 3233 Twenty-Ninth Avenue North.

Tours can be arranged by calling (205) 324-8489 or by visiting *https://thehistoricbethel.org/*. Tours are offered Monday to Saturday, from 9 a.m. until 3 p.m. For groups of six or more, the cost per person is $10 for adults and $5 for students; smaller groups are $20 per person.

Reverend Fred Lee Shuttlesworth

At the 2007 annual crossing of the Edmund Pettus Bridge in Selma, then–US senator Barack Obama pushed a man in a wheelchair across that famous bridge. That man was Rev. Fred Lee Shuttlesworth, about to celebrate his eighty-fifth birthday. A younger Rev. Shuttlesworth is pictured below sitting between Dr. King and the Rev. Ralph David Abernathy.

Rev. Shuttlesworth was in the forefront of the civil rights movement from the mid-1950s on. In 1956, when Alabama banned the NAACP from conducting activities inside the state (based on the technicality of not registering as an out-of-state group), Shuttlesworth formed an Alabama-based organization, the Alabama Christian Movement for Human Rights, to continue the same work. That same year, he accompanied Autherine Lucy and her attorney when Ms. Lucy tried to enroll at the University of Alabama.

In 1957, he was part of a group of civil rights icons (including Dr. King, Rev. Abernathy, and others) who formed the Southern Christian Leadership Conference (SCLC). In

1961, Rev. Shuttlesworth supported the Freedom Riders by alerting authorities and the press of the need for police protection as well as arranging for drivers to rescue the injured riders in Anniston and bring them to University Hospital in Birmingham.

Descriptions of Rev. Shuttlesworth often include adjectives like "fiery," "inspiring," "tireless" and "blunt." When sixteen sticks of dynamite blew up outside his bedroom window intending to kill him, a Klan-affiliated police officer suggested Shuttlesworth move away. Undeterred, the minister told him, "I wasn't saved to run."

He was a man of vision. It was Shuttlesworth who invited Dr. King to Birmingham at the time of the 1963 campaign. He was prescient when he told King, "If you come to Birmingham, you will not only gain prestige, but really shake the country. If you win in Birmingham, as Birmingham goes, so goes the nation."[125]

President Bill Clinton awarded Rev. Shuttlesworth the Presidential Citizens Medal in 2001.

When Rev. Shuttlesworth died in 2011, another civil rights icon, John Lewis, called him "a fearless, determined, courageous leader for civil rights and social justice" and "the last of a kind."[126] A statue of the reverend stands outside the Birmingham Civil Rights Institute, and the Birmingham International Airport now bears him name.

When you drive from the BCRI–Kelly Ingram Park area or the Birmingham jail marker to Historic Bethel Baptist Church, you will likely pass Oak Hill Cemetery (1120 Nineteenth Street North). Rev. Fred Shuttlesworth is buried there. Find his grave in Block 10, Lot 22, Section A (the northeast corner of the cemetery). Look for the nearby twenty-five-foot-tall obelisk at the grave of Birmingham industrialist and Confederate Army colonel James Sloss. Even in the grave, Rev. Shuttlesworth apparently needs to be looking over his shoulder for Confederates.

CHAPTER 16

Anniston

As your journey winds down, the museums you have visited have displayed powerful images from the cameras of many news photographers. Some photographs are probably seared into your memory. It's difficult to forget some of the images that captured and exposed the cruelty of segregation:

- David Jackson's photo of Emmett Till's open casket that appeared in *Jet* in September 1955.
- The photo by Will Counts that captured the angry white teenager shouting hate in the ears of Elizabeth Eckford as she walked toward Little Rock Central High School.
- Associated Press photographer Bill Hudson's timely shot of a German shepherd lunging for the midsection of seventeen-year-old Walter Gadsden during the 1963 Birmingham demonstrations.
- Freelance photographer Bob Adelman's images of children and teenagers sheltering themselves as best they could from the high-pressure fire hoses in the streets of Birmingham.

Bob Adelman was a volunteer photographer for the movement. This insider status often put him in just the right place at the right time. Adelman aptly noted in *Jet* in 2014, "In a profound sense, the movement revealed how segregation was ugly and un-American. The photographs were the evidence."[127]

The shout-out to these and other photographers who put themselves in harm's way to bring to the nation and the world the truth and determination of the change agents of the 1950s and 1960s is overdue in this book. It is also to some extent intentional, since Anniston produced one of the most stunning and disturbing photographs of the era: the image of the burning Greyhound bus that Klansmen attacked in Anniston in 1961. The Klansmen set upon the bus and its Riders when it arrived, flattened its tires, chased it to just outside the city limits, and set it on fire with a bunch of burning, gas-soaked rags jammed into a soda bottle.

The photographer was Joe Postiglione, a freelancer for the *Anniston Star.* Questions:

- How did Mr. Postiglione know to be at the Greyhound station on Mother's Day, May 14, 1961?
- How did he handle a curious Klansman at the bus depot regarding why he was carrying a camera that morning?
- What happened to the negatives of his famous shots? Who has them now?

All these queries are answered during what is likely to be a half day in Anniston. Before laying out the plan for this brief stay, let's provide some background on the Freedom Rides.

You may recall reading about unsung hero Irene Morgan in chapter 14. Her challenge to a 1944 arrest for refusing to move to the back of an interstate bus resulted in the 1946 US Supreme Court ruling in *Morgan v. Virginia.* That decision struck down a Virginia law requiring racial segregation on commercial interstate buses. Another Supreme Court ruling (*Boynton v. Virginia*) in 1960 affirmed that segregated services—restaurants and waiting rooms, for example—intended for use by interstate bus passengers were also unconstitutional.

Like their initial refusal to adhere to the Supreme Court's *Brown v. Board of Education* decision, some southern states and cities ignored the court on the topic of interstate bus travel. The Congress of Racial Equality (CORE) recruited a group of white and Black activists in 1961 to ride on interstate buses from Washington, DC, to New Orleans. The goal was to draw attention to the lack of state and federal law enforcement. The initial group of thirteen Freedom Riders ranged in age from eighteen-year-old Charles Person to sixty-one-year-old Walter Bergman.

The idea behind the Freedom Rides wasn't new but the name was. First conceived in 1947 by CORE and the Fellowship of Reconciliation (FOR) to test the *Morgan* decision, the rides were called the "Journey of Reconciliation." For the 1961 effort, James Farmer, CORE's national director, selected "Freedom Rides" to garner more media attention and to capture what was truly at stake.

The thirteen original Riders split into two groups in Washington on May 4, 1961: six boarded a Greyhound bus and the other seven hopped on a Trailways bus. The goal was to reach New Orleans by May 17 in order to celebrate the seventh anniversary of the *Brown* school desegregation decision.

For the most part, things went smoothly as the group traveled through Virginia. On May 8, in Charlotte, North Carolina, the first arrest occurred when young Charles Person decided to get a shoeshine in a whites-only chair. However, Person wasn't the one arrested; the Riders thought it would be better if another Black Rider, Joe Perkins, was the first to go to jail.

That's what happened when Perkins stayed in the shoeshine chair when told to move. He refused to pay the fifty-dollar bail and opted for a couple of days in jail and a trial. At trial, the unexpected happened: the judge followed the law and pronounced Perkins not guilty.

Violence against the Riders reared its ugly head when the Greyhound bus pulled into Rock Hill, South Carolina, on May 9. Twenty-one-year-old John Lewis (then a theology student, now an icon who passed away in 2020) and his white fellow Rider Albert Bigelow (the Riders typically rode in Black-white pairs) headed to the whites-only waiting room.

Two white thugs stopped Lewis and told him to go down the hall to the other waiting area. One of the goons responded with blows when Lewis asserted that it was his right to enter any waiting room. Fists to the face were followed by kicks in the ribs when Lewis hit the floor. The dangers associated with the Riders heading deeper into the South became apparent.

By May 13, the Riders reached Atlanta, where they were hosted by Dr. Martin Luther King Jr. While King offered them encouragement and praise for what they were doing, privately he voiced concern about the harm they faced. Dr. King told reporters from *Jet* and *Ebony* that the group "will never make it through Alabama." Anniston was their next stop.

The next day was Mother's Day, May 14. Freedom Rider James Peck—age forty-six, white, and a veteran of the 1947 Journey of Reconciliation rides—called Rev. Fred Shuttlesworth to let him know when the bus should arrive in Birmingham. Rev. Shuttlesworth shared that Birmingham was buzzing with rumors of Klan attacks on the buses when they arrived in town. Peck let the other Riders know about those rumors, but they all were united that the rides must continue.

The Greyhound bus carrying seven Freedom Riders departed Atlanta about 11 a.m. Besides the Freedom Riders, two journalists were on board as well as two undercover Alabama Highway Patrolmen, Ell Cowling and Harry Sims. Cowling and Sims were spies, there to listen in on what the Riders were saying to each other. However, the pair would actually do their jobs and protect the Riders when the bus was attacked in Anniston.

Anniston was a scheduled intermediate stop prior to the Greyhound's arrival in Birmingham. As the bus crossed into Anniston, the Riders saw the streets full of people, yet when the bus arrived at the Greyhound depot, the crowds were gone. But not for long.

About fifty men carrying pipes, clubs, and chains suddenly surrounded the bus. No policemen were in sight. One Klansman lay down in front of the bus to prevent it from driving off. The two undercover cops blocked the Klansmen from getting on board, but they could not stop the mob from breaking some windows and hurling rocks at the Riders inside. Twenty minutes went by before police arrived on the scene. They broke up the mob but arrested no one. When the crowd dispersed, the bus was able to leave the station. No one on the bus realized that two of its tires were slashed. The bus did not get far.

That's a good place to stop for now. The story continues as we cover Anniston's top sites.

The Plan for Anniston in 300 Words or Less

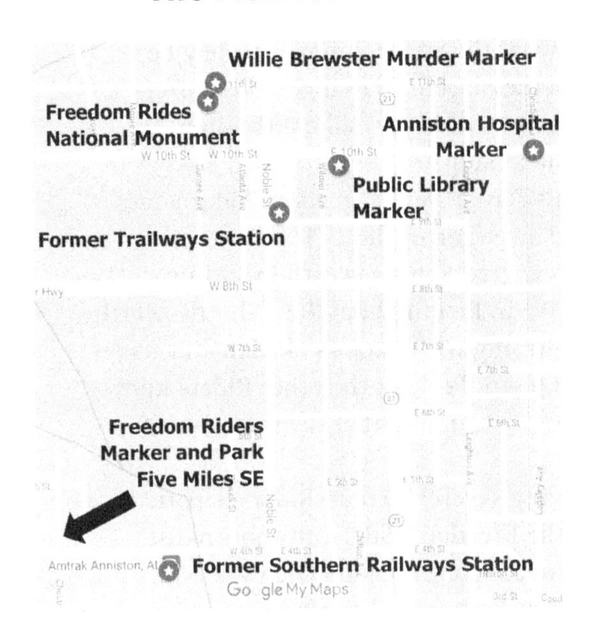

Eight locations are recommended in and around Anniston. They require about a half day. Five of them relate to the Freedom Rides of 1961; the other three tie to non–Freedom Rides events.

Visit the six locations in the heart of Anniston first, a mix of Freedom Rides memorials and other markers related to civil rights–era events. Except for the marker describing the beating that college student Art Bacon received at the hands of five whites at what is now the Amtrak station, the other five are relatively close together.

Park your car near the NPS Freedom Rides site on Gurnee and walk to the next four spots, ending at the marker in front of the Calhoun County Courthouse. This walk is a little over a mile, ending back near your car. Drive to the marker at today's Amtrak station on Fourth Street.

Moving outside of the city, continue to two places just off Highway 202, where that Greyhound bus was firebombed. This approach puts the Freedom Rider events in essentially chronological order. If seeing the Freedom Riders locations in chronological sequence doesn't matter to you, you can start at the two locations near Highway 202 as you drive to Anniston from Birmingham.

Former Site of the Greyhound Station, 1031 Gurnee Avenue

The story of what occurred on the afternoon of May 14, 1963, is well told here. Officially, the NPS site is called the Freedom Riders National Monument. A timeline describes key events—from the planning meeting of Klan members in Birmingham the day before, through the arrival of the bus, the attack in the terminal, and the bus's departure from the depot. There is also good content on who the Riders were and how they were selected.

Less familiar to me before this visit were details on Joe Postiglione, the *Anniston Star* photographer. His well-known and shocking images of the burning Greyhound bus and the stunned Riders moved the nation and the world. The wall boards on the brick wall dealing with Mr. Postiglione and his work share who tipped him off that trouble was coming to the bus depot and also how he outsmarted a Klansman to stay in position to capture history. His negatives for the photos went missing for quite awhile, but you will learn how they were found. Today, those negatives are the property of the Birmingham Civil Rights Institute.

The city of Anniston has a memorial marker here. It's another one where the word choice seems inaccurate, even a bit offensive. Recall previous issues on word choice at the Memphis marker for Echol Cole and Robert Walker, the sanitation workers whose deaths were a spark igniting the strike in 1968. The powers that put up markers control the content on them.

The marker at the Greyhound depot location states that the Freedom Riders "were attacked by a mob of whites who were protesting the desegregation of public transportation facilities." To associate the actions of the mob here with the word "protest" is distressing. The mob was defying the law. They were lawbreakers, not protesters. The Freedom Riders had every right to be on that bus and sit wherever they wanted.

This NPS site is outdoors, on a brick wall of a building adjacent to the original terminal. The wall mural and educational boards can be accessed at any time on any day, no admission fee required. Parking is easy near this and the next destination: the Trailways station where the so-called other bus arrived from Atlanta. These first two destinations are a five-minute walk apart.

At the time of publication, the NPS was working to add more visitor amenities and information here, so what is already a good site may get even better.

Former Site of the Trailways Station, 901 Noble Street

The Trailways bus depot was near the corner on Noble and East Ninth Street. On a wall at that intersection is another wall mural and descriptive boards for the "other bus," the words used on the wall to describe the Trailways bus. The Trailways incident here on Mother's Day 1961 is less well known than what happened to the Greyhound bus because the Trailways bus wasn't firebombed. However, more physical harm came to the seven Freedom Riders on the Trailways bus, a significant point.

The Trailways bus departed from Atlanta about an hour after the Greyhound bus left. Several Klansmen got on the bus in Atlanta. En route, the Klansmen began to harass the Riders; the threats increased as they crossed into Alabama. The bus arrived in Anniston, and a few of the Riders went into the depot to buy sandwiches.

Returning to the bus, the driver, accompanied by several "hoodlums" (as Freedom Rider James Peck called them), told the Riders about what happened to the Greyhound bus. The driver told the group that the Trailways bus wasn't leaving Anniston until the Black Freedom Riders moved to the back of the bus.

The Freedom Riders told the driver of their rights; he left the bus shaking his head. That's when the Klansmen ordered Black college students Charles Person and Herman Harris to get in the back. When neither moved, the brutes punched both Riders, dragged them into the aisle, and kicked them until forty-six-year-old James Peck and sixty-one-year-old Walter Bergman tried to stop the violence. They became the next victims of the Klansmen's blows. Both older Riders were knocked unconscious.

Other Klansmen dragged Person and Harris to the back of the bus. Then Peck and Bergman were dragged there as well. Their brutal violence done for now, the Klansmen sat down in the middle of the bus to make sure no one tried to violate their human color line.

The driver returned with a police officer. With the Jim Crow seating arrangements in place, the officer exited the bus, and the driver headed out of Anniston using back roads to get to Birmingham. The Freedom Riders did not realize it, but another welcoming party awaited them there: a collaboration between the Klan and Bull Connor's police department. The police had agreed to give the Klansmen a fifteen-minute window to "welcome" the bus's arrival in Birmingham.

If you are wondering why you were not directed to visit the former site of Birmingham's Trailways station (1900 Fourth Avenue North), it's simple. Today, the location on the northwest corner of the intersection of Fourth Avenue and Nineteenth Street North is a Wells Fargo drive-thru. There is a marker there, though, if you want to add this to your Birmingham day.

Former Anniston Memorial Hospital, Tenth Street and Christine Street

After the firebombing attack on the Greyhound bus, the Riders needed medical attention. While they escaped the bus, they had breathing issues from all the smoke. One Freedom Rider, nineteen-year-old Hank Thomas, also had a head wound from one of the attacking white clubbing him with a baseball bat.

When ambulances arrived to take the Riders to the hospital, their drivers showed how far the lunacy of Jim Crow extended; they initially refused to take the Black Riders to the local hospital. The ambulance drivers eventually relented when the white Freedom Riders were not willing to leave their Black colleagues.

At Anniston Memorial Hospital, the doctors treated the injured, but the hospital's superintendent told them, once treated, they had to leave. Joe Perkins, the Freedom Rider who went to jail in Charlotte less than a week prior, called Rev. Fred Shuttlesworth. The minister arranged a caravan of his followers to head to Anniston and get the Riders back to the relative safety of his home in Birmingham.

The marker is at the corner of Tenth and Christine Streets. Drivers will find it easier to park on Christine Street.

Public Library of Anniston and Calhoun County, 108 East Tenth Street

Another marker on Tenth Street is in front of the Public Library of Anniston and Calhoun County. This memorial plaque is not associated with the Freedom Rides but rather with the actions of two little-known ministers to integrate the local library in 1963: Revs. William B. McClain and Nimrod Quintus Reynolds. The marker stands near the east end of the building, perhaps a bit hidden by the crepe myrtle trees if they are in bloom. Park in the library lot on Wilmer Avenue.

Unsung Heroes: Revs. William B. McClain and Nimrod Quintus Reynolds

If you were Black in Anniston before September 1963, you couldn't go into the library any time you wanted. You could if it was during special hours set aside for African Americans on Thursday and on the first Sunday of the month. Beyond those short windows, you were out of luck.

In the summer of 1963, a group of African Americans came to the library, called the Carnegie Library in those days, to request library cards, but their request was denied. The library board was waiting for city officials to decide whether Blacks could have a library card. Other attempts to open library services to all regardless of race had failed that summer.

Eventually, the city and the library board decided to open the public library to everyone. Sunday, September 15, 1963, was to be the starting date for integration.

On that day, two African American ministers came to the Carnegie Library. Revs. William McClain and Nimrod Q. Reynolds had been working with the library board to desegregate the facility. When the clergymen arrived at the library, a mob of around one hundred angry whites attacked them with sticks, fists, and a chain. When the pair tried to escape, their car was blocked in. When they ran, a motorist picked up McClain and Reynolds and helped them escape.

They were taken to Anniston Memorial Hospital.

Does that date—September 15, 1963—sound familiar? It was the same day four young girls were killed in the Sixteenth Street Baptist Church bombing in Birmingham.

The next day, city officials, members of the library board, and Rev. J. Phillips Noble (who was chair of the Anniston Human Relations Council) accompanied Rev. McClain and another African American minister, George Smitherman, to the library. Rev. Smitherman took the place of Rev. Reynolds, who was still in the hospital. Both men were issued library cards.

Eventually, police arrested four men who were part of the mob attack at the library. One was found guilty; however, *at the request of the victims*, the case was dismissed.

Murder of Willie Brewster, 34 West Eleventh Street

Willie Brewster worked the nightshift at a local foundry. Driving home with coworkers on July 13, 1965, Mr. Brewster was shot in the neck and died three days later. White supremacist Hubert Damon Strange was arrested in the shooting and convicted of second-degree murder. Strange's conviction was the first time in Alabama history an all-white jury found a white man guilty of killing a Black man. The jury sentenced Strange to ten years in prison but he never served a day. While his appeal was pending, Strange was killed in a fight in 1967.

The Willie Brewster marker is near the corner of West Eleventh Street and Gurnee Avenue at the Calhoun County Courthouse. Willie Brewster's name is also on the list of civil rights martyrs at the Southern Poverty Law Center in Montgomery. Your car is 250 feet away if you left it on Gurnee near the NPS site. Drive to the next stop.

Former Southern Railways Train Station, 144 Fourth Street

It was January 2, 1961. The violence against the Freedom Riders was just over four months away. Talladega College student Arthur Bacon was waiting for a ride at the Southern Railways station in Anniston. The twenty-three-year-old Bacon happened to be waiting for that ride back to the college in the whites-only area of the station. Segregated facilities at transportation centers had been outlawed by the Supreme Court. He had every right to sit there.

For his simple, *legal* action, Bacon was beaten by five men and ended up at the same Anniston Hospital that would treat the Freedom Riders four and a half months later.

Art Bacon finished his education at Talladega, went to Howard University, and earned a PhD in zoology. Dr. Bacon returned to Talladega College to become, in time, the dean of the Math and Sciences Departments and a vice president for academic affairs at the university.

You can't miss the marker at what now is the Amtrak station. Go inside for a trip back in time.

Greyhound Bus Burning Site: Freedom Riders Park, Old Birmingham Highway

This site is a work in progress, a collaboration of the NPS and the Calhoun County Chamber of Commerce. It is near the site of the attack on the Greyhound bus in 1961. The actual part of the highway where the bus was engulfed in flames was paved over to expand Highway

202 to accommodate traffic to the nearby Anniston Army Depot.[128]

To reach this spot, enter 5062 Old Birmingham Road into your mapping software. This should direct you where to turn off State Highway 202 (the Albert P. Brewer Highway) and park safely. The next and final destination is close by.

Burn marks on the sign reveal that not everyone is happy to have this site memorialized.

Freedom Riders Marker, Old Birmingham Highway

Park your car near the future site of the Freedom Riders Park. Walk about one hundred yards to the west to see a privately funded marker, placed by the Theta Tau chapter of the Black fraternity Omega Psi Phi. This marker is on a triangle of land controlled by the Alabama Department of Transportation. Walk toward where Old Birmingham Highway dead-ends; the marker is along the guard rail. It is much safer to view it from this side, not from the much busier Highway 202.

This Freedom Riders marker is not only the last covered in Anniston but the final memorial in Part 2 of this book. So many of the places you have visited relate to despicable acts fueled by hatred. The attacks on the Greyhound bus and the Freedom Riders would rank high on the list of the segregationists' depraved and evil actions.

However, because of the brave actions of a young girl, we can end with a story of compassion in the midst of such hatred.

The Greyhound bus was firebombed in front of a small family-run store, Forsyth and Son Grocery. A Molotov cocktail explosive was tossed into the bus, setting it on fire, with the passengers inside. When the bus's fuel tank exploded, the attacking mob backed off and Officer Ell Cowling on board managed to get the bus door open, allowing the passengers to escape. As choking Freedom Riders tumbled out of the burning vehicle, they were beaten by the mob. Cowling's raised weapon, the heat from the bus, and a second fuel tank explosion caused the mob to disperse.

Some nearby residents helped the Freedom Riders, but the actions of the grocery store owner's daughter that provided a ray of hope on such a terribly dark day. Twelve-year-old Janie Forsyth plunged into "a scene from hell," as she described it years later. She hauled buckets of water, again and again, out to those sprawled around the lawn. She washed the Freedom Riders' faces.

Janie Forsyth paid a price for her acts of kindness that Mother's Day, ridiculed by her fellow white students at school. In an interview done around the fiftieth anniversary of the May 14, 1961, events, she remembered her reaction: "I didn't feel like I belonged, like I fit in," she said. Janie Forsyth McKinney eventually left Alabama and moved to the West Coast.

There's something about the actions of twelve-year-old Janie Forsyth. Perhaps it was because I was also twelve in 1961. Perhaps I wonder: If I grew up in Anniston, Alabama, would I have had the courage to do what she did? Exercise the "power of one"?

The power of one is a key lesson for all of us from the American civil rights movement. We owe such a debt to the brave individuals—well-known or otherwise—who chose to sit in, to march, to face the punishing force of water from fire hoses, and to take part in so many actions to make the words of the Declaration of Independence really mean something: that all men are created equal. As Janie Forsyth McKinney wrote,

> "When you get the opportunity to do the right thing against great odds, you have to do it. If you don't, it will diminish you as a person. On the other hand, if you do it, you can know that you passed at least one hard test, and it helps define you as a stronger person."[129]

PART THREE

TRAVELING FREEDOM'S ROAD BEYOND THE LOOP DESTINATIONS

Overview: Parts 3 to 5

The *Journal of Happiness Studies* (yes, that's a thing) reported that the ideal length of a vacation is eight days—too short if you want to take the full civil rights loop trip. It demands more: two dedicated, focused weeks on the road—a long trip by any yardstick.

Despite the time commitment required to visit the cities already covered, this rest of the book takes us beyond the destination cities already covered to offer even more locations of possible interest. We group them as follows:

- More *within* the five states covered so far (chapters 17–21)
- More in the nine states that *border* these five states (Chapters 22–29)
- More in the rest of the United States (Chapter 30)

The first grouping recognizes that, to one degree or another, you will be traveling within Georgia, Alabama, Mississippi, Arkansas, and Tennessee on the loop tour. Some people will be there as temporary tourists; others as residents. For both, laying out additional relevant options may be appealing. Some of these locations are just a slight detour from the recommended loop route, while others require a significant diversion.

A slight-detour example would be the Safe House Black History Museum in Greensboro, Alabama. It is only twenty miles beyond Marion, Alabama, making it a possible add-on stop following time in Marion. On the other hand, some notable sites are not so close to the recommended route.

An example of that would be Hattiesburg, Mississippi. Hattiesburg is over an hour and a half southeast of Jackson, making it an unlikely side trip for those already traveling the ten-stop loop. However, Hattiesburg is on the way for travelers coming from the southern parts of Mississippi, Louisiana, or Alabama. A Hattiesburg stop on the way to Jackson affords the chance to learn more about two lesser-known heroes of the movement, Vernon Dahmer and Clyde Kennard.

This idea of stopping on the way to start the two-week journey is also a reason to note historical locations and museums in the nine states that border the states on the loop. That's the focus of Part 4. These nine states open many possibilities for civil rights and African American history enthusiasts in cities like Columbia, Greensboro, Nashville, Richmond, St. Louis, Louisville, and more.

The on-the-way approach is only a partial reason for going beyond just covering the cities on the loop. Relevant history occurred and is remembered elsewhere, affording folks who cannot make the lengthy journey the chance to visit that history closer to home. Hopefully, these closer-to-home experiences might whet the appetite to make the full civil rights tour trip one day.

That's why Part 5 (chapter 30) presents options in the rest of the country, covering twenty-four of the remaining thirty-six states plus Washington, DC, which could be a civil rights and African American history destination in its own right.

MARCH ON WASHINGTON FOR JOBS AND FREEDOM

AUGUST 28, 1963

LINCOLN MEMORIAL PROGRAM

1. The National Anthem	*Led by* Marian Anderson.
2. Invocation	The Very Rev. Patrick O'Boyle, *Archbishop of Washington.*
3. Opening Remarks	A. Philip Randolph, *Director March on Washington for Jobs and Freedom.*
4. Remarks	Dr. Eugene Carson Blake, *Stated Clerk, United Presbyterian Church of the U.S.A.; Vice Chairman, Commission on Race Relations of the National Council of Churches of Christ in America.*
5. Tribute to Negro Women Fighters for Freedom Daisy Bates Diane Nash Bevel Mrs. Medgar Evers Mrs. Herbert Lee Rosa Parks Gloria Richardson	Mrs. Medgar Evers
6. Remarks	John Lewis, *National Chairman, Student Nonviolent Coordinating Committee.*
7. Remarks	Walter Reuther, *President, United Automobile, Aerospace and Agricultural Implement Wokers of America, AFL-CIO; Chairman, Industrial Union Department, AFL-CIO.*
8. Remarks	James Farmer, *National Director, Congress of Racial Equality.*
9. Selection	Eva Jessye *Choir*
10. Prayer	Rabbi Uri Miller, *President Synagogue Council of America.*
11. Remarks	Whitney M. Young, Jr., *Executive Director, National Urban League.*
12. Remarks	Mathew Ahmann, *Executive Director, National Catholic Conference for Interracial Justice.*
13. Remarks	Roy Wilkins, *Executive Secretary, National Association for the Advancement of Colored People.*
14. Selection	Miss Mahalia Jackson
15. Remarks	Rabbi Joachim Prinz, *President American Jewish Congress.*
16. Remarks	The Rev. Dr. Martin Luther King, Jr., *President, Southern Christian Leadership Conference.*
17. The Pledge	A Philip Randolph
18. Benediction	Dr. Benjamin E. Mays, *President, Morehouse College.*

"WE SHALL OVERCOME"

CHAPTER 17

Georgia beyond Atlanta

Five Georgia cities beyond Atlanta are covered here, with the highest-profile civil rights activity occurring in Albany in late 1961. There, Dr. King faced off against Police Chief Laurie Pritchett and learned lessons that he would apply when the campaign for freedom moved into Birmingham and his adversary was Theophilus Eugene "Bull" Connor. Albany, Macon, and Cairo are south of Atlanta; Savannah and Midway are in the eastern part of the state.

Albany

Three hours and 180 miles south of Atlanta lies Albany, Georgia. It could be a day trip for Atlantans, an add-on to civil rights movement tourists visiting Atlanta, or a possible stopping point for those leaving Atlanta and driving back to various points in Florida. Unlike Montgomery and Birmingham, where Dr. King's efforts successfully produced change despite intense local opposition, Albany turned out a little differently for him—a teachable moment, if you will.

Dr. King would reflect on the Albany campaign, labeling some of his decisions at the time "mistakes" but a valuable learning experience in the long run. King acknowledged that "what we learned from our mistakes in Albany helped our later campaigns in other cities to be more effective."[130]

Albany Civil Rights Institute, 324 Whitney Avenue

This former home of Mount Zion Baptist Church is now the site of the Albany Civil Rights Institute (ACRI). Here on November 25, 1961, the first mass meeting was held following several arrests at the Continental Trailways bus station, at the corner of East Oglethorpe Boulevard and Jackson Street. Three high school students and two local college students were arrested for violating the segregation laws at the bus station.

The institute is open Tuesday to Saturday from 10 a.m. to 4 p.m. Adult admission is $6, less for seniors, students, and military. Groups of ten or more must make arrangements to visit at least a week in advance.

Shiloh Baptist Church, 325 Whitney Avenue

In mid-December 1961, Dr. Martin Luther King Jr. spoke at a mass meeting at Shiloh Baptist Church, offering his support to what became known as "the Albany Movement." A historical marker in front of the church asserts that "the Albany Civil Rights Movement Started Here." No tours are offered.

So many came to hear Dr. King that the overflow filled Mount Zion Baptist Church across the street. (That's right: two Baptist churches across the street from one another.) King walked across the street when he finished at Shiloh and energized a similarly packed house at Mount Zion.

The day after Dr. King spoke at the two churches, he, Rev. Ralph Abernathy, and others were arrested following a mass march. Initially, the leaders refused to post bail. When the city pledged to desegregate the train and bus stations and made some other concessions, Dr. King and Rev. Abernathy posted bond and returned to Atlanta. When they returned for their trial they were given the option of paying a $178 fine or receiving a forty-five-day jail sentence. They chose jail time. However, they didn't serve much of it as a then-unknown person posted bail, later identified in Taylor Branch's *Parting the Waters* as Albany attorney B. C. Gardner.[131] Albany's police chief Laurie Pritchett said he allowed bail here as "a matter of strategy." He admitted he feared continued trouble in Albany if King stayed in jail.

Dr. King and others were eventually banned from further marches in Albany by a federal court; King obeyed that order. He viewed the Albany campaign with disappointment, saying "the mistake I made there was to protest against segregation generally rather than against a single distinct facet of it. Our protest was so vague that we got nothing."[132]

Charles Sherrod Civil Rights Park, Jackson Street and Highland Street

A block from Shiloh and Mount Zion Baptist churches is Charles Sherrod Civil Rights Park. A black granite memorial there shares some of the civil rights history in the city. Notice the footprints along the Jackson Street side of the park; they follow the protest route that thousands took to their arrest at City Hall.

Charles Sherrod arrived in Albany in late 1961 as a field secretary for the Student Nonviolent Coordinating Committee (SNCC). Instrumental in the Albany Movement and the Selma Voting Rights Campaign, Rev. Sherrod served as a city councilman in Albany from 1976 to 1990. He and his wife to this day provide leadership at the *Southwest Georgia Project for Community Education*.

Macon

About halfway between Atlanta and Albany is the city of Macon. While some associate Macon with the Allman Brothers Band, the most important musical act to come out of the city is Richard Wayne Penniman. Who? You know him as Little Richard. You can go by his boyhood home, which the expansion of nearby interstate highways caused to be relocated to 416 Craft Street.

Macon is also home to the massive (forty-nine-thousand square feet) Tubman Museum. The building was a warehouse that was falling apart but salvaged.

Tubman Museum, 310 Cherry Street

Besides a gallery devoted to the museum's namesake, Harriet Tubman, visitors will find content dealing with African American inventors, local civil rights history, courageous women in the fight for freedom, and more. A fifty-five-foot mural provides more on African American heritage. The Tubman's halls and galleries also display a significant amount of art and sculpture.

Adult admission is $10 with $2 discounts for seniors, educators, military, college students, AARP/AAA members, and groups of fifteen or more; children and teens cost $6. Open Tuesday to Saturday from 9 a.m. to 5 p.m.

Cairo

Tiny Cairo is fifty-five miles south of Albany and just north of the Florida/Georgia state line. Its most famous former resident is Jackie Robinson, the first Black player to don a Major League uniform.

Jackie Robinson Birthplace Historical Marker, Hadley Ferry Road, north of Meridian Road

The first African American to play Major League Baseball, Jackie Robinson was born in Cairo on January 31, 1919. In 1920, he and his family moved to California. In 1947, Robinson joined the Brooklyn Dodgers, breaking Major League Baseball's color barrier. Robinson died in 1972. Sadly, the house in which he was born burned in 1996. A museum honoring the great number "42" is in development in New York City.

Savannah

Savannah is the oldest city in Georgia, its first state capital, and home of the state's oldest African American community. Following Savannah's settlement in 1733, enslaved people were brought here from South Carolina despite a slavery ban from General James Oglethorpe of Georgia. (Besides slavery, Oglethorpe also banned lawyers and Catholics.) By the late 1740s, humans were openly sold in Savannah.

Following his march to the sea, General William Tecumseh Sherman issued Special Field Order 15 here in 1865; it subdivided four hundred thousand acres of southern land into forty-acre plots to be provided the formerly enslaved. Apart from on-duty military personnel, no whites were to be allowed to live on those four hundred thousand acres.

The phrase "forty acres and a mule" came from Sherman's Field Order 15, even though the field order itself made no mention of mules. A "History of Emancipation" marker commemorating the order is near the corner of Harris and Bull Streets in Savannah's Madison Square. Sherman's order was countermanded by President Andrew Johnson after he assumed the presidency upon Lincoln's assassination.

In the 1960s, like other southern cities, Savannah was the site of store boycotts, mass marches, lunch-counter sit-ins, and even wade-ins at popular tourist destination Tybee Island, previously reserved for whites. Two markers commemorating the Tybee Island wade-ins were installed in March 2021 between the Tybee Island Lighthouse and Fort Screven.

Ralph Mark Gilbert Civil Rights Museum, 460 Martin Luther King Jr. Boulevard

The Gilbert Civil Rights Museum chronicles the civil rights struggle in Savannah. Three floors of photographic and interactive exhibits provide insight and education on the civil rights movement in Savannah and in Georgia. Start with the short film to get a good overview.

The building itself was constructed in 1914 for the African American–owned Wage Earners Bank. Dr. Ralph M. Gilbert was pastor of First African Baptist Church from 1939 until his death in 1956 and a leader in the civil rights movement in Savannah.

The pandemic closed the museum for some time but the website indicates it plans to re-open. Its hours were 10 a.m. to 5 p.m. except on Sunday, Monday, and the usual holidays. Admission fees: Adults, $8; seniors, $6; students, $4.

The African-American Monument, Rousakis Riverfront Plaza

This monument depicts a family of four embracing after emancipation. Chains representing slavery lie at their feet. This was the first monument in Savannah to recognize the contributions made by African Americans. Designed by Savannah College of Art and Design professor Dorothy Spradley, the inscription from poet Maya Angelou reads:

> "We were stolen, sold and bought together from the African continent. We got on the slave ships together. We lay back to belly in the holds of the slave ships in each other's excrement and urine together, sometimes died together, and our lifeless bodies thrown overboard together. Today, we are standing up together, with faith and even some joy."

The monument is a little over a one-mile walk from the Gilbert Museum.

First African Baptist Church, 23 Montgomery Street (on Franklin Square)

This church has one of the oldest Black congregations in the United States. Founded by enslaved preacher George Leile in 1773, First African Baptist Church was formally recognized in 1788, at that time meeting in a barn on a nearby plantation. In 1794, the congregation moved to the city but split over doctrinal differences in 1832. The name First African (originally First Colored) was retained by the group of congregants who moved onto Franklin Square in the 1830s, initially into a structure vacated by the white Baptist church and later into a building of their own.

Rev. Ralph Gilbert, for whom the local civil rights museum is named, was the pastor of the church during the civil rights era. The church served as the largest gathering place for Blacks and whites to meet during the time of segregation.

Recognized as a National Historic Landmark and registered with the National Register of Historic Places, one can reserve a tour of the inside of the church by calling (912) 233-0636. Tours are given Wednesday to Saturday at 3 p.m.

Outside the church is another part of Savannah's Black history: the **Haitian Monument**. It is dedicated to more than five hundred Black troops who fought in the 1779 Siege of Savannah during the Revolutionary War.

Midway

Historic Dorchester Academy Museum of African-American History, 8787 East Oglethorpe Highway

Founded after the Civil War as a school for the formerly enslaved, this site, thirty-five miles southeast of Savannah, was used by Dr. Martin Luther King Jr. and his SCLC colleagues as they planned the 1963 Birmingham Campaign.

The museum here is open Tuesday to Friday from 11 a.m. to 2 p.m. and on weekends from 2 p.m. to 4 p.m. Group tours can be arranged by calling (912) 884-2347. Markers and content boards on the grounds tell the story of this place should you arrive after closing time.

CHAPTER 18

Alabama beyond the Loop

Six communities around the state of Alabama outside of our six recommended loop tour stops merit mention. Scottsboro, Decatur, and Danville are north of Birmingham; Tuscaloosa and Greensboro are northwest of Montgomery; and Mobile is along the state's Gulf Coast.

The sites in the first three cities—the two locations of the Scottsboro Boys trials of the 1930s and the birthplace of the hero of the 1936 Olympics, Jesse Owens—predate the civil rights era but are certainly important events in African American history. The prejudice evident in the prosecution of the Scottsboro Boys was still evident in the 1980s as local officials debated where to place a memorial honoring Jesse Owens in Oakville.

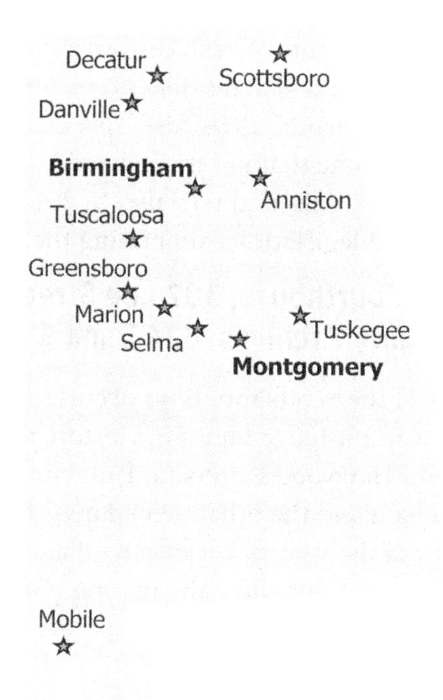

Scottsboro and Decatur

The Scottsboro Boys Museum and Cultural Center, 428 West Willow Street, and Scottsboro Boys Trial Marker at the Jackson County Courthouse, Scottsboro

Located in a former United Methodist church, the museum is just a few blocks from the Jackson County Courthouse, where nine young African American men were first tried when accused of raping two white women in 1931. Eight of the nine were convicted in the initial trial in Scottsboro. However, an appeal of the initial convictions led to the landmark Supreme Court decision (*Powell v. Alabama*) that affirmed the right of defendants to legal counsel. New trials were ordered, and the trial venue changed to nearby Decatur.

The museum is open 10 a.m. to 4 p.m. on the second and third Saturdays of each month and by appointment (call 256-609-4202). Adults, $3; others, $2.

A marker describing the multiple trials of the Scottsboro Boys is on the East Peachtree Street side of the Jackson County Courthouse in Scottsboro.

The 1931 verdict was hardly the end of the injustice brought against the young defendants. As the University of Missouri's website called Famous Trials (*https://famous-trials.com/scottsboroboys*) observed about the Scottsboro Boys case, "No crime in American history—let alone a crime that never occurred—produced as many trials, convictions, reversals, and retrials." In 2013, Alabama governor Robert Bentley signed legislation exonerating the Scottsboro Boys.

Morgan County Courthouse, 302 Lee Street NE, and Morgan County Archives, 624 Bank Street NE, Decatur

The retrials of the Scottsboro Boys occurred in Decatur. Presided over by Circuit Judge James E. Horton, the first retrial involved defendant Haywood Patterson. Patterson's new attorneys argued that Patterson and the other defendants could not receive a fair trial by a jury of their peers because no Blacks were allowed on juries. Judge Horton did not allow the motion. This triggered appeals eventually leading to another major US Supreme Court decision in

Norris v. Alabama. The ruling guaranteed the inclusion of Blacks in jury rolls.

Even after Patterson's defense team got one of his accusers to refute her previous testimony and deny that any rape had occurred, an all-white jury still convicted Patterson. Judge Horton stepped in and set aside the jury's guilty verdict. Eventually, all the defendants were set free.

At Morgan County Courthouse, visitors will find a marker on the Scottsboro Boys trials here on the Ferry Street side. Inside the building, Judge Horton's bench is preserved in the first-floor courtroom. The judge is remembered with a statue in front of the Limestone County Courthouse in Athens, Alabama (about fifteen miles from Decatur). Athens is where the judge wrote his decision overturning the jury's guilty verdict. That decision cost Horton his judgeship, as he was voted out in the next election.

The Morgan County Archives on Bank Street maintains an exhibit of photographs and the witness chair from the trial of Haywood Patterson. There is no charge to visit, and the archives are available weekdays from 8 a.m. to 4:30 p.m. Group guided tours can be arranged by calling archivist John Allison at (256) 351-4726. Decatur also has a self-guided African American Heritage tour of the Old Town Historic District; pick up a map at the local tourism office or download it at https://www.decaturcvb.org/

In October 2019, local media in Decatur reported that a Scottsboro Boys Museum was in the works, but progress has been slowed by the COVID-19 pandemic. The museum will be located at 815 Sycamore Street NW in Decatur. Check *https://sbcmuseum.org/* for updates.

The Scottsboro Boys were arrested in Paint Rock, a community between Scottsboro and Decatur. There is an Alabama historical marker near the site of the arrest. Find the marker on Church Street near the Paint Rock Senior Center, just off Lee Highway.

Danville

Jesse Owens Memorial Park and Museum, 7019 County Road 203

Adolf Hitler planned for the 1936 Berlin Olympics to be a showcase for his views on the superiority of the Aryan race. By winning four gold medals at the Olympic Games, Black American Jesse Owens spoiled Hitler's party.

In 1983, local residents (finally) wanted to honor their hometown hero by putting a monument on the lawn of the Lawrence County Courthouse. The all-white county commissioners denied that request and put one six miles away. Some vandals didn't want it in that less visible spot either; later in 1983, they hooked a chain around the monument and tried to pull it down.

Today, the Owens monument, a statue, a replica of the Olympic torch, and more are in this memorial park. A museum here relates Mr. Owens's accomplishments as an athlete and humanitarian.

The museum is open Monday to Saturday from 10 a.m. to 4 p.m., and Sunday from 1 p.m. to 4 p.m. The park gates are always open, giving visitors access to the playgrounds, sports facilities, and picnic areas.

Tuscaloosa

Foster Auditorium, University of Alabama, Sixth Avenue

This is the site of Governor George Wallace's stand in the schoolhouse door in 1963: his unsuccessful attempt to preclude Black students Vivian Malone and James Hood from enrolling at the University of Alabama.

The Malone-Hood Plaza is adjacent to Foster Auditorium; the plaza's centerpiece is the forty-foot Autherine Lucy Clock Tower. Ms. Lucy was the first Black to enroll at the university in 1956. Her 1956 enrollment lasted three days; she was expelled when the university said it could not protect her. In 1989, she enrolled here again with her daughter. They graduated together in 1992.

Four large bronze plaques at the clock tower tell the story of Autherine Lucy Foster, James Hood, and Vivian Malone Jones and the courage they displayed in opening doors rather than standing in front of them.

No hall, building, or plaza is named for George Wallace on the Tuscaloosa campus. His name was taken off a building on the Birmingham campus in February 2021.

Greensboro

The Safe House Black History Museum, 518 Martin Luther King Drive

Two weeks before his assassination, Dr. Martin Luther King Jr. sought refuge from the Ku Klux Klan inside this shotgun-style home. The late Theresa Burroughs, a close friend of the King family and an active participant in the civil rights movement, turned this house into a museum documenting the local struggle for equality. Displayed here are many unpublished photos of the civil rights struggle in Alabama's Black Belt.

All tours are by appointment (334-624-2030), ideally with two weeks' notice. Admission is $5 for adults.

Mobile

The 2018 discovery of the *Clotilda* in the Mobile River holds new possibilities for cultural tourism here in 2022 and beyond. The *Clotilda* was the last known ship to bring enslaved Africans illegally into the country in 1860, over fifty years after importing captured humans was banned. Water- and land-based tours are in the planning stages, as are an Africatown Welcome Center and a Heritage House to showcase relics pulled from the ship; an NPS site is also likely.

The Dora Franklin Finley African-American Heritage Trail

This downloadable tour covers over forty sites in Mobile related to the long history of African Americans here. Find the map and information on their guided bus and walking tours at *https://www.dffaaht.org/index.php*. The range of tour sites is broad, including the Slave Market marker on North Royal Street, Africatown, and the homes of baseball legends Leroy "Satchel" Paige and Henry "Hank" Aaron. Locations tied to the civil rights era are part of the tour; three are noted below.

Unity Point Park, 900 Spring Hill Avenue at North Broad Street

This triangular park is home to a statue of civil rights leader John LeFlore and former mayor Joseph Langan. LeFlore was a postal employee who founded the city's NAACP chapter in 1925 and remained a tireless civil rights advocate until his death in 1976.

The name of the park and the presence of this statue of the two men shaking hands suggest that the interracial cooperation that desegregated the city's buses, police department, and other local institutions was easy here. Historians can tell you it wasn't quite that way.

The post office across the street is a good place to park when visiting Unity Point.

Former Site of the Non-Partisan Voters League Office, 558 St. Francis Street

When Alabama expelled the NAACP in 1956, John LeFlore and others formed the Non-Partisan Voters League. Mr. LeFlore and the league won lawsuits concerning how city commissioners were selected and the desegregation of Mobile County's schools. A marker at this site honors Mr. LeFlore's civil rights activism. In June 1967, LeFlore's Chatague Avenue home was bombed. No one was injured in the blast; a yearlong investigation failed to produce any arrests. Perhaps Mobile wasn't quite a place of unity as the park mentioned earlier would have you believe.

Michael Donald Historical Marker, near 114 Michael Donald Avenue

Nineteen-year-old Michael Donald was one of the last lynching victims in America when members of the United Klans of America hung him from a tree on what is now Michael Donald Avenue in 1981. Two Klansmen were convicted for the murder.

A civil suit was brought against the United Klans of America (UKA), and a $7 million judgment was awarded to Mr. Donald's mother. The size of the judgment bankrupted the UKA, an organization also linked to the 1963 Sixteenth Street Baptist Church bombing in Birmingham and the 1965 murder of Viola Liuzzo near Selma.

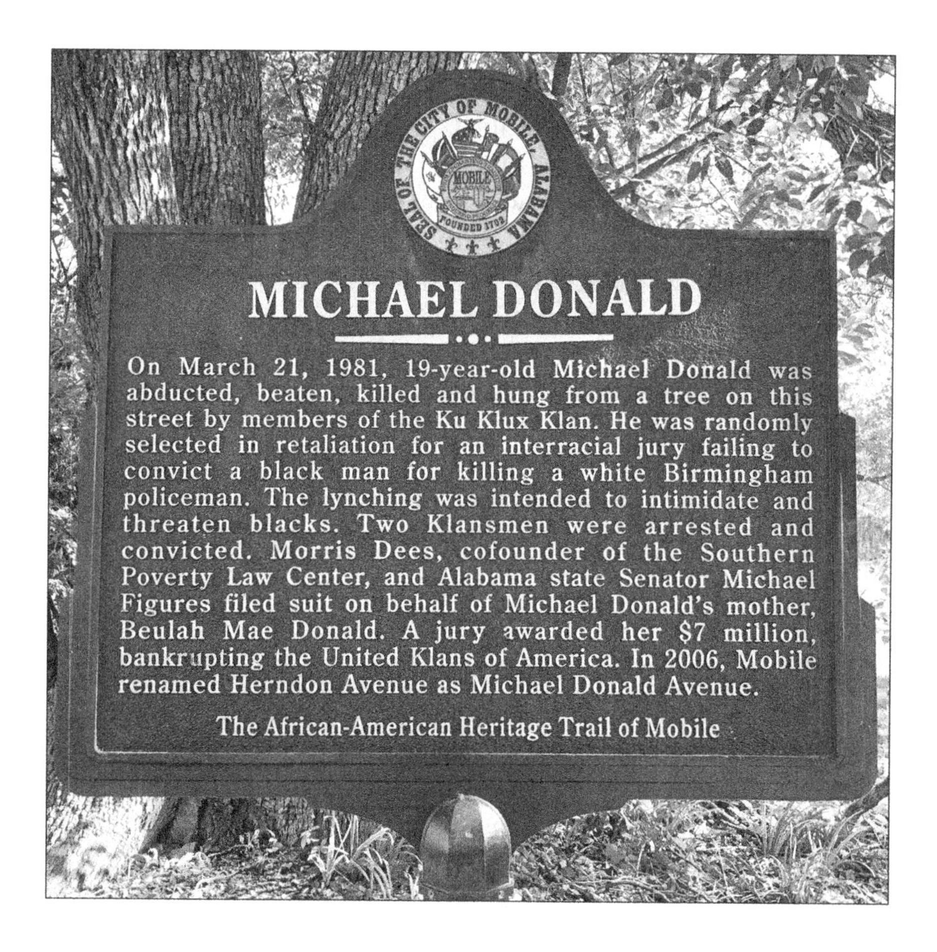

CHAPTER 19

Mississippi beyond the Loop

The recommended route takes you to Jackson and Philadelphia as well as to several locations in the Mississippi Delta. Some other relevant sites in Mississippi were covered in other chapters: Meridian in the Selma chapter and Holly Springs in the Memphis chapter. Several more cities within the state have important history. Nine are highlighted here.

We start in the southern half of the state, covering Biloxi, Hattiesburg, McComb, Brookhaven/Union Church, and Byram. Then, moving north of Interstate 20, which slices through Mississippi's mid-section, we visit two towns close to the Tennessee border: Hernando and Blue Mountain, a site with a serene-sounding name that was anything but that one night in 1964.

The final stories shift to two university towns: Oxford and Starkville. While Starkville is a spot lacking relevant markers, the university there is part of an important civil rights–era story.

Southern Mississippi

Biloxi

Biloxi Beach Wade-In Historical Marker, Beach Boulevard

Two months after the February 1960 Greensboro lunch-counter sit-ins, Dr. Gilbert Mason tried to lead a peaceful wade-in at the public beach in Biloxi on April 24, 1960. A not-so-peaceful white mob with bats, chains, clubs, and pipes had a different idea. Police at the scene acted as spectators, not protectors. The next month, Robert F. Kennedy's US Department of Justice (DOJ) brought a lawsuit to integrate the beaches. The DOJ eventually prevailed years later, long after the beaches were finally open to all.

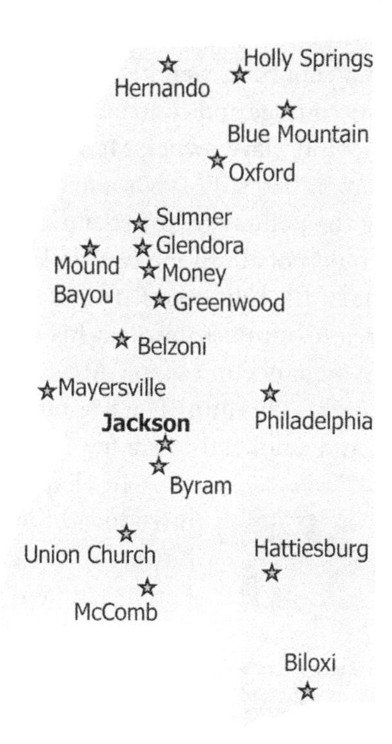

The marker is across from the Biloxi Lighthouse in the parking lot by the beach, to the right of the pier as you face the gulf. A section of Beach Boulevard you will likely drive on near the beach is named the Dr. Gilbert Mason Sr. Memorial Highway after the leader of the wade-in.

Hattiesburg

Freedom Summer Sites Driving Tour, Various Locations

Home to the University of Southern Mississippi (USM) and "some of the saddest civil rights stories in Mississippi,"[133] Hattiesburg hosted one of the state's largest groups of Freedom Summer volunteers in 1964. Hattiesburg's tourism bureau has prepared an extensive self-driving tour of Freedom Summer sites. Download the brochure at *http://hburgfreedomtrail.org/*. There is also an audio guide for the ninety-minute tour.

Vernon Dahmer Marker, 796 Monroe Road

Vernon Dahmer may not be as well known as others in the civil rights movement, but his courage and contributions deserve attention. The great-grandson of a white slave owner, Mr. Dahmer provided shelter to Freedom Riders in the early 1960s and led voter registration campaigns, even paying the poll tax, required at the time if you wanted to vote, for those who could not afford the two-dollar assessment.

At 2 a.m. on January 10, 1966, the Ku Klux Klan firebombed his home in rural Forrest County. To protect his wife and three children and give them a chance to escape, Mr. Dahmer ran through the burning house firing his shotgun. The fire burned him badly and he inhaled flames and smoke, dying a few hours later.

In chapter 12, we introduced the name Samuel Bowers in the context of Parchman Penitentiary. Bowers was tried four times for ordering the attack on Mr. Dahmer; all trials ended without a verdict. Finally, in 1998, an integrated jury sent this imperial wizard of the Klan to prison for life.

Vernon Dahmer's former homesite and this marker are six miles north of the first stop on the Freedom Summer Sites driving tour, the former site of the True Light Church. Entering "796 Monroe Road, Hattiesburg" into your GPS software will get you here but slow down as you near the marker; there is no shoulder on the road here.

Vernon Dahmer's grave is in the Shady Grove Baptist Church cemetery, located just north of the homesite marker. The church's address is 101 Church Street. The gravestone, which is near the edge of the parking lot, reads, "Husband, father, community leader, voting rights activist. If you don't vote, you don't count."

Clyde Kennard Marker, Kennard-Washington Hall, University of Southern Mississippi (USM)

Clyde Kennard's tragic story is also not well known. After serving in the Korean War as a distinguished paratrooper, Mr. Kennard enrolled at the University of Chicago. In his senior year, his stepfather became ill, forcing him to return to Mississippi to take over the family farm. Interested in completing his college degree, Kennard applied to the closest college, the all-white state school then called Mississippi Southern College in Hattiesburg, now USM.

Three times he tried to enroll but was repeatedly turned down. On the day of his last rejection in 1959, Mr. Kennard was arrested on campus. The charges were reckless driving and illegal possession of whiskey. Despite the fact Kennard was a devout Baptist and didn't drink, the judge convicted him and assessed a six-hundred-dollar fine.

The local White Citizens' Council was out to ruin him. After the bank foreclosed on his family farm, he was arrested when a well-known local thief accused Mr. Kennard of hiring him to steal chicken feed. The actual burglar was released, but Kennard was sentenced to seven years of hard labor at Parchman. There he complained of stomach pains, a condition that was left undiagnosed and untreated for months before a doctor found he had colon cancer. Even then, he was sent back to work in the prison's fields.

Comedian and activist Dick Gregory heard all of this from Medgar Evers and began a push to get Mr. Kennard out of Parchman; he raised the story in the national media. The adverse publicity convinced Governor Ross Barnett to pardon Mr. Kennard in the spring of 1963; however, on July 14, 1963, he died in a Chicago hospital, three weeks after he had turned thirty-six years old.

In 2006, Mr. Kennard was exonerated of the charges that led to his imprisonment in 1960—another case of justice severely delayed. In May 2018, Clyde Kennard was awarded a posthumous Honorary Doctorate from USM.

The Clyde Kennard marker is in front of the building on the USM campus named after him and Dr. Walter Washington (former president of Alcorn State University, a historically Black college): Kennard-Washington Hall. In December 2017, a portrait of Clyde Kennard joined the gallery of civil rights legends at Busboys and Poets at 2021 Fourteenth Street NW in Washington, DC.

Mount Zion Baptist Church, 900 Spencer Street

Dr. Martin Luther King Jr. visited Hattiesburg two weeks before his assassination in Memphis. He spoke at this church, one of several local churches important in the civil rights movement and known locally as "the civil rights church." The original church was demolished in 1993 but rebuilt at the same Spencer Street location where this marker stands.

McComb

C. C. Bryant Marker, 1521 C. C. Bryant Drive

McComb is just north of the Louisiana/Mississippi border. Labeled "the most violent city in Mississippi,"[134] it is a railroad town named for railroad man H. C. McComb. Many of its citizens were employed by the Illinois Central Gulf Railroad. A leading civil rights movement figure here, Curtis Conway (C. C.) Bryant was a railroad crane operator.

Mr. Bryant became the head of the NAACP in Pike County in 1954. In 1961, he invited civil rights organizer Bob Moses to launch a voter registration effort here, four years before the Voting Rights Act became law. Mr. Bryant arranged for the local Masonic Hall (no longer there) to be used by Mr. Moses and Medgar Evers in August 1961 to motivate residents to register to vote.

The summer of 1964 was a particularly violent one in McComb. Mr. Bryant dubbed it "hell on earth" for good reason: his home and a nearby barbershop he owned were bombed on June 22, 1964; the same night, two other homes of Black leaders were also bombed. Violence against Blacks and their property continued through the summer. The marker honoring Mr. Bryant's commitment and persistence is on the road named in his honor.

Brookhaven/Union Church

Lamar Smith Gravesite, Former Mount Carmel Cemetery, Union Church

In 1955, Lamar Smith, a sixty-three-year-old Black World War I veteran, was trying to help people to vote. On August 13, Mr. Smith went to the Lincoln County Courthouse to get absentee ballots for

African American registered voters who feared going to the polls in person. There, on the courthouse lawn and in front of many witnesses, he was beaten by three men and shot, at 10 a.m.! A later FBI investigation reported the attackers killed Mr. Smith "in front of the sheriff."[135]

A grand jury convened in Brookhaven while national attention was focused on the Emmett Till murder. On September 13, 1955, the grand jury failed to indict the three men for any crime in connection to the attack on Mr. Smith.

No marker in Brookhaven makes sure people remember the work of Lamar Smith and that his murder went unpunished. Mr. Smith is buried in Union Church, Mississippi (Lincoln County), in what used to be called Mount Carmel Cemetery. It is near the intersection of Coleman Lane NW and Mississippi Highway 550. Addresses are tricky in this rural area. Use GPS coordinates 31.67009, -90.68961 to locate the small cemetery, eighteen miles northwest of Brookhaven.

Mr. Smith's name is on the list of Civil Rights Martyrs on the memorial at the Southern Poverty Law Center in Montgomery, Alabama.

Byram

Other cities in the southern part of Mississippi produced unsung heroes in the struggle for equality like Vernon Dahmer, Clyde Kennard, Lamar Smith and C. C. Bryant. Byram's inclusion here raises the name of one of the movement's haters: Byron De La Beckwith. At a Pearl River fishing camp in Byram, he bragged to his fellow Klansman, and to Delmar Dennis, an undercover FBI informant, that he was Medgar Evers's killer.

His admission here is reported by Bobby Delaughter, the prosecutor who finally convicted Byron De La Beckwith for the Evers murder in 1993, in his book *Never Too Late: A Prosecutor's Story of Justice in the Medgar Evers Case.* In it, Delaughter writes about interviewing former Klansman turned FBI informant Dennis about a Klan meeting in Byram in August 1965. To get to the meeting, Dennis recalled walking across "a rickety bridge." Delaughter asked, "The swinging bridge?" "Yeah," replied Dennis.[136]

The swinging bridge in Byram is on the National Registry of Historic Places, not for this meeting but rather for its engineering. Find the bridge by putting "Byram Swinging Bridge" into Google Maps.

Northern Mississippi

Hernando

The March against Fear Marker, 4243 State Highway 51

On June 5, 1966, James Meredith left Memphis to begin his 220-mile march through Mississippi. He called the trek the March against Fear, seeking to encourage Black voter registration throughout the state; the Voting Rights Act had been signed by President Lyndon Johnson the previous year. The next day, Mr. Meredith was shot.

If you locate Hernando on a map, you notice that he hadn't gotten too far into Mississippi. A thirty-year-old Klansman emerged from the woods and shot Mr. Meredith with a 16-gauge shotgun. The shooter served eighteen months of a five-year sentence.

Others continued the march while Mr. Meredith recovered from his wounds. As the marchers neared Jackson, the capital, he was able to rejoin the march on June 25 and walked arm in arm with Dr. Martin Luther King Jr. On the next day, an estimated fifteen thousand strong proceeded into Jackson, making this the largest civil rights march in Mississippi history.

The marker can be found at the VFW Post 7531 building at 4243 Highway 51, south of Hernando, near the small tank on the property. Plenty of parking.

Oxford

James Meredith Enrollment Memorials,
University of Mississippi Campus Locations

Until 1962, the University of Mississippi had been an all-white institution for 114 years. James Meredith, an Air Force staff sergeant, wanted to change this by transferring here from Jackson State University. His application was rejected. On September 13, 1962, a federal court ordered that Mr. Meredith be admitted.

Resistance to the court order was massive, from Governor Ross Barnett on down. Retired general Edwin Walker (whom we first met on the other side of an integration battle in Little Rock) rallied segregationists to protest the admission of Mr. Meredith. A riot occurred on Sunday, September 30, and two people were killed, one a French journalist (Paul Guihard), and 160 marshals were hurt.

Protected by National Guardsmen and federal troops, James Meredith enrolled on October 1, 1962. Despite ongoing harassment, he graduated on August 18, 1963, with a degree in political science.

A marker for what happened at the university in the fall of 1962 is on campus between the Lyceum and the library. While near the Lyceum, a hospital during the Civil War, note the bullet marks on the front columns. They are remnants of the 1962 violence, not the Civil War.

There is also a statue of James Meredith on campus. Unveiled in October 2006, forty-years after the historic enrollment, the statue depicts Mr. Meredith passing through a doorway marked "Courage." This monument is also located between the Lyceum and the library. In 2014, a student was sentenced to six months in prison, followed by twelve months' supervised release, for putting a noose around the neck of the statue of Mr. Meredith.[137]

Not Bryon De La Beckwith *Again*?

The segregationist General Edwin Walker had a fan in Byron De La Beckwith, the man ultimately convicted in 1993 of murdering Medgar Evers in 1963.

When the court ordered James Meredith to be enrolled at the University of Mississippi in 1962, Byron De La Beckwith knew where he needed to go. He headed to Oxford. Even though the trouble at the university took place months before Medgar Evers was assassinated, De La Beckwith had a reputation. As he traveled to Oxford, he was stopped by "some friendly police" who were expecting him. With some difficulty, they convinced him to go back.[138]

Byron De La Beckwith has a connection to another state university, Mississippi State. The school was known as Mississippi State College in 1940. In the fall of that year, the man who would murder Medgar Evers enrolled at the Starkville institution.

Byron De La Beckwith had finally graduated from high school, at twenty years old. With college grades so poor, he dropped out after the midterm.[139]

Blue Mountain

The Carpenters for Christmas Marker, Antioch Baptist Church, 3651 County Road 700, 5 Miles East of Blue Mountain in Tippah County

This intriguingly named location is admittedly off the beaten path. And it doesn't celebrate a Christmas recording by a famous 1970s brother-and-sister singing duo.

What happened here, however, is so representative of the determination and unity of disparate groups of people within the movement. On October 30, 1964, Fannie Lou Hamer of Ruleville spoke at a Mississippi Freedom Democratic Party rally at this small, rural church. The rally included a voter registration push as an election was coming up the following week. The church was to be a polling place.

Later that same night, the church was burned to the ground. Antioch Missionary Baptist Church was one of many churches set on fire in 1964 across the South. At Oberlin College in Ohio, students and faculty decided something needed to be done to call attention to the destruction of southern churches. They organized a rebuilding project and chose this church for their initial effort.

With local help, volunteers, donated material, and national media attention, the church was sufficiently rebuilt to hold Christmas services there in 1964. The building was fully operational the first week of January. Search "Antioch Missionary Baptist Church, Tippah County" to locate the marker.

"A Game That Should Not Be Forgotten"

That is how ESPN described an NCAA basketball game played in 1963. Who played? Was the championship at stake? What made the game so important? Why mention it in this book?

The game was an NCAA tournament regional semifinal between Mississippi State University (MSU) of Starkville and Loyola University of Chicago. Loyola had four Black players in its starting five.

In Mississippi, the races were separated in schools, buses, lunch counters, movie theaters, and more. A basketball court wasn't going to be an exception. In fact, Mississippi had an unwritten but then adhered-to law prohibiting state schools from participating in sports competitions against integrated teams. This presented a big problem for MSU in the NCAA tournament.

The state's vocal segregationist governor, Ross Barnett, didn't hide his intentions to keep the team from playing Loyola. A judge issued a temporary injunction to prevent the team from leaving Mississippi. However, some fans, Coach James "Babe" McCarthy, and Mississippi State president Dean Colvard wanted the team to play.

But then what ESPN senior writer Dana O'Neil called "perhaps the best end-around in sports history" occurred.

continued

continued from previous page

Colvard told Coach McCarthy to head to Tennessee and stay in Memphis. To prevent the injunction from being served on him, President Colvard went to Alabama for a speaking engagement. Ms. O'Neil described the rest of the subterfuge to get the team out of the state: "The next day, an assistant coach ferried the freshmen and some of the reserve players to a private plane as decoys and, when they saw that the coast was clear, called for the rest of the team to join them."[140]

With coaches and players together in Tennessee, they flew on to East Lansing, Michigan, for what some refer to as the "Game of Change" on March 15, 1963.

In Chicago, the Loyola team was receiving hate mail—at their dorm addresses, no less. Having played teams in the South, Loyola was accustomed to vitriol from fans at these games. However, personally addressed hate mail ratcheted the tension up a notch.

The game began with a handshake between team captains Jerry Harkness (Loyola) and Joe Dan Gold (Mississippi State). That didn't go over well with many of MSU's fans.

Loyola won 61-51 and went on to win the national title that year. There are no memorials in Starkville to the loss. The championship trophy is in an appropriate case in Chicago.

While the contest was often referred to as the "Game of Change," it didn't usher in much change in Mississippi. As you've read, many brutal acts occurred in Mississippi in 1963 and 1964. The first Black basketball player didn't suit up for MSU until 1972.

CHAPTER 20

Arkansas beyond Little Rock

The school desegregation crisis of 1957 is the major civil rights–era event that occurred in Arkansas. Other civil rights actions—sit-ins and Freedom Rides—were largely centered in and around Little Rock. In fact, all thirty-six locations noted on the Arkansas Civil Rights History app are Little Rock–centric.

Five Arkansas communities beyond the state capital have places a civil rights enthusiast may want to visit. One of these, Helena, is a possible stop between the Mississippi Delta area and Little Rock; another, Tyronza, is between Little Rock and Memphis. The other three (Pine Bluff, Arkansas City, and Rohwer) are downstate from the capital city.

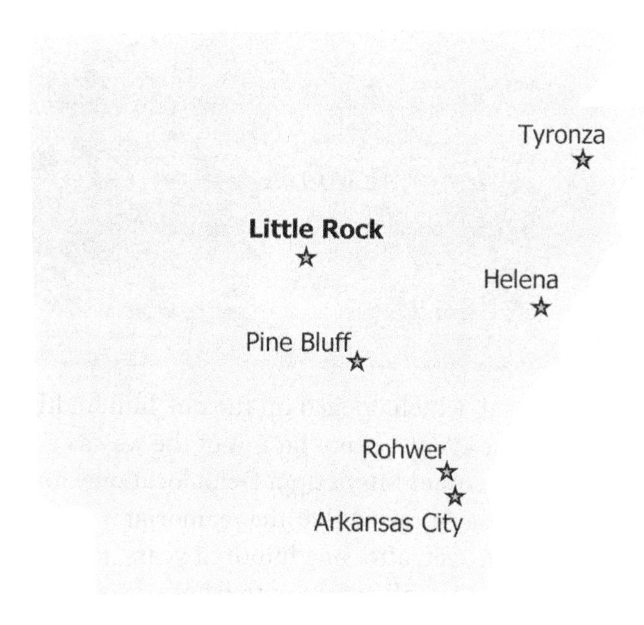

Helena

The Elaine Massacre Memorial, 622 Walnut Street

In September 1919, cotton prices were favorable. African American sharecroppers wanted their fair share of those good prices from their landowners. A group of sharecroppers met in a church in Hoop Spur, just north of Elaine to discuss how to do just that. Outside of that church, there were armed Black guards to protect those inside. Also nearby were two white law officers. No one is sure who fired the first shot, but when gunfire erupted, one officer lay dead.

Fearing a Black uprising, Helena officials sent armed white posses to the area and asked the governor to send troops. In this charged atmosphere, posses, mobs from neighboring counties, and federal troops murdered an unknown number of African Americans; estimates range from 100 and up. An estimated 300 African Americans were jailed, and 122 were charged with first-degree murder, intent to kill, or a lesser charge.

This memorial, which opened on the one hundredth anniversary of these events, is not far out of the way as you travel between Sumner (or other Mississippi Delta locations) and Little Rock. Concern has been raised that the memorial is in Helena and not in or near Elaine; yet, after one hundred years, it is good that something is in place to call attention to what occurred in 1919.

Tyronza

Southern Tenant Farmers Museum, 117 South Main Street

The Elaine Massacre resulted from the exploitation of labor by landowners. Landowners provided little transparency on the price they received for what sharecroppers grew. At this museum in Tyronza, you will learn about the highly unlikely alliance of white and Black sharecroppers. In 1934, they formed the racially integrated Southern Tenant Farmers Union.

The museum is open from Tuesday to Saturday, 9 a.m. to 3 p.m. A donation of $3 to $5 per person is requested.

Pine Bluff

University Museum and Cultural Center (UMCC), Childress Hall, University of Arkansas at Pine Bluff

At this historically Black university, visitors experience exhibits describing the challenges its staff and students faced in segregated Arkansas. Check the UMCC's website for special exhibits. A prepandemic exhibit focused on the Student Nonviolent Coordinating Committee's role in organizing grassroots efforts in the Mississippi Delta region within Arkansas.

There is no charge to visit the center; open weekdays from 8 a.m. to 5 p.m. Groups larger than ten should call in advance at (870) 575-8230.

Arkansas City, McGehee, and Rohwer

John H. Johnson Cultural and Educational Museum, Arkansas City

John H. Johnson founded the major publishing company bearing his name and launched significant magazine titles like *Ebony* and *Jet*. The museum, a replica of Mr. Johnson's boyhood home, contains memorabilia of his early years in Arkansas City as well his legendary business career. Visit on weekdays between 9 a.m. and 3 p.m.

Japanese American Internment Museum, 100 South Railroad Street, McGehee and the Rohwer Relocation Center Memorial Cemetery, State Highway 1, Rohwer

Discrimination can take many forms and materialize in different ways. Though not directly related to the Black struggle for freedom, the events memorialized here constitute another case of discrimination and injustice against American citizens.

On February 19, 1942, President Franklin Roosevelt signed Executive Order 9066; the order and a subsequent act of Congress caused some areas in the western United States to be designated as exclusion zones, meaning that the military could prohibit any person from being within them. As a result, an estimated 120,000 people of Japanese descent, two-thirds of them American citizens, were forced to move from their homes and were held in relocation or internment camps as far east as Arkansas.

This museum is twelve miles west of Arkansas City. It's open Tuesday to Saturday from 9 a.m. to 4 p.m. Admission is $5 and free for children and college and school groups. The actual internment camps in Arkansas were in Jerome (eighteen miles south of McGehee and in Rohwer, thirteen miles north of McGehee. The Rohwer Relocation Center Memorial Cemetery is off Arkansas Highway 1. A riveting documentary on the treatment of Japanese Americans during World War II is *Silent Sacrifice: Stories of Japanese American Incarceration.*

CHAPTER 21

Tennessee beyond Memphis

The assassination of Dr. Martin Luther King Jr. in Memphis in 1968 dominates civil rights history within Tennessee, and the National Civil Rights Museum at the Lorraine Motel is the primary site in the state to visit. As in other southern states, activism in the form of school desegregation, lunch-counter sit-ins, and Freedom Ride participation took place throughout the civil rights period, and many sites are memorialized across the (very wide) state.

An important aspect of Tennessee's contribution in the fight for equality was the training of civil rights leaders who provided inspiration to others through their unwavering courage and strategic brilliance. Just over the state's southern border with Alabama and Georgia is the town of Monteagle, the former home of the Highlander Folk School. There, in the 1950s, leaders like Rosa Parks and John Lewis received training in nonviolence. Others who came to Highlander included Septima Clark, Dr. King, and Ralph Abernathy.

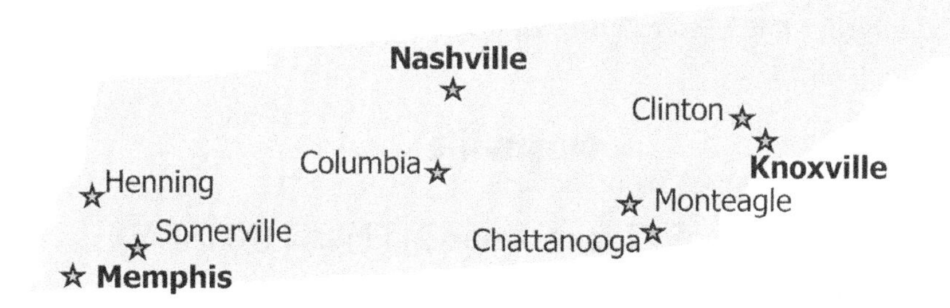

Nashville was a major source of movement organizers. The Nashville Student Movement (NSM) produced young leaders who were on the front lines of some of the major civil rights events of the time. Blessed with talent from Nashville's four historically Black colleges (American Baptist Theological Seminary, Fisk University, Meharry Medical College, and Tennessee Agricultural & Industrial), the NSM's mark came from heroes who included the following:

- *James Lawson*—inspirational leader of the NSM, who provided strategic direction during the Memphis sanitation strike.
- *Congressman John Lewis*—Freedom Rider, speaker at the 1963 March on Washington, a victim of police violence on Bloody Sunday in Selma, and an ever-present warrior for social justice.
- *Diane Nash*—Founding member of the Student Nonviolent Coordinating Committee (SNCC), veteran of sit-ins in Nashville and Rock Hill, South Carolina, where she was arrested and jailed.
- *C. T. Vivian*—Freedom Rider, key lieutenant to Dr. King in the Southern Christian Leadership Conference (SCLC).
- *Bernard Lafayette*—SNCC leader in Selma, victim of racial violence as a Freedom Rider, jailed over two dozen times for civil rights activities.

This chapter begins with civil rights locations in Nashville and then branches out to other relevant sites across Tennessee. With several interstates leading into and out of Nashville and with its reasonable proximity (three to four hours) to loop cities Memphis, Birmingham, and Atlanta, Nashville makes a good stopping point for travelers from midwestern cities that are over a day's drive to one of those loop cities.

Nashville

National Museum of African American Music (NMAAM), 510 Broadway

Located across from the Ryman Auditorium, this is one of the newest museums (as of 2021) covering African American history and achievement. With interactive content focused on every musical genre from spirituals to hip-hop inside this fifty-thousand-square-foot facility, there is something for everyone. Of particular interest to those interested in the civil rights era is the *One Nation under a Groove* gallery, covering 1940 to the current day.

The museum suggests blocking out ninety minutes for a visit. That will not be long enough for true music lovers, especially when you begin to build your own playlist here. Admission is $24.95 for adults; $18.75 for students, teachers, and seniors; $13.50 for guests ages 7 to 17; and free for those under 7. NMAAM is open from 9 a.m. to 5 p.m., Wednesday through Monday, with a 7 p.m. closing on Thursday. Tickets are timed-entry, and tours are self-guided.

Former Office Site of the Nashville Student Movement, 1905 Jefferson Street

A historical marker is located on the south side of Jefferson Street. Another marker noting the work of the NSM to desegregate the city's lunch counters is at the intersection of Dr. D. B. Todd Jr. Boulevard and Jefferson Street, right next to the Fisk University sign at this side of campus.

Three sites within a half-mile walk of the former NSM office are also worthy of note:

- *The Looby Home at 2010 Meharry Boulevard.* Z. Alexander Looby played an important role in desegregating Nashville public schools and defending those involved in the 1960 lunch-counter sit-ins. His home at this address was bombed on April 19, 1960; a marker here memorializes Mr. Looby's critical but too often overlooked contributions.

- *St. Anselm's Episcopal Church, 2008 Meharry Boulevard.* Three lynching victims are remembered on a marker in the front yard of this church to the left of the red doors. Brothers Henry and Ephraim Grizzard were murdered by separate mobs in April 1892, while Samuel Smith was killed in December 1924. The church's website has a detailed account of these racial violence incidents.

- *The Jubilee Singers of Fisk University*. Fisk counts many notables among its alums, including W. E. B. Du Bois, Ida B. Wells, and John Lewis. On the campus next to Jubilee Hall is a marker commemorating the Jubilee Singers and their 1871 tour of the United States and Europe to raise funds for the university.

Clark Memorial United Methodist Church, 1014 Fourteenth Avenue North

The church is three tenths of a mile from Jubilee Hall at Fisk University. At Clark Memorial, Rev. James Lawson held training sessions in nonviolence in 1958; three years later, Dr. King conducted SCLC's annual meeting here. The marker here honors Dr. Matthew Walker, a graduate of Nashville's Meharry Medical College. He was instrumental in securing a 1968 federal grant to start the Meharry Neighborhood Health Center. Today, the Matthew Walker Neighborhood Health Center at the Meharry Medical College is named in his honor.

Woolworth on Fifth Avenue, 221 Fifth Avenue North

This registered historic site saw the first lunch-counter sit-ins in Nashville in 1960. On several occasions between February 13 and April 11, 1960, groups of African American college students sought to desegregate Nashville lunch counters here and elsewhere. They were denied service, and many were arrested.

Civil rights attorney Z. Alexander Looby defended the students who were arrested. As mentioned, the Looby home was bombed. Neither Looby nor his wife were hurt but over one hundred windows were blown out at the nearby Meharry Medical College, injuring some students. That same day, thousands of students marched to the local courthouse. Diane Nash is credited with confronting Mayor Ben West on whether segregation of lunch counters was moral. He replied that it was not, and the process of desegregating downtown lunch counters began.

Part of the Fifth Avenue Historic District, the former Woolworth's building today is a restaurant and event venue; it's a short walk from the National Museum of African American Music.

The Civil Rights Room at the Nashville Public Library, 615 Church Street

Nashville doesn't have a civil rights–focused museum, but this would come closest to serving as an option for anyone wanting to provide children a glimpse at the city's role in the civil rights era. Black-and-white photos show local activism and activists, and there's a timeline of national and local civil rights events—and a replica lunch counter.

The room is open during regular library hours. Groups must reserve in advance (615- 862-5782). Tours can be tailored to different age groups and arranged via the library's website.

Z. Alexander Looby and the Columbia "Race Riot" of 1946

World War II was only over for about six months when Black navy veteran James Stephenson accompanied his mother, Gladys, to a Columbia department store. They were picking up her repaired radio. The white clerk was abusive toward Mrs. Stephenson when a dispute arose about the repair. James stepped in. The clerk ended up going through a window, and both Stephensons ended up under arrest. They pled guilty and paid a fifty-dollar fine.

That should have been the end of the story, but the clerk's father pressed for charging Stephenson with felony assault with the intent to commit murder. Bond was posted, and Stephenson returned home that evening.

Overnight, trouble began. A white mob assembled, and four white police officers went into the Black business district. A shout for the officers to stop came from a group of African American citizens, including many World War II veterans. When they didn't stop, shots were fired, and the four officers were wounded.

Reinforcements from the state highway patrol came to Columbia. With some of the town's whites, the highway patrolmen surrounded the Black business district. During

continued

continued from previous page

the early morning of February 26, the patrolmen entered the district, firing into buildings. They stole cash and goods, searched homes without warrants, and took any firearms they found.

As the sweep ended, over one hundred Blacks were under arrest; none were granted bail. About three hundred weapons were confiscated. The "riot" grabbed local and national attention. NAACP attorneys Thurgood Marshall and William White went to Columbia to mount a defense for those accused. Z. Alexander Looby was part of the defense team.

Two days after the police sweep, police were interrogating three of those arrested. When the prisoners allegedly went for the guns of the officers, two of the prisoners ended up dead and the third was wounded. None of the policemen were charged by an all-white grand jury. As for the dozens of Blacks arrested on February 26, twenty-five were tried. Only one conviction resulted, on charges of shooting at a police officer.

The marker memorializing these events of 1946 is located at 115 East Eighth Street in Columbia.

Chattanooga

The Bessie Smith Cultural Center, 200 East Martin Luther King Boulevard

The center, affectionately called "The Bessie" by locals, showcases the contributions of African Americans to the development of Chattanooga. In particular, visitors can enjoy exhibits featuring the "Empress of the Blues," Bessie Smith.

The center, formerly known as the Chattanooga African American Museum / Bessie Smith Performance Hall, is open Tuesday to Friday, 10 a.m. to 5 p.m., and Saturday from 10 a.m. to 3 p.m. Adult admission is $10, with discounts for seniors and those under 12. Tours are available with advanced reservations.

Henning

Alex Haley Museum, 200 South Church Street

The eight-part TV miniseries based on Mr. Haley's Pulitzer Prize–winning book *Roots* captivated audiences in 1977. The story of the captured Mandingo youth, Kunta Kinte, began on the porch of this home five decades earlier. Here, young Alex would absorb the tales of Kunta Kinte from his grandmother and other relatives.

After viewing a short documentary film, visitors can tour the restored boyhood home of Alex Haley which contains some of the author's childhood memorabilia and family artifacts.

Open Tuesday through Saturday, 10 a.m. to 5 p.m., and Sunday by appointment only for groups. Adults, $10; seniors, $9; students ages 5 to 18, $8; under 5 are free.

Fort Pillow State Park, 3122 Park Road

This park is twenty miles west of the Alex Haley Museum. A Civil War–era attack by the Confederate Army at the fort gives the site relevance in African American history,

In 1864, Union forces held this fort along the Mississippi with 570 troops; nearly half were formerly enslaved. The Confederates attacked Fort Pillow, eventually retaking it and training their assault on the Black Union soldiers, killing 90 percent of them. Word of this spread to Black soldiers in other units within the Union forces. "Remember Fort Pillow" became a battle cry, motivating Black troops for the rest of the Civil War.

A Fort Pillow marker is about a half mile from the Alex Haley Museum, at the intersection of Jefferson Davis Highway (US 51) and Graves Street (State Highway 87). Another Fort Pillow marker is in the **Memphis National Cemetery**, 3568 Townes Avenue, nine miles east of the National Civil Rights Museum.

Clinton

Green McAdoo Cultural Center, 101 School Street

It was August 1956, two years after the *Brown v. Board of Education* desegregation decision and a year after the Supreme

Court's ambiguous clarification that school desegregation should proceed "with all deliberate speed." And, of course, it was a year before the Little Rock Nine first entered Central High School. A dozen courageous Black students enrolled at previously all-white Clinton High School and gave it the distinction of becoming the first desegregated high school in the South.

The museum here, located in the former elementary school which the Clinton 12 attended, tells the story of this less well-known chapter of post-*Brown* desegregation. It is open Tuesday through Saturday from 9:30 a.m. to 5:30 p.m. Outside the center are a dozen life-sized bronze statues honoring each of the twelve young civil rights pioneers.

Located about six miles from Interstate 75, the center is a possible stop for those heading to Atlanta from Cincinnati, Dayton, Cleveland, Detroit, and other cities.

Monteagle

Highlander Folk School Memorial Marker, on Tracy Road at Justus Street Intersection

Only two miles off Interstate 24 if you are traveling between Nashville and Atlanta is this marker near the former location of the Highlander Folk School. This nonprofit institution was important before and during the civil rights era as a training ground for social justice activists. Rosa Parks attended Highlander in the months before her refusal to change seats on a Montgomery bus, and Dr. Martin Luther King Jr. delivered the keynote address here for the school's twenty-fifth anniversary in 1957.

Knoxville

Beck Cultural Exchange Center, 1927 Dandridge Avenue

This facility serves as the state's primary repository of Black history and culture in East Tennessee. One permanent exhibit is the *Pioneer Stairway*, which is lined with photos and the achievements of Black individuals. A recent temporary exhibit focused on the musical contributions of African Americans from the state.

The museum is open Tuesday to Saturday, 10 a.m. to 6 p.m., and admission is free.

"Oh, Deep in My Heart, I Do Believe"

Recognize those lyrics? Of course, you do. They are words from the anthem of the civil rights era, "We Shall Overcome."

It's a simple song. Sing it and every syllable of every word is slowly enunciated. As simple as the song is, its lineage is more complex. One thing that music historians agree on is the role that the Highlander Folk School in Monteagle, Tennessee, played in adapting a pre–Civil War spiritual to become one of the most recognizable pieces of music of the twentieth century.

The enslaved sang a spiritual called "I'll Be All Right." During a strike at a South Carolina tobacco processing plant in the 1940s, that song boosted the morale of striking Black workers. A version of the song ended up at a workshop at the Highlander Folk School, where the school's cultural director, Zilphia Horton, was particularly taken by the repeated lyric "I'll overcome" in the song.

Ms. Horton changed that lyric to "We will overcome," slowed down the tempo, and added more verses. In 1947, she introduced the tune to folksinger Pete Seeger, who changed the main lyric to "We shall overcome" to make it easier to sing.

Over a decade passed before Seeger strummed the tune for Guy Carawan, who became the music director at Highlander after Ms. Horton's death. Carawan tried different arrangements before teaching the song in February 1960 at Highlander to those who would lead sit-ins in Nashville. In April 1960, he taught the song to the activists at the founding meeting of the Student Nonviolent Coordinating Committee (SNCC) at Shaw University in Raleigh, North Carolina. From there, the song caught fire across the civil rights movement.

By 1971, the Highlander Folk School had been reincorporated as the Highlander Research and Education Center and in that year moved to New Market, Tennessee. The state of Tennessee, which stripped the Highlander Folk School of its nonprofit status in 1961 and sold off its property and land in Monteagle, later put up a marker near the site of the school.

Somerville

Marker at the Former Site of the Fayette County Tent City, Intersection of TN Highway 76 and Lagrange Road

When African American citizens sought to register to vote, a common intimidation tactic by white landowners was to push Black sharecroppers off their property. That happened in Lowndes County, Alabama, and it happened here and in adjacent Haywood County, Tennessee. In Lowndes County and here in Somerville (just east of Memphis), tent cities (sometimes called "freedom villages") came into existence for the displaced Black citizens.

In July 1962, the US Department of Justice won a court injunction banning retaliation against citizens who wanted to exercise their right to vote.

281 We Will Overcome

By FTA-CIO Workers
Highlander Students

This simple and moving hymn tune becomes especially thrilling when you consider where the song was first sung. It was learned by Zilphia Horton of the Highlander Folk School, in Tennessee, from members of the CIO Food and Tobacco Workers Union. Many a visitor to the south has never forgotten hearing the rich harmonies of some little band, and the determination in these words, even though surrounded on all sides by hate, Jim Crow and all the forces of power and money.

Zilphia writes: "It was first sung in Charleston, S.C., and...one of the stanzas of the original hymn was...'we will overcome'...At school here they naturally added other verses...Its strong emotional appeal and simple dignity never fails to hit people. It sort of stops them cold silent."

The Lord will see us through,
The Lord will see us through,
The Lord will see us through, some day,
(CHORUS:)

We're on to victory . . .
(CHORUS:)

We will overcome . . .
(CHORUS:)

PART FOUR

TRAVELING FREEDOM'S ROAD ELSEWHERE IN THE SOUTH

Muhammad Ali mugs for Malcolm X
at the Hampton House in Miami

CHAPTER 22

Florida

Juan Ponce de Leon landed in Florida in 1513. His crew included Juan Garrido, identified by Harvard professor Dr. Henry Louis Gates Jr. as the first African to arrive in what would become America. The history of Blacks in today's Florida is very long, and not always pleasant. As you travel the state visiting sites associated with African American history, you learn that this history was often marked by racial discrimination and violence. Examples include

- The fiery destruction of the Black-dominant town of Rosewood in 1923.
- A bombing in Mims on Christmas Day 1951 that claimed the life of the first NAACP official killed in the modern civil rights era.
- An ugly incident at a motel pool in St. Augustine in 1964 that played a role in passage of the Civil Rights Act of 1964.

This chapter guides readers to these sites and a dozen more.

Your Florida travels will bring you into contact with some of the most important people in the movement for equality. Daytona Beach is the birthplace of Howard Thurman, an author and philosopher who had a

Did You Know?

Florida Georgia Line was more than a musical duo.

Before 1821, the Florida-Georgia line was an international boundary. Florida was a Spanish colony, while Georgia was a British colony, and after the American Revolution, a part of the United States.

Florida remained a Spanish colony until the Adams-Onis Treaty was ratified in 1821. The state was admitted to the Union in 1845.

major impact on Dr. Martin Luther King Jr. Other major figures like educator Mary McLeod Bethune and baseball Hall of Famer Jackie Robinson have connections to the state, with sites honoring both of them as well as Dr. Thurman in Daytona Beach.

The chapter divides the state into North, Central, and South regions. In the northern part of the state, one could start in Panama City in the Panhandle and the Central Time Zone. A court case there established the principle that those accused of a crime are entitled to legal representation. Traveling east and moving into Eastern Time, visitors to Tallahassee can learn about a bus boycott there in 1956 modeled after the successful Montgomery action that began in 1955.

Further east on the Atlantic Ocean side of the state are two more cities of historical note:

- *Jacksonville* is the site of the "Ax Handle Memorial." The name alone suggests another act of racial violence.

- *St. Augustine* has history ranging from Florida's Spanish colonial period in the 1500s to the twentieth-century's civil rights era.

The drive across northern Florida on I-10 is long. From Panama City to Jacksonville and then south on I-95 to St. Augustine requires five hours of driving, not including any other stops, so just these visits alone are likely more than a day trip.

Central Florida provides heritage tourists and Floridians a wide range of experiences as well. Within this section of the chapter, we cover

- *Along the Atlantic Coast*: Daytona Beach, New Smyrna Beach, and Mims
- *Inland*: Orlando, Eatonville, and Tavares
- *On the Gulf*: St. Petersburg and Sarasota

Among the things you can see are the stadium where Jackie Robinson made his debut with the Brooklyn Dodgers organization in Daytona Beach. There, he played in an exhibition game as a member of the Dodgers' farm team, the Montreal Royals, on March 17, 1946.

In Tavares, a memorial maker tells a story sadly too similar to that of Alabama's Scottsboro Boys. The Groveland Four were accused of rape in 1949, although eventually pardoned by the state's governor seventy years later. Harry Moore of Mims, Florida, investigated the shooting death of one of the Groveland Four. He and his wife were victims of the bombing referenced earlier. Learn more about the Moores at a museum named after them in Mims.

Residents and tourists can find modest museums focused on aspects of the quest for equality in Orlando, New Smyrna Beach, and St. Petersburg.

The southern part of the state currently has fewer opportunities to connect with African American history, so after pointing out a nightclub and hotel of historical importance in the Jim Crow era plus three possible locations to visit in Fort Lauderdale, the chapter ends with a discussion of convict leasing. This practice of turning those convicted of trumped-up charges like vagrancy into laborers—leased out by various governmental entities to private companies—played a major but not well-known role in developing Florida. The *Washington Post* called the use of convict leasing here "the whitewashed history of the Sunshine State."[141] Convict leasing was not unique to Florida by any means.

Northern Florida

Panama City

The Gideon v. Wainwright Marker, 300 East Fourth Street

How many times have you heard these words in a television drama? "You have the right to an attorney. If you can't afford an attorney, one will be provided for you." This civil right, important to all Americans, was established for noncapital felonies by a case first tried at the Bay County (Florida) Courthouse, the site of this marker.

Clarence Gideon was charged with stealing fifty dollars and a bottle of wine from a local pool hall. His request for an attorney was denied. He was forced to defend himself and he lost. From prison, he wrote to the US Supreme Court, sharing the denied request for legal help. The high court took the case, and in a 1963 unanimous decision affirmed the right of criminal defendants to have an attorney. Gideon received a second trial and was acquitted.

This marker is on the McKenzie Avenue side of the courthouse. Also on the same McKenzie Avenue side of the building is a small memorial to Dr. Martin Luther King Jr.

Tallahassee

John Gilmore Riley Center and Museum, 419 East Jefferson Street

The Riley Center and Museum takes visitors back in time to the post–Civil War Reconstruction era. The Riley House built in 1890 now represents the once-thriving Black neighborhood of Smokey Hollow. Born enslaved, John Riley died a millionaire and had an impact on Tallahassee and beyond. He was the principal of the Lincoln Academy, the first area public high school for Blacks. Riley was also an officer in Florida's NAACP chapter.

The facility opens at 10 a.m. from Monday to Saturday and closes at 4 p.m. except for Friday and Saturday, when closing time is 2 p.m. Admission is $5.

Southeastern Regional Black Archives Research Center and Museum, Carnegie Library on the Campus of Florida A&M University

Billing itself as a "specialty museum," this facility's exhibits cover a wide range of people, groups, and topics important to African American history, spanning from ancient Africa to the present. The archives' resources and artifacts are vast.

The museum is open weekdays from 9 a.m. to 5 p.m. and has no admission fee.

Tallahassee Bus Boycott Marker, 1764 South Martin Luther King Boulevard

Everyone knows Rosa Parks. Sadly, very few know Wilhelmina Jakes and Carrie Patterson. The actions of these two Florida A&M students in 1956 led to another successful economic boycott. The two young women boarded a crowded city bus and sat down in open seats in the front of the bus. They refused the driver's order to move and were arrested for "placing themselves in a position to incite a riot." A ten-month boycott followed their arrest.

This marker on the Florida A&M campus is a quarter-of-a-mile walk from the Research Center at the Carnegie Library.

Jacksonville

Ax Handle Saturday Memorial, Southwest Corner of Hemming Park

In another instance of young people's commitment and courage, the Youth Council of the Jacksonville NAACP chapter had been trying to desegregate lunch counters at various establishments around this downtown park. On Saturday, August 27, 1960, the demonstrators were attacked by about two hundred white men wielding ax handles and baseball bats. Police watched the violence until a Black street gang (the Boomerangs) intervened to protect the demonstrators.

Besides the Hemming Park memorial, this ugly incident is also the subject of a mural wrapping around the Eastside Brotherhood building at 915 A. Philip Randolph Boulevard, one and a half miles from this park.

John Jordan "Buck" O'Neil Statue, J. P. Small Memorial Stadium, 1701 Myrtle Avenue North

If you watched the Ken Burns documentary *Baseball*, you met—and likely couldn't get enough of—"Buck" O'Neil. Mr. O'Neil played for and managed the Kansas City Monarchs of the Negro American League. He was the first African American to be named a coach in the Major Leagues, by the Chicago Cubs in 1962, and a driving force behind the Negro Baseball Leagues Museum in Kansas City.

Mr. O'Neil's story inspires well beyond the baseball diamond. Denied the chance to attend high school due to racial discrimination near his rural home in Carrabelle, Florida, he enrolled at Jacksonville's Edward Waters College, where he completed high school and two years of college.

His baseball career was interrupted when he served in the navy from 1943 to 1945 during World War II, yet he still had a batting average over .300 for two seasons after his military service.

St. Augustine

The ACCORD Civil Rights Museum and the ACCORD Freedom Trail, 79 Bridge Street

At this location was the office of Dr. Robert B. Hayling, a local dentist and civil rights leader. Dr. Hayling and three other activists were beaten by Klan members in September 1963. His home was fired upon, killing the family dog. The following year, he asked Dr. Martin Luther King Jr. to come to the city to inspire lunch-counter sit-ins, beach wade-ins, and protest marches.

Visitors must call (904) 347-1382 to schedule an appointment. A Freedom Trail tour of over thirty locations can be found at *https://www.accordfreedomtrail.org/phase1.html.*

Lincolnville Museum and Cultural Center, 102 Martin Luther King Avenue

Featuring exhibits about St. Augustine's African American heritage, this museum (at a former high school for Blacks) traces the history from how those escaping captivity built Fort Mose for the Spanish through the struggle for civil rights and on to current times. Its major exhibit is *Journey: 450 Years of the African-American Experience*, originally developed to commemorate the fiftieth anniversary of the signing of the Civil Rights Act of 1964.

The museum is open from 10:30 a.m. to 4:30 p.m., Tuesday to Saturday. Adult admission is $10; everyone else gets in for $5.

Fort Mose Historic State Park, 15 Fort Mose Trail

Fort Mose is the site of the first free African settlement in what is now the United States. Founded in 1738 by Spanish colonists offering asylum to the enslaved escaping the British colonies, it is also one of the original sites on the southern route of the Underground Railroad. The timeline in the park's museum sheds light on its history.

Open daily from 9 a.m. to 5 p.m., and there is no fee to visit.

Former Site of the Monson Motor Lodge (Now the Bayfront Hilton), 32 Avenida Menendez

Dr. King and others were refused access to the restaurant and arrested at this motel in 1964. In response, white and Black protesters staged a wade-in at the motel's swimming pool on June 18, 1964. James Brock, the owner, responded by pouring a jug of acid into the water and near the heads of the protesters.

As noted in the Anniston chapter, photos of racially motivated hatred had an impact on public opinion. Photos of Brock dumping acid in the pool were published in newspapers around the world. The US Congress was then debating civil rights legislation, and this St. Augustine incident influenced some lawmakers to vote in favor of the Civil Rights Act of 1964. President Lyndon B. Johnson signed the act into law on July 2, 1964, two weeks after Brock's display of intolerance.

The Monson Motor Lodge was demolished in 2003. However, the steps from the motel were salvaged and remain here at the Bayfront Hilton in tribute to Dr. King's arrest while he was standing on them in 1964.

Rosewood, Florida: Racial Violence Wipes Out a Town

In one respect, Rosewood isn't close to any of the Florida cities mentioned in this chapter. Tallahassee, St. Augustine, and Orlando are each over two hours away.

In another respect, Rosewood isn't close to anyplace—because it is really not there any longer. Certainly, Rosewood isn't what it was as the calendar turned to January 1923, when white mobs burned the town to the ground.

That violence was triggered by an accusation by Fannie Taylor, a white woman from nearby Sumner. Taylor claimed a Black man assaulted her. The area's whites fingered a recent escapee from a road crew named Jesse Hunter. The Black citizens of Rosewood believed that Taylor's boyfriend had beat her up and she blamed a Black man to hide her affair from her husband.

Taylor's husband gathered some vigilantes to search for Jesse Hunter. On January 4, unable to find Hunter, the searchers assumed the Blacks were hiding him. A group of whites stormed a house they suspected of hiding him. Shots were fired, and two whites and two Blacks were killed.

The next day, hundreds of whites converged on Rosewood, their numbers boosted by a KKK rally that happened to be going on in Gainesville. Black homes and churches were burned to the ground. The number killed is unknown.

In 1994, Florida's passed the Rosewood Claims Act, which compensated any survivor who "was present and affected by the violence . . . and who was evacuated the week of January 1, 1923." While only a few old-timers could claim the monetary compensation, the act provided scholarships for Rosewood descendants. Director John Singleton's 1997 film *Rosewood* was based on the events of that first week of January 1923.

There is a Rosewood marker on State Road 24, about two and a half miles north of Sumner and just north of Rosewood Baptist Church; it is on the right as you travel north. The marker is near the only remaining home in what was Rosewood. The home was owned by John Wright, a white shopkeeper who assisted Black residents hiding from the vigilantes in 1923.

Central Florida

Daytona Beach

Mary McLeod Bethune Home and Gravesite, 640 Dr. Mary McLeod Bethune Boulevard

A National Historic Landmark, this is the former home of civil rights leader, educator, and founder of Bethune-Cookman University, Dr. Mary McLeod Bethune. There is no admission fee. Guided tours were suspended during the COVID emergency but hopefully will resume on the former schedule: Monday through Friday, 10 a.m. to 3 p.m., and Saturday by appointment. Visitors to Washington, DC, can learn about Dr. Bethune at the Mary McLeod Bethune Council House National Historic Site.

Howard Thurman Home, 614 Whitehall Street

In the Atlanta chapter, you read how Dr. Howard Thurman and his book *Jesus and the Disinherited* had a powerful influence on Dr. King and provided an intellectual framework for the civil rights movement. Here, you can learn more about the man and his impact. The Howard Thurman Home is open for tours on Friday from 11 a.m. to 4 p.m., and on Saturday from 10 a.m. to 2 p.m. For other times, call for an appointment—(386) 258-7514—or send an email to *info@howardthurmanhome.org*.

Jackie Robinson Ballpark and Museum, 105 East Orange Avenue

On March 17, 1946, history happened here. Then-named City Island Ballpark, this was the site for the first integrated professional baseball game in the United States. Jack Roosevelt (Jackie) Robinson broke the so-called color barrier in America's pastime when he played for the Montreal Royals against his eventual Major League club, the Brooklyn Dodgers.

Daytona Beach renamed the stadium Jackie Robinson Ballpark in 1990, erected a statue of him and created the Jackie Robinson Museum. The museum is free and open daily from 9 a.m. to 5 p.m. **Dodgertown in Vero Beach**, two hours south of Daytona Beach, was the spring training camp for the Brooklyn and Los Angeles Dodgers through 2008. The Vero Beach facility became the first sports facility to become part of the U.S. Civil Rights Trail in 2019.

Hopefully in 2022, another museum to Mr. Robinson is supposed to open, this one in lower Manhattan, much to the dismay of Dodger fans from Brooklyn, I suspect.

New Smyrna Beach

Mary S. Harrell Black Heritage Museum, 314 North Duss Street

This free-to-the-public museum educates visitors about the history of race relations in small-town Florida through photos, oral histories, memorabilia, and artifacts. Closed on Sunday.

Tavares

Groveland Four Monument, Lake County Historical Museum, 317 West Main Street

Like the Scottsboro Boys' accusations in Alabama, a white woman accused four Black men of raping her in 1949. During the hunt for the accused, one Black man was killed. The other three were caught and convicted; two received the death penalty, and the lone minor was sentenced to life. The US Supreme Court overturned these convictions and ordered a new trial for the three men.

As the second trial date approached in November 1951, the Lake County sheriff was transporting the two men originally sentenced to death and the minor. Even though the adult prisoners were handcuffed together, the sheriff claimed they jumped him; he shot them both. One died immediately; the other was seriously injured but survived. That man and the minor were convicted by an all-white jury in the second trial. Both men were paroled, however, in the 1960s, and after many years, pardoned by the governor.

The granite memorial in front of the Lake County Courthouse and Historical Museum features a bronze plaque with an account of this largely unknown travesty of justice.

Orlando

Wells'Built Museum, 511 West South Street

Dr. William Monroe Wells built a hotel and entertainment venue for African Americans visiting Orlando during the 1920s. Now a small museum and on the US National Register of Historic Places, the facility offers visitors the chance to see how the hotel hosted such famous African American performers as B. B. King and Ray Charles.

The Wells'Built Museum, just west of Interstate 4, is typically open weekdays from 9 a.m. to 5 p.m. and is a worthwhile side trip when you visit Orlando for the city's main tourism magnets. The museum's operations were reduced to Monday, Wednesday, and Friday as the book went to press. Adult admission is $5.

Mims

Harry T. and Harriette V. Moore Cultural Center, 2180 Freedom Avenue

The Moores were both teachers. Mr. Moore became active in the NAACP in the 1930s. By 1941, he was the executive secretary of the Florida NAACP, then an unpaid position. His focus expanded from issues like segregated schools and unequal pay for Black teachers to the spate of lynchings occurring across the state. When this caused the Moores to lose their teaching jobs in 1946, Mr. Moore became a paid organizer for the NAACP.

One of the lynching cases Mr. Moore investigated involved the shooting death of one of the Groveland Four at the hands of the Lake County sheriff. That killing occurred in November 1951. On Christmas Day 1951, a bomb exploded under the Moores' bed, killing the couple. Despite an extensive FBI investigation plus two later investigations, the murders have never been solved. Harry Moore was the first NAACP official killed in the civil rights struggle, and the couple are the only husband and wife to give their lives together to the movement.

The cultural center bearing their name is open Monday to Thursday from 10 a.m. to 7 p.m., Friday from 9 a.m. to 6 p.m., and Saturday from 10 a.m. to 2 p.m.

Eatonville: The Oldest Black Municipality in the United States?

Eatonville is eight miles north of Orlando and where celebrated Harlem Renaissance author Zora Neale Hurston grew up. Her works include *Their Eyes Were Watching God*. Eatonville served as the setting for several of Ms. Hurston's stories, and the town honors her with an annual Zora! Festival as well as an art museum named after her.

Eatonville claims to be the first incorporated all-Black city in the nation; so does Princeville, North Carolina. If you simply judge by papers of incorporation, Princeville would win the title, having been incorporated in 1885, two years before Eatonville. However, Eatonville makes its claim based on the fact that it was a *planned* Black community, drawing residents from other states who wanted to be part of an all-Black town. In fact, Zora Neale Hurston's parents moved here from Alabama in 1894.

St. Petersburg

Dr. Carter G. Woodson African American History Museum, 2240 Ninth Avenue South

Three years after earning a PhD from Harvard, Dr. Woodson and some colleagues founded the Association for the Study of Negro Life and History in 1915. In 1926, Dr. Woodson proposed an annual February observance of "Negro History Week"; the idea evolved to become Black History Month in 1976.

The museum is open Tuesday to Friday, noon to 5 p.m.

Sarasota

Newtown African American Heritage Trail

This fifteen-marker trail commemorates the Newtown neighborhood's role in pushing for racial justice from 1914 to the present. Newtown Alive, through its website, offers guided, two-hour trolley or bus tours at $40 per person. Guests hear stories of the 1950s beach integration campaigns, the history of the Newtown

African American community, and personal accounts of courage from civil rights trailblazers. The Newtown markers are mapped on the Newtown Alive app should you want to tour on your own.

Sarasota County Beach Segregation Marker, West Side of the Lido Beach Pavilion

Blacks here in the early 1950s wanted a "Negro" beach. The county preferred to build a swimming pool in the Newtown community. This beach-pool debate went on for several years, resulting in protests at city-owned Lido Beach in the fall of 1955 led by NAACP president Neil Humphrey.

There never was an official "Negro" beach established, and in November 1957, the city opened a community pool at Newtown Recreation Center. The 1964 Civil Rights Act put an end to separate beaches, though the shoreline took some time to become integrated.

The Practice of Convict Leasing

This discussion could appear in any number of chapters. Florida was not the only state to use the so-called Black Codes to charge Black people with "crimes" like vagrancy. Once convicted, the state would put "offenders" into forced labor with no compensation, renting them out to private companies. Historian Douglas Blackmon called this practice *Slavery by Another Name*, the title of his Pulitzer Prize–winning book.

In some respects, convict leasing was often more dangerous than slavery to the physical well-being of those subjected to it. Enslavers had a selfish incentive to treat the enslaved at least well enough to keep them productive. Those who leased convicts did not. They could work the prisoners hard, in terrible conditions, and often beat or kill them with little risk of punishment. The title of a book by Matthew Mancini suggests the overseers' typical attitude: *One Dies, Get Another.*

continued

continued from previous page

Florida leased convicts to plantations, turpentine farms, and lumber camps. However, this information appears here specifically because one of the ways Florida used leased convicts was to build roads to enhance tourism. One such road where convict labor was used was the Tamiami Trail, which runs east-to-west from Miami to Naples, right through the Everglades, and then north to Tampa.

Florida was one of the last states to end convict leasing. The practice ceased here in 1923 when the flogging death of a white prisoner from North Dakota resulted in negative publicity for the state. The North Dakota man was arrested for not having a train ticket and fined twenty-five dollars. His parents sent the money to pay the fine to the Leon County prison system (plus another twenty-five dollars for a return ticket to get their son back to North Dakota). Somehow, none of this cash made it to the proper authorities. Their son was whipped to death in a logging camp.

Southern Florida

Fort Lauderdale

African American Research Library and Cultural Center, 2650 Sistrunk Boulevard

A branch of the Broward County library system, the African American Research Library and Cultural Center (AARLCC) is much more than your typical library. It is a state-of-the-art facility for research, lifelong learning, and community gatherings. The library's programming focuses on the cultural influence of the African diaspora in the Americas as well as African influence on world civilizations. The interior supports this holistic vision with its African-centric design. The exhibit area is on the first floor of this sixty-thousand-square-foot building.

The facility is open from 11 a.m. to 7 p.m. on Monday and Wednesday; from 10 a.m. to 6 p.m. on Tuesday, Thursday, and Saturday; and closed on Friday and Sunday.

Sistrunk Park and the Sistrunk Historical Wall, 200 Sistrunk Boulevard

Two miles east of the AARLCC lies this park and its thirty-six-panel, 123-foot-long wall mural painted by Charles Mills, a local artist and historian. The vibrantly colored work has vignettes from African American history, including people and places of local importance. The park and the boulevard are named for Dr. James Sistrunk, a pioneering physician who practiced in Fort Lauderdale for forty-four years. His community service merits more national attention.

Dr. Sistrunk arrived in Fort Lauderdale in 1922 after graduating from Meharry Medical College in N sashville and serving in World War I. Since Black doctors and patients were denied full access to the community's hospitals then, Dr. Sistrunk, a trained surgeon, was not allowed to perform surgery here. He and Dr. Von Mizzell founded Provident Hospital, Broward County's first Black hospital. A bridge over the North Fork River is also named in Dr. Sistrunk's honor.

Old Dillard Museum, 1019 NW Fourth Street

In 1907, Old Dillard was the city's first school for African Americans. Listed on the National Register of Historic Places, the museum promotes the heritage of African Americans in Broward County by providing enriching exhibitions and cultural activities.

The museum is open Monday to Friday, 11 a.m. to 4 p.m., except in the summer when the museum is closed on Friday. The location is about a mile from Sistrunk Park.

Miami

Historic Hampton House, 4240 NW Twenty-Seventh Avenue #3010

This segregation-era motel and lounge has been reenergized as a cultural center celebrating Black culture and pride. In its Jim Crow–era heyday, this Brownsville landmark was where Black visitors felt safe. The Hampton House welcomed Black celebrities and leaders who could not overnight at the Miami Beach hotels, as Regina King's film *One Night in Miami* showcased.

The Hampton House has a museum, offering three tours daily. The museum operates Thursday to Sunday, 10 a.m. to 6 p.m. Advanced booking suggested at *Historichamptonhouse.org*. Adult admission is $25; less for students, seniors, and youth.

CHAPTER 23

South Carolina

The Palmetto State offers a rich range of experiences for the cultural heritage tourist. From Charleston and the Carolina Lowcountry to and around Columbia, the state capital, to cities near the North Carolina border, those seeking to connect with civil rights and African American history will find much to explore in South Carolina.

- There are sites where significant events occurred in the civil rights era—lunch-counter sit-ins, Freedom Rides, and a young woman who refused to give up her seat on a public bus, months before Rosa Parks did the same thing in Montgomery.
- Freedom fighters like Civil War hero Robert Smalls as well as twentieth-century heroines' struggling for equality, like Septima Clark and Modjeska Monteith Simkins, hailed from the Palmetto State.
- Travel the roads of Johns Island, where one of the civil rights movement's anthems—"Keep Your Eyes on the Prize, Hold On"—had its roots. Visit the site of a 1945 tobacco workers' strike in Charleston that played a role in the transformation of "We Shall Overcome" into the most popular movement anthem.

Did You Know?

South Carolina's General Assembly was the first state legislative body in the nation where the majority of its members were Black.

When the state's General Assembly convened on July 6, 1868, Black lawmakers outnumbered their white counterparts by more than a two-to-one margin. There were eighty-seven Blacks and forty whites in the lower house.

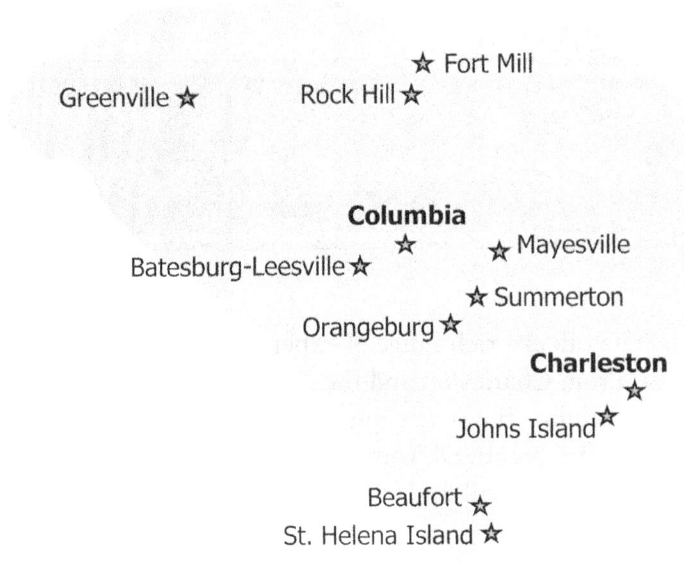

- Expected in 2022 is the world-class International African American Museum in Charleston. Visit it after paying your respects at the historic Mother Emanuel A.M.E. Church just up Calhoun Street.

In Columbia, the stunning African American History Monument at the state capitol is not to be missed. Designed by former astronaut candidate Ed Dwight, the bronze relief panels here artistically relate the story of the African American experience from slavery to the present. In the capital city, take the Columbia '63 Walking Tour and learn about Sarah Mae Flemming, the nineteen-year-old South Carolinian who refused to give up her seat on a city bus, well before Rosa Parks.

A four-city driving circle from Columbia takes you first to Batesburg-Leesville, where a marker recounts the police beating of Sergeant Isaac Woodard in 1946, described later in the chapter.

An hour southeast of the Woodard marker is Orangeburg. In 1968, state highway patrol officers shot into a crowd of two hundred protesting the segregation policies of a local bowling alley, killing three African American students. This occurred two years before the National Guard shooting of four Kent State University students at an antiwar protest, but the Orangeburg killings generated a fraction of the attention of the Ohio incident.

From Orangeburg, travel forty minutes east to Summerton, where you can visit sites related to the *Brown v. Board of Education* (1954) school desegregation case; one of the five named plaintiffs in that landmark case was the Briggs family from Summerton.

About a half hour north of Summerton is Mayesville, the birthplace of educator, humanitarian, and activist Mary McLeod Bethune. Her home and the university bearing her name were covered in the Florida chapter. In this chapter, we direct you to the historic marker memorializing this local civil rights champion.

Mayesville is about an hour from the capital city if Columbia is your base. However, one could head north from Mayesville and stay in the Rock Hill–Fort Mill area along Interstate 77. Rock Hill has two important distinctions in civil rights history:

- McCrory's lunch counter there was the site of one of the early sit-ins in February 1960. Those arrested employed a tactic that eventually became common in the movement: "jail, no bail."
- In May 1961, Rock Hill was the first stop in the Deep South for one of Freedom Rider groups trying to integrate interstate bus travel. The beating that John Lewis and others suffered here drew national attention to the Freedom Rider initiative.

A fifteen-minute drive from Rock Hill is Fort Mill, site of one of the more distressing memorials in the country: a monument dedicated to the "Faithful Slaves." The monument went up in 1895—a bit late for a sincere expression of gratitude.

Another possible stop in the northern part of the state is Greenville. There, a smartphone app guides you to a dozen African American sites of significance. One of them is the former site of the Claussen Bakery, where a strike by African American workers drew the support of Dr. Martin Luther King Jr. in 1967, foreshadowing his support of the Memphis sanitation workers. Less than a half mile from the Claussen site is the boyhood home of the Reverend Jesse Jackson, a Southern Christian Leadership Conference (SCLC) protégé of Dr. King.

Old and new come together on the opposite side of the state, in coastal Carolina. Charleston's highly anticipated International African American Museum is likely to open in 2022, located near the wharf where many captured Africans first set foot in America. Driving south from Charleston, heritage tourists encounter Gullah Geechee culture on Johns Island and three sites related to the Citizenship Schools designed to assist Blacks with voting eligibility.

The next options in Lowcountry South Carolina are about an hour and a half from Charleston. Plan a stop in Beaufort, where you can learn more about Robert Smalls's journey from enslaved man to Civil War hero (for the Union side, of course) to the halls of Congress. From Beaufort, it is fifteen minutes to the historic Penn School and the York W. Bailey Museum. The grounds here were home to a Quaker school in 1862—part of the not-well-known Port Royal Experiment, explained later— and were used by Dr. King as a planning retreat during the civil rights movement.

From end to end geographically and across centuries historically, South Carolina delivers tremendous opportunities to connect with so many threads in the fabric of the African American story. From a thwarted rebellion by the enslaved in Charleston to the civil rights activism of major figures like Septima Clark and Modjeska Monteith Simkins to a lunch-counter sit-in in Rock Hill that introduced a successful, new tactic in the struggle for civil rights, South Carolina has it all.

Capital Region

Columbia

Columbia '63 Walking Tour, Various Locations in the General Vicinity of Main Street

Columbia wanted to recognize the contribution of countless citizens who demonstrated for freedom in the early 1960s. The result was a self-guided walking tour accessible on the Columbia '63 website, *https://columbiasc63.com*. You can also arrange docent-led tours through the website.

On the tour, you pass the intersection of Main and Washington Streets. There, seventeen months before Rosa Parks refused to give up her bus seat in Montgomery, Sarah Mae Flemming took a similar stand on a Columbia city bus.

The Columbia '63 website is an excellent place to discover the many civil rights actions taken in South Carolina; most are not widely known. The site has an engaging decade-by-decade rundown that takes you through these actions chronologically.

Unsung Trailblazer: Sarah Mae Flemming

Sarah Mae Flemming's entrance into civil rights history came on the morning of June 22, 1954. The nineteen-year-old took a seat in what the driver viewed as the whites-only section on a segregated city bus. In Columbia, the color line on city buses shifted based on whether more whites than Blacks were on board.

The white bus driver thought that Ms. Flemming, who was on her way to work, was on the wrong side of this fluid, invisible line. He ordered her to move; she started to leave the bus, by the front door. The driver viewed that as a second transgression; Black riders were supposed to depart using the back door.

The driver blocked the front door and struck Ms. Flemming. Some reports say she was ejected from the bus; others say she left on her own. In any case, her ride that morning ended at Main and Washington Streets. Today, at that intersection, there is a street sign renaming the corner "Sarah Mae Flemming Way," in honor of this civil rights trailblazer.

With the aid of another unsung civil rights leader, Modjeska Simkins, and the NAACP, Ms. Flemming filed a lawsuit. In July 1955, the US Fourth Circuit Court of Appeals reversed a lower-court ruling that sided with the bus company. The Fourth Circuit Court ruled that the integration principle the Supreme Court applied to schools in the *Brown* decision also applied to public transportation. Flemming's heroic actions and her lawsuit desegregated Columbia's city buses and provided an important legal precedent for the Montgomery Bus Boycott, which began on December 5, 1955, 531 days after Ms. Flemming's activism.

Desegregation Commemorative Garden, Osborne Administration Building, University of South Carolina

In the fall of 1963, a year after riots broke out when James Meredith enrolled at the University of Mississippi and three months after Governor George Wallace stood in the schoolhouse door at the University of Alabama, the University of South Carolina was desegregated. A US District Court judge ordered the school to admit the first Black students since Reconstruction. The university appealed but lost, and Henrie Monteith, James Solomon, and Robert Anderson enrolled.

On the fiftieth anniversary of this event, the three African American students were welcomed back to campus and this garden was dedicated. A granite monument in the garden is etched with an original poem, "The Irresistible Ones," written by university poet Nikky Finney.

African American History Monument, Capitol Grounds, 1100 Gervais Street

This artistic gem from Ed Dwight is a moving teaching instrument, tracing African American history from slavery through today via twelve detailed scenes in bronze relief. At the base of the monument's twenty-three-foot-tall obelisk are four rubbing stones from regions of Africa where humans were captured: Senegal, Sierra Leone, the Republic of Congo, and Ghana.

We discuss sculptor Ed Dwight again, as his artwork is in public places around the country. He also holds an important distinction in American history, one having nothing to do with his talent as a sculptor. In the early days of the country's space program, Mr. Dwight became the first Black astronaut candidate. The PBS series *Chasing the Moon* noted that, despite having the backing of President Kennedy and his brother Robert, Mr. Dwight was not chosen as cuts were made to determine the seven Mercury program astronauts. As Tom Wolfe wrote in *The Right Stuff*, the Mercury astronauts were "seven patriotic God-fearing small-town Protestant family men with excellent backing on the home front."[142] And all white.

The Museum of the Reconstruction Era at the Woodrow Wilson Family Home, 1705 Hampton Street

President Woodrow Wilson lived here when he was fourteen. Inside the museum, however, the emphasis is on Reconstruction, not the twenty-eighth president whose record on racial matters was miserable. Visitors are immersed in the Columbia of the 1870s.

Historic Columbia offers tours of this facility as well as four other historic sites: the Robert Mills House, the Mann-Simons Site, the Hampton-Preston Mansion, and the Modjeska Monteith Simkins Home. The Simkins Home is likely to generate the most interest from Freedom's Road travelers. (Mrs. Simkins assisted in Sarah Mae Flemming's city bus lawsuit and her involvement in school desegregation is presented later in this chapter.) If you can't tour the Simkins Home, see the historic marker in front of it at 2025 Marion Street.

Tours cost $10 per home per adult ($5 for those ages 6 to 12). Tour days and times vary by site. Buy tickets at the Mills House Gift Shop at 1616 Blanding Street. Historic Columbia also offers a ninety-minute guided bus tour of African American heritage sites.

Modjeska Monteith Simkins: Matriarch of the South Carolina Civil Rights Movement

Modjeska Monteith Simkins coauthored the brief in Summerton's *Briggs v. Elliott* school desegregation case. Mrs. Simkins and the Reverend Joseph DeLaine led a drive to gather signatures from Summerton citizens on a petition advocating equality in education. She was a founding member of the state's NAACP.

A graduate of Columbia's Benedict College, Mrs. Simkins did not confine her civic engagement to the field of civil rights. She was a leader in women's rights, health care (particularly the treatment of tuberculosis), and the environment.

In 1990, South Carolina honored Mrs. Simkins with its highest civilian award, the Order of the Palmetto. Selected posthumously by her home city of Columbia as a 2019 "City of Women" honoree, a portrait of Mrs. Simkins hangs in the South Carolina State House, about a mile from her home at 2025 Marion Street in Columbia.

Batesburg-Leesville

The Blinding of Isaac Woodard Marker, Intersection of West Church Street and Fulmer Street

Sergeant Isaac Woodard was returning home from his World War II service, having just been honorably discharged at Fort Gordon, Georgia. The decorated veteran, still in uniform, was pulled off the bus here on February 12, 1946, by Police Chief Lynwood Shull. Shull hit the sergeant with his nightstick, and the beating continued in a nearby alley with other officers joining in.

The attack left Sergeant Woodard blind. The police chief and other officers were tried for their actions; an all-white jury found them not guilty after deliberating half an hour. Judge Julius Waties Waring, covered later in the chapter, presided over the trial. The case had a profound impact on later pro–civil rights decisions made by the judge.

President Harry Truman learned of the Woodard beatings. He ordered the Justice Department to investigate, leading to indictments for Shull and others. Based in part on this attack and similar ones on other Black veterans, Truman sent civil rights legislation to the Congress in 1947 and integrated the US military by Executive Order in 1948.

Orangeburg

Orangeburg Massacre Memorial, 300 College Street

The stone monuments here pay homage to Samuel Hammond Jr. and Henry Smith (both South Carolina State University students) and Delano Middleton (a student at local Wilkinson High School). The three were killed by gunfire when state highway patrol officers fired on students attempting to desegregate the all-white All Star Bowling Lane on February 8, 1968. Twenty-seven others were wounded.

Nine officers were tried for using excessive force on the protesters. None were convicted. In fact, the only person convicted because of the shooting was SNCC leader Cleveland Sellers for being the alleged instigator of the protest. Sellers was one of the twenty-seven wounded. He received a full pardon twenty-five years later.

The location of the former All Star Bowling Lane is 1543 Russell Street, about one and a half miles from the Orangeburg Massacre Memorial. The facility closed in 2007, but the building is on the National Register of Historic Places.

Summerton

Liberty Hill A.M.E. Church, 2310 Liberty Hill Road

A marker in front relates how nineteen congregants became plaintiffs in the *Briggs v. Elliott* case. Led by the Reverend Joseph DeLaine, the group initially sought bus transportation for their children to the Blacks-only Scott's Branch School. When vulgarly denied by white school board chairman R. W. Elliott, Thurgood Marshall and the NAACP turned the case from one focused on school transportation to one about school desegregation. Ultimately, the Summerton case became one of the five components of the landmark *Brown v. Board of Education* decision of 1954.

Scott's Branch School, 1154 Fourth Street

Not only was this school central to the *Briggs* case, but the research conducted here by psychologists Kenneth and Mamie Clark was persuasive to the Supreme Court justices who voted unanimously to end school segregation in 1954.

The research presented white and Black dolls to children of both races and asked which dolls were "nice" or "bad," which dolls were "preferred," and which were "most like them." Writing the court's opinion in *Brown*, Chief Justice Earl Warren seemed to rely on the Clarks' research in stating that the legal separation of Black children gave them "a feeling of inferiority as to their status in the community that may affect their hearts and minds in a way unlikely to ever be undone."

The school was designed as an "equalization school," built in the early 1950s as part of a state plan to "equalize" Black facilities. The intention was to preemptively comply with the separate-but-equal prescription of the 1896 *Plessy v. Ferguson* decision upholding segregation. It replaced an older wooden schoolhouse, which stood when the *Briggs* lawsuit began. There is a brick memorial (erected when it was Scott's Branch High School) on the Larry King Highway side of the building.

Briggs-DeLaine-Pearson Foundation, 9355 Alex Harvin Highway

This community center houses artifacts from the *Briggs v. Elliott* school desegregation case. Request a visit by calling (803) 485-2196.

Mayesville

Birthplace of Mary McLeod Bethune Marker, On the Island at the Intersection of Florence Highway and South Lafayette Street

Mary McLeod Bethune was born on a rice and cotton farm about five miles north of Mayesville, the fifteenth of seventeen children. Mrs. Bethune founded and served as president of Bethune-Cookman College, a historically Black college in Daytona Beach, Florida. She also founded the Washington, DC–based National Council of Negro Women (NCNW) in 1935. Her role at the NCNW brought her visibility in the nation's capital; she was selected to be part of the so-called Black Cabinet, a group of Black appointees who advised

President Franklin D. Roosevelt. She also played a role in drafting the charter for the United Nations.

Northern Region

Rock Hill

McCrory's Sit-In Marker, 135 East Main Street

The first sit-ins at McCrory's in Rock Hill occurred on February 12, 1960, just days after four North Carolina A&T students (Joseph McNeil, Franklin McCain, Ezell Blair Jr., and David Richmond) staged the landmark sit-in in Greensboro, North Carolina. About eleven months later, South Carolina's sit-in movement contributed an important first to the arsenal of the civil rights movement.

On January 31, 1961, ten students from Friendship Junior College were refused service at McCrory's lunch counter. They were arrested when they refused to leave. Rather than pay the fine typically associated with the offense of ordering lunch while Black, nine of the ten students chose thirty days of hard labor on a county chain gain.

The nine students became the first sit-in protesters to do jail time when they refused to post bail. This "jail, no bail" strategy of the group, the Friendship Nine, became a model for the 1961 Freedom Rides and many subsequent civil rights actions during the 1960s.

Fort Mill

To the Faithful Slaves Monument, Intersection of Main Street (State Highway 160) and Academy Street

This thirteen-foot marble obelisk was the most viewed marker on the US Historic Marker Database in 2020. As its name suggests, it is "dedicated to the faithful slaves who, loyal to a sacred trust, toiled for the support of the army, with matchless devotion, and sterling fidelity guarded our defenseless homes, women and children."

A quick fact check on the "toiled for the support of the army" inscription: The Confederate Congress did not let African Americans serve until mid-March 1865, about three weeks before Richmond fell.

Will this monument still be in place if you visit, given the removal of so many Confederate memorials? Press reports as of publication time suggest that the descendants of the enslaved people named on the monument want this memorial to stay. The descendants may not have a voice, though, in whether the monument stays or goes. Sole authority to remove monuments like this in the state rests with the legislature, thanks to the South Carolina Heritage Act of 2000. The constitutionality of that act was challenged in July 2020 and arguments heard by the state's Supreme Court in May 2021.

Greenville

African American History Tour, Various Greenville Locations

This fifteen-location route brings some truth-telling to what some see as an incomplete image of the city of Greenville and Greenville County. The sanitized version of local civil rights history overlooks facts such as that Greenville County was the last county in the nation to recognize the mid-January Martin Luther King Jr. national holiday.

The tour website notes that "the dominant white narrative summarized the civil rights movement . . . as inconsequential here, compared to Alabama, Mississippi, or even Orangeburg and other areas of South Carolina." It concludes, "By the end of the tour, you should see things differently." The tour covers five miles. However, eight of the locations are in the heart of downtown Greenville, a relatively easy stroll. Drive to the other seven.

Coastal Region

Charleston

Emanuel A.M.E. Church, 110 Calhoun Street

Perhaps now best known for the tragic shooting of nine church members and leaders in 2015, Mother Emanuel, as the church is often called, has a major place in American history, African American history, and civil rights history. Founded in 1817, it is the oldest African Methodist Episcopal church in the South.

The church paid a price in 1822 when a church leader, Denmark Vesey, led a slave insurrection in Charleston. The uprising was quashed, Vesey was hanged, and the city destroyed the church, then located at Reid and Hanover Streets in Charleston.

In 1962, Dr. Martin Luther King Jr. preached here, urging congregants to register and vote. In 1969, Coretta Scott King led fifteen hundred demonstrators to the church in support of striking hospital workers in Charleston. At the church, they faced bayonet-wielding members of the state's National Guard; the church's pastor and nine hundred demonstrators were arrested.

For group tours, contact (854) 444-3856 or *tours@emanuelamechurch.org*.

Denmark Vesey House, 56 Bull Street

Denmark Vesey was a leader at Mother Emanuel in the early 1800s. When he allegedly planned a rebellion of the enslaved in 1822, Vesey was a free man, having purchased his freedom thanks to some lottery winnings. Despite the comfortable life provided by his carpentry business, he identified with those not yet free.

Vesey's insurrection plan was crafted with precision and efficiency. His plot became known when word was leaked by an enslaved man. The military was alerted, causing Vesey's plan to lose the element of surprise. Once revealed, Vesey's scheme caused hysteria within Charleston; whites were in the minority at the time.

Vesey and over three hundred others were arrested. In all, sixty-seven were convicted and thirty-five executed. Vesey was sentenced to death on July 2, 1822. His plot was not the first such uprising in the state. The more well-known Stono River Rebellion occurred in 1739. Its marker (covered in the Virginia chapter) is located about fourteen miles west of Charleston, near Rantowles.

The Vesey House at 56 Bull Street was designated a National Historic Landmark in 1976. However, Vesey's carpentry business and residence were found in old records to be at 20 Bull Street, not 56 Bull Street. The National Historic Landmark status of the structure at 56 Bull Street remains (the author is resisting puns based on the street name).

International African American Museum, 113 Calhoun Street

Down Calhoun Street from the Mother Emanuel Church grounds will be this major addition to the nation's museums honoring African American history. The International African American Museum (IAAM) is slated to open in early 2022, according to the museum's website.

One feature at the museum will be free and open to the public: the African Ancestors Memorial Garden, commemorating the sacred site (Gadsden's Wharf) where many enslaved people first stepped onto American soil. The website promises "a place to reflect, experience botanic gardens, artistic installations, a huge infinity fountain on the edge of the original wharf, a soundscape that explores diverse African languages, performances, programs and more."

The IAAM estimates that 60 to 80 percent of African Americans can trace an ancestor back to Gadsden's Wharf. Given this, the museum will also house the Center for Family History, a research center with a special focus on African American genealogy.

Avery Research Center for African American History and Culture, 125 Bull Street

The Avery Research Center acquires, preserves, and makes available materials that promote the history and culture of the African diaspora, with an emphasis on Charleston and the South Carolina Lowcountry. The center, part of the College of Charleston, is located just a few blocks from campus and a two-minute walk from the Denmark Vesey House.

Hours of operation have been affected by the pandemic but hopefully will return to their normal times: Monday through Friday from 10 a.m. to 5 p.m., but closed from 12:30 p.m. to 1:30 p.m. Tours are available on the half hour during these hours. Admission is free; donations are welcome.

Septima Poinsette Clark Fountain and Historical Marker, Liberty Square, 340 Concord Street

Septima Clark may be South Carolina's most important contributor to the civil rights movement. Her connections and contributions to the struggle for freedom were many and spanned over seven decades. The brief sidebar on Mrs. Clark as a fighter for equality does not do justice to her full impact. Learn more in her two autobiographies (*Echo in My Soul* [1962] and *Ready from Within: Septima Clark and Civil Rights* [1987]). Ms. Clark is buried at Charleston's Old Bethel United Methodist Church Cemetery.

Septima Poinsette Clark: "Mother of the Movement"

From humble beginnings in Charleston at the turn of the twentieth century, Septima Clark became a giant in civil rights history, and no less a figure than Dr. King called her "the mother of the movement."

When financial issues blocked her from going to college initially, she became a teacher on Johns Island, east of Charleston. There, Ms. Clark became familiar with the NAACP, then a relatively new organization. She joined the NAACP when she returned to Charleston in 1919. One of her first successes was her involvement in the NAACP's effort to allow Black educators to become school principals.

During summers in her teaching years, she attended Columbia University in New York and Atlanta University, where she studied with W. E. B. DuBois. During the first half of the 1940s, she earned a bachelor's degree from Benedict College in Columbia and a master's from Hampton University in Virginia. In 1947, she moved back to Charleston to care for her mother.

Ms. Clark was named vice president of the Charleston NAACP branch in 1956. That same year, the state legislature banned city and state employees from being part of civil rights organizations. She refused to leave the NAACP and paid a dear price. Not only was she was fired from her teaching job in 1956, but she also lost her pension (it was restored in 1976). However, as that door closed, another opened.

Ms. Clark was active with the Highlander Folk School in Tennessee, attending her first workshop there in 1954. Soon she was teaching there and developed its adult

continued

continued from previous page

literacy program, which led to the formation of Citizenship Schools across the Deep South. These schools, a response to legislation in southern states requiring literacy in order to vote, eventually became a program of Dr. King's SCLC in 1961. Ms. Clark became the SCLC's director of education and the first woman on the SCLC's board.

An educator since 1916, her most prominent student came out of a workshop she conducted while serving at the Highlander Folk School. In the summer of 1955, Rosa Parks attended one of Septima Clark's workshops. A few months later, Rosa Parks would refuse to give up her seat on a Montgomery city bus, triggering the Montgomery Bus Boycott, one of the crucial early successes of the civil rights movement.

Old Slave Mart Museum, 6 Chalmers Street

Rescued from the demolition ball in 1960 by two sisters who had just moved to Charleston, the building was used for buying and selling human beings before the Civil War. After the war, the structure was a tenement house; in the 1920s, it became an auto showroom.

Today, the Old Slave Mart Museum is owned by the City of Charleston. Operating hours are Monday through Saturday, 9 a.m. to 5 p.m. General admission: $8; children 6 to 12, military members, seniors, teachers, and students: $5.

US Courthouse and Post Office and Briggs v. Elliott *Marker, 83 Broad Street*

It may seem odd that a marker associated with Summerton's important school desegregation case is in Charleston; Summerton is an hour and a half away. However, this marker (on the Meeting Street side of this Renaissance Revival building) is here because, in this courthouse, Thurgood Marshall argued the case.

One of three judges hearing Mr. Marshall was Julius Waties Waring. Judge Waring was the only one siding with the case Mr. Marshall made for Eliza and Harry Briggs and the other Clarendon

County residents. In his dissent, Waring argued that segregation "must go and must go now. Segregation is per se inequality." Judge Waring's brave stance in the *Briggs* case had adverse repercussions for him. In time, however, South Carolina honored the judge, naming the J. Waties Waring Judicial Center at 83 Meeting Street after him.

Julius Waties Waring: Unlikely Advocate for Equality

As an eighth-generation South Carolinian, the son of a Confederate soldier, and a politically well-connected member of the Democratic Party of the early twentieth century, one might have bet against Judge Waring writing these words in 1951: "Segregation was an evil that must be eradicated."

Yet Judge Waring did just that in his *Briggs v. Elliott* dissent. His open-mindedness on matters of race was evident in earlier rulings. Before the *Briggs* case, he delivered decisions that brought parity to the salaries of Black and white teachers, and he directed the state to integrate its law school or create an equivalent one for Blacks.

South Carolinians were angered. And it wasn't just how the judge ruled from the bench. He divorced his first wife, a member of Charleston's social elite, and married a twice-divorced northerner. An attempt was made to impeach him, a cross was burned at his home, and rocks shattered its windows as well. He and his second wife eventually moved to New York City. When he died in 1968, over two hundred Blacks but fewer than a dozen whites attended his burial in Charleston's Magnolia Cemetery.

In time, attitudes shifted. In October 2015, the Hollings Judicial Center in Charleston was renamed the J. Waties Waring Judicial Center (83 Meeting Street). In front of this building bearing his name, visitors can see a statue of the judge, a marker, and a nice, shaded spot to sit down and reflect on his forward-thinking perspective.

Cigar Factory and "We Shall Overcome" Marker, Intersection of Drake and Columbus Streets

Low wages, poor working conditions, and the lack of advancement opportunities spurred an October 1945 strike at this former American Tobacco Cigar factory. The labor protest lasted for five months. The October 1945 date is meaningful because the workers had pledged not to strike while the country was at war. However, long-simmering anger over discriminatory practices at the factory and the firing of a Black worker in early October pushed over one thousand workers to join the picket line.

The end of a day on the picket line would often be signaled by one of the strikers, Lucille Simmons, singing her adaptation of a 1901 composition by the Reverend Charles Albert Tindley. Tindley's song, based on a hymn from pre–Civil War praise houses, was "I'll Overcome Someday."

Lucille Simmons changed the song's lyrics a bit, singing "We Will Overcome" to reflect the solidarity and determination of the strikers. Another slight change to the song, inserting "Shall" in place of "Will" at the Highlander Folk School in Monteagle, Tennessee, would further transform the composition from a gospel hymn dating before the Civil War to the civil rights movement protest anthem we know today.

Johns Island

Moving Star Hall, South River Road and Hunter Road

Moving Star Hall is an unmarked, one-room building where locals were taught citizenship skills in order to meet the voting eligibility requirements of the 1950s. The building was listed on the National Register of Historic Places in 1982. The hall was built through the efforts of the Moving Star Association, a mutual-aid society set up to care for a wide range of community needs.

The Progressive Club Marker, 3377 River Road

The Progressive Club became another Citizenship School after the building was restored by the Highlander Folk School. Septima Clark and her cousin Bernice Robinson ran classes here in the 1960s.

Severely damaged by Hurricane Hugo, funds have been raised to restore this landmark and build a museum and community center across River Road.

Johns Island and Another Civil Rights Anthem

In the Tennessee chapter, we noted the role the Highlander Folk School and Guy Carawan played in the evolution of "We Shall Overcome." Earlier in this chapter, you learned how tobacco plant strikers in Charleston played a role in the evolution of the song in the mid-1940s.

The Oxford American website describes Guy Carawan's role in popularizing another movement song: "Keep Your Eyes on the Prize, Hold On." At the Johns Island Progressive Club, local resident Alice Wine heard Carawan singing a spiritual with the lyric "Keep your hand on the plow, hold on."

Mrs. Wine said she knew an alternative lyric and sang a version of the song we know today. Carawan began using the "eyes on the prize" lyrics with young activists, transforming another spiritual into an inspirational freedom movement song. Today, Alice Wine's name appears on the composition's copyright.[143]

Esau Jenkins Gravesite, 2726 River Road

Esau Jenkins was the first president of the Progressive Club. He played a major role in establishing the Citizenship Schools on Johns Island, led by Septima Clark and Bernice Robinson.

Mr. Jenkins drove a 1966 Volkswagen station wagon all over the South as he worked for equality. The back panels of the Volkswagen displayed Mr. Jenkins's motto: "Love is Progress, Hate is Expensive." That restored Volkswagen will be in the planned Progressive Club museum. When you visit his gravesite in the church cemetery, you'll note the same statement on his gravestone.

Beaufort

Reconstruction Era National Historical Park, 706 Craven Street

Reconstruction was the twelve-year period following the Civil War. The country grappled with integrating newly freed African Americans into its social, political, economic, and labor systems. "Hope" and "disappointment" are words aptly describing the era. This park is open Tuesday through Saturday, 10 a.m. to 4 p.m. As an NPS site: no admission fees.

Robert Smalls Home, 511 Prince Street

Five-term congressman Robert Smalls was born into slavery, and this home initially belonged to his enslaver. While enslaved, Mr. Smalls worked the docks in Charleston and learned navigation skills. In 1862, with his family and other crew members on board, he commandeered a sidewheel steamship and piloted it past several Confederate watchtowers, eventually reaching the Union ship blockade of Charleston's harbor. His bravery won freedom for his family and a place in the Union Navy for himself. After the war, Smalls returned to Beaufort, bought this house, and eventually represented South Carolina in the US House of Representatives.

A bronze plaque here designates the home as a National Historic Landmark. Smalls is buried in the churchyard of **Tabernacle Baptist Church** (911 Craven Street), a two-minute walk from the Reconstruction Era NHP. A bust of Mr. Smalls is in the churchyard.

St. Helena Island

Penn School and York W. Bailey Museum, 16 Penn Center Circle West

Founded in 1862 and named for Quaker William Penn, the Penn School was one of the first schools in the South established by northern missionaries. The school, first established in the plantation house, was soon moved to Brick Baptist Church (85 Martin Luther King Jr. Drive), a historic landmark close to the Penn Center entrance. The church has served St. Helena's Black community since 1855.

The Penn School came into existence shortly after the Union captured South Carolina's Sea Islands, causing the white population to flee. The Quakers and other northern charitable organizations provided a formal education to the formerly enslaved as they successfully took over farming the land abandoned by the whites and earned wages for the first time. This initiative to bring economic opportunity to the now-freed Blacks was called the Port Royal Experiment, providing a glimpse of what Reconstruction could have been. President Andrew Johnson, however, ended the Port Royal Experiment in 1865.

Port Royal itself was the site of Camp Saxton, where five thousand African Americans were trained to serve in the Union Army. Stationed at Camp Saxton was a nurse whose fame was established elsewhere in the freedom movement before the Civil War: Harriet Tubman, whose connections to South Carolina and the Port Royal Experiment are not widely known.

The school closed in 1948 but Penn became the first site in South Carolina whose primary purpose was to safeguard the heritage of a Gullah Geechee community.

The grounds here are also tied to the civil rights movement. Dr. Martin Luther King Jr. held SCLC leadership retreats here to plan the forward progression of the movement. The Gantt Cottage offers a pictorial exhibit of Dr. King and SCLC staff during their Penn Center retreats.

The Bailey Museum chronicles the Penn Center's history as a place of education, activism, and community building. It is typically open Monday to Saturday, 9 a.m. to 4 p.m. but hours have been reduced to 10 a.m. to 2 p.m. during the summer of 2021; adult admission is $10 and a docent-led tour is $15.

HARRIET TUBMAN.

CHAPTER 24

North Carolina

It wasn't the most thoroughly planned civil rights action, but it may have been the most widely copied, other than marching. The idea for the Woolworth lunch-counter sit-in in Greensboro, North Carolina, on February 1, 1960, emerged from a dorm room conversation between four freshmen at North Carolina Agricultural and Technical University the previous night. The four were the same age as Emmett Till in 1955, the year he was murdered.

The college students discussed what they could do about how African Americans were treated. As historian Frye Gaillard wrote, "Finally, in the early morning quiet of February 1, just an hour or two before dawn, Joe McNeil looked at the others and demanded simply: 'Let's do something.'"[144]

The "something" happened later that afternoon. Ezell Blair Jr. (now Jibreel Khazan), Joseph McNeil, Franklin McCain, and David Richmond went to the local Woolworth's store, bought some everyday items, and went to the lunch-counter area. Rather

Did You Know?

One of the first narratives about the struggle for freedom by enslaved females was written by Harriet Jacobs of Edenton, North Carolina. She escaped from Edenton to Philadelphia by boat in 1842. Her autobiography, *Incidents in the Life of a Slave Girl*, was published in 1861.

In Edenton, a marker honoring Harriet Jacobs stands outside of the visitors' center. Inside the center, you can learn more about her and pick up a map of sites relating to her life. One location on this self-guided tour is Colonial Waterfront Park, part of the NPS Underground Railroad Network to Freedom program. Here, African American watermen identified sympathetic seamen and arranged passage for enslaved persons to a free state.

than use the stand-up counter where Blacks would receive service, they sat down.

Greensboro was not the first use of the sit-in tactic to call attention to discrimination. However, the courage of the Greensboro Four sparked similar actions across the South and motivated other civil rights–era legends. For example, in his book on Freedom Summer, Bruce Watson points out how Robert Moses was influenced by the Greensboro sit-ins. Four months afterward, Moses headed south to begin his long commitment to social justice.

This chapter kicks off in Greensboro at the International Civil Rights Center & Museum (ICRCM). Greensboro is part of North Carolina's Central Piedmont region, which includes most of the municipalities covered in this chapter. Besides the museum in Greensboro, Piedmont-area residents and travelers can visit

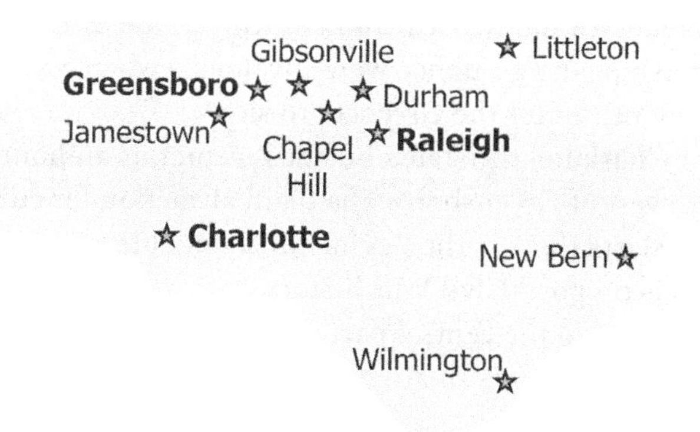

- A Quaker farm in Jamestown that harbored runaways; the farm has one of the few remaining false-bottom wagons used to conceal freedom seekers.
- A museum in Gibsonville honoring the work of Dr. Charlotte Hawkins Brown, whose mission was educating African Americans.
- The campus of Shaw University in Raleigh, where one of the most consequential civil rights–era organizations, the Student Nonviolent Coordinating Committee (SNCC), was founded.

Also in Raleigh is the North Carolina Museum of History, an excellent place to connect with a wide range of the state's history (from NASCAR to civil rights).

- A section of Durham that earned "Black Wall Street" designation in the early 1900s along with similar neighborhoods in Richmond, Virginia, and Tulsa, Oklahoma.
- A Chapel Hill tribute to those who participated in 1947's Journey of Reconciliation, a precursor of the Freedom Rides of 1961.

If you start in Jamestown, the farthest west of the six cities noted above, and traveled east to Raleigh, making all intermediate stops, that would roughly be one hundred miles of driving. After covering Greensboro, these other Piedmont cities are presented in west-to-east order. Along the way, we recognize Ella Baker, who worked with the NAACP and Dr. King at the SCLC. Her experience, leadership, and guidance were invaluable when SNCC was founded two months after the Greensboro sit-in.

Charlotte, the state's business center, is an hour and a half southwest of Greensboro. The main attraction for cultural heritage enthusiasts there is the Levine Museum of the New South, where the focus is on post–Civil War history.

Leaving the central part of the state and heading toward the coast, two cities merit attention:

- Wilmington, just north of the South Carolina border, was the site of an armed coup d'état by white supremacists. The overthrow of the city's legitimate government took place in 1898 and represents another example of post-Reconstruction violence against Blacks. Also in Wilmington, learn about the Wilmington Ten, a group of civil rights activists wrongly convicted of arson and conspiracy in 1971. Their sentences were voided in 1980, and the governor extended pardons on December 31, 2012.
- New Bern, the birthplace of Pepsi-Cola, offers a twelve-stop African American Heritage walking tour.

A quick North Carolina connection with Dr. King closes out this overview. Dr. King spoke at a high school in Rocky Mount, North Carolina, on November 27, 1962. Claims have been made that King previewed parts of his "I Have a Dream" speech at Booker T. Washington High School (now a city recreational center and gym). There are similarities between the Rocky Mount speech and the well-known one delivered at the March on Washington in 1963. Drew Hansen's book on Dr. King's 1963 speech, *The Dream*, points out that the themes in the March on Washington address also were evident in speeches King gave in other cities.

Greensboro

International Civil Rights Center and Museum, 134 South Elm Street

Of all the locations outside the five states making up the loop tour, this one arguably has the highest historical profile. Make every effort to visit this museum, which displays the actual lunch counter where the 1960s sit-in movement began. Despite earlier lunch-counter sit-ins (like in Lexington, Kentucky), the actions here on February 1, 1960, directly inspired a tidal wave of similar protests.

The courage displayed by the Greensboro Four sparked other nonviolent affirmations of equality, not only at lunch counters across the Jim Crow South but also at libraries, public beaches, swimming pools, and other segregated places.

Open Monday through Saturday from April to August, 9 a.m. to 6 p.m.; during other months, the museum is open Monday through Saturday from 10 a.m. to 6 p.m. Admission fees: Adults, $15; seniors, $12; students (13 years to college), $10; youth (6 to 12 years), $8; children 5 and under, free with paying adult.

Also, not far from the museum is the Walkway of History (corner of South Elm Street and February One Place). Markers here relate six chapters in Greensboro's Black history from the Underground Railroad to the Woolworth sit-in. Also on the corner of South Elm and February One Place is the *Cup of Freedom* sculpture, one of eight bronze works around Greensboro commemorating the 1960 sit-in.

February One Monument at the Dudley Memorial Building, North Carolina A&T State University

This sculpture honors the Greensboro Four with ten-foot-tall bronzes of the young men. Created by James Barnhill and unveiled in 2002, it's an excellent spot for a photo to commemorate your stop in Greensboro.

Jamestown

Mendenhall Homeplace, 603 West Main Street

This former Quaker farm, fifteen miles southwest of Greensboro, is a wonderful place to learn about the Underground Railroad and transporting enslaved people to freedom. One method used false-bottom wagons to hide runaway slaves. False-bottom wagons are hard to find, but visitors can see one here.

The Mendenhall Homeplace operates March through December from Tuesday to Friday, 11 a.m. to 3 p.m., and on Saturday from 1 to 4 p.m.; in January and February: Friday and Saturday and by appointment. Advance notice requested for groups. Adult admission is $5, less for seniors, students, and children.

Gibsonville

Charlotte Hawkins Brown Museum at the Palmer Memorial Institute, 6136 Burlington Road

Charlotte Hawkins Brown founded the Palmer Memorial Institute in 1902. The school educated over two thousand African Americans. The museum links Dr. Brown and Palmer Memorial Institute to African American, women's, and social history, emphasizing the contributions of African Americans to North Carolina.

There is no charge to visit. The museum is open Tuesday to Saturday, 9 a.m. to 5 p.m.

Chapel Hill

The Journey of Reconciliation Marker, Intersection of North Columbia Street and East Rosemary Street

In June 1946, the US Supreme Court struck down segregation in interstate bus travel in *Morgan v. Virginia*. Later that summer, Greyhound, the largest interstate bus service provider, issued an internal memo on seating passengers that seemed to ignore the court's ruling.

In 1947, the Congress of Racial Equality (CORE) and the Fellowship of Reconciliation (FOR) decided to test compliance with the segregated seating ban. On April 9, 1947, a racially mixed group of sixteen CORE members departed Washington, DC, on Greyhound and Trailways buses.

On April 12, both buses arrived in Chapel Hill. The next day, as the buses were departing Chapel Hill for Greensboro, four of the Riders were arrested: two Blacks for refusing to move to the rear of the Trailways bus, and two whites for interfering. The commotion attracted spectators, one of whom attacked white rider James Peck as he went to pay his bond at the police station across the street. In 1961, James Peck would join a similar mixed-race group of nonviolent protesters on a similar mission but with a much better name: the Freedom Rides.

As this marker points out, some of those arrested in Chapel Hill were sentenced to thirty days on chain gangs. Even though the Supreme Court had banned racial discrimination in the seating arrangements on interstate buses, the judge here found that, since this bus was headed to Greensboro, this part of the trip was not interstate travel.

Durham

James E. Shepard Memorial Library, North Carolina Central University

One week after the lunch-counter sit-in in nearby Greensboro, another occurred at a Woolworth's store in Durham. A small section of that lunch counter from the February 8, 1960, protest is part of a civil rights exhibit in the library's lobby.

At the request of a local civil rights leader, the Reverend Douglas Moore, Dr. Martin Luther King Jr. and Rev. Ralph David Abernathy came to Durham shortly after the Woolworth's sit-in. On the evening of February 16, Dr. King delivered his "Fill Up the Jails" speech at White Rock Baptist Church, which was demolished but rebuilt a short distance from its former site.

Black Wall Street Marker, North Mangum Street and West Parrish Street

Durham's West Parrish Street was a hub of Black-owned business in the early 1900s. Like areas within Tulsa, Oklahoma, and Richmond, Virginia, Durham's West Parrish neighborhood became known as the "Black Wall Street."

Practically next to this marker is another titled "A Black Capital for the World to See." Among the Black-owned companies mentioned on that marker is the North Carolina Mutual Life Insurance Company, founded here in 1898; its original headquarters (114-116 West Parrish) is a short walk from these markers.

Raleigh

Founding of the Student Nonviolent Coordinating Committee Marker, Shaw University, 809 South Wilmington Street

No story of the civil rights movement in the United States is complete without including the work of the Student Nonviolent Coordinating Committee (SNCC; pronounced "snick"), which was instrumental in the Freedom Rides, Mississippi Freedom Summer, the March on Washington, and more. Superior leadership also came from SNCC members including Ella Baker, John Lewis, Diane Nash, Julian Bond, Stokely Carmichael, and others. It all began here at Shaw University on Easter weekend in 1960.

Organized and inspired by Ella Baker, then a director at the Southern Christian Leadership Conference, SNCC set its own course apart from the SCLC. Following the April meeting, she labeled as "refreshing" the inclination of those at the Shaw University sessions to embrace "group-centered leadership" rather than a "leader-centered group pattern of organization," the latter phrase describing her view of the King-led SCLC.

The 1960 meetings at Shaw University were held in Greenleaf Hall (118 East South Street) and at the then Memorial Auditorium (2 East South Street), now the Duke Energy Center for the Performing Arts. Besides the SNCC marker on South Wilmington Street, another one is near Greenleaf Hall.

Dr. Martin Luther King Jr. Memorial Gardens, 1215 Martin Luther King Jr. Boulevard

Raleigh claims this was the first public park in the United States solely devoted to Dr. King and the civil rights movement. Find the larger-than-life bronze statue of King in clerical robes here as well as a granite water monument honoring the area's notable movement pioneers—a good place for reflection.

Not far from this park is a larger one (twenty-nine acres) honoring John Chavis. Mr. Chavis was a Black man who fought for three years in the Revolutionary War, earning him "free Black" status. He was a teacher and preacher to both whites and Blacks. **Chavis**

Memorial Park (505 Martin Luther King Jr. Boulevard) has many amenities, including the historic Allan Herschell Carousel, making this a terrific stop for travelers with kids.

North Carolina Museum of History, 5 East Edenton Street

This highly rated Smithsonian affiliate provides a wide range of content on state history in its impressive space. There truly is something for everyone here. While some explore African American history in North Carolina, others can dive into the rich sports history of the state (think NASCAR and basketball, for starters).

Check out the temporary exhibits too. Examples of past displays include *Freedom! A Promise Disrupted: North Carolina, 1862–1901* and *The Green Book*. *The Green Book* was a guide for Black travelers during the Jim Crow era. Officially titled *The Negro Motorist Green Book*, it provided listings of hotels, restaurants, and other businesses that served the needs of African Americans.

No charge to visit; the museum is open Monday through Saturday, 9 a.m. to 5 p.m., and Sunday from noon to 5 p.m.

City of Raleigh Museum, 220 Fayetteville Street

Raleigh's journey toward equality is explored here along with other topics related to the city's history. The museum is closed on Monday but open other days until 4 p.m. Doors open at 9 a.m. except Sunday (1 p.m. opening). Admission is free; donations are welcomed.

Charlotte

Levine Museum of the New South, 200 East Seventh Street

Using a variety of interactive and immersive exhibits, the museum covers the New South from 1865 to today, including content on the civil rights era. The Levine's centerpiece exhibit, *Cotton Fields to Skyscrapers*, shares stories from Reconstruction to the rise of contemporary Charlotte.

Open Friday to Monday only (at 10 a.m. except for Sunday's noon opening). Closing time is 5 p.m. (except Saturday at 4 p.m.). Adults, $10; seniors, students, educators, and active military, $8.

Ella Baker: "Daring Us to Go Further"

Born in Norfolk, Virginia, and raised in Littleton, North Carolina, Ella Baker's formative years were influenced by the stories of her formerly enslaved grandmother. Ms. Baker attended Shaw University and was the valedictorian of the class of 1927. She moved to New York City and joined the Young Negroes Cooperative League (YNCL). Her leadership abilities were recognized early, and before long, she was serving as the YNCL's national director.

Her activism grew in the 1940s when she worked as a field secretary for the NAACP, served as its director of branches from 1943 to 1946, and became the director of the New York chapter in 1952. In 1957, Baker moved to Atlanta and helped Martin Luther King start the SCLC. She served as the SCLC's interim executive director until 1960 and battled the sexism that existed there during her tenure.

Then came the April 1960 formation of SNCC. Fifty-six years old at the time, she became an inspirational leader for SNCC's young activists. The list of SNCC members who made a significant difference across the civil rights era is long, and much of the credit goes to the guiding hand and vision of Ella Baker. As John Lewis put it, "She kept daring us to go further."[145]

Markers honoring this dedicated, long-serving advocate for social justice can be seen

- In Littleton, North Carolina, near the intersection of East South Main Street and Kirkland Street.
- At the intersection of Fremont and Church Streets in her birth city of Norfolk, Virginia.

Littleton is between I-85 and I-95, not far from the Virginia border but not near any of the cities in this chapter.

Wilmington

The 1898 Coup Marker, 409 Market Street, and 1898 Memorial Park, 1081 North Third Street

When you think of an armed coup d'état, you typically don't think of the United States, yet Wilmington had one in 1898. Armed whites overthrew the duly elected mayor and the entire city government of whites and Blacks. The mob installed its leader as the new mayor and torched the local Black newspaper's office. The coup was inspired by inflammatory speeches by white supremacist Charles Aycock, who was elected North Carolina's governor two years later, receiving 60 percent of the vote.

The marker on Market Street is in front of the former armory of the Wilmington Light Infantry, many of whose members participated in the insurrection. Today, the building is owned by the adjoining First Baptist Church.

A mile from this marker is the 1898 Memorial Park (1081 North Third Street). See the unique abstract sculpture by Odeleye Sculpture Studios commemorating the Wilmington tragedy.

Alex Manly Marker, South Third Street and Church Street

Alex Manly was editor of the *Wilmington Daily Record*, the newspaper the white mob attacked during the coup. Whites in Wilmington were pushing a variety of falsehoods about Blacks into the public discourse during the local November 1898 election. Manly ran an editorial response to these stereotypes, setting off many local whites. He left Wilmington, escaping the ensuing violence that may have killed as many as three hundred. This marker is on the right if you are traveling south.

Wilmington Ten Marker, Gregory Congregational Church of Christ, 609 Nun Street

The Wilmington Ten (nine Black men and one white woman) were wrongly convicted of firebombing a grocery store in 1971. The incident occurred when school desegregation was a hot issue in Wilmington and this church was a meeting place for civil rights activists.

Their sentences were commuted in 1978 but not pardoned. The convictions were overturned in 1980 because of perjury and legal misconduct; pardons eventually came in 2012, forty years after the conviction.

New Bern

African American Heritage Walking Tour, Various Locations

This city on the Neuse River offers residents and visitors two walking tours that connect with the history and heritage of New Bern's African American community. The first African American Heritage Trail Guide highlights ten points of interest within the Craven Terrace and Dryborough neighborhoods. Panels at these locations explain an aspect of the community's history. One major event was the tragic Great Fire of 1922, which displaced thousands of Black residents.

The second self-guide tour, very similarly named to the first, is the African American Heritage Tour. This tour includes the sites of homes, churches, and other buildings that played important roles in New Bern Black history. Included on this tour, for example, is St. Peter's A.M.E. Zion Church. The church was destroyed in the Great Fire of 1922 and painstakingly rebuilt by its persistent congregation over the next two decades.

There is no prescribed order to either tour. Get copies of both and integrate the few overlapping stops on them as you tour. Maps of each one can be downloaded at *https://visitnewbern.com/african-american-heritage-tour/.*

CHAPTER 25

Virginia

In August 1619, the English privateer *White Lion* set its anchor in the James River off the coast of the present-day Hampton, Virginia. The English pirates had stolen some enslaved Africans from a Portuguese ship. In exchange for provisions for the *White Lion*, the pirates sold twenty to thirty Africans to the colonists. Enslaving human beings in the British colonies had begun.

The arc of African American history in Virginia is long. One of the largest trading companies selling men, women, and children in the United States, Franklin and Armfield, was based in Alexandria, and that location is now a city-run museum. Rebellions by the enslaved in Virginia are memorialized in Richmond, Courtland, and Capron. Black soldiers, remembering Fort Pillow in Tennessee, equipped themselves well in the final campaign that ended the Civil War.

This chapter spotlights the contributions of three women trailblazers:

- *Maggie Walker*. Her business acumen led her to become the first Black women to charter a bank and earn millionaire status. The National Park Service operates the Maggie L. Walker National Historical Site in Richmond's historic Jackson Ward neighborhood.

Did You Know?

As late as December 2020, one of two statues representing Virginia in Statuary Hall in the US Capitol was that of Robert E. Lee, who led the Confederate forces in rebellion against the United States. Replacing Lee's statue will be one of Robert Russa Moton High School student Barbara Johns.

The other Virginian in Statuary Hall? George Washington.

- *Irene Morgan*. Her refusal to move from her seat on an interstate bus in 1944 produced a Supreme Court decision forbidding restrictive practices on interstate buses. A marker in Saluda, east of Richmond, commemorates Ms. Morgan's brave act. The Freedom Rides over a decade and a half later pushed the federal government to enforce that decision.
- *Barbara Johns*. She led a student walkout protesting the substandard facilities at her high school in Farmville. That 1951 protest spurred a lawsuit that became part of the plaintiff class of the five cases resolved in the 1954 *Brown v. Board of Education* Supreme Court case. A visit to Farmville's Robert Russa Moton Museum is the best way to learn more about the leadership of this sixteen-year-old hero.

Despite the decision in *Brown*, southern states certainly did not rush to comply with the desegregation order. In fact, in Virginia, a movement known as Massive Resistance fought for more than a decade against integrating schools. Led by US senator Harry Byrd, this campaign to delay the implementation of the *Brown* ruling caused entire public school systems to close and state funds to be denied to systems that integrated.

The final blow to Massive Resistance came in 1968 with another important desegregation case before the Supreme Court. In *Green v. County School Board of New Kent County*, the high court established five factors—faculty, staff, transportation, extracurricular activities, and facilities—as criteria by which courts should evaluate progress on desegregation. A historical marker in Quinton is in front of the formerly all-Black high school at the center of the *Green* case.

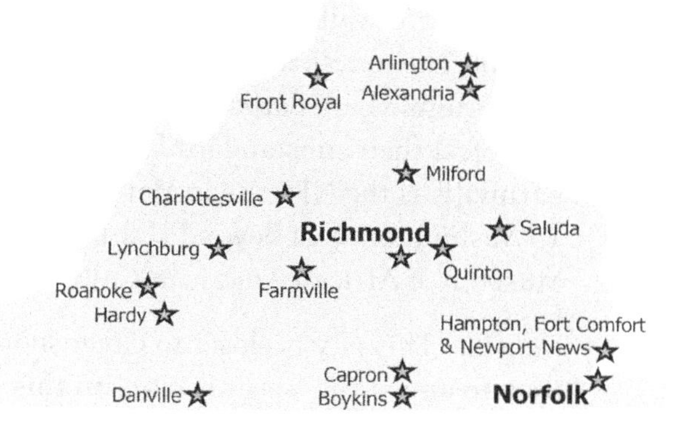

This chapter divides Virginia's relevant sites into five regions:

- *Northern Virginia*: Two cities here can be easily added to any Washington, DC, trip. Alexandria's city-run museum at the former northern headquarters of Franklin and Armfield affords visitors the chance to hear reports on the practices of the two notorious merchants. The *Washington Post* labeled them the cruelest slave traders in America. The Arlington National Cemetery hosts the gravesites of African American heroes including Thurgood Marshall, Medgar Evers, and others.
- *Richmond area:* In Virginia's capital, visit the previously mentioned NPS site honoring Maggie L. Walker and sites near Capitol Square: the Commonwealth's Civil Rights Memorial and a marker related to the *Loving v. Virginia* case, which overturned bans on interracial marriage. Not far from Richmond are markers commemorating two other court cases that propelled the quest for equality: one on Irene Morgan's interstate bus travel case and the other putting an end to Massive Resistance.
- *Coastal Virginia / Hampton Roads area:* Highlights here include visiting Fort Monroe to understand both the introduction of slavery to the colonies and an emancipation event here as the Civil War began. Historic Hampton University is home to the oldest African American museum in the nation and the sprawling and stirring Emancipation Tree. Two markers related to the Nat Turner Rebellion are in Southampton County, an hour west of Norfolk.
- *Central Virginia:* West of Richmond is Farmville, site of the 1951 student walkout from the Robert Russa Moton High School. The excellent museum here lets you sit in the same auditorium where Barbara Johns rallied her fellow students to protest their substandard facility. Two hours west of Farmville is the NPS site in Hardy at the birthplace of Booker T. Washington. Just beyond Hardy is Roanoke and its Harrison Museum of African American Culture.
- *Danville:* This city is closer to Greensboro, North Carolina, than to any of the Virginia cities in this chapter. In 1963,

Dr. King led protests in Danville after the city's police staged a Birmingham-style attack on civil rights marchers. Nearly one hundred years earlier, Jefferson Davis fled here as his Confederacy was falling apart. The chapter guides you to the home where Davis stayed, now a small museum.

Northern Virginia

Alexandria Black History Museum, 902 Wythe Street

Located in the library established for Black citizens during segregation, this modest-sized, city-sponsored museum has a gallery for permanent exhibits and another for temporary exhibits, like one on the city's "contraband" heritage of protecting those who escaped captivity.

Hours: Tuesday to Saturday, 10 a.m. to 4 p.m. Donations requested, not required.

The Contrabands and Freedmen Cemetery Memorial, 1001 South Washington Street, Alexandria

Federal troops occupied Alexandria in 1861, making the city a haven for the newly freed. Many arrived in poor health; disease spread through their living quarters, and many people died. This land was confiscated in 1864 to create a cemetery.

The history of the cemetery and the twists and turns of finding it and preserving it are fascinating. Come to learn more and reflect on the lives of those buried here. Mario Chiodo's stunning sculpture, *The Path of Thorns and Roses*, greets visitors.

Freedom House Museum, 1315 Duke Street, Alexandria

This building was once the northernmost headquarters of Franklin and Armfield. From 1828 to 1861, as many as fifty thousand enslaved adults and children from the Chesapeake Bay area were transported from here to ports in the Deep South.

John Armfield, based here, bought enslaved people at depressed prices when tobacco growers no longer could keep them, having depleted their soil by continually planting tobacco. Armfield shipped humans to his partner, Isaac Franklin, based in Mississippi. Franklin sold these enslaved people at considerable profit, making him and Armfield millionaires.

The city of Alexandria purchased the museum in March 2020, and renovations were under way at the time of publication. Check *https://www.alexandriava.gov/FreedomHouse* for updates on the reopening.

Arlington National Cemetery, Memorial Avenue

The graves of many individuals important to civil rights and African American history are at Arlington National, including

- Mississippi activist Medgar Evers: Section 36, Grave 1431
- Supreme Court Justice Thurgood Marshall: Section 5, Grave 40-3
- Heavyweight boxing champion Joe Louis Barrow: Section 7A, Grave 177
- US Army Lieutenant Colonel Lemuel A. Penn: Section 3, Grave 1377-LH
- Mark Matthews—The last Buffalo Soldier to pass away, Sergeant Matthews lived to age 111 and served in both world wars: Section 69, Grave 4215
- "Contrabands": An estimated three thousand Civil War–era liberated captives are interred in Section 27.

Make the visitors' center your first stop to pick up a map or use the ANC Explorer app, which lets users access a Civil Rights Figures listing under the Most Visited Graves tab. Open year-round for gravesite visitation from 8 a.m. to 5 p.m.

Richmond

Maggie L. Walker National Historical Site, 600 North Second Street

Born in 1864, Mrs. Walker became the first African American woman to charter and run a bank, the St. Luke Penny Savings Bank. Located in the Jackson Ward Historic District, Mrs. Walker's elegant brick home and surrounding buildings serve as an NHS Visitors' Center and exhibit hall. The house is at 110 1/2 Leigh Street, and the visitors' center is around the corner at 600 North Second Street.

Open Tuesday to Saturday, 9 a.m. to 4:30 p.m. No charge to visit.

About a half mile from the NHS site, at West Broad and Adams Streets, is a ten-foot bronze statue of Mrs. Walker, appropriately holding a checkbook.

A statue of another prominent Richmond trailblazer is three miles from the Walker home. Tennis legend Arthur Ashe's memorial is on Monument Avenue at Roseneath Road.

Lieutenant Colonel Lemuel A. Penn: Another Victim of Civil Rights-Era Violence

A World War II veteran and Bronze Star recipient, Lt. Col. Penn was returning home from Fort Benning, Georgia, on July 11, 1964, with two other officers. Penn, an assistant superintendent in the Washington, DC, schools and a father of three, had just taken over driving duties as he and his fellow army reservists headed back to the nation's capital.

Local Ku Klux Klansmen pulled up in a car next to Penn's vehicle. As the cars approached the Broad River Bridge separating Madison and Elbert Counties in Georgia, gunshots rang out. The driver's side windows were shattered, and Lt. Col. Penn was killed.

The driver of the shooters' car admitted his role in the murder and identified two Klan members, Howard Sims and Cecil Myers, as the ones who fired the fatal shots.

Sims and Myers were tried in Georgia Superior Court, but an all-white jury found them not guilty. The date of the murder is significant: July 11, 1964. Nine days before the murder, the Civil Rights Act of 1964 went into effect. Federal prosecutors charged Sims and Myers with violating Penn's civil rights. A federal district court jury found them guilty of conspiracy, and the two served about six years in federal prison.

Besides paying respects to Lt. Col. Penn at Arlington National Cemetery, you can also do so at a historical marker honoring him on Georgia Highway 172, where he was murdered. The marker is just south of the Broad River Bridge in Madison County. Turn in at Roy Woods Road to safely view this marker.

St. Luke Building, 10 West Baker Street

The Independent Order of St. Luke (IOSL) was a benevolent society that provided financial assistance to the newly freed when founded in 1867. The IOSL moved here from Baltimore in 1903. Maggie Walker became involved in the Richmond chapter of the organization in the 1880s at age fourteen. In 1899, Mrs. Walker took on the title of "Right Worthy Grand Secretary" and applied her business acumen to save the financially struggling IOSL.

Here, Mrs. Walker started the St. Luke Penny Savings Bank, becoming the first African American woman to charter a financial institution in the United States. The IOSL served Richmond's Black community for over a century before disbanding in the 1980s.

Black History Museum, 122 West Leigh Street

Located in the stunning Leigh Street Armory and a six-minute walk from the Maggie L. Walker NHS, this museum is an example of a local facility that does an excellent job covering relevant content on national topics (Reconstruction, the Jim Crow era, etc.) as well as local history (Massive Resistance in Virginia, the Richmond 34 sit-in, etc.).

The museum is open Wednesday to Saturday, 10 a.m. to 5 p.m. Adults: $10, with discounts for seniors, students, and children.

Virginia Civil Rights Memorial, Virginia State Capitol

This sculpture by Stanley Bleifeld portrays Barbara Johns, the leader of the student walkout at Farmville's Robert Russa Moton High School, as well as other students, community members, and the lawyers who were part of this historic event. The memorial is located near the entrance to the Executive Mansion in Capitol Square. It is a short walk from this memorial to the *Loving v. Virginia* marker.

Loving v. Virginia Marker, East Broad Street and North Eleventh Street

In June 1958, Richard Loving and Mildred Jeter were married in Washington, DC. They returned to their home in Caroline County, Virginia. In July, both were arrested for violating Virginia's Racial Integrity Act. Enacted in 1924, the law banned interracial marriages, and the Lovings had broken the law.

An appeal to the US Supreme Court led to a 1967 ruling overturning the interracial marriage ban. The marker at the Patrick Henry Building commemorates this historical decision.

Near Richmond

Three Supreme Court decisions, all with either Virginia or one of its local governments on the losing end, are memorialized at these three locations. Each marker is under an hour's drive from Richmond:

- *Milford, US 301 and Sparta Road.* Another *Loving* decision marker, this one is closer to where the couple lived.
- *Quinton, in front of the George W. Watkins Elementary School, 6501 New Kent Highway.* The school, formerly an African American–only high school, is a National Historic Landmark due to its association with the 1968 Supreme Court case of *Green v. County School Board of New Kent County.*
- *Saluda, on the New Street side of the Middlesex County Courthouse on Virginia Highway 33.* Irene Morgan's Supreme Court case and victory are celebrated here.

Coastal Virginia / Hampton Roads

Hampton University Museum and Archives, 14 Frissell Avenue, Hampton

Founded three years after the Civil War as Hampton Normal and Agricultural Institute, today's Hampton University is home to the oldest African American museum in the nation. From the Children's Curiosity Room to an extensive fine arts collection, there is something here to fascinate everyone.

The museum offers excellent campus tours, which include the sprawling and inspiring Emancipation Oak—a sacred place where the first southern reading of President Lincoln's Emancipation Proclamation occurred. The tour also includes a monument to one of the university's most well-known alumni, Booker T. Washington.

Like so many museums, it was closed temporarily during the pandemic. Visitors can hopefully explore this fine facility when normal operations resume: Monday to Friday, 8 a.m. to 5 p.m., and on Saturday from noon to 4 p.m. No charge to visit.

Fort Monroe National Monument and Casemate Museum, 41 Bernard Road, Fort Comfort

So much history on these 565 acres of land! Occupied by Indigenous people before the arrival of the British and the arrival point for the first enslaved people in British North America in 1619, Fort Monroe played a key role during the Civil War as a Union stronghold.

In 1861, three enslaved men escaped the Confederate Army and fled to the fort. Union General Benjamin Butler refused to return the slaves, and before long, the fort became known as "Freedom's Fortress" since those escaping captivity who made it there were not returned. Visitors can't miss the irony of the 1619 and 1861 events happening in the same place. The book discusses this 1861 encounter at Fort Monroe when we cover the Rokeby Museum in Vermont. Jump ahead now if you are curious about why it is presented there and not here.

These two Fort Monroe facilities are run by the NPS (the National Monument) and the Commonwealth of Virginia (the museum). The Casemate Museum provides most of the services and programming for visitors, presenting the complex history of Old Point Comfort and Fort Monroe since 1619. Of special interest may be a series of annual commemorative events held here in late August surrounding the anniversary of the first Africans' arrival in the British Colonies.

The grounds are open from 5 a.m. to midnight daily. The museum is open Thursday to Saturday, 10 a.m. to 3 p.m.

Hampton History Museum, 120 Old Hampton Lane, Hampton

This city museum offers a range of content on Hampton from its nautical roots to its involvement with NASA. However, as the city's roots go back to Point Comfort, where the first captives arrived in the British colonies, exhibits for those interested in African American history are also available.

Operates every day from 9 a.m. to 5 p.m., except Sunday when hours are 1 p.m. to 5 p.m. Adult admission is $5.

Newsome House Museum and Cultural Center, 2803 Oak Street, Newport News

J. Thomas Newsome was an attorney, journalist, and civic leader. From his elegant Queen Anne residence, he rallied the local Black community to fight for social justice in the first part of the twentieth century. The museum shares Mr. Newsome's story and his contributions amid authentic period home décor.

Open Thursday to Saturday, 10 a.m. to 5 p.m.; a $2 donation per person is requested.

Elsewhere in Newport News is an impressive sculpture of Dr. Martin Luther King Jr. in a plaza bearing his name. The bronze bas relief titled *The Unfinished March* by Ed Hamilton is at Twenty-Fifth Street (Martin Luther King Jr. Way) and Jefferson Avenue.

Nat Turner Insurrection Markers—Meherrin Road (Virginia Route 35), South of Cross Keys Road near Boykins, and in Courtland, Virginia, on US 58 at Buckhorn Quarter Road near Capron, Virginia

Nathaniel "Nat" Turner's group killed fifty to sixty whites in August 1831 before his rebellion against enslavement was put down. Turner was caught, tried, and hanged. The event led to legislation prohibiting the education, movement, and assembly of enslaved people.

The Route 35 marker that focuses on Turner's rebellion was on the east side of the highway but agricultural equipment knocked it out of place in 2020. A new marker with new text is supposed to be in place in 2022.

A second marker relating to the insurrection is on US 58. This Buckhorn Quarters marker claims that Turner hid near this location when the militia ended the rebellion.

Next to the Buckhorn Quarters marker is one relating to Dred Scott, who lived on a plantation near here in the early 1800s. In 1830, Scott was sold to an army officer stationed in free territories; Scott sued for his freedom in 1846 because he had lived where slavery was illegal. In 1857, the US Supreme Court ruled Congress could not outlaw slavery; that Scott was property, not a citizen; and that all Blacks—whether free or enslaved—could never be US citizens. The so-called Dred Scott decision is often listed as the high court's worst, outraging abolitionists and further dividing the nation. However, Frederick Douglass had the foresight to see that this ruling, which he labeled the "judicial incarnation of wolfishness," would push the slavery issue even more to the forefront of public debate and eventually lead to its end. Said Douglas in an *1857 speech*, "My hopes were never brighter than now."[146]

"The *Only* Effective, Sustained Revolt"?

In 1967, William Styron won a Pulitzer Prize in Fiction for *The Confessions of Nat Turner.* The novel is based on an 1831 document containing what is represented as Turner's "confession" to a local white lawyer. In the book, Styron labels Turner's rebellion as "the only effective, sustained revolt in the annals of American Negro slavery."[147]

This characterization appears in resources as wide ranging as the Encyclopedia Britannica and the website of Virginia's tourism bureau. It's not entirely true. While not every rebellion may have been sustained as long as others, Styron's claim and other characterizations in his book have been challenged. In any case, several uprisings are memorialized across the South, including those in the following three locations:

- *Richmond, Virginia.* Gabriel's Rebellion (1800) is remembered on a marker in the median in front of 5405 Brook Road. Detail on this effort is available on an information board and map of related places in the parking lot of the Spring Park Historic Site (2000 Park Street).
- *Rantowles, South Carolina.* The Stono Rebellion (1739) was the largest slave revolt staged in the colonies. Dozens of captives planned to march to freedom in Florida (then Spanish-held), picking up more support along the way. They fought off the British for a week over a fifteen-mile stretch. The Stono Rebellion marker is on US 17 just south of the Wallace River on the right. Find it near 4256 Savannah Highway, Ravenel, South Carolina.
- *Destrehan, Louisiana.* Inspired by a successful revolt by slaves in Haiti, Charles Deslondes led the German Coast Uprising in 1811. It has been called the largest, most sophisticated slave revolt in the post–Revolutionary War period.[148] Learn more about it at the Destrehan Plantation, covered in the chapter on Louisiana.

Historian Herbert Aptheker in *American Negro Slave Revolts* found records of 253 rebellions and conspiracies by enslaved individuals in the country.

Central Virginia

Robert Russa Moton Museum, 900 Griffin Boulevard, Farmville

Students at the all-Black Moton High School had put up with overcrowding and substandard conditions long enough. On April 23, 1951, led by sixteen-year-old Barbara Johns, some students walked out of school and began a two-week strike. The students contacted the NAACP for assistance, and with the agreement that the case would be about desegregation and not school conditions, the NAACP wove in this case with four others that collectively were decided in *Brown v. Board of Education*.

There is a real feeling of stepping into history here. Particularly meaningful is being in the auditorium where Barbara Johns addressed her fellow students in 1951 and, in so many words, said, "Enough." It may not be every visitor's good fortune during a visit to meet individuals who were part of this history, or to hear firsthand the effects of Virginia's Massive Resistance policy, shutting down the state's public schools when the Supreme Court ruled in *Brown*. However, that was my own experience, adding so much to the Moton Museum visit. A stop here is highly recommended.

The museum is open from noon to 4 p.m., Monday to Saturday and by appointment. There is no admission fee. Farmville also has a civil rights walking tour; the seventeen locations are listed and mapped on the museum's website.

Virginia's Response to *Brown v. Board of Education*: Massive Resistance

After the Supreme Court ruled in *Brown* and clarified a year later that school integration should proceed with "all deliberate speed," southern states and cities interpreted that phrase differently. Little Rock is a high-profile example of one interpretation. In Virginia, the reaction was given a name: Massive Resistance. Virginia's senior US senator Harry F. Byrd was instrumental in both creating and naming the strategy.

The state General Assembly passed a package of laws in 1956 that, among other things, stopped state funding to any public school that moved to integrate. The governor was authorized to close any school that desegregated.

In September 1958, the governor used that authority to close several schools in Warren County (Front Royal), Charlottesville, and Norfolk. Court cases challenged and overturned the law; Governor J. Lindsay Almond conceded. Despite that, pockets of resistance remained. The most extreme resistance came from Prince Edward County, where Farmville is the county seat. There, public schools remained closed for five years! Even by 1964, only 5 percent of Black students in Virginia were attending integrated schools.

Massive Resistance markers and memorials can be found in these four locales:

- In Farmville at one of the entrances to Prince Edward County High School off Zion Hill Road (the high school's address is 35 Eagle Drive).
- In Front Royal at today's Warren County Middle School (240 Luray Avenue).
- In Charlottesville at Venable Elementary School (Fourteenth Street NW and Gordon Avenue).
- In Norfolk at 322 Shirley Avenue (Maury High School).

Legacy Museum, 403 Monroe Street, Lynchburg

Housed in a two-story Victorian in Tinbridge Hill, a historically Black neighborhood near downtown Lynchburg, the museum displays artifacts, documents, and memorabilia on the contributions of African Americans in the Lynchburg area.

Hours: Wednesday to Saturday, 12 to 4 p.m.; Sunday, 2 to 4 p.m. Admission is $5 for adults, $3 for seniors, and $2 for students and young people.

Booker T. Washington Monument, 12130 Booker T. Washington Highway, Hardy

This chapter noted Booker T. Washington's education at Hampton, and the Montgomery chapter lauded his leadership at the Tuskegee Institute. This NPS site is where he was born in 1856. A short film in the visitors' center as well as an interactive exhibit educate visitors on the life of this educator and adviser to presidents.

The facility is open from 9 a.m. to 5 p.m. daily. The rangers offer a thirty- to sixty-minute walking tour. Groups should reserve that tour in advance to ensure sufficient staffing.

The Harrison Museum of African American Culture, 1 Market Square SE, Second Floor, Roanoke

This museum celebrates the art and history of African Americans for Roanoke Valley citizens and visitors. A wide range of programming is offered here, from a discussion of the challenges of Green Book–era travel to an exhibit titled *Black Citizenship in the Age of Jim Crow.*

The Harrison Museum is open Wednesday through Saturday, 10 a.m. to 3 p.m. Adult admission is $8; $4 for children ages 5 to 17.

Danville

Bloody Monday Memorial Marker, Patton Street in Front of the Danville Circuit Court

The most violent episode of the civil rights movement in Virginia occurred here on June 10, 1963. Only a month after TV images of Bull Connor using charging dogs and high-pressure fire hoses against young demonstrators in Birmingham, police in Danville clubbed and hosed marchers in this tobacco and textile town. About six hundred protesters were arrested in what became known as Bloody Monday. Dr. Martin Luther King Jr. came here on July 11, 1963, to offer his support to the nonviolent protests.

Danville: The Last Capital of the Confederacy?

Swing by the Danville Museum of Fine Arts and History at 975 Main Street. In the 1860s, this was the mansion of Major William T. Sutherlin. However, for a week in April 1865, it was the temporary residence of Confederate president Jefferson Davis. Here, Davis authored his last official proclamation as leader of the Confederacy. His government stayed in Danville until news of Lee's surrender at Appomattox arrived on April 10.

That evening, Davis and his fugitive government left Danville for Greensboro, North Carolina, and Danville earned the distinction of being the last capital of the Confederacy.

During the civil rights era, this was the city's public library. Now a museum, it has an exhibit on the civil rights movement in Danville.

CHAPTER 26

Louisiana

This chapter highlights nine Louisiana cities where Freedom's Road travelers can discover African American history from the earliest days of slavery to the modern civil rights movement. New Orleans provides a good home base for most of the nine locations covered. The majority of them are within an hour and a half of the French Quarter.

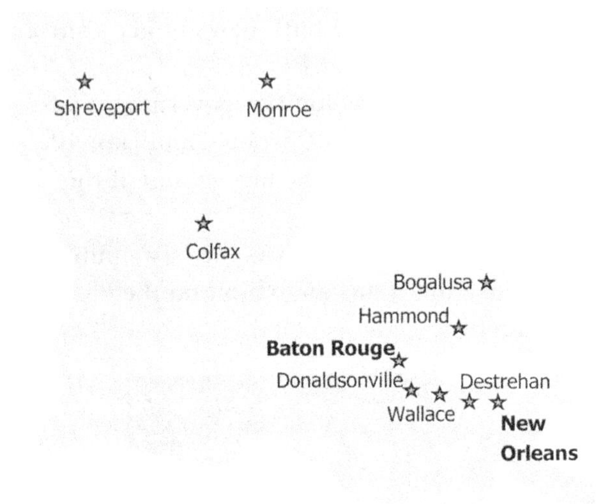

In New Orleans itself, visit the former William Frantz Elementary School, which one of the youngest heroes of the civil rights era, Ruby Bridges, desegregated in 1960. A Louisiana Civil Rights Museum has been proposed for New Orleans, providing another first-rate facility devoted to this era of American history.

French colonists introduced slavery to Louisiana in the early 1700s. The invention of the cotton gin in 1793 and the Louisiana Purchase ten years later accelerated the demand for forced labor in Louisiana. Two Mississippi River plantations west of New Orleans offer the opportunity to learn more about the lives of the enslaved.

- At the Destrehan Plantation, take a guided tour to explore dependency buildings and the grounds. In a museum on the plantation, the 1811 slave revolt mentioned in the Virginia chapter is covered.
- The Whitney Plantation in Wallace bills itself as "a museum of slavery on the grounds of a historical sugar, rice and indigo plantation." As a result, this plantation's tours are more focused on the lives of the people forced to work in the fields, kitchens, and elsewhere.

Twenty-five miles from Wallace is Donaldsonville. The city, the state capital from 1829 to 1831, has a modest African American museum and a beautiful historic district. Part of Donaldsonville's history is the fact that it elected Pierre Caliste Landry, a Methodist minister, the first African American mayor in the United States.

Louisiana's capital, Baton Rouge, would be the next logical stop after visiting Donaldson or seeing one or both of the plantations above. Baton Rouge had its own bus boycott, two years before the one

Did You Know?

Descendants of the principals in the 1896 *Plessy v. Ferguson* case have joined forces to promote equality in education and awareness of the African American history of New Orleans. That Supreme Court decision allowed racial segregation based on the principle of "separate but equal." Keith Plessy and Phoebe Ferguson now are partners in the Plessy and Ferguson Foundation, which hosts an annual Plessy Day on June 7 to commemorate the anniversary of Homer Plessy sitting in a whites-only train car in 1892.

The foundation has also erected several historical markers, including one at the intersection of Press and Royal Streets in New Orleans, where Homer Plessy was arrested. The city renamed Press Street as Homer Plessy Way in 2018.

in Montgomery. The Baton Rouge boycott, settled much more quickly than the Montgomery boycott, was led by the Reverend T. J. Jemison, one of the founding pastors of the Southern Christian Leadership Conference.

To the east of Baton Rouge is Hammond and the Tangipahoa African American Heritage Museum. Its multiple galleries include content on the Underground Railroad as well as the history of the so-called Florida parishes of Louisiana. These eight parishes were considered West Florida by the British, who took over the area after winning the French and Indian War in the mid-1700s.

Bogalusa, the next potential stop, is across the Lake Pontchartrain Causeway. To be honest, the history here is bigger than how it is remembered. That history is a 106-mile march from Bogalusa to Baton Rouge to protest violence against Louisiana's Black citizens. The march in 1967 was twice as long as the well-known Selma-to-Montgomery March.

Not only has the Bogalusa march gained scant attention in the history books, but it hasn't even garnered much tribute in Bogalusa. Two markers are in the neighborhood of the two march organizers, Robert "Bob" Hicks and A. Z. Young. Later we discuss more on the courage of these two men and the events in Bogalusa.

Much farther from New Orleans (three-plus hours) than Bogalusa but similarly dealing with violence brought against African Americans is Colfax. Here, amid growing local displeasure with Reconstruction-imposed rule, "the bloodiest single instance of racial carnage in the Reconstruction era" occurred in 1873.[149] (More on this later as well.)

Northeast of Colfax is Monroe and the Northeast Louisiana Delta African American Museum, another example of a local effort to share local Black history with residents and travelers.

Finally is Shreveport. Right now, no marker memorializes what occurred here in October 1963. However, the chapter concludes relating this event, with its significance for both music and civil rights history: the origin story of Sam Cooke's classic "A Change Is Gonna Come."

New Orleans

William Frantz Elementary School (Now the Akili Academy), 3811 North Galvez Street

Visitors to the Robert Russa Moton Museum in Virginia are struck by the leadership of sixteen-year-old Barbara Johns inspiring her fellow students to walk out of their high school in 1951. Sightseers are certainly impressed by the courage displayed by the Little Rock Nine as they desegregated Little Rock Central High School in 1957. In New Orleans, a few years later, a similarly brave student integrated her school. This time it was an elementary school, and the courage came from six-year-old Ruby Bridges.

Ruby was the daughter of sharecroppers from Mississippi who moved to New Orleans to find better educational opportunities for their four children. Accompanied by federal marshals, she integrated Frantz Elementary School on November 14, 1960. Her school year started late because the school district dragged its feet on her admission.

A smart way to help children understand the civil rights movement is to introduce them to the Ruby Bridges story. Several children's books about Ruby are available. A statue honoring her stands in the school's courtyard, and a classroom has been restored to its vintage 1960 appearance. Schedule a tour via the Akili Academy website's contact page.

Proposed Louisiana Civil Rights Museum

Approximately eight hundred thousand dollars has been secured for this project according to Louisiana lieutenant governor Billy Nungesser. Sites are being scouted for the museum's future home. One possible location is the planned expansion of the Ernest N. Morial Convention Center, where as much as forty thousand square feet could be set aside for the museum.

One point of distinction for this proposed museum is the broader definition of "civil rights" that could be applied here. Besides the struggle for freedom of African American citizens in the Crescent City, the focus may also include Native Americans, the Acadians, Creoles, and other cultures as well.

Destrehan

Destrehan Plantation, 13034 River Road

At this plantation on the east bank of the Mississippi, you can learn about general plantation life and the enslaved's 1811 German Coast uprising. Two tours are offered: a general forty-five-minute plantation tour available several times daily and a two-hour tour focused on "Unheard Voices," available on Saturday and Monday at 10:15 a.m.

Open daily from 9 a.m. to 4:30 p.m. Admission (including the general plantation tour): $23, with discounts for AAA, active military, and seniors; ages 7 to 17: $12; free under 6. The "Unheard Voices" tour is $28 for adults and not recommended for children.

Wallace

Whitney Plantation, 5099 Louisiana Highway 18

Located on the Mississippi River's west bank, the Whitney Plantation is dedicated to explaining the facts about slavery in Louisiana. An hour from New Orleans and Baton Rouge, here you see plantation life through the eyes of the enslaved people who lived and worked here. The Whitney Plantation commissioned sculptor Woodrow Nash to memorialize the enslaved killed during or after the 1811 German Coast revolt; it will be hard to get Mr. Nash's work out of your mind after seeing it.

Open Thursday to Monday, 9:30 a.m. to 4:30 p.m. The admission fee includes a self-guided ninety-minute tour using the Whitney Plantation app. Adults: $25 with a $2 discount for seniors, students, and military; youth ages 6 to 18: $11; under age 6, free.

Baton Rouge

The Baton Rouge African-American Museum, 805 St. Louis Street

Following the murder of its founder, activist Sadie Roberts Joseph, the museum moved from its former South Boulevard location to a city-parish building. The location change puts the operating schedule and features of the facility up in the air. Check online for updates.

In the past, the museum showcased the contributions of local African Americans in music, cuisine, education, politics, and business. Part of the visitor experience was boarding a colorful bus from the early 1950s to explore Baton Rouge's civil rights past. In 1953, there was an eight-day bus boycott in Baton Rouge, the first such large-scale action in the South.

A Bench by the Road Marker, McKinley High School Alumni Center, 1520 Thomas H. Delpit Drive

This marker memorializes the civil rights actions of residents of South Baton Rouge and the role of the Reverend T. J. Jemison. Rev. Jemison was a founding member of the Southern Christian Leadership Conference along with Dr. King and Revs. Abernathy and Shuttlesworth.

Rev. Jemison led the 1953 Baton Rouge boycott, protesting segregation on city buses. It demonstrated that collective action can produce change and served as a model for the Montgomery Bus Boycott that began two years later.

New Zion Baptist Church, 2319 Third Street

Once pastored by Rev. Jemison, New Zion is where Dr. King and his colleagues met in February 1957 to form the SCLC. A historical marker is to the right of the church's front door. A memorial is planned across from the church to note New Zion's role in the SCLC's founding and other civil rights events.

Donaldsonville

River Road African American Museum, 406 Charles Street

Located in the town that served as Louisiana's capital in 1830, the staff and exhibits here receive high marks for an engaging and educational experience, particularly for a museum of this size. Expect solid content on the Underground Railroad, as the museum is a member of the NPS's National Underground Railroad Network to Freedom.

Open Wednesday to Saturday, 10 a.m. to 5 p.m. Adult admission is $10; children under 6 are free.

Hammond

Tangipahoa African American Heritage Museum, 1600 Phoenix Square

The eight galleries here cover different aspects of the African American experience, including life in Louisiana's Florida parishes, the Underground Railroad, and prominent Blacks in diverse fields. Over two dozen large color murals depict the history of African Americans in the United States from their West African homelands to the civil rights movement.

Open weekdays 10 a.m. to 5 p.m. General admission, $10; seniors, $7; students, $5; and children 5 and under, $2.

Bogalusa

Robert "Bob" Hicks Marker, 924 Robert "Bob" Hicks Street
A. Z. Young Marker, 1119 Young Brothers Road

Bogalusa is on the Mississippi/Louisiana border and in the 1960s was a hotbed of Klan activity. Like many places, it chose to ignore the integration mandates of the Civil Rights Act of 1964. Klan membership grew here when the act became law.

Robert Hicks was president of the segregated union representing the Black workers at the local paper mill. One night in February 1965, the police chief visited Mr. Hicks to warn him that the Klan was going to bomb his home unless two white civil rights workers staying there left. The chief also told him the police could not protect him or his family if the two white men didn't leave.

At the time of the chief's visit, not many months had passed since the 1964 murders of three civil rights workers in Philadelphia, Mississippi. Yet Mr. Hicks refused to back down, later recalling that those two men would never be seen alive again if they left his home. Calls went out for help, and soon many Blacks with shotguns were at the Hicks home, taking by surprise the two policemen who had stayed out front. They left, and no white mob ever materialized.

This event is noteworthy for three reasons. First, it was a clear departure from the nonviolent approach advocated by Dr. King. Next, it was the start of the Bogalusa chapter of a self-defense group that doesn't get much attention in civil rights history: the Deacons for Defense and Justice. Third, Bogalusa became a test case for the enforcement of the Civil Rights Act of 1964.

In August 1967, Mr. Hicks and fellow activist A. Z. Young began a 106-mile march to Baton Rouge to raise awareness of violence against African Americans. The march ended with a six-hundred-person rally at the Louisiana state capitol. There they received protection from more than two thousand National Guardsmen and police officers, suggesting some resolve to enforce the still relatively new civil rights law.

The two historical markers honoring Hicks and Young at their former homes are four tenths of a mile apart.

Colfax

Colfax "Riot" Marker and Monument, 300 Main Street (Marker) and Faircloth and Fifth Street (Monument)

These two "memorials" paint an inaccurate picture of what happened in Colfax on Easter Sunday, 1873. Louisiana, like other states that seceded from the Union, was governed during the Reconstruction era by interracial Republican administrations. These officials were often called "carpetbaggers" by the local, bigoted Democrats of the time (and by the history books many of us had in twentieth-century classrooms).

The Colfax massacre, a more accurate description of what happened here, stemmed from the disputed 1872 gubernatorial election. President Ulysses Grant, a Republican, recognized a member of his party as Louisiana's governor. Local white Democrats with significant firepower, upset with Grant's choice, created mayhem around Colfax and Grant Parish; local Blacks fled to the parish courthouse for protection. The whites attacked the courthouse and an estimated 150 Blacks were killed, many of whom were executed by the whites *after they were captured.*

The misnamed "Colfax Riot" marker at 300 Main Street states that the "event on April 13, 1873 marked the end of carpetbag misrule in the South." False! Reconstruction ended via a political compromise that settled the 1876 presidential election.

One item on this marker, erected in 1950 by the Louisiana Department of Commerce and Industry, is that three whites were also killed. That is true, though some sources indicate that one was killed by one of his fellow attackers. On a tall monument in a nearby local cemetery, these dead white men are called "heroes . . . who fell in the Colfax Riot fighting for white supremacy." That monument is on the Fifth Street side of the cemetery opposite Colfax Baptist Church (409 Faircloth Street).

Monroe

Northeast Louisiana Delta African American Museum, 1051 Chennault Park Drive

A mix of African American art and history is present here. On the history side, there are artifacts from cabins that housed the enslaved plus many farming tools. Lifelike models of African American leaders like Frederick Douglass and Mary McLeod Bethune provide good teaching opportunities for young visitors.

Hours: Tuesday to Saturday, 10 a.m. to 4 p.m. Admission: Adults 18 and older, $7; students and senior citizens, $5.

Intolerance and Bigotry Spurs an Anthem for the Ages

"A Change Is Gonna Come"[150] was written by Sam Cooke in late 1963 following an incident in Shreveport. Mr. Cooke, his wife, and other members of his entourage had phoned in reservations at a local Holiday Inn. However, when the group arrived at the front desk, the clerk denied them the rooms they reserved, saying there were no vacancies.

Hits like "You Send Me," "Cupid," and "Wonderful World," as well as TV appearances and concert tours made Sam Cooke a household name in the early 1960s. None of that mattered in the Shreveport Holiday Inn lobby in October 1963. The only thing that mattered was his skin color.

Mr. Cooke was understandably angry and protested so much that his wife, Barbara, cautioned him that "they'll kill you."[151] Eventually, Mr. Cooke and his group went to the Castle Motel in town, where they were welcomed, but the trouble wasn't over yet. The Holiday Inn folks complained to the police about the horn-honking by Mr. Cooke's party as they left. The police arrested Sam Cooke for disturbing the peace, an arrest that even made it into the *New York Times*.

If something good can emerge from blatant discrimination, then "A Change Is Gonna Come" is it. The denial of accommodations and the arrest for disturbing the peace caused Mr. Cooke to want to write from this personal experience. Three months later, the song was finished and recorded at the RCA Studios in Hollywood. Mr. Cooke performed it on *The Tonight Show with Johnny Carson* on February 7, 1964. Little attention came from the Friday night performance since two nights later the Beatles appeared on *The Ed Sullivan Show*. Mr. Cooke never performed the song

continued

continued from previous page

again in public, viewing the song's arrangement as complex and its mood as dark.

The song was released on an album in March 1964 and was scheduled for release as a single in December 1964. Tragically, on December 11, 1964, just before the single was to come out, Sam Cooke was shot to death in Los Angeles. He never saw how the civil rights movement picked up the forward-looking optimism of the last line of the chorus and turned it into a powerful social justice anthem.

While the song only rose to the thirty-first spot on the *Billboard* 100 after its release, its stature grew in time. *Rolling Stone* magazine ranked the song number three on its 2021 Five Hundred Greatest Songs of All Time listing. Fittingly, the song was performed at celebrations during Barack Obama's first inauguration.

When you visit the Smithsonian's National Museum of African American History and Culture, you will see "A Change Is Gonna Come" on one of the walls in the facility's Contemplative Court, along with similarly inspiring words of Dr. King, Nelson Mandela, and African American abolitionist and suffragist Frances Ellen Watkins Harper.

No marker in Shreveport explains how bigotry in 1963 resulted in a song that continued to have enormous social impact for decades. While officials in the city of Shreveport apologized in 2019 to Mr. Cooke's daughter for how her father was treated, there should be a marker bringing this event to light for the general public. The site of the former Holiday Inn (1906 North Market Street) would be a perfect spot.

CHAPTER 27

Kentucky

The ten cities covered in this chapter do not subdivide in a logical way geographically. There are no neat clusters as in South Carolina or Virginia. The ten Kentucky cities are, for the most part, spread out. Two of the ten do not even have a place for a heritage traveler to visit but are included in the chapter nonetheless as we will explain shortly.

The ten places covered are

- *Louisville.* The state's largest city offers the popular Muhammad Ali Center. The center is more than a tribute to the great boxing champion, offering important exhibits like *Truth Be Told: The Policies That Affected Black Lives*. Also in Louisville, one can explore the Kentucky Center for African American Heritage, Freedom Park at the University of Louisville, and a walkable downtown civil rights trail.
- *Simpsonville.* East of Louisville, this city is the birthplace of National Urban League president Whitney Young and where Berea College created the Lincoln Institute in response to legislation passed in Kentucky banning interracial education.

Did You Know?

African Americans were some of the first guides at Mammoth Cave, Kentucky's biggest tourist draw today, with over two million visitors.

The first guide was an enslaved man named Stephen Bishop. In 1838, Mr. Bishop was not only tasked with guiding visitors through the known parts of the cave but also with the dangerous task of exploring unseen passages.

One of the highlights of a cave tour today, the Mammoth Dome, was a Bishop discovery. Mammoth Cave is a national park and located about thirty minutes northeast of Bowling Green.

- *Newport.* This Ohio River city, ninety minutes from Louisville, included in our Kentucky compilation to call attention to what is across the river in Cincinnati: the National Underground Railroad Freedom Center. We mention the center here, and in Ohio too, not only because of its proximity to Kentucky but also because of its outstanding presentation of Underground Railroad content.

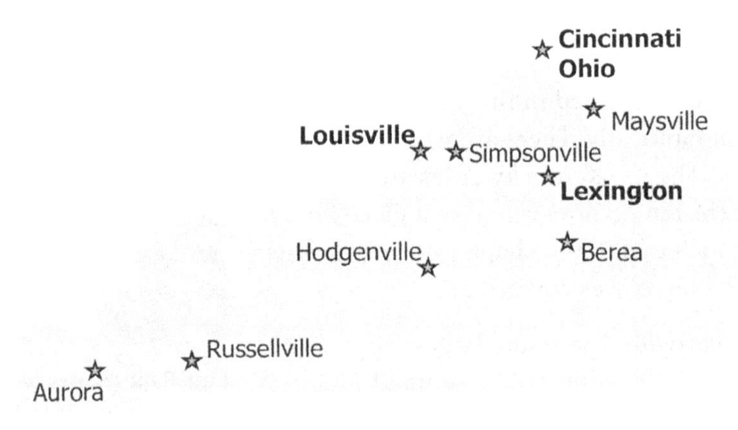

- *Maysville.* A smaller museum on the Underground Railroad is located here in the Bierbower House, a documented safe house from the period before Emancipation.

- *Lexington.* Home to the Commonwealth's largest state university, Lexington has a heritage trail. At the university in front of a hall named in his honor, a marker notes how Lyman Johnson's lawsuit brought an end to segregation at the school in 1949.

- *Frankfort.* A significant march in 1964 drew Dr. King, Jackie Robinson, other luminaries, and ten thousand protesters to this capital city. No marker commemorates this event. This omission by the Kentucky Historical Society might seem more baffling when we relate some of the seemingly less important events that the society recognized.

- *Berea.* Berea College was founded before the Civil War and dedicated to the mission of interracial education. That mission was interrupted for many decades by a law the state's legislature passed in 1904. Visiting this historic college sheds more light on the school's history, importance, and unique approach to education.

- *Hodgenville.* The Abraham Lincoln Birthplace National Historical Site is here, eleven miles off I-65 if you happen to be traveling between Nashville and Louisville.
- *Russellville.* About an hour north of Nashville, Russellville has the SEEK Museum and its two locations; one primarily focuses on slavery and Emancipation while the other picks up after Emancipation and goes through the civil rights era. Learn about pioneering journalist Alice Allison Dunnigan, the first African American woman to be admitted to the White House press corps.
- *Aurora.* On the western side of Kentucky Lake, Aurora was the site of Cherokee State Park. Opened in 1951, the park was for Black Kentuckians, a consequence of the separate-but-equal mentality of the times. While not expecting readers to drive to the western part of the state to see the marker at this now-closed park, we include the park to show the lengths that some went in order to segregate the races during the Jim Crow era.

One final note before we begin: Kentucky is a two-time-zone state. All of the cities we cover *except for westernmost Russellville and Aurora* are in the Eastern Time Zone. The two in the Central Time Zone are one hour behind the rest of the group.

Louisville

Kentucky Center for African American Heritage, 1701 West Muhammad Ali Boulevard

This four-building complex was once a city trolley barn (another fascinating aspect of this center) and is part museum and part event venue. Located in the culturally relevant Russell community, the museum includes a Rotunda of the Ancestors and an exhibit titled *Two Centuries of Black Louisville.*

Gallery hours: Monday to Friday, 10 a.m. to 4 p.m. Free admission.

Louisville Downtown Civil Rights Trail, Various Locations

Driven by the late Dr. J. Blaine Hudson of the University of Louisville (UL), these eleven detail-rich markers memorialize sites and events important to Louisville's civil rights past; each marker is headed by the artwork of sculptor Ed Hamilton. Maps are available at the Louisville Visitors' Center (301 South Fourth Street) or on the UL website.

Other markers of relevance not on this trail include:

- **Smoketown** (the only remaining post–Civil War African American neighborhood in Louisville, according to this marker): corner of East Broadway and South Hancock Street
- **The Campaign to End Segregation in Louisville**: 572 South Fourth Street
- **Slave Trading in Louisville**: South Second Street, near West Main Street
- **Site of Arterburn Brothers Slave Pens**: 209 South First Street

Muhammad Ali Center, 144 North Sixth Street

The athletic prowess, charm, courage, and humanity of this worldwide hero shine through for visitors at this award-winning facility. Ali's rejection of his slave name, Cassius Clay, helped to fuel a widespread Black Pride movement.

The permanent exhibits are built on the six core principles of Ali's life: *Confidence*, *Conviction*, *Dedication*, *Giving*, *Respect*, and *Spirituality*. Recent temporary exhibit topics include women's fight for the right to vote and a truth-telling exhibit exploring policies linked to systematic racism in America.

Open Wednesday to Sunday, noon to 5 p.m. Admission for adults is $14, with discounts for seniors, military, students, and children over 6 (under 6: free). The Muhammad Ali Center is a half mile from the Louisville Visitors' Center.

Charles H. Parrish Jr. Freedom Park, Cardinal Boulevard between Second and Third Streets

This compact park tells the story of African Americans in Louisville on ten black obelisks starting at the Third Street corner. Glass panels featuring nine Kentucky civil rights defenders embellish the pergola on the north end of the park, including one honoring Charles H. Parrish Jr., the first Black professor at UL.

No fees. Park at the Speed Art Museum garage or in metered spaces along Second Street.

Simpsonville

The Whitney M. Young Jr. Birthplace and Marker, 8460 Shelbyville Road

Dr. Whitney Young led the National Urban League for ten years until he drowned in 1971. A recipient of the Presidential Medal of Freedom, Dr. Young transformed the Urban League into one of the most important organizations during the civil rights era, particularly due to its work to end employment discrimination. His birthplace is a National Historic Landmark and open to the public by request. Call the Lincoln Foundation at (502) 585-4733.

Besides the Whitney Young marker, a second one memorializes the Lincoln Institute. The institute was established here when state law prevented Berea College from carrying through on its mission to provide interracial higher education.

Newport

National Underground Railroad Freedom Center, 50 East Freedom Way, Cincinnati, Ohio

This terrific museum is across the river in Cincinnati, but noted here for the convenience of readers planning civil rights travel in Kentucky. The center is reviewed in the Ohio section, and a visit is highly recommended.

Maysville

National Underground Railroad Museum, Bierbower House, 38 West Fourth Street

This documented safe house provides visitors a view into how those escaping captivity were protected and hidden as they traveled the Underground Railroad. Artifacts, documents, and memorabilia detail Maysville's role in the abolitionist movement.

Open Friday and Saturday, 10 a.m. to 3 p.m. Admission: $5 for adults, less for students.

Lexington

Downtown African-American Heritage Interpretive Sign Program, Various Locations

The eleven signs on this route deal with slavery, the Jim Crow era, and the civil rights movement. Sign #3 on Main Street relates to the Lexington lunch-counter sit-in movement; the first occurred in 1959, before the Greensboro action. A map and listing of the locations is at *https://visitlex.com*.

Desegregation of the University of Kentucky Marker, 340 Hilltop Avenue

Lyman T. Johnson sued to attend the university in 1948; a federal judge ruled in his favor. The result was that over two dozen Black students entered graduate and professional programs in 1949. Five years later, undergraduate classes desegregated.

The marker is in front of Lyman T. Johnson Hall. Mr. Johnson became an educator and continued his activism, serving as president of the Louisville NAACP.

Frankfort

On March 5, 1964, Dr. Martin Luther King Jr., Rev. Ralph David Abernathy, and baseball great Jackie Robinson led over ten thousand marchers to the Kentucky capitol. Popular folk singers Peter, Paul, and Mary performed. The march sought to end discrimination in Kentucky's stores, restaurants, theaters, hotels, and other public accommodations via a bill being considered by the state legislature. The bill did not pass in that session but did two years later. Sometimes absence can be instructive. No marker in Frankfort memorializes this event.

The Kentucky Historical Society, which administers the historical marker program, has over twenty-six hundred markers in place. In recent years, markers were put in place to commemorate a commercial nursery in Lexington, a jeans manufacturing facility in Louisville, a mid-air plane collision over Hardinsburg, and the Downtown Commercial District in Winchester (presented by the Beer Cheese Festival). Perhaps a marker for the historic 1964 march at the capitol can be in place before its sixtieth anniversary in 2024.

Berea

Berea College Marker, Intersection of State Highway 21 and US Highway 25

Berea was named by the Reverend John Fee after a biblical town whose citizens were tolerant and open-minded. Founded in 1855 based on Oberlin College's model for interracial learning, the school delivered on that mission until 1904, when the Kentucky legislature passed the Day Law, banning interracial education.

Berea was the only institution impacted by that legislation, and the college fought the Day Law (named after the legislator who pushed the bill) for four years. The college ultimately lost in the US Supreme Court (*Berea College v. Kentucky*), resulting in a four-decade hiatus in Black enrollment at Berea. The year before the Day Law passed, Carter Woodson—father of the concept of Black History Month—graduated from Berea. The Day Law was repealed in 1950.

The historical marker for the college and its mission is near historic Lincoln Hall and the Boone Tavern Hotel. Another marker that deals with Rev. John Fee, the college's founder, is in front of Union Church (200 Prospect Street), a two-minute walk.

Hodgenville

Abraham Lincoln Birthplace National Historical Park, 2995 Lincoln Farm Road

The park commemorates the birth and early years of our sixteenth president. It consists of two separate units located ten miles from each other:

- The Birthplace unit shows Mr. Lincoln's humble beginnings, displaying a symbolic cabin within the neo-classic Memorial Building. The visitors' center with exhibits and a short orientation film is located here at 2995 Lincoln Farm Road.
- The Boyhood Home unit at Knob Creek is northeast of the Birthplace unit; its physical address is 7120 Bardstown Road in Hodgenville.

Start at the visitors' center at the Birthplace unit: open 9 a.m. to 5 p.m. The Boyhood Home unit is open from dawn to sundown. No fee to visit.

Russellville

The SEEK Museum, 183 West Eighth Street

Located in western Kentucky, an hour north of Nashville, the SEEK Museum has two locations. At the Bibb House, the focus is primarily on slavery and emancipation. The SEEK Museum at the Bottom is where visitors can learn, among other things, about pioneering journalist Alice Allison Dunnigan, the first female African American to be admitted to the White House, congressional, and Supreme Court press corps.

Tours of the two sites are available Wednesday to Saturday from 10 a.m. to 4 p.m. with prior email notification through the website's contact form. Cost: $8 per person.

Another marker honoring Ms. Dunnigan resides in the small park at the intersection of South Main Street and East Fourth Street in Russellville.

Overcoming Double Bias: Alice Allison Dunnigan

Listen to any established woman journalist today speak of the early days of her career and you are likely to hear stories of trying to become successful in the face of gender bias and the good-ol'-boy network. Now imagine if you were a woman of color, battling a second type of discrimination.

Not only is that what faced Alice Allison Dunnigan when she decided that journalism would be her career path, but she took her first writing job in 1919 when racial tensions and hostilities were very high. Racial violence, for example, sparked Red Summer in 1919 in Chicago, Washington, D.C., and several other cities including the previously mentioned massacre in Elaine, Arkansas.

Born in 1906 in Russellville, Alice was the daughter of a sharecropper. Her first job came at age thirteen as a reporter for the local Black newspaper, the *Owensboro Messenger-Inquirer.* After college, she taught in the segregated schools of Todd County. There, on seeing how unaware her students were of the contributions of Blacks in Kentucky, she wrote on that subject, but her work was not published until much later.

The call for workers in Washington, DC, during World War II brought her to the nation's capital, where she took night classes at Howard University. After the war, she landed a job as Washington correspondent for the *Chicago Defender.* Initially, she earned less than her male peers but that situation changed when she proved how good she was. The position with the Chicago paper prepared her for her next career move: a writer for the Associated Negro Press. In that position, she sought credentials to cover the US

continued

continued from previous page

House and Senate. Initially denied on the grounds that she did not work for a daily paper, this decision was reversed six months later. Mrs. Dunnigan became the first African American woman to gain congressional press accreditation. After covering the 1948 Truman presidential campaign, she was assigned to the White House, received those press credentials, and chalked up another first.

Over her career, Mrs. Dunnigan garnered dozens of journalism awards and was inducted into the Black Journalist Hall of Fame in 1985. To learn more about this trailblazer, read her 1974 autobiography, *A Black Woman's Experience: From Schoolhouse to White House*.

Aurora

Cherokee State Park Marker, Cherokee Lane at the Intersection with US Highway 68

This marker provides a teaching moment on the lengths some went to keep Blacks and whites separate in the Jim Crow era. Cherokee State Park opened in 1951 as the only state park in Kentucky developed specifically for African Americans. It was closed in 1964 after an order from the governor ended segregation in public facilities.

CHAPTER 28

Missouri

What Missouri lacks in the number of places relevant to Black history, the state more than makes up for in the variety of historic people and places one can visit within its borders. For instance, Missouri has connections to

- An enslaved man born late in the eighteenth century whose case seeking his freedom ended with perhaps the most egregious decision ever made by the US Supreme Court.
- A scientist, born into slavery prior to Emancipation and famous for his work on peanuts, who became the first nonpresident to be honored with a national monument.
- The growth of the Negro Baseball Leagues, which showcased the athletic talent of Black players before the sport was integrated in the 1940s.

Did You Know?

When Lewis and Clark departed St. Louis on May 14, 1804, to explore the territory acquired by the United States in the Louisiana Purchase, a Black man was part of the twenty-eight-month trip.

His name was York, and he wasn't on the trip by his own choice. He was the property of William Clark via his father's will.

York's hunting skills, his ability to barter with Native people, and other talents made him a valuable member of the expedition. Despite how key York was to the journey's success, Clark did not free him at the trip's end—but did sometime later, likely between 1811 and 1815.

There is a mural on the Lewis and Clark Expedition in Liberty, Missouri, at the intersection of South Water Street and East Mill Street. It does feature York.

- The long-overdue landmark decision to integrate the US military in 1948.
- The 2014 shooting of a young African American by a Ferguson, Missouri, police officer, which gave impetus to the Black Lives Matter movement

The history that is covered in this chapter centers around five Missouri cities. Four of the five lay out along a 250-mile stretch of Interstate 70, the highway that bisects the Show Me State from east to west. Let's begin on the east side with St. Louis.

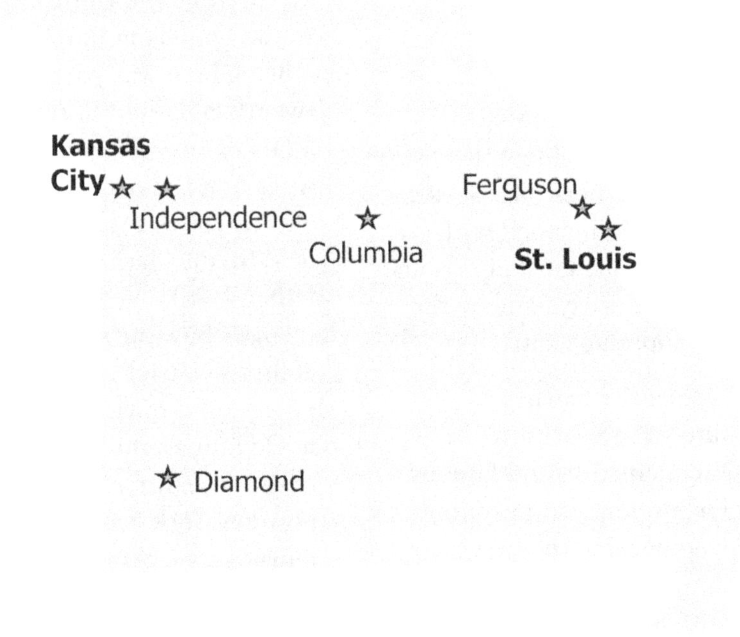

St. Louis is located on the Mississippi River, which plays an important role in the tale of a problem-solving St. Louis minister, the Reverend John Berry Meachum. Rev. Meachum's work included educating Black people. However, Missouri law prohibited this activity after the territory was admitted to the Union as a slave state by the Missouri Compromise; Maine became a state then as a free state.

With the education of Blacks banned in Missouri, Rev. Meachum needed to be resourceful, and the river came in handy. Across the river was the free state of Illinois. The boundary line was in the middle of the river, which was a mile wide at St. Louis.

To skirt the prohibition, the clever clergyman established a "Floating Freedom School" in 1847 on a steamboat anchored in free territory, right in the middle of the Mississippi River. In some ways, it was an early version of the schools created during Freedom Summer 1964 in Mississippi.

Reverend Meachum also was a founder of the oldest Black church in Missouri, the African Church of St. Louis (later renamed First Baptist Church of St. Louis). Learn more about this ingenious man at the Griot Museum of Black History in St. Louis.

Also on your list of places to visit in St. Louis should be the Old Courthouse, not far from the iconic Gateway Arch. At this courthouse, the enslaved Dred Scott sued for his freedom. Mr. Scott argued that the free states he lived in for four years had laws that took away slaveholders' ownership rights after a period of time.

The 1857 Supreme Court decision that came to bear his name not only denied Mr. Scott his freedom but also held that Black people "are not included, and were not intended to be included, under the word 'citizens' in the Constitution." The Missouri History Museum, also in St. Louis, sheds more light on the Dred Scott case.

Fifteen minutes north of the Old Courthouse is the suburb of Ferguson and the site of the 2014 police shooting of Michael Brown. Two memorials are on Canfield Drive, where the shooting occurred.

West of St. Louis is Columbia, home to the University of Missouri. A two-mile-long heritage trail here has over three dozen locations to visit and an ever-expanding number of markers at the locations.

On the western side of the state are two cities with wonderful educational museums. In Kansas City, visit the Negro Leagues Baseball Museum, where you can learn about the various leagues in which talented Black athletes played from 1920 to 1948 when prejudice kept them from the Major Leagues. In December 2020, Major League Baseball (MLB) added statistics from the Negro Leagues' players to the sport's record book. In doing so, MLB called its action "correcting an oversight." As ESPN senior writer Howard Bryant correctly pointed out, the exclusion of Black players prior to Jackie Robinson was not an "oversight" but rather a conscious, ongoing decision.

Harry S. Truman was hardly someone whom one might associate with the quest for civil rights. The thirty-third president grew up in Missouri when segregation was widely accepted. In fact, both sets of his grandparents were slaveowners. At the Harry S. Truman Presidential Library and Museum, learn about how Truman's Executive Orders led to prohibiting discrimination in federal employment and ending segregation in the nation's military. The Truman Library and Museum is located in Independence, a suburb of Kansas City.

A possible final stop in Missouri is the birthplace of scientist, inventor, and educator George Washington Carver. The National Park Service has a facility in Diamond, ten miles outside of Joplin; the national monument to Mr. Carver was put in place in 1943.

St. Louis and Ferguson

Missouri History Museum, 5700 Lindell Boulevard

Permanent exhibits like *Seeking St. Louis* make this museum a worthwhile stop. That exhibit introduces visitors to Jeanette Forchet, a free Black woman who lived in St. Louis around 1790. Learn what her life was like as one of only a few dozen free Blacks in the city at the time. The gallery includes content on Dred Scott's unsuccessful quest for freedom. The civil rights movement in St. Louis is also covered.

A special exhibit running through June 2022 features groundbreaking St. Louis women including Annie Turnbo Malone, a Black entrepreneur and philanthropist, whose beauty products company grew to employ seventy-five thousand women worldwide.

The museum is open Tuesday to Sunday from 10 a.m. to 5 p.m. Admission is free.

Old Courthouse, 11 North Fourth Street

Well-maintained inside and out, this is the courthouse where Dred Scott first filed his lawsuit seeking freedom for himself and his family. Missouri was admitted as a slave state via the Missouri

Compromise of 1820. Mr. Scott had lived in the free state of Illinois and filed his petition for freedom on that basis.

Normally open daily, 8 a.m. to 4:30 p.m., this NPS facility, close to the Gateway Arch, was undergoing renovations as the book went to press.

Griot Museum of Black History, 2505 St. Louis Avenue

In Africa, a griot preserves and shares stories from the past. This museum performs this function through artifacts, memorabilia, and life-sized wax figures of prominent African Americans. Their History Hunt makes a visit more engaging for young people.

Hours: Wednesday to Saturday, 10 a.m. to 5 p.m. Admission: $7.50 for ages 13 and above; $3.75 for ages 5 to 12.

George B. Vashon Museum Home, 2223 St. Louis Avenue

George Vashon was an abolitionist and legal scholar whose family moved to St. Louis after his death in 1878. Calvin Riley, the museum's curator, collected the memorabilia on display here, some of which Mr. Riley acquired from the Vashon family.

Closed December to February; open other months, Wednesday to Saturday, from 10 a.m. to 4 p.m.

Michael K. Brown Memorials, 2943 and 2973 Canfield Drive, Ferguson

On August 9, 2014, Ferguson police office Darren Wilson killed Michael Brown in this St. Louis suburb. Many aspects of the incident are in dispute, but these are not: Mr. Brown had six bullet wounds and his body was left on Canfield Drive for four hours. Office Wilson has not been charged by local authorities in the shooting.

In front of 2943 Canfield Drive, note the dove imprinted on the sidewalk and the repaved asphalt section where Mr. Brown lay in the street. The section of the street where he lay was removed at the request of Mr. Brown's family and given to them. Near 2973 Canfield Drive (about one hundred yards from the dove marker) is a bronze plaque imbedded in the sidewalk honoring Michael Brown.

The deaths of Michael Brown here and Eric Garner in New York City (by an illegal chokehold by police) provided more sparks to the Black Lives Matter movement, which began in 2013 after the shooting of Trayvon Martin by George Zimmerman in Florida.

Columbia

African American Heritage Trail, Various Locations

The city has an ever-growing, two-mile-long Heritage Trail consisting of thirty-six historical markers. Find a map with these locations on the city's website (www.como.gov).

Kansas City

Negro Leagues Baseball Museum, 1616 East Eighteenth Street

Racism and the Jim Crow laws of the late 1800s put an end to Blacks and whites playing professional baseball together for nearly a half century. Black players formed their own teams and traveled the country competing against any challenger. In 1920, the Negro National League was organized, and other leagues followed over the next twenty-five years.

The integration of Major League Baseball by Jackie Robinson in 1947 ultimately led to the demise of the Negro Leagues. However, the legacy of these leagues and their players is presented at this popular museum (three hundred thousand visitors annually). Don't miss the documentary that tells the story of the leagues, narrated by actor James Earl Jones.

Open Tuesday to Saturday, 10 a.m. to 5 p.m., and Sunday, noon to 5 p.m. Admission: $10 for those 13 to 64; $9 for 65 and older; $6 for children 5 to 12 years.

A five-minute walk from the museum is the Buck O'Neil Tribute Park (at Nineteenth Street and The Paseo). Mr. O'Neil was a player and manager for the Kansas City Monarchs in the Negro American League. He was a driving force behind the Negro Leagues Baseball Museum; learn more here about this recipient of the Presidential Medal of Freedom.

Leroy "Satchel" Paige Gravesite, Forest Hill and Calvary Cemetery, 6901 Troost Avenue

About eight miles south of the Negro Leagues Baseball Museum is the grave of Hall of Fame pitcher Leroy "Satchel" Paige, one of many star players in the Negro League. Mr. Paige, a teammate of Jackie Robinson on the Kansas City Monarchs, was the first Black pitcher in the American League.

His gravestone, located on its own "island" between sections 38 and 51, includes an explanation of how he earned the nickname "Satchel" and six of his tips for staying young. Worth the trip.

Black Archives of Middle America, 1722 East Seventeenth Terrace

Located three minutes from the Negro Leagues Baseball Museum, the Black Archives named its central permanent exhibit *With My Eyes No Longer Blind*, a line from the Langston Hughes poem "I Look at the World." The exhibit tracks the African American experience in Kansas City through six time periods, including the civil rights movement.

There is no charge to visit; open Monday to Friday, 10 a.m. to 5 p.m., and on Saturday, 10 a.m. to 3 p.m.

Independence

Harry S. Truman Presidential Library

From the Revolutionary War onward, African Americans have always fought in the nation's wars. However, in most instances, they fought in segregated units. Harry Truman changed that when he signed an Executive Order on July 26, 1948, to integrate the country's armed forces. This decision, made as the 1948 Presidential campaign began, is one aspect of our thirty-third president's life presented at the newly renovated museum.

The museum is open from Monday to Saturday at 9 a.m. and Sunday at noon. Closing is at 5 p.m. every day. Admission: $12 for adults; $10 for seniors; $5 for teens 13 to 18; and free for children 12 years and under.

Diamond

George Washington Carver National Monument, 5646 Carver Road

This National Park Service site, the first to honor an African American, commemorates the birthplace of famous scientist and inventor George Washington Carver; he spent his childhood here. Located sixteen miles from Joplin, the 240-acre park has a visitors' center, theater, museum, interactive exhibit area for kids, and short nature trail. In 1896, Mr. Carver joined the Tuskegee Institute in Alabama, where he conducted his groundbreaking research.

The park is open daily from 9 a.m. to 5 p.m. Guided tours are offered at 10 a.m. and 2 p.m. The NPS site is free.

CHAPTER 29

Oklahoma and Texas

The three most populous cities in Oklahoma offer varied and important opportunities to better understand people and events that shaped Black history.

Tulsa. As the year 1921 began, the Greenwood section of Tulsa was one of the most prosperous neighborhoods in the country. Greenwood was one of those sections of a US city that gained "Black Wall Street" status. That came to a tragic end in June 1921 when whites burned the Greenwood District to the ground. Learn more about the Tulsa Race Massacre at the two locations covered here.

Oklahoma City. Here, you can get to know Clara Luper, another often-overlooked champion of freedom. Mrs. Luper was a tireless advocate for equal rights, creating her own Children's Crusade long before that tactic was used successfully in Birmingham in 1963. A civil rights center bearing her name is in development. Also,

Did You Know?

The Lone Ranger character of radio and 1950's television fame may have been based on a Black lawman.

That's what professor Art Burton hypothesizes in his book on Bass Reeves. Reeves, born enslaved in Arkansas, became the first Black deputy marshal west of the Mississippi. Whether he served as a prototype for the masked man is uncertain, but Reeves's exploits are admirable. With legendary shooting skills and an uncompromised integrity, he cleverly captured bad guys across the Southwest.

One story suggested he dressed as a beggar running from authorities as he searched for two outlaw brothers. Finding them, he was taken in by the pair's sympathetic mother and allowed to spend the night under the same roof as his targets. By sunrise, her sons were in handcuffs.

in this state's capital, visit the church that *didn't* hire a particular recent seminary graduate, twenty-four-year-old Martin Luther King Jr. Might things have been different if Dr. King started his career here?

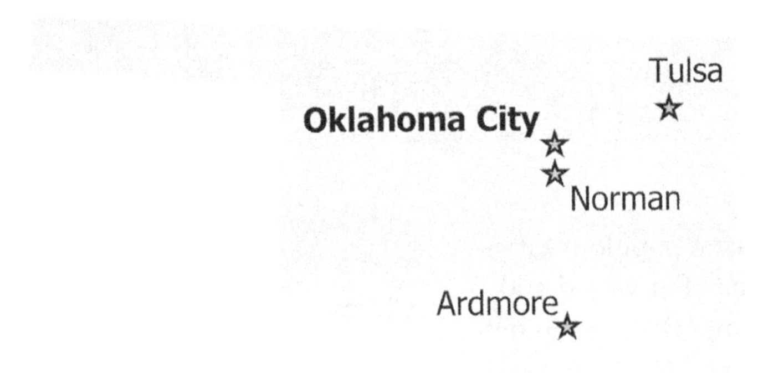

Norman. The University of Oklahoma figures into a 1950 US Supreme Court decision that opened up educational opportunities at the graduate-school level for African Americans. Go to the library on campus to learn more about the precursor to 1954's *Brown v. Board of Education* decision.

Tulsa and Oklahoma City are ninety minutes apart. Norman is essentially a suburb of the capital city, a half-hour drive.

A fourth possible stop in Oklahoma is Ardmore, roughly halfway between Oklahoma City and Dallas, where one can visit a building on the National Register of Historical Places that recalls the time when Blacks were not allowed to attend whites-only movie theaters. The Black Theatre of Ardmore served its community for two decades before being converted to a church.

Turning to Texas provides the opportunity to note a civil rights–era school desegregation attempt in 1956 that is not as widely known as others like Little Rock, yet the situation was just as ugly, if not even more so.

The incident took place in Mansfield, outside of Fort Worth, as the 1956 school year began. The schools were ordered to desegregate, the school board concurred, but some white parents gathered at Mansfield High School to prevent three Black students from going to class. They hung three Blacks in effigy and roughed up some of the students' supporters. The governor, Allan Shivers, a segregationist, sent in the Texas Rangers to keep the Black students out.

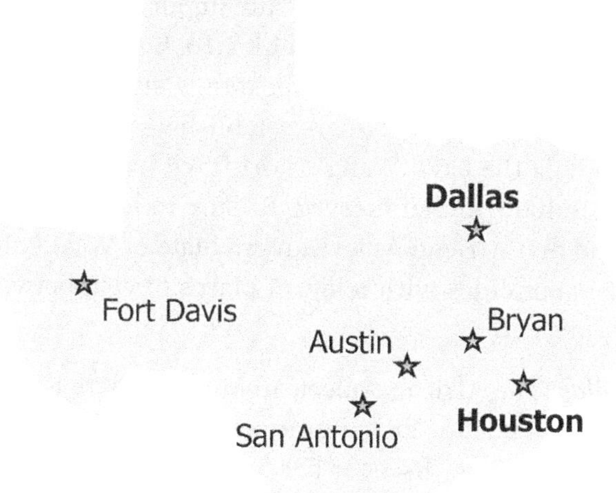

The Rangers in Mansfield were captained by E. J. (Jay) Banks. Banks also was the Ranger commander at a similar mob action at Texarkana Junior College the same school year. Two Blacks, an eighteen-year-old female and a seventeen-year-old male, were prevented from enrolling at the junior college by the white mob that blocked their path. The Rangers led by Banks did nothing to prevent the mob from beating up the young Black man.

Five years after these incidents, a statue with a likeness of Banks went up at Love Field, the main airport serving Dallas and Fort Worth at the time. Except for a period when the airport was modernized, the statue remained at Love Field until June 2020. A book titled *Cult of Glory: The Bold and Brutal History of the Texas Rangers* by Doug Swanson laid out Banks's participation in these ugly incidents. The statue named *One Riot, One Ranger* was removed from the now city-owned airport in June 2020.

Incidents like those at Mansfield High and Texarkana Junior College factored into the state passing segregation laws in 1957. These laws delayed local integration for several years. In fact, it wasn't until 1965 when, faced with the loss of federal funds, the Mansfield school district quietly desegregated.

The Texas part of the chapter focuses on seven cities, from Houston in the east out to historically important Fort Davis, almost on the state's western border with Mexico. Both places describe the work of the Buffalo Soldiers. In Houston, visit a museum named for these regiments of Black soldiers established as peacekeepers in the West following the Civil War. At Fort Davis, see the restored base where the Buffalo Soldiers served. Be sure to learn about Henry O. Flipper, the first African American graduate of West Point.

The major cities with relevant places to visit between Houston and Fort Davis are

- *Dallas*. The African American Museum here is a must-see. Also recommended is an appointment-required visit to the Juanita J. Craft House to discover her role in civil rights and her service to Dallas as a member of the city council. Be sure to tour the Wheatley Place neighborhood near her home.
- *Austin*. Two sites, the Bullock Texas History Museum and the Texas African American Monument at the state capitol, are just a half-mile apart. The monument is another stunning creation of sculptor Ed Dwight.
- *Bryan and San Antonio*. These cities host modest museums largely focused on local African American history.

Oklahoma

Tulsa

Greenwood Cultural Center, 322 North Greenwood Avenue

The center describes itself as "the keeper of the flame" for Tulsa's Black Wall Street era and the violence that came here in 1921, fueled by racial hatred. The Greenwood District was quite prosperous in the early 1900s, one of the wealthiest African American neighborhoods in the United States.

That prosperity was interrupted on June 1, 1921, when white mobs attacked Blacks and burned thirty-six blocks of the Greenwood District to the ground. The Tulsa Race Massacre was investigated by a state commission in 2001, which estimated that as many as three hundred people may have lost their lives, making it one of the single deadliest acts of racial violence and domestic terrorism in the nation's history. The commission also found indications that the city government at the time was complicit in the massacre.

Exhibits here relate both the antecedents to the violence and the recovery of the Greenwood District. Part of a visit to the center can include stopping at the Mabel B. Little Heritage House. The home originally belonged to two survivors of the massacre, Sam and Lucy Mackey. It was rebuilt by 1925 and gives visitors a glance at life in the historic Greenwood District.

Open weekdays from 9 a.m. to 5 p.m. There is no fee to visit the cultural center or the Mabel B. Little Heritage House.

John Hope Franklin Reconciliation Park, 321 North Detroit Avenue

This beautifully laid-out park, with flower gardens and a soothing water feature, is charged with telling the ugly story of the 1921 Tulsa Race Massacre. Reconciliation Park is one result of the 2001 report titled *Tulsa Race Riot: A Report by the Oklahoma Commission to Study the Tulsa Race Riot of 1921*. The park's twenty-seven-foot bronze, *Tower of Reconciliation*, is another stunning work by sculptor Ed Dwight.

Dr. John Hope Franklin, born in Oklahoma in 1915, had a seven-decade-long career of scholarship, teaching, and advocacy. President Bill Clinton awarded him the Medal of Freedom in 1995. It is fitting for a park whose theme is reconciliation to be named for Dr. Franklin.

Free guided tours of the park can be arranged via a contact form on the park's website. Tours are available on Tuesday and Thursday from 9 a.m. to 3 p.m. (no tour at noon) and on Saturday from 10 a.m. to 1 p.m.

African American Resource Center, Rudisill Regional Library, 1520 North Hartford Avenue

While providing the usual library services, the center also serves as a genealogical resource and presents exhibits such as *Portraits of Historic African-American Leaders.*

The center is open Monday to Saturday at 10 a.m.; closing time is 7 p.m. through Thursday, with earlier closings on Friday and Saturday.

Oklahoma City

Clara Luper Civil Rights Center (in Development), 2609 North Martin Luther King Avenue

In December 2019, voters in Oklahoma City approved a temporary one-cent sales tax to fund several community projects, including the construction of the Clara Luper Civil Rights Center and the renovation of the Freedom Center. During the civil rights era, the Freedom Center served as the headquarters of the NAACP Youth Council, which Clara Luper led. A monument in front of the Freedom Center honors other local activists.

Clara Luper was one of the Black students who integrated the University of Oklahoma in 1950, completing a master's in history education in 1951. Influenced by the success of the Montgomery Bus Boycott and the nonviolent approach of Dr. King, Ms. Luper took on the role of mentor at the NAACP Youth Council. One of her noteworthy initiatives was desegregating the lunch counter at the Katz Drug Store in downtown Oklahoma City. This success occurred on August 19, 1958, eighteen months before the more widely known lunch-counter protest in Greensboro, North Carolina, on February 1, 1960.

Former Site of Calvary Baptist Church, 300 North Walnut Avenue

This church, built in 1921 in the Deep Deuce section, has important connections to civil rights history beyond being a social and religious center for the city's Black population:

It was instrumental during the 1958 lunch-counter sit-ins that Clara Luper led. Mrs. Luper would meet with her NAACP Youth Council members and plan their ultimately successful sit-in efforts.

Calvary Baptist chose not to hire a new seminary graduate named Martin Luther King Jr. to serve as its pastor in 1951. Dr. King came here seeking a position, preached, but came up short.

Historian Currie Ballard interviewed one of the senior deacons involved in that decision and reported that the deacon said, "The reason we didn't hire Dr. King is he didn't have enough gravy." Ballard asked what "gravy" meant. The deacon replied, "He just wasn't old enough." King was twenty-four at the time.

A law firm has restored the historic brick building for its offices. The blue neon sign out front is not the original, but use your imagination to bring yourself back to the 1950s to see Dr. King leaving the church to continue his job search in 1951 or Clara Luper heading in to strategize with her teenage heroes who pulled off those sit-ins at segregated lunch counters in 1958.

There are no tours of the building per se; however, you can see the inside of the restored sanctuary by asking the Dan Davis Law Firm in advance with an email to *receptionist@dandavislaw.com*.

Oklahoma History Center, 800 Nazih Zuhdi Drive

Among the many permanent exhibits at this general state history museum is one titled *The African American Experience*, located on the third floor. The center has five traveling African American history exhibits that can be booked by other museums.

Admission: Monday through Saturday, 10 a.m. to 5 p.m. Adults $10; seniors and students $5; children under 5 and active-duty military, veterans, and their dependents (with ID) are free.

Norman

Bizzell Library at the University of Oklahoma, 401 West Brooks Street

In one respect, this building could be the largest memorial to a single event in civil rights history. In 1948, George McLaurin applied to the doctoral program at the university. After a court fight, the retired Black professor won the right to enroll, but on a segregated basis. That meant that he had to eat separately from whites in the cafeteria, sit separately in classes, and study at a designated desk on the mezzanine level of the Bizzell Library.

Mr. McLaurin sued again, with his case decided by the US Supreme Court in 1950. In *McLaurin v. Oklahoma Board of Regents*, the court unanimously ruled that, because of segregation, McLaurin was "handicapped in his pursuit of effective graduate instruction. Such restrictions impair and inhibit his ability to study, to engage in discussion and exchange views with other students, and in general to learn his professions."

The case capped the NAACP's suits to overturn the separate-but-equal doctrine in graduate and professional schools. Then it was on to challenge that same flawed concept in elementary and secondary education.

Ardmore

The Former Black Theater of Ardmore, 536 East Main Street

Precluded from patronizing "white" theaters, the Black citizens of Ardmore had their movie entertainment needs satisfied here from 1922 to 1944. The building was sold to Metropolitan A.M.E. Church and is listed on the National Register of Historic Places.

Texas

Austin

Bullock Texas History Museum, 1800 Congress Avenue

This museum presents a wide range of programming on Texas history and often has content of interest to Black history. In 2021, an exhibit titled *Black Citizenship in the Age of Jim Crow* centered on how African Americans pursued democratic ideals during Reconstruction and then persevered after it ended as they faced Jim Crow laws and policies promoting racial inequality.

Open Wednesday to Sunday, 10 a.m. to 5 p.m. Admission: Adults, $13; seniors, military, and students, $11; youth ages 4 to 17, $9.

George Washington Carver Museum, 1165 Angelina Street

This thirty-six-thousand-square-foot facility houses four galleries, including a Families Gallery, highlighting ten Central Texas families. The core exhibit, *The African American Presence in 19th-*

Century Texas, tracks the path from African homeland to servitude to freedom.

Admission is free. The museum opens every day except Sunday at 10 a.m., closing at 6 p.m. every day except Thursday (9 p.m. close) and Sunday (4 p.m. close).

Texas African American Monument, State Capitol Grounds, 100 West Eleventh Street

Bold sculptures by former astronaut candidate Ed Dwight can be seen in Reconciliation Park in Tulsa; at the state capitol in Columbia, South Carolina; and many other places. The bas-relief work by Mr. Dwight in Austin traces the African American experience in Texas, from Spanish colonial times to the present. Narrative plaques describe each era.

Always open and always free. Find the display on the expansive capitol grounds near where West Eleventh Street and Congress Avenue meet.

African American Cultural Heritage Facility, 912 East Eleventh Street

This restored historic house serves as an African American visitors' center. It was once owned by one of the first freedmen in Travis County. The modern building here is home to the Greater

Austin Black Chamber of Commerce and the Office of Arts & Cultural Resources.

African American Historical Landmarks Trail, Various Locations

Find a listing of the eleven locations on this trail at the Visit Austin website *https://www.austintexas.org*.

Dallas

The African American Museum at Fair Park, 3536 Grand Avenue

Plan a couple of hours to experience the four floors of this facility. Along with many artistic works, there are exhibits on slavery, the civil rights movement, Blacks in the fields of sports and music, and more.

Admission is free. Open Tuesday to Friday, 11 a.m. to 5 p.m., and Saturday, 10 a.m. to 5 p.m.

Dallas Civil Rights Museum, 2922 Martin Luther King Boulevard

This museum is part of the five-building Martin Luther King Jr. Community Center, which includes a social services center and a library. The museum focuses on four primary topics: the Underground Railroad, the civil rights movement, Black Wall Street, and the Trail of Tears. The museum is in Building A, Suite #118.

The center is open Monday to Friday, 8 a.m. to 5 p.m., and Saturday, 8 a.m. to 3 p.m.

Juanita J. Craft Civil Rights House, 2618 Warren Avenue

Juanita Craft's contributions to the civil rights movement far outdistance her renown. Mrs. Craft played a crucial role in integrating the University of Texas Law School and what is now the University of North Texas. Besides desegregating these institutions, she successfully pushed for integration at the Texas State Fair and at Dallas theaters, restaurants, and lunch counters. The first Black woman to vote in Dallas County in 1944, Mrs. Craft served two terms on the Dallas City Council in the 1970s.

Appointments are necessary to visit the house; contact the Dallas Office of Cultural Affairs (214-670-3687). A marker in front of the house honors Mrs. Craft. Tour the entire Wheatley Place Landmark District, a predominantly African American area on the National Register of Historic Places.

Houston

The African American Library at the Gregory School, 1300 Victor Street, and the Houston Museum of African American Culture (HMAAC), 4807 Caroline Street

In his first term as Houston's first Black mayor, Lee Brown formed a committee to explore establishing an African American museum. The committee recommended two separate facilities: one focused on history, the other on art and culture. The Gregory School was selected to be the history repository as it was the first public school for African Americans in Houston. A restored classroom from its 1926 inception is one of three permanent exhibits. The HMAAC is two miles from the Gregory School location and collects, preserves, exhibits, and encourages artistic expression appealing to all races.

Both facilities are free. The library is open Tuesday to Saturday, 10 a.m. to 4 p.m. The culture museum is open Friday and Saturday, 11 a.m. to 6 p.m.

Buffalo Soldiers National Museum, 3816 Caroline Street

A half mile from the Houston Museum of African American Culture, this institution pays tribute to the first Black professional soldiers to serve in a peacetime army. The Buffalo Soldiers came from varied backgrounds, including formerly enslaved men, some who served during the Civil War. At several Texas forts where the Buffalo Soldiers served, memorials are also installed.

Open Tuesday to Saturday, 10 a.m. to 4 p.m. Admission is $10; students and military, $5; children 5 and under, free. Thursday after 1 p.m. is free, and closing is at 5 p.m.

Bryan

Brazos Valley African American Museum, 500 East Pruitt Street

This museum offers a mix of art and history; one 2020 exhibit featured Congressman John Lewis's Brazos Valley connections.

Open Tuesday to Friday, 10 a.m. to 5 p.m., and Saturday, 10 a.m. to 4 p.m. Adult admission is $5.

San Antonio

San Antonio African American Community Archive and Museum, Building 20, 218 South Presa Street

Located in the La Villita Historic Arts Village, the museum collects and shares stories of people and events related to the city's Black citizens. One goal of the museum is to build a community-based digital archive.

Open from 10 a.m. to 6 p.m., Monday to Saturday and 11 a.m. to 4 p.m. on Sunday and by appointment.

Fort Davis

Fort Davis National Historic Site,
Junction of Texas Highways 17 and 118

West Texas visitors and residents encounter an important slice of African American history here. For nearly two decades after the Civil War, the only troops garrisoned here were the Buffalo Soldiers. In Houston's Buffalo Soldiers Museum, one learns their history; at this NPS site, you can see where they served.

Fort Davis was one of the first to receive African American troops, among them the first Black graduate of West Point, Lieutenant Henry Ossian Flipper. Lieutenant Flipper experienced discrimination throughout his career, including here. He was accused of embezzlement at Fort Davis, court-martialed, and dishonorably discharged from military service.

While he sought to clear his name for years, he died in 1940 with the stigma of a dishonorable discharge still in effect. When his case gained more attention as a result of the civil rights movement, his reputation began to be restored. Reviews of Lieutenant Flipper's dismissal led the army to reverse his dishonorable discharge. In 1999, President Bill Clinton granted a full and unconditional pardon to Lieutenant Flipper.

Your visit should include viewing a fifteen-minute film as well as touring the ample grounds and its nicely restored buildings. Wear comfortable footwear.

Open daily 8 a.m. to 5 p.m. Admission is $10 per person over age 15, or $20 per vehicle. NPS passes for seniors, military, and others are honored.

PART FIVE

TRAVELING FREEDOM'S ROAD ELSEWHERE IN THE UNITED STATES

CHAPTER 30

Traveling Freedom's Road in the Rest of the United States

Civil rights and African American history can be explored beyond the South and closer to home for Americans in or near their home state. While high-profile civil rights–era events were less likely to have occurred outside the South, some took place. Think of the 1963 March on Washington for one and the assassination of Malcolm X in New York for another.

Major figures in the civil rights movement have connections to the places covered here. Just consider Dr. King. His name comes up in conjunction with Washington, DC, Chicago, Cleveland, Indianapolis, and Seattle.

Significant events that occurred in the 1950s and 1960s have their origin stories connected to other states. *Brown v. Board of Education* has its roots in Topeka, Kansas. The volunteers who worked in Mississippi during Freedom Summer 1964 were trained in Oxford, Ohio. Many of the people and tactics that helped the civil rights movement succeed were part of the Pullman Porters' quest for justice. A terrific museum in Chicago focuses on this union of railcar porters and its longtime leader, A. Philip Randolph.

So, while well-known civil rights events are less common as you move away from the South, you can still learn about the broader struggle for freedom everywhere from New England to Hawaii. These learning opportunities occur in museums both modest and massive, at National Park Service (NPS)–managed sites, in the homes that once housed great women and men of the movement, and at parks and other memorials honoring significant people, events, and moments in time.

Ponder these questions, as they'll give an idea of what you can see outside the South:

- Where's the original bus that Rosa Parks rode in when she refused to give up her seat? Hint: It's over eight hundred miles from Montgomery.
- How about Malcolm X's birth home? Maybe New York City? Nope, try going twelve hundred miles west.
- Where will a man born enslaved prior to the American Revolution end up living out his life and have his homestead there connect with one of the highest-profile individuals in African American history? No hint on this one: just read on!

As with the book so far, the listings here are not exhaustive. Crossing the vast expanse of the United States, not to mention the civil rights movement, requires some judgment calls in terms of the states covered and how many sites are presented.

Thirty-six states have not yet been covered in the book; we suggest places to visit in two dozen of them, plus the District of Columbia, an outstanding civil rights history destination on its own. Residents of the states in the lower 48 that did not get a listing just need to cross a state line to connect with relevant history.

Within these twenty-four states, we limit ourselves to no more than three potential sites. Some states may only have a location or two that merit a mention. When a state has more than one potential destination, we try to present geographically dispersed locales within that state. The three-location limit applies only to states; DC is exempt because there's so much to see.

To research what might be near your hometown, think about these approaches:

- Start with your state's historical society and state history museum. Find out what they offer on civil rights or African American history.
- Search the internet using terms like "civil rights museums" or "African American museums" and your city or your state name. Use the quote marks around "civil rights museums" and "African American."

- The Historical Marker Database website (*www.hmdb.com*) has an easy-to-use search tool to find memorial markers near you. Put your city in the search bar to find what is close to home.
- Consult local and state visitors' bureaus. They may have designed relevant walking or driving tours.
- Explore nearby universities and libraries, particularly around the MLK National Holiday and Black History Month for exhibits or lectures.

The three geographic sections we cover are

- The District of Columbia and eastern states
- The central states
- The western states

The District of Columbia and Eastern States

Washington, DC

The National Museum of African American History and Culture, 1400 Constitution Avenue NW

A stunning success since opening in late 2016, the museum is part of the Smithsonian Institution's collection of world-class museums and galleries. The number of artifacts on display and the array of subjects covered can keep you engaged on five exhibition floors for hours. To be honest, don't plan anything else on the day you visit. Securing an admission pass is hard enough, so take advantage of all that is offered once you enter.

So much is here that one could write a book on this collection alone. In fact, the Smithsonian has authorized one: *Official Guide to the Smithsonian National Museum of African American History and Culture*. The Smithsonian also offers an excellent smartphone app.

Located on the National Mall, the museum uses a timed-entry

system for admitting visitors. These passes can be reserved thirty days in advance; they become available at 8 a.m. daily for the date thirty days in the future. Some same-day timed passes are sometimes available online at 8:15 a.m. daily. Admission is free.

From time to time, different approaches are used to manage visitor demand, so check the museum's website often. For example, in 2019, the museum began making walk-up entry available after 1 p.m. on the days it was open. That policy or a similar one may return after the pandemic.

Other Sites in Washington, DC

The Martin Luther King Jr. Memorial, 1964 Independence Avenue SW.

The thirty-foot *Stone of Hope* pink granite sculpture by Lei Yixin dominates this four-acre memorial; included are fourteen quotes from Dr. King carved into the north and south walls.

The Lincoln Memorial, Dr. Martin Luther King Jr. Plaque, 2 Lincoln Memorial Circle NW.

Count down eighteen steps from the top landing of the Lincoln Memorial and you will find an inscription marking the spot where Dr. King stood as he delivered his "I Have a Dream" speech in 1963. Of the many sacred places of the civil rights era, this is likely to be at or near the top of the list.

A. Philip Randolph Bust, Union Station, 50 Massachusetts Avenue, NW.

A driving force behind the Brotherhood of Sleeping Car Porters union in the 1930s, the desegregation of the US military in the 1940s, and the March on Washington in 1963, Mr. Randolph is honored here with a bust by Ed Dwight. It's located in the Amtrak waiting area between Gates A and B.

African American Civil War Memorial Museum, 1925 Vermont Avenue NW.

Learn the often-overlooked tales of heroism of the two hundred thousand African Americans who fought for the United States in the Civil War.

Anacostia Museum, 1901 Fort Place SE.

Part of the Smithsonian family of museums, exhibitions here focus on current issues facing urban communities.

Frederick Douglass National Historic Site, 1411 W Street SE.

While anyone can go to the NPS site's visitors' center, one must be on a ranger-led guided tour to be inside this historic house. Half-hour tours are limited to ten people and given daily at scheduled times. Reservations are strongly encouraged.

Mary McLeod Bethune Council House National Historic Site, 1318 Vermont Avenue NW.

This building was the headquarters for the National Council of Negro Women, led by Mrs. Bethune from 1935 to 1949. This National Historic Site is open for tours Thursday through Saturday. Note: A statue honoring Mrs. Bethune (the first of a Black woman in a DC public park) stands at 1301 East Capitol Street SE.

Carter G. Woodson Home, 1538 Ninth Street NW.

Readers may recall Dr. Woodson's role in establishing Black History Month. He also cofounded the Association for the Study of Negro Life and History, whose goal was to inform Americans about the contributions of Black Americans in the nation's formation. The association used the first floor of his home as its headquarters, now a National Historic Site. Free tours of the home are given from Thursday to Saturday.

Mary Church Terrell House, 326 T Street NW.

A decade before four North Carolina A&T students held their Greensboro sit-in, Mary Church Terrell employed that tactic in the nation's capital. When she and her colleagues were refused service at the segregated Thompson Restaurant in February 1950, she took the case to court, winning a 1953 judgment that segregation at restaurants in the District was unconstitutional.

The house, a National Historic Landmark, was being restored and not open to the public at the time of publication. Another place to visit would be Terrell Place at the intersection of F Street NW and Seventh Street NW. More information on Mrs. Terrell's civil rights work in the 1950s and a large picture of her are located there. Another marker honors Mrs. Terrell at G Street NW and Fourteenth Street NW, a half mile away and not far from the White House.

Blanche Kelso Bruce House, 909 M Street.

Blanche Bruce may not be as well known as Frederick Douglass, Mary McLeod Bethune, and others mentioned earlier. However, he was the first African American to serve a full term as a US senator and the only formerly enslaved person to be elected to that position. Senator Bruce was also the first Black to preside over the Senate. His restored home is not open to the public, but a plaque adorns the home's ironwork in front.

John Philip Sousa Junior High School, 3650 Ely Place SE.

Now a middle school, this was the site of one of the five cases that were rolled up into the *Brown v. Board of Education* decision. The school, a National Historic Landmark, is not open to the public. There is information on the school's role in the landmark 1954 case to the left of the front door.

Maryland

Banneker-Douglass Museum, 84 Franklin Street, Annapolis

From Benjamin Banneker—the surveyor who helped set the boundaries of Washington, DC—to Harriet Tubman to Thurgood Marshall and Gloria Richardson (a SNCC leader during the 1963 civil rights protests in Cambridge, Maryland), this state's sons and daughters have made their mark on history. The Banneker-Douglass Museum is housed in the former Mount Moriah A.M.E. Church (itself on the National Register of Historic Places) and is Maryland's official museum for the preservation of African American history and culture.

Open Tuesday to Saturday, 10 a.m. to 4 p.m. While admission is free, guided tours are $5 per person.

Harriet Tubman Underground Railroad State Park, 4068 Golden Hill Road, Church Creek

Another state-run facility, these seventeen acres let visitors experience the world of Harriet Tubman from her early years on

Maryland's Eastern Shore to her role as liberator and humanitarian in the Underground Railroad resistance movement.

The visitors' center is open Thursday to Sunday, 10 a.m. to 4 p.m.; no fee to see the exhibits.

Download the Harriet Tubman Byway app to go deeper on the topic of the Underground Railroad on the Eastern Shore by visiting thirty-six local spots.

Reginald F. Lewis Museum, 830 East Pratt Street, Baltimore

Four hundred years of African American history are conveniently located in the city's Inner Harbor area. This is Maryland's largest museum on African American history.

Open Thursday to Monday until 5 p.m. General admission is $8.

Less than a mile from this museum is a statue honoring Justice Thurgood Marshall. Walk west on Pratt to South Sharp Street, at the US District Courthouse. Baltimore's native son, the nation's first Black Supreme Court Justice, is similarly honored at the Maryland State House.

Delaware

Howard High School (now Howard High School of Technology), 401 East Twelfth Street, Wilmington

So far, we have covered three of the five schools involved in the *Brown v. Board of Education* decision: one in Summerton, South Carolina; another in Farmville, Virginia; and John Philip Sousa Junior High School just a moment ago in Washington, DC. Howard High School's role in the 1954 decision traces back to a local case (*Belton v. Gebhart*) in which the parents of Black students living in Claymont, Delaware, filed a suit so that their children could attend a local all-white high school.

The Black students in Claymont were being bused to Howard High School, nine miles away. The Delaware chancery and supreme courts actually sided with the Black parents, making this case unique among the five that were decided in *Brown*. The state courts nullified local segregation. However, Delaware's attorney general appealed that ruling.

A marker stands in front of the school, but the inscription focuses on the school's historic role as the first Delaware school to offer Black students a complete high school education. The attorney who argued on behalf of the Black parents, Louis Redding, is honored in Wilmington outside the government complex (800 North French Street) named for him with a life-size bronze statue of him and two school children, one Black and one white.

The Cannon/Johnson Kidnapping Gang Marker, West Stein Highway, Reliance (Sussex County)

History books speak of the Underground Railroad, but few describe the practice of whites kidnapping free Blacks and selling them into slavery. This marker calls attention to the "reverse underground railroad" that came to be after Congress banned the importation of enslaved people in 1807. The memoir and film *12 Years a Slave* brought attention to this practice.

The Cannon/Johnson gang referred to on this marker, located just over the Maryland/Delaware border, operated their racial kidnapping ring in several counties along this line. One of the gang leaders was murderer Patty Cannon, who in her day was called "the wickedest woman in America." She was so notorious that a century and a half after her death by suicide, parents would warn their children, "Behave or Patty Cannon will get you."

Pennsylvania

African American Museum in Philadelphia, 701 Arch Street, Philadelphia

This Smithsonian affiliate museum was the first such institution funded and built by a major US city. Its four galleries offer exhibitions anchored to three dominant themes: the African Diaspora, the Philadelphia Story, and the Contemporary Narrative. One 2020 exhibit, *Through His Eyes: Youth Activism in Philadelphia's Civil Rights Era*, spotlighted photographs from the forty-year career of Jack T. Franklin, who covered many major civil rights events. That exhibit is available online.

Open Thursday to Sunday from noon to 5 p.m. Adult admission is $14, with discounts for seniors, students, and children. Check the two-museum discount offered with its partner, the National Constitution Center, located a block away at 535 Arch Street.

Mother Bethel African Methodist Episcopal Church, 419 South Sixth Street, Philadelphia

The church is the oldest continuously Black-owned property in the United States, purchased through the initiative of Richard Allen. Reverend Allen preached at another church in Philadelphia in 1786, but that congregation insisted on segregated services. Objecting to this practice, he established his own church and in 1787 bought the land on which this church stands. In 1816, Rev. Allen was elected the first bishop of the African Methodist Episcopal Church, the oldest and largest formal institution in Black America.

The church has a museum; tours can be arranged via a form on the church's website. They are available Tuesday through Saturday from 10 a.m. to 3 p.m. and after church services on Sunday. The tours are free, but donations are welcome.

Senator John Heinz History Center, 1212 Smallman Street, Pittsburgh

A wonderful option for those in western Pennsylvania is this Smithsonian affiliate. Its award-winning permanent exhibit *From Slavery to Freedom* mixes artifacts, documents, and interactive displays to deliver an excellent visitor experience. The sports-focused section of the center has an exhibit on Negro League baseball.

The museum is open daily from 10 a.m. to 5 p.m.; adult admission is $18; $15 for seniors; and discounts for military, students, and children.

New York

Two new museums are in the works in New York City, their progress slowed by the pandemic:

- The Jackie Robinson Foundation has raised over 80 percent of the funds needed for its planned museum in lower Manhattan.
- Ground was broken in March 2021 for the Urban Civil Rights Experience Museum on 125th Street in Harlem; it will focus on the civil rights movement in the North.

Niagara Falls Underground Railroad Heritage Center, 825 Depot Avenue West, Niagara Falls

With Canada on the opposite bank of the Niagara River, the center's permanent exhibit *One More River to Cross* is aptly named. The museum presents accounts of the Underground Railroad in Niagara Falls and its critical location on the journey to freedom. The center's website links to an app outlining walking and driving tours of local sites that helped shepherd freedom seekers to safety.

Open Tuesday to Sunday at 10 a.m. and closes at 5 p.m. every day except Sunday (4 p.m.). Adult admission is $10; seniors and students, $8. The center is a stop on the Free Discover Niagara Shuttle that runs from May to October.

Harriet Tubman National Historical Park, 180-182 South Street, Auburn

This park has three separately located sites, all in Auburn and managed by the Harriet Tubman Home Inc. The National Park Service provides visitor services.

- The Tubman Home and the Home for the Aged are on South Street.
- Thompson Memorial A.M.E. Zion Church, one mile away at 49 Parker Street, is known as the "Freedom Church." Its membership included Harriet Tubman, Frederick Douglass, and Sojourner Truth.
- Fort Hill Cemetery, the location of Harriett Tubman's gravesite, is at 19 Fort Street. Enter the cemetery on Fitch Avenue through the Underwood Gate; take an immediate left turn. The gravesite is a short distance farther on the right under a large spruce tree.

This is one of many stops on the New York Underground Railroad Heritage Trail. Search the trail's name to locate a map of all the stops statewide.

National Abolition Hall of Fame, 5525 Pleasant Valley Road, Peterboro

This facility honors over two dozen antislavery abolitionists, some well-known and more who are not. Located in the building where the first meeting of the New York Anti-Slavery Society met in 1835, the museum covers these advocates' work to end slavery and the legacy of that struggle.

Cost for adults: $5; everyone else is free. Closed during the week; open on weekends from 1 p.m. to 4 p.m.

Massachusetts

The Robert Shaw and the 54th Massachusetts Regiment Memorial (across from the State House on Beacon Street) and the Boston Black Heritage Trail, Boston

This memorial, honoring the first company of African Americans to fight in the Civil War, is one of fourteen stops on the city's Black Heritage Trail. The trail explores the history of the city's nineteenth-century African American community and is a mile and a half long. Do a self-guided tour any time using maps available at the Museum of African American History, at the Faneuil Hall Visitors' Center, or on the NPS website. Free ranger-led tours operate seasonally.

Museum of African American History, 46 Joy Street, Boston

The museum's two properties (the Abiel Smith School and the African Meeting House) are open year-round, Monday to Friday, 10 a.m. to 4 p.m. Adults $10; seniors and students $8; 12 and under are free. Ranger talks are available daily inside the African Meeting House and are included with museum entry.

Birthplace of W. E. B. DuBois,
612 South Egremont Road, Great Barrington

An all-volunteer effort keeps alive the legacy of this prolific author and thought leader from the first half of the twentieth century. Dr. DuBois was one of the founders of the NAACP and editor of the influential publication *The Crisis* from 1910 to 1934.

There is a self-guided interpretive trail here; it is closed in the winter. Also, a seventeen-stop walking and driving tour covers other Great Barrington aspects of Dr. DuBois's life. More details at *https://www.duboisnhs.org/*.

Vermont

Rokeby Museum, 4334 Route 7, Ferrisburgh

The permanent exhibit, *Free & Safe: The Underground Railroad in Vermont*, shares the story of Simon and Jesse, two fugitives from bondage who found shelter here in the 1830s. The exhibit introduces guests to the Robinsons, the abolitionist family that called Rokeby home. The turbulent decades prior to the Civil War are well covered.

The historic residence, fully furnished with two hundred years of household belongings, provides a glimpse into four generations of the Robinson family. Rokeby's nine historic farm buildings are filled with agricultural artifacts. A hiking trail and picnic tables afford some outdoor options.

The Rokeby Museum is open daily 10 a.m. to 5 p.m. from mid-May to late October. Guided tours of the house are available Friday through Monday at 11 a.m. and 2 p.m., and by appointment. Adults are $10; others over the age of 5 are $5.

William Lloyd Garrison Marker, in the Triangle of Land Formed by West Road, Park Way, and Monument Avenue, Bennington

One of leading abolitionists during the first half of the nineteenth century, William Lloyd Garrison founded the antislavery weekly *The Liberator* in Boston in 1831. He was also an advocate of women's suffrage. The marker is in Bennington because Mr. Garrison's *Journal of the Times* was produced here before he founded *The Liberator*.

The marker is close to the Bennington Museum (75 Main Street).

John Wheeler House, 133 South Prospect Street, Burlington

The antislavery traditions in Vermont go back to the days before it was a state and its existence as an independent republic. In 1777, its constitution explicitly forbade slavery. Among Vermont's antislavery advocates was the Reverend John Wheeler, the sixth president of the University of Vermont.

Dr. Nancy Curtis's compilation *Black Heritage Sites* states that oral tradition suggests that Rev. Wheeler "assisted fugitive slaves who were fleeing to Canada."[152] If true, the Wheeler House may have been part of the Underground Railroad.

Today, this building, which is on the National Register of Historic Places, houses the university's History Department. Visit on weekdays by appointment.

A Young Vermont Sentry's Momentous Decision in Virginia

On May 23, 1861, Frank Baker, Shepard Mallory, and James Townsend arrived at the entry gate to Fort Monroe in Virginia. They wanted to come in. They wanted safety and freedom. The three enslaved men had escaped from their forced labor by rowing across the James River to the fort.

The Civil War had only been under way for a month. Though Virginia had seceded from the Union, the fort remained in Union hands. With Confederate soldiers across the river, guards were posted at the entry. When Baker, Mallory, and Townsend arrived, a young sentry from the 1st Vermont Regiment was at the guard house. When the men asked for an audience with the fort's general, the sentry had a decision to make. Would he let them in or turn them away?

He let them in.

Reflect on that young man's decision for a moment. What thoughts ran through his head when the three men appeared? Did he worry this was a set-up by the Confederates? How much experience had he had with Blacks in Vermont?

continued

continued from previous page

Now reflect on what was going on in the minds of Baker, Mallory, and Townsend. What kind of reception would they get at the fort? Were these people going to be any different than the white folks across the river? What punishment waited for them if they were forced to return?

Everyone made unbelievably brave, history-changing decisions that night. In the midst of covering Vermont, this amazing tale fits perfectly.

The rest of the story lives up to the drama of the young sentry's encounter with the three freedom seekers. The next day, the men met with General Benjamin Butler. Two things about General Butler: First, he was a dour-looking man, certainly not the face you'd pick to have on the other side of an asylum request. Second, he had only arrived as the commander of the fort *one day ahead* of the fugitives. What kind of risk-taker might he be? After all, the Fugitive Slave Act of 1850 was in force, and it required the return of runaways to their enslavers.

Butler was a lawyer by training, and one could make the case that his legal training helped him deal with the return-or-don't-return decision he now faced. Confederate Colonel John Cary, bearing a truce flag, showed up at the fort seeking the three escapees on May 24, 1861. General Butler met him on horseback and the two rode off to discuss the situation.

Butler refused to return the men. Cary pointed out that the Fugitive Slave Act required him to do so. Butler countered that the law applied in the United States, not in Virginia, which had seceded. In fact, the referendum approving Virginia's secession passed by an 80/20 margin on the very day the men arrived at Fort Monroe. The men were "contrabands of war," said Butler; they would be staying right where they were.

It wasn't clear then whether Butler's superiors would see things the same way once Butler's decision was communicated up the line. He began writing his report on the incident on Saturday. On Sunday, eight more runaways arrived, then forty-seven more came on Monday. Word was out. The die had been cast, not by the political establishment in Washington who did not overturn Butler's decision, but by the volume of freedom seekers arriving at Fort Monroe.

Maine

Harriet Beecher Stowe House, 63 Federal Street, Brunswick

In 1852, Harriet Beecher Stowe took what she had published as a serial in the abolitionist newspaper, *National Era*, and released perhaps the most successful example of antislavery literature as a book. *Uncle Tom's Cabin* introduced the horrors of slavery to the American public, and the work became an instant sensation here and in Europe.

The impact that *Uncle Tom's Cabin* had on the public's psyche was significant enough that, when President Lincoln met the author, he is reported to have said, "You're the little lady who started this great war."

The Harriet Beecher Stowe House, a National Historic Landmark, is where this book was written. The house is now owned by Bowdoin College, and most of the house is used for faculty offices. A historical marker appears out front.

Popular tours on Harriet Beecher Stowe are offered by Cathi Belcher, a local expert on Mrs. Stowe. Check out *www.harrietlives.com* for details.

Central States

Ohio

Freedom Summer 1964 Marker, Miami University Campus, Western College Drive, Oxford

Chapter 10 noted that training for about eight hundred Freedom Summer volunteers took place at the Western College for Women, now the Western Campus of Miami University. This marker honors the legacy of the work done by these volunteers to assist voter registration in the South. Particular attention on the marker is given to the ultimate sacrifice made by Michael Schwerner, James Chaney, and Andrew Goodman. The marker is on Western College Drive, near the small amphitheater honoring the Freedom Summer workers; it is to the right of Kumler Chapel.

The National Underground Railroad Freedom Center, 50 East Freedom Way, Cincinnati

This wonderful museum is appropriately located on the north bank of the Ohio River, the boundary between bondage in the South and freedom in the North. Your experience here begins with an orientation film that draws on the talents of three separate animators. Don't think you're just going in to watch a cartoon; it is terrific.

After the film, exhibit after exhibit provides educational content on the brave and determined men and women who sought to be free. Perhaps the most striking single image in the museum is an actual slave pen. Built in the early 1800s, the massive structure served as a holding pen for Kentucky enslaver Captain John W. Anderson.

Open Wednesday to Sunday, 10 a.m. to 5 p.m. Adults $15; seniors $13; children 3 to 12 $10.50; free if under 3.

African American Civil Rights Trail (in Progress), Various Locations in Cleveland

The Cleveland Restoration Society, aided by a National Park Service grant, will be installing ten historical markers in Cleveland at sites associated with the civil rights struggle from 1954 to 1976. The project is titled *In Their Footsteps: Developing an African American Civil Rights Trail in Cleveland, OH.*

While the final list of locations is being discussed, one of the first selected was Cory United Methodist Church (1117 East 105th Street). On separate occasions, Dr. King and Malcolm X addressed the congregation here in the 1960s, the latter giving his "The Ballot or the Bullet" remarks here. Also likely to merit a marker is Carl Stokes, the first elected African American mayor of a major city in 1967. Mayor Stokes is already honored on a marker at Kinsman Road and East 147th Street in a small plaza at the Andrew J. Rickoff School.

Michigan

The Henry Ford Museum of American Innovation, 20900 Oakwood Boulevard, Dearborn

The highlight here for civil rights enthusiasts is the restored Montgomery city bus on which Rosa Parks was riding when she refused to move seats to accommodate a white rider. The story of how the bus was found, confirmed to be the "real one," acquired by the Ford Museum, and restored is fascinating; learn more about it at *https://www.americanheritage.com/power-2857*.

The Rosa Parks bus is part of the *With Liberty and Justice for All* exhibit, which also contains other artifacts relevant to the civil rights movement and African American history. The museum has much to offer visitors, so plan for a long day.

Open daily from 9:30 a.m. to 5 p.m. General admission for those 12 to 61 is $25; seniors, $22.50; youth ages 5 to 11, $18.75; under 5, free.

Jim Crow Museum of Racist Memorabilia, Ferris State University, 1010 Campus Drive, Big Rapids

The name should give parents pause in bringing young children here. The images here are graphic and disturbing, but they have been gathered to accomplish the museum's mission of using "objects of intolerance to teach tolerance and promote social justice." The museum recommends only those twelve and above visit and suggests that those under eighteen be accompanied by an adult. No photography is allowed.

The museum features six exhibit areas: *Who and What Is Jim Crow?*, *Jim Crow Violence*, *Jim Crow and Anti-Black Imagery*, *Battling Jim Crow Imagery*, *Attacking Jim Crow Segregation*, and *Beyond Jim Crow*.

Regular hours are Tuesday through Friday, noon to 5 p.m.; no charge to visit.

Charles H. Wright Museum of African American History, 3 15 East Warren Street, Detroit

And Still We Rise is a permanent exhibit at the Wright, providing a comprehensive look at the African American resilience from the brutality of the Middle Passage to the bravery of the civil rights movement and beyond. No surprise that another gallery (*Detroit Performs!*) recalls the rich performing arts history of the Motor City. *Stories in Stained Glass* by artist Samuel A. Hodge captures the contributions of African Americans in a wide range of endeavors. This large facility merits at least a two-hour visit.

Open Thursday to Saturday, 9 a.m. to 4 p.m., and Sunday noon to 5 p.m. Admission: Adults, $10; seniors, $7; youth ages 3 to 12, $7; under 3 free.

Indiana

Civil Rights Heritage Center,
1040 West Washington Avenue, South Bend

The center is housed in a former city-owned swimming pool. Despite being a public pool, entry was denied local Black citizens in the 1950s. Learn more about the facility's transformation and other local civil rights achievements during a free guided tour. Check the website for the operating schedule.

A sixteen-location heritage tour of homes and institutions that played a significant role in the history of the area's Black residents can be found at *https://www.theclio.com/tour/470*.

Freetown Living History Museum,
625 Indiana Avenue, Indianapolis

Self-described as a "museum without walls," 1870s-era costumed Freetown Village players present a wide range of programs that showcase African American history and culture in unique, entertaining formats and varying lengths. The programs, some of which are free, occur at museums, libraries, and other venues around the city. Check the organization's website to learn what is being offered, where, and whether there is a charge or not.

King-Kennedy Memorial, Dr. Martin Luther King Jr. Park, 1702 North Broadway Street, Indianapolis

On April 4, 1968, Dr. King was assassinated. That evening, presidential candidate Robert F. Kennedy was holding a rally at this park. When he arrived, he learned that the mostly Black crowd had not been told of Dr. King's murder. Drawing on the tragedy that befell his brother John in 1963, urging calm and compassion, and quoting from the Greek writer Aeschylus, Kennedy delivered short remarks that some have labeled one of the best speeches of the twentieth century. Indianapolis, unlike other American cities, was quiet that night; many credit that to the words Kennedy delivered here.

The *Landmark for Peace* memorial here features Dr. King and Robert Kennedy reaching out to each other. Designed by Indiana artist Greg Perry, the bronze casts of King and Kennedy were created by Indianapolis sculptor Daniel Edwards.

Robert F. Kennedy, April 4, 1968

"...We have to make an effort in the United States, we have to make an effort to understand, to go beyond these rather difficult times.

My favorite poet was Aeschylus. He wrote: "In our sleep, pain which cannot forget falls drop by drop upon the heart until, in our own despair, against our will, comes wisdom through the awful grace of God."

What we need in the United States is not division; what we need in the United States is not hatred; what we need in the United States is not violence or lawlessness; but love and wisdom, and compassion toward one another, and a feeling of justice toward those who still suffer within our country, whether they be white or they be black."

Read and listen to Senator Kennedy's complete remarks on the website of the John F. Kennedy Library under Robert Kennedy speeches *https://www.jfklibrary.org/learn/about-jfk/the-kennedy-family/robert-f-kennedy/robert-f-kennedy-speeches/statement-on-assassination-of-martin-luther-king-jr-indianapolis-indiana-april-4-1968.*

Sundown Towns

"Sundown Towns" sounds like it could be the name of a chain of Florida retirement communities or a series of west-facing resorts on the shores of Lake Michigan. The reality that lies under this pleasant-sounding description is quite ugly, however.

The term refers to the practice of excluding African Americans from living in cities and towns across the country or even being welcome there after the sun went down. Some sundown towns passed ordinances to prevent Black citizens from being able to buy or rent housing there, while others accomplished the same end through harassment and violence. Often, the practice was not just confined to discriminating against African Americans, with people of Jewish, Chinese, Native American, and other descents facing similar restrictions and treatment.

Dr. James Loewen's book *Sundown Towns: A Hidden Dimension of American Racism* notes that "independent sundown towns are fairly common in the East, frighteningly so in the Midwest, nontraditional South and Far West, but rare in the traditional South."[153]

As Loewen suggests, housing discrimination against Blacks was real across the nation, yet Midwestern states were major offenders. Loewen points out that jurisdictions of every size were sundown towns as late as 1970: from tiny communities like DeLand, Illinois, to Warren, Michigan, a suburb of Detroit, which had just twenty-eight minority families out of a total population of 180,000, and most of those minority families lived on an army base.

An assumption that this type of discrimination began right after the Civil War would be incorrect. African Americans moved all over the United States after the war ended. Loewen notes that things changed between 1890 and 1930. One of many cities that pushed Black citizens out during these years was Decatur, Indiana. Loewen quotes a *New York Times* article from July 14, 1902, reporting that

"the last Negro has left Decatur. . . . His departure was caused by the anti-Negro feeling. About a month ago, a mob of 50 men drove out all the Negroes who were making that city their home. Since that time the feeling against the Negro race has been intense, so much so that an Anti-Negro Society was organized."[154]

Illinois

The A. Philip Randolph Pullman Porter Museum, 10406 South Maryland Avenue, Chicago

At the turn of the twentieth century, travel meant getting on a train. Moreover, traveling in style meant riding in one of the luxurious cars owned by George Pullman. Pullman hired only Black men to be porters (many were formerly enslaved) to accommodate the passengers booking his fancy sleeper cars. Pullman's reasons for hiring only Blacks were not at all altruistic, as you might imagine.

The railway unions of the day would not allow Blacks to join, so in 1925, A. Philip Randolph, an important social activist, organized the Brotherhood of Sleeping Car Porters (BSCP). The idea of a union for the porters did not sit well with Pullman. Mr. Randolph and his union members fought for over a decade to secure a collective bargaining agreement. They succeeded in 1937, and the agreement was the first ever between a union of Black workers and a major US company.

At this museum, learn how the organizational and leadership skills developed by the BSCP served well the goals of the civil rights movement of the 1950s. One porter leader, Edgar D. Nixon, led the local BSCP chapter in Montgomery. He played a key role in the 1955–1956 bus boycott there, paying Rosa Parks's bail after her arrest and enlisting a young minister, Martin Luther King Jr., to organize the boycott.

Hours vary by season; check the website for details. A $5 donation is requested as an admission fee.

Less than five minutes from the museum, the National Park

Service manages a visitors' center at 11141 South Cottage Grove for the Pullman National Historic District. While there is memorabilia on the Pullman porters, the NPS site is about the "company town" aspect of the Pullman District, a fascinating story in itself.

The DuSable Museum of African American History, 740 East Fifty-Sixth Place, Chicago

Named after Jean Baptiste Point DuSable—a Haitian fur trader and the first non-Native-American permanent settler in Chicago and, as such, viewed as "the founder of Chicago"—the DuSable is a Smithsonian affiliate.

The main exhibit areas include

- *South Side Stories: The Art and Influence of Margaret T. Burroughs* (educator, artist, and the founder of the Ebony Museum, which became the DuSable)
- *The Harold Washington Story*, where an animatronic version of Chicago's first Black mayor "talks" to visitors about his 1983 election and his battles with the entrenched white city councilors.
- *Freedom, Resistance, and the Journey towards Equality*, providing an overview of Blacks in America from the transatlantic slave trade to the election of Barack Obama.

The DuSable is open Wednesday to Sunday from 11 a.m. to 4 p.m. The museum costs $12.50 for adults, $9 for seniors and students.

Plans call for the Obama Presidential Center to be in Jackson Park, less than three miles from the DuSable. There is no date certain for the opening.

Springfield and Central Illinois African American History Museum, 1440 Monument Avenue, Springfield

Downstate Illinois benefits from the content at this popular museum. Exhibits of local interest include *Early African American Pioneers of Central Illinois* and a past exhibit on a race riot that occurred in Illinois's capital in 1908. The museum also brings in content from other museums (like one on the Negro Professional Baseball Leagues on loan from the Negro League Baseball Museum in Kansas City).

Open Thursday to Saturday, noon to 4 p.m. The museum is free; a donation of $3 per person is requested, especially with groups of fifteen or more.

Former Chicagoans: Ida B. Wells-Barnett, Emmett Till, and . . . Martin Luther King?

Yes, Dr. King lived in Chicago. In late January 1966, he moved his family into a third-floor apartment at 1550 South Hamlin Avenue in the city's North Lawndale community. He came to Chicago to call attention to the unacceptable living conditions and poverty African Americans faced in the urban North and highlight housing segregation in northern cities. Today, on the ground floor of the King Legacy Apartments (built in 2011) at 1550 South Hamlin, there is a modest Martin Luther King Fair Housing Museum featuring artifacts and exhibits from the civil rights leader's time in North Lawndale.

Besides Dr. King's apartment location, three other Chicago stops to consider are the homes of the following:

Ida B. Wells-Barnett. The former home of this crusader for justice is at 3624 South Martin Luther King Drive in Chicago. She moved to Chicago after her work documenting lynching in America and the resulting threats forced her to leave Memphis. Her former residence, a National Historic Landmark, is not open to the public, however, as it is privately owned. About four hundred feet south of the home, at Thirty-Seventh Street and King Drive, there is a large stone paying tribute to her. Funds for another monument to Mrs. Wells-Barnett have been raised; it will be installed in the Bronzeville section of the city.

Emmett Till. The murdered fourteen-year-old lived on the South Side of Chicago. Roberts Temple Church of God (4021 South State Street) was the site of his funeral service. A school is named in his honor at 6543 South Champlain, and his gravesite is in the Burr Oak Cemetery in Alsip, Illinois (twenty-two miles south of Chicago).

continued

continued from previous page

Fred Hampton. Mr. Hampton— at the time, the twenty-one-year-old head of the Illinois chapter of the Black Panther Party— was asleep in his bed at 2337 West Monroe Street when a tactical unit of the state's attorney's office broke in and shot him and Mark Clark to death in December 1969. Even though only one of the ninety to one hundred bullets exchanged during the raid came from a nonpolice gun, the deaths were ruled a "justifiable homicide."

Wisconsin

Wisconsin Black Historical Society, 2620 West Center Street, Milwaukee

The exhibits here are true to the mission of highlighting the social and economic events that affected African Americans in Wisconsin. The exhibits, however, are not solely Wisconsin-focused. A case in point is the *NAACP Civil Rights Tribute Bus* exhibit, depicting both local and national civil rights pioneers. The cost to visit is $10 for non-members. Open Monday to Friday, 11 a.m. to 4 p.m., and Saturday, 10 a.m. to 12:30 p.m.

American Black Holocaust Museum, 401 West North Avenue, Milwaukee

In mid-2021, the galleries at the museum's new location and the museum were virtual only. Touring its exhibits reveals diverse educational content arranged chronologically from *African People before Captivity* to *Now—Free at Last?*"

Interested in visiting once the physical museum reopens? Check the website or sign up for their newsletter. Admission prices and operating hours are not yet announced.

Milton House Museum, 18 South Janesville Street, Milton

Originally a stagecoach inn that opened in 1845, this building was a station in the Underground Railroad. Visitors can walk through a tunnel that, prior to Emancipation, allowed freedom seekers transit from the main inn to a log cabin behind the structure. Some sources indicate that Sojourner Truth was a guest at the Milton House during one of her preaching tours.

Open Memorial Day to Labor Day, Tuesday to Sunday at 10 am; the last tour begins at 3:30 p.m. Adults, $10; seniors, $8; youth ages 5 and up, $6; discounts for AAA and military.

Minnesota

Minnesota African American Heritage Museum, 1256 Penn Avenue North, Fourth Floor, Minneapolis

Located in the gleaming Regional Acceleration Center building, this is a relatively new museum, founded in 2018. A permanent exhibit titled *Unbreakable* celebrates the resilience of the state's African American citizens, from settlers in the 1800s to southern Blacks who moved to Minnesota during the Great Migration to African American soldiers who fought for freedom abroad but faced discrimination upon their return.

A photography exhibit, *Gather in His Name*, centers on the protests that followed the George Floyd murder; it will run at least to the end of 2021.

Free admission and free parking (accessed via the ramp behind the building). The museum is open Tuesday to Friday from 1 p.m. to 5 p.m. and on Saturday from 10 a.m. to 1 p.m.

St. Paul African American Heritage: Points of Entry Tour, Various Locations, St. Paul

This sixteen-stop tour highlights the history of the state's African Americans going back to the 1790s. The first stop on the tour relates to Dred Scott and the infamous Supreme Court decision of 1857 precluding Black people from becoming US citizens. Recall that, after Mr. Scott's Virginia-based owner died, Scott and his wife moved with subsequent enslavers to locations where slavery was illegal. One location was Fort Snelling in current-day Minnesota.

Search for "St. Paul African American Heritage Tour." You may find two: the one mentioned here and one with six African American churches in the Frogtown area.

Clayton Jackson McGhie Memorial, East First Street and North Second Avenue, Duluth

On June 15, 1920, nearly one hundred years to the day before the murder of George Floyd in Minneapolis, three Black men were lynched in Duluth. Elias Clayton, Elmer Jackson, and Isaac McGhie were falsely accused of raping a white woman, forcibly taken from their jail cells, and lynched before as many as ten thousand onlookers. This crime took place at the intersection where the Clayton Jackson McGhie Memorial now stands. No one was convicted of the three men's murders, and only three whites received any punishment at all—convicted of rioting.

The outdoor memorial is always open, and there is no charge to visit. Learn more about this largely unknown atrocity on the Minnesota Historical Society's website *https://www.mnhs.org/duluthlynchings/*.

Iowa

African American Museum of Iowa, 55 Twelfth Avenue SE, Cedar Rapids

This is a terrific museum with a sophisticated website. The museum was started in 1993 by members of Mt. Zion Missionary Baptist Church in Cedar Rapids. The current building opened a decade later, only to be badly flooded in 2008. Resilience is a common characteristic of those honored in African American museums, and resilience certainly was true of the board, staff, and volunteers here in Cedar Rapids. Despite five feet of water in the building, the museum was back open in 2009.

The museum has a permanent exhibit titled *Endless Possibilities* and a second temporary exhibit. The permanent exhibit covers from life in West Africa over four centuries ago to present-day America. One part of *Endless Possibilities* is a lunch counter recognizing the 1948 sit-ins at Katz Drug Store in Des Moines. Yes, 1948—over a decade before the Greensboro sit-in. Iowa had a civil rights law prohibiting discrimination in public accommodations since 1884; the management at Katz repeatedly ignored it, and lower courts in the state tended to take a narrow interpretation of the law's intent.

The actions of Edna Griffin pushed the state to enforce the law. An

Iowa Supreme Court decision, *State of Iowa v. Katz*, in 1949 ruled against Katz, stating that denial of service based on race was indeed illegal.

Open Thursday to Saturday, 10 a.m. to 4 p.m. Adults, $6; seniors, $5; students, $3.50.

Edna Griffin: A Sit-In Pioneer

When Edna Griffin's name was mentioned in connection with the 1948 sit-in at Katz Drug Store, you may have never heard of her. That is even more surprising given when her sit-in occurred relative to the much more well-known actions in 1960 in Greensboro.

Edna Mae Griffin was born in Kentucky in 1909 but grew up in New England. She attended Fisk University and studied sociology.

She and her husband, Stanley, moved to Des Moines in 1947 so Stanley could study medicine. Edna had her first of three children but that did not slow down her activism as she held leadership roles with both the Iowa Progressive Party and the Communist Party.

On July 7, 1948, Edna took her one-year-old daughter to the Katz Drug Store and ordered an ice cream soda. Along with fellow African Americans, John Bibbs and Leonard Hudson, they were denied service. She asked to speak with the manager, who took the position that the lunch counter was "not equipped to serve colored people."

Mrs. Griffin brought two successful suits against the Katz Drug Store. One was a criminal trial for violating Iowa's Civil Rights Act; Katz was fined $50 on October 7, 1948. The other was a civil suit, and an all-white jury found for Griffin, awarding her $1 in damages. The size of the damages awarded were far less important than the principle established that race-based discrimination was illegal.

Her activism continued for decades. She founded the Iowa chapter of the Congress for Racial Equality, organized a group of Iowans to go to Washington for the 1963 march, and, at age seventy-five, protested nuclear armaments being shipped

continued

continued from previous page

to a Nebraska army base. All of this earned Mrs. Griffin an FBI file as part of COINTELPRO (COunter INTELligence PROgram), the covert surveillance program that also included the Black Panther Party and Dr. King's SCLC as targets.

Mrs. Griffin passed away in 2000. She is in the Iowa Women's Hall of Fame and the Iowa African-American Hall of Fame. Just prior to her death, the former Flynn Building, where the Katz Drug Store was once located, was renamed to honor Mrs. Griffin. There's a plaque on the Locust Avenue side of the building at 319 Seventh Street in Des Moines.

Henderson Lewelling Quaker House, 401 South Main Street, Salem

Basements were not too common when Henderson Lewelling built this home in 1840. Mr. Lewelling had a reason for putting one in his stone house in Salem: he wanted to provide a safe hiding place for the enslaved escaping from nearby Missouri. Today, visitors can see the trap doors that led to the basement.

The house is open to the public from May to September but on Sunday only, 1 to 4 p.m. During the rest of the year, tours are given by appointment; call (319) 258-2000.

Jordan House Museum, 2001 Fuller Road, West Des Moines

This Victorian home was built by James Jordan in 1850; Mr. Jordan was instrumental in Underground Railroad activities in Polk County. Abolitionist John Brown stayed in the home at least twice, including in early 1859 as he planned his raid on Harper's Ferry.

The local historical society runs the museum and offers tours every Friday and Sunday at 11 a.m. and 1 p.m.; cost $5, plus fees. Check for special events too.

Nebraska

Malcolm X Birthplace, Visitors' Center and Marker, 3463 Evans Street, Omaha

Malcolm X was born Malcolm Little in Omaha on May 19, 1925; his boyhood home was torn down, but he is remembered at this fourteen-acre site funded by the Malcolm X Foundation. Lectures, concerts, and other community events happen here. Nebraska honors its consequential native son with a historical marker.

Visitors can enjoy the outside amenities anytime, but the visitors' center is open Saturday from noon to 4 p.m. and by appointment at (800) 645-9287.

Great Plains Black History Museum, 2505 North Twenty-Fourth Street, Omaha

The museum is proof that one person's drive and vision can make a difference. In 1976, Bertha Calloway founded the museum, dedicating it to publicizing and preserving the achievements of the region's African American heritage. Open Thursday to Saturday, 1 to 5 p.m., and by appointment. No admission fee.

Homestead National Historical Park, 24405 Southwest 75th Street, Beatrice

When President Lincoln signed the Homestead Act of 1862, it opened up millions of acres of public land to settlement, as long as those staking a claim had not taken up arms against the United States. The law and subsequent homesteading-related acts of Congress are controversial; what these laws saw as empty land, Native Americans saw as their tribal home.

At this NPS site, visitors can learn about how Black homesteaders set up communities in places like Nicodemus, Kansas, and DeWitty, Nebraska. This is a large park; the address above directs you to the Heritage Center. There, interactive exhibits inform visitors on how homesteading affected immigration, Native people, the ecosystem, and more. Summer hours are weekdays from 8:30 a.m. to 6:00 p.m.; weekend opening time is 9:00 a.m. Other months have a 5:00 p.m. closing.

Kansas

Brown v. Board of Education National Historic Site, 1515 SE Monroe Street, Topeka

This NPS facility brings us to the last and most widely known of the five plaintiff locations involved in the 1954 school desegregation decision. You know how the Supreme Court ruled, but do you know the case's origin? Thirteen parents in Topeka volunteered to work with the local NAACP chapter to push for public school integration. In the summer of 1950, they visited nearby schools to enroll their children. All were refused admission and forced to attend one of four city schools for African Americans.

The parents filed suit in 1951 against the Topeka Board of Education on behalf of their children. Oliver Brown, a minister, was the first parent listed in the suit, so the case bears his last name.

The US District Court ruled against the African American plaintiffs, but the court placed in the record its acceptance of the psychological evidence from Drs. Kenneth and Mamie Clark indicating how African American children were adversely affected by segregation. The research findings by the Clarks in Summerton, South Carolina, later were quoted in the Supreme Court's 1954 opinion.

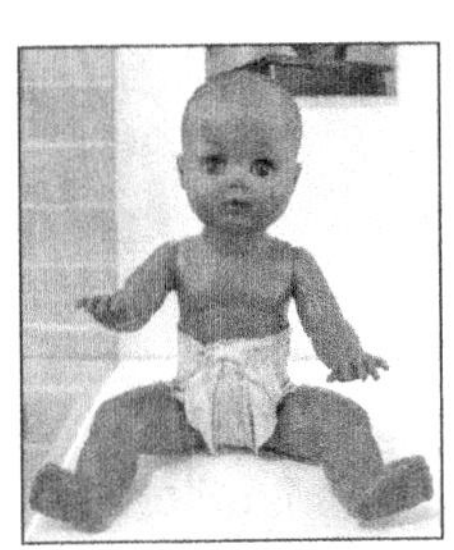

Visitors to this NPS site can see one of the Black dolls the Clarks used. Fifty years after the decision, the National Park Service received a call from someone who had the doll, given to them by a student of Dr. Clark. The NPS acquired this important artifact from American judicial history.

Open daily from 9 a.m. to 5 p.m.; no cost to visit. *https://home.nps.gov/brvb/index.htm*

Kansas Museum of History, 6425 SW Sixth Avenue, Topeka

The museum captures the history of the Sunflower State, of course, and material on and artifacts from African Americans are part of that history: African American Civil War flags, a chair from the Underground Railroad, and a shackle from an escaping freedom seeker. Learn about the town of Nicodemus, Kansas, mentioned earlier in conjunction with the Homestead National Park. The entire town is a national historic site, the oldest town west of the Mississippi founded by African Americans. (The town is 240 miles west of Topeka; it has an NPS site south of the roadside park off Highway 24.)

The Kansas Museum of History is open Wednesday to Saturday, 10 a.m. to 4 p.m. Adults, $10; seniors / active military / college student with ID, $9; children ages 2 to 17, $5. *https://www.kshs.org/.*

The John Brown Museum, Tenth and Main Streets, John Brown Memorial Park, Osawatomie

The Reverend Samuel Adair and his wife, Florella, settled near Osawatomie, eighty miles southeast of Topeka in 1855. John Brown was Florella Adair's half-brother. Osawatomie was an abolitionist community, the center of conflict during Bleeding Kansas. "Bleeding Kansas" described the period of pre–Civil War violence between pro- and antislavery forces when the Kansas territory was being settled.

The Adair cabin was a station on the Underground Railroad; John Brown used this cabin as his headquarters. There are several John Brown artifacts at the museum.

The hours are listed as "subject to change" and "usually open 10 a.m. to 5 p.m. from Tuesday to Saturday." As a result, call (913) 755-4384 to confirm prior to your arrival. Admission is free. *https://www.kshs.org/john_brown.*

Western States

Colorado

Black American West Museum and Heritage Center, 3091 California Street, Denver

The museum promotes understanding of the role African Americans played in the settlement and growth of the American West. Located in the former home of Dr. Justina L. Ford, the first licensed African American female physician in Colorado, the museum presents life stories of Black cowboys and others who came west as entertainers, miners, tradesmen, and more.

Open Friday and Saturday, 10 a.m. to 2 p.m. Adults, $10; students, $8; children ages 6 to 11, $7. *https://www.bawmhc.org/.*

Fort Garland Museum and Cultural Center, Colorado Highway 159, South of US 160, Costilla

Learn about Buffalo Soldiers of the Ninth Cavalry here. The Buffalo Soldiers were the first peacetime all-Black regiments in the regular US Army. They were stationed here from 1876 to 1879. Tour the nineteenth-century fort and five original adobe buildings.

Open Monday to Saturday, 9 a.m. to 5 p.m. Check winter hours. Adult admission is $5; others less. *https://www.historycolorado.org/*.

Barney Ford House Museum, 111 East Washington Avenue, Breckenridge

Most people going to Breckenridge aren't there for a museum experience, yet visitors have positive comments about their under-an-hour visit to this museum. Mr. Ford was raised by an enslaved mother who placed a high value on education. He was a successful entrepreneur, judging from his lovely Victorian home. Mr. Ford is also honored in the state capitol.

The museum is open year-round, but the schedule varies. Check *https://www.breckheritage.com/barney-ford-victorian-home*. Admission is free; a $5 donation is requested.

Arizona

George Washington Carver Museum and Cultural Center, 415 East Grant Street, Phoenix

The name may lead visitors to think that the Carver Museum centers on the work of the great scientist—plus there is a bronze statue of Dr. Carver standing out front. The mission is broader: collecting, preserving, and disseminating the history and culture of Americans of African descent in Arizona.

The Carver Museum connects with the 1960s civil rights movement via a Sculpture Garden memorial to the four young Black girls killed in the Sixteenth Street Baptist Church bombing in Birmingham and featured exhibit titled *That Which Might Have Been: Birmingham 1963*.

Located in the historic Warehouse District of Phoenix, the museum's building has an interesting history of its own. Opened in 1926 as the Phoenix Union Colored High School, it served two

African American neighborhoods in south Phoenix. The location angered the parents whose children were assigned to go there because the school was on contaminated land. Renamed George Washington Carver High School in 1943, it closed in 1954 when the local courts ended segregated education.

Open Thursday to Saturday, 10 a.m. to 4 p.m. No admission fee but donations support the museum's mission.

Nevada

Former Site of the Moulin Rouge Hotel and Casino, 900 West Bonanza Road, Las Vegas

Let's call this a hopeful entry because, at this writing, there is no museum here, just a vacant lot. Yet the Moulin Rouge holds a place in the civil rights history of Las Vegas, and attempts have been made to memorialize the hotel's role in some fashion.

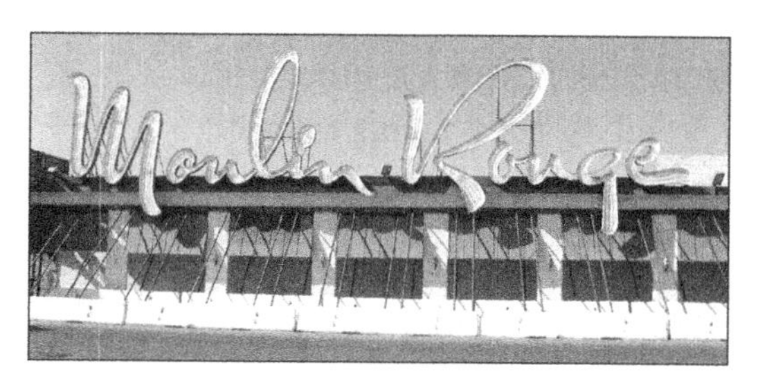

The Moulin Rouge had a short run in the Las Vegas limelight in the mid-1950s. At the time, casinos were segregated. Black entertainers could perform at segregated resorts but had to find other lodging. The Moulin Rouge was the solution as the city's first integrated hotel. Primarily white-owned, African American boxer Joe Louis was, however, a part-owner of the property. On March 26, 1960, local NAACP chapter officials and city representatives met and unofficially ended segregation in Las Vegas.

Multiple attempts to rebuild a structure here have fallen short. In 2018, a Los Angeles–based firm bid to "build a revived Moulin Rouge and a civil rights museum on the site."[155] However, the company missed a financial deadline, ending their plans at least temporarily.

Today, the only remnant of the Moulin Rouge is its neon sign. That sign, a classic by Betty Willis, who designed the "Welcome to Fabulous Las Vegas" sign, lives at the Neon Museum (770 Las Vegas Boulevard North). General admission at the popular Neon Museum is $20.

Idaho

Idaho Black History Museum, 508 Julia Davis Drive, Boise

Idaho has the second-lowest percentage of Black-to-total population (0.6 percent) in the Union, second to neighboring Montana, yet this museum in Julia Davis Park brings Black history to Idaho citizens. Housed in the historic former St. Paul Baptist Church, the museum presents exhibits like *From Slave to President*, featuring bold portraits by local artist Pablo Rodriguez of Black champions from Frederick Douglass to Barack Obama.

Open Friday and Saturday, 11 a.m. to 4 p.m., and Wednesday, 5:30 to 7:30 p.m. Donations welcome.

Washington

Northwest African American Museum (NAAM), 2300 South Massachusetts Street, Seattle

This museum opened in March 2008 with a feature that is perhaps unique in the museum world. Besides having a stated mission to "spread knowledge, understanding, and enjoyment of the histories, arts and cultures of people of African descent for the enrichment of all," the building offered thirty-six affordable apartment units above the museum when it opened. Also likely unique is that the historic Colman School that houses the NAAM was occupied in 1985 by several local activists who broke into the closed school, set up camp, and claimed the site for the museum.

The Charles Colman School was built in 1909 and overlooks a beautiful, sprawling green park, named after rock legend, Jimi Hendrix.

Open Wednesday through Sunday, 11 a.m. to 5 p.m., with a 7 p.m. closing on Thursday. Adults, $7; seniors, students, and children ages 4 to 12, $5.

Martin Luther King Jr. Civil Rights Memorial Park, 2200 Martin Luther King Jr. Way South, Seattle

The four-and-a-half-acre city park calls to mind Dr. King's last public remarks, his ""I've Been to the Mountaintop" speech. The park is designed around a dramatic, thirty-foot black granite mountainlike sculpture set in a reflecting pool. Surrounding the pool are twelve bronze plaques commemorating key dates in Dr. King's life. Dr. King's inspirational words are engraved in tiles placed along the pavement. .

The park is set on a terraced hill, providing many quiet spots for reflection; open from dawn until 11:30 p.m.

Oregon

Oregon Black Pioneers, 117 Commercial Street NE, Salem

This is an all-volunteer nonprofit based in Salem. Lacking a dedicated museum space, its exhibits have been showcased at the Oregon Historical Society, the state capitol, and elsewhere. The group's activities reflect a commitment to conduct research on and educate Oregonians about African Americans' contributions to Oregon's history.

The group's exhibit *Racing to Change: Oregon's Civil Rights Years* exemplifies that commitment. After touring the state, the exhibit (and others) is available online at *https://oregonblackpioneers.org/racing-to-change/.*

Oregon Historical Society Museum, 1200 SW Park Avenue, Portland

Like similar state historical society facilities, this museum's mission is broad. Yet as it covers Oregon's history, Black history topics are not overlooked. One example is a 2021 exhibit, *I Am My Story*, focused on six African women who recently immigrated to Oregon. The traveling exhibit, *Black Athletes Disrupting White Supremacy in Oregon*, is another.

The museum is open seven days a week, from 10 a.m. to 5 p.m., except on Sunday when the doors open at noon. Multnomah County residents are free; otherwise, adults are $10; seniors, students, and teachers $8; and youth ages 6 to 18, $5.

Three miles north of the museum and across the Willamette River is the Harriet Tubman Middle School (2231 North Flint), where a mural pays tribute to the brave woman called the "Moses of Her People," born nearly three thousand miles from Portland on Maryland's Eastern Shore

California

Oakland Museum of California (OMCA), 1000 Oak Street, Oakland

The Black Panther Party was founded in 1966 in Oakland which served as the party's base. Oakland's citizens benefited from Panther programs like food distribution and free medical clinics. In the OMCA's Gallery of California History, visitors learn more about the party and its leaders. The permanent exhibit *Black Power* not only focuses on the Black Panther Party, but it also covers the history of Black Power movements in the state. Find a listing of a dozen Oakland sites related to the Black Panther Party at *https://www.visitoakland.com/blog/post/black-panther-party/.*

The museum has three large galleries. Besides the extensive Gallery of California History, areas are devoted to art and the natural sciences.

Open Friday to Sunday, 11 a.m. to 5 p.m. Adults, $16; seniors and students $11; youth ages 9 to 17, $7.

California African American Museum (CAAM), 600 State Drive, Los Angeles

This forty-four-thousand-square-foot, state-supported museum is in Exposition Park near the California Science Center and the state's Natural History Museum. Established in its current location in 1984, Lonnie Bunche, the first director of the Smithsonian National Museum of African American History and Culture, curated CAAM's first exhibit, *The Black Olympians 1904-1984*.

A more recent exhibit indicating the quality of content here is *California Bound: Slavery on the New Frontier, 1848–1865*. California entered the Union in 1850 as a free state as part of the Compromise of 1850, which also included the Fugitive Slave Act. The exhibit presented how the reality of statehood was more complex. Despite being a free state and prohibiting slavery, California wavered on the status of enslaved people in its early history, and the exhibit revealed this lesser-known history of slavery in the Golden State.

CAAM is open Tuesday to Saturday, 10 a.m. to 5 p.m., and Sunday, 11 a.m. to 5 p.m. Admission is free; parking is not ($15 during the day and $18 after 5 p.m.).

Allensworth Historic Town Site, 4011 Grant Drive, Earlimart

This historic site lies about halfway between Visalia and Bakersfield. The town of Allensworth was founded in 1908 by Colonel Allen Allensworth and several associates. Colonel Allensworth and the town named after him are not widely known.

The town of Allensworth began when the Pacific Farming Company offered the colonel and his group the chance to purchase land in Solito, California. It seemed perfect—with a depot on the main Santa Fe Railroad line from Los Angeles to San Francisco, fertile soil, seemingly abundant water, and plentiful and reasonably priced land. Like Mound Bayou in Mississippi, the town was to be self-sufficient and all Black.

The town grew into a thriving community, its success touted in Black and general-readership newspapers. Then the company that sold Allensworth the land reneged on its contractual obligation to supply the town with water for irrigation.

The railroad created problems also. It would only hire Blacks for menial-labor jobs, and it built a spur rail line through another town, allowing much of the rail traffic to bypass Allensworth. As bad as all of that, the major blow to the town occurred when the man whose vision created it was killed in September 1914, struck by a motorcycle.

Much of the former town has been preserved as the Colonel Allensworth State Historic Park. As the state gradually restores some buildings, two important structures already reflect their historical period: the schoolhouse and the colonel's home.

The visitors' center, featuring a film about the site, is open daily, 10 a.m. to 4 p.m.; the park is open from 9 a.m. to sunset and is bike-friendly.

Allen Allensworth: Freedom Seeker, Union Soldier, Army Chaplain, Town Founder

Born in 1842 in Louisville, Kentucky, Allen Allensworth learned to read and write despite laws prohibiting the enslaved from receiving education. Undeterred by two unsuccessful attempts to escape, he managed to find his way to an Illinois infantry unit camped in Louisville in the early days of the Civil War. He served with that unit but eventually became part of the Union Navy, rising to the rank of first-class petty officer.

After the war, he studied theology at Roger Williams University in Nashville and became a minister. This moved him into the political realm, and he served as a Kentucky delegate to the 1880 and 1884 Republican National Conventions. During the 1880s, Buffalo Soldier units were assigned to western outposts and needed chaplains. In April 1886, Allensworth became the chaplain to the 24th Infantry Regiment. Over the next twenty years, the colonel ministered to the needs of the soldiers of the 24th as they moved from the Arizona Territory to California and to Fort Missoula in Montana. Education, so important to him as an enslaved young man in Louisville, was just as important to him as he worked with the soldiers in his role as chaplain.

Colonel Allensworth retired in 1906. He and his family relocated to Los Angeles. However, this man who served his country in the Civil War, served his God as a minister, and served his flock in the 24th Infantry was not going to settle into an ordinary retirement. He not only wanted to improve the lot of his race, but he also wanted to change the prevailing attitude of whites toward Blacks. Those combined desires drove him to establish Allensworth as a town run by and for his fellow Black citizens.

Hawaii

Proposed President Barack Obama Historical Markers, Various Locations

In February 2021, the Hawaii State Legislature considered a bill requiring the state's Department of Land and Natural Resources to place historical markers throughout the state memorializing significant sites in the life of President Barack Obama.

Among the sites proposed in the bill are the Baskin-Robbins shop at 1618 South King Street, where Barry Obama scooped ice cream as a teen, and the Punahou School at 1601 Punahou Street—both in Honolulu. Punahou is the college preparatory school the future president attended from fifth grade through high school.

Anthony D. Allen (aka Alani) Historical Marker, Washington Middle School, 1633 South King Street, Honolulu

Anthony Allen was born in upstate New York (then a British colony) in 1774. As an enslaved young man, he worked for a small family. Around age twenty-four, sensing he was about to be sold, he escaped to Boston (a free city) and eventually began a life of adventure on the seas. He traveled throughout the world—the Caribbean, Europe, even China—but he put down roots when he arrived in Hawaii.

Given a parcel of land by the high priest serving King Kamehameha I, Alani (as native Hawaiians called him) not only made a comfortable place for his family but also established a hospital for sailors. His entrepreneurial acumen created everything from a dairy to a slaughterhouse to a bowling alley. The bowling alley was so popular that a friend of Alani rented a cart and ran a ride-share type of service to bring people to bowl. In the process, the bowling alley and ride-share service created one of the first roads on Oahu—what is now Punahou Street.

Washington Middle School now sites on Alani's land, and a marker here memorializes the life of this man born into slavery in pre–Revolutionary War America.

Close readers may have already picked up on two coincidences in the lives of Anthony D. Allen and Barack Obama. They conclude our journey and represent an amazing arc connecting a young enslaved man born in the eighteenth century and the man who became our forty-fourth president in the twenty-first.

Look at the addresses of the two proposed Barack Obama marker sites in Honolulu. The Baskin Robbins where Obama worked as a teen is 1618 South King Street, literally across the street from the school built on the land given to Anthony Allen and where he raised his family and ran his businesses.

At the time, the future president lived with his maternal grandparents at the corner of Beretania and Punahou Streets, just two blocks from where Anthony D. Allen had his home and businesses.

Now consider that one of Anthony Allen's businesses was a bowling alley, a popular one at that—so popular, in fact, that one of Alani's friends, Stephen Reynolds, created his own business carting people to and from the location.

Five years after Anthony Allen's death, missionaries opened a school less than a mile from Alani's homestead—on the road created, in part at least, by the popularity of Alani's business. The school and the road are named Punahou after land won in battle by King Kamehameha I, the same ruler who deeded land to Alani.

In 1971, a young man entered the Punahou School as a fifth grader, thanks to a scholarship. Barack Obama attended Punahou through high school. He helped the school win the state basketball championship in 1979, his senior year there. In 2008, he was elected as the first African American president of the United States and its forty-fourth president, winning by nearly ten million votes. Barack Obama won the Nobel Peace Prize the following year and reelection in 2012.

Think for a moment about all the somewhat improbable series of time-separated events that come together on a stretch of land less than a mile long near the south coast of the island of Oahu.

This sweep of history in our most remote and fiftieth state amazed me. For Freedom's Road to stretch all the way to the middle of the Pacific Ocean was uplifting and frankly gave me goose bumps.

What are the odds that all the following would happen in this small area?

What are the odds that a man born into slavery before the American Revolution would:

- Successfully escape captivity?
- Sail the world?
- Buy his freedom?
- Decide to end his days as a mariner and settle in Hawaii?
- Be granted six acres of land there from the island's king?
- Set up his home and successful businesses on that land (including a bowling alley at that!)?
- Have his bowling alley be the impetus for one of the first roads on Oahu?
- Five years after his death, have the same king who granted him land do the same for missionaries just down that road so they could open a school?

Then, what are the odds that a young man well over a century and a quarter later would:

- Live at the corner of Beretania Street and the same road (now called Punahou Street) initially created by the successful business of that former runaway?
- Enroll as a fifth grader in 1971 in the same school established by the missionaries in 1841?
- Live two blocks from the "Old Allen Place" (as it was referred to in documents from the 1840s) with his grandparents when his mother went to study in Indonesia?

- Get a job as a teenager scooping ice cream at the Baskin Robbins store directly across King Street from the Old Allen Place?
- Continue at that school (the Punahou School) through high school, playing on the school's state basketball championship team in 1979, the year of his graduation?
- Be elected to the US Senate a quarter century after his high school graduation?
- Be inaugurated the forty-fourth president of the United States in 2009, becoming the nation's first African American president?

The journey taken in this book may end, but the desire to know the past does not. Discovering the well-known and lesser-known people and events that shaped our history, particularly the history of and antecedents to the civil rights movement, can be transformative. Awareness can lead to understanding, which can generate greater tolerance. Connecting with the past, however, painful it may be, is of great significance and richly rewarding.

The book began with a quote from James Baldwin. Another of his thoughts aptly provides a fitting directive to all of us as we conclude: "Not everything that is faced can be changed, but nothing can be changed until it is faced."[156]

The past is there for us to find. Make the journey. Get traveling on Freedom's Road.

Endnotes

Chapter 1

1. *I Am Not Your Negro* (dir. Peck), Magnolia Pictures, 2016.
2. Ibid.
3. David M. Rubenstein, *The American Story: Conversations with Master Historians* (New York: Simon & Schuster, 2019), 253.
4. Clayborne Carson, David J. Garrow, Gerald Gill, Vincent Harding, and Darlene Clark Hine, eds., *The Eyes on the Prize Civil Rights Reader: Documents, Speeches, and Firsthand Accounts from the Black Freedom Struggle, 1954–1990* (New York: Viking Penguin, 1991), 48.
5. "Transcript of President Obama's Selma Speech," Bloomberg, March 7, 2015, *https://www.bloomberg.com/news/articles/2015-03-07/transcript-of-president-obama-s-selma-speech.*
6. *I Am Not Your Negro.*

Chapter 3

7. Holland Cotter, "The New Mississippi Civil Rights Museum Refuses to Sugarcoat History," *New York Times*, December 18, 2017.
8. Ibid.
9. Elaine Glusac, "Learning about the Civil Rights Era through Travel," *New York Times*, April 20, 2018.
10. Oprah Winfrey, "Inside the Memorial to the Victims of Lynching," *60 Minutes*, CBS, April 8, 2018.

Chapter 7

11. Dagmawi Woubshet, "Revisiting One of King's Final and Most Haunting Sermons," *The Atlantic*, April 1, 2018.
12. Charles E. Cobb Jr., *On the Road to Freedom: A Guided Tour of the Civil Rights Trail* (Chapel Hill, NC: Algonquin Books, 2008), 177.
13. Ibid., 167.
14. Tomiko Brown-Nagin, *Courage to Dissent: Atlanta and the Long History of the Civil Rights Movement* (New York: Oxford University Press, 2011).
15. Cobb, *On the Road to Freedom*, 174.

Chapter 8

16. Frye Gaillard, *A Hard Rain: America in the 1960s: Our Decade of Hope, Possibility, and Innocence Lost* (Montgomery, AL: NewSouth Books, 2018), 258.
17. Susan Neiman, *Learning from the Germans: Race and the Memory of Evil* (New York: Farrar, Straus and Giroux, 2019), 279.
18. Diane McWhorter, *A Dream of Freedom: The Civil Rights Movement from 1954 to 1968* (New York: Scholastic, 2004), 72.
19. Lydia Bjornlund, *Rosa Parks and the Montgomery Bus Boycott* (Farmington Hills, MI: Lucent Books, 2008), 47.
20. Rosa Parks and Jim Haskins, *Rosa Parks: My Story* (New York: Dial Books, 1992), 136.

21. Martin Luther King Jr., *Stride toward Freedom: The Montgomery Story* (New York: Harper, 1958).
22. Gaillard, *A Hard Rain*, 65.
23. Ibid.
24. Ann Bausum, *Freedom Riders: John Lewis and Jim Zwerg on the Front Lines of the Civil Rights Movement* (Washington, DC: National Geographic Society, 2006), 46.

Chapter 9

25. Gaillard, *A Hard Rain*, 250.
26. Ibid., 251.
27. Ibid., 255.
28. Rubenstein, *American Story*, 258.
29. McWhorter, *Dream of Freedom*, 122.
30. Gaillard, *A Hard Rain*, 247.
31. Peniel E. Joseph, *The Sword and the Shield: The Revolutionary Lives of Malcolm X and Martin Luther King Jr.* (New York: Basic Books, 2020), 225.
32. Andrew Beck Grace and Chip Brantley, "A Dangerous Kind of Self-Delusion," *White Lies*, National Public Radio, https://www.npr.org/podcasts/510343/white-lies.

Chapter 10

33. Don Mitchell, *The Freedom Summer Murders* (New York: Scholastic Press, 2014), 112.
34. Seth Cagin and Philip Dray, *We Are Not Afraid* (New York: Nation Books, 2006), 29.
35. Ibid., 30.
36. Bruce Watson, *Freedom Summer: The Savage Season That Made Mississippi Burn and Made America a Democracy* (New York: Viking Penguin, 2010), 16–17.
37. Ibid., 83.
38. Robert Moses and Charles E. Cobb Jr., *Radical Equations* (Boston: Beacon Press, 2002), 3.
39. Jerry Mitchell, *Race against Time: A Reporter Reopens the Unsolved Murder Cases of the Civil Rights Era* (New York: Simon and Schuster, 2020), 15.
40. Claude Sitton, "Graves at a Dam," *New York Times*, August 5, 1964.
41. Neiman, *Learning from the Germans*, 305.
42. Watson, *Freedom Summer*, 193.
43. Ibid.
44. Cagin and Dray, *We Are Not Afraid*, 396.
45. Mitchell, *Race against Time*, 120.
46. Howard Ball, *Murder in Mississippi: United States v. Price and the Struggle for Civil Rights* (Lawrence: University Press of Kansas, 2004), 48.

Chapter 11

47. Calvin Trillin, *Jackson, 1964* (New York: Random House, 2016), 4.
48. Cotter, "New Mississippi Civil Rights Museum."
49. Calvin Trillin, "Back on the Bus: Remembering the Freedom Riders," *New Yorker*, July 18, 2011.
50. Vollers, *Ghosts of Mississippi*, 88.

51. M. J. O'Brien, *We Shall Not Be Moved: The Jackson Woolworth's Sit-In and the Movement It Inspired* (Jackson: University Press of Mississippi, 2013), 4.
52. Unita Blackwell, with JoAnne Prichard Morris, *Barefootin': Life Lessons from the Road to Freedom* (New York: Crown Publishers, 2006), 8.
53. Robert Weisbrot, *Freedom Bound: A History of the Civil Rights Movement* (New York: Plume, 1991).
54. Ibid., 200.
55. "Negro Leader Dies in Odd Accident," *Clarion-Ledger* (Jackson, MS), May 7, 1955.
56. Weisbrot, *Freedom Bound*, 199.
57. Vollers, *Ghosts of Mississippi*, 51, and Timothy B. Tyson, *The Blood of Emmett Till* (New York: Simon & Schuster, 2017), 95.
58. Susan Goldman Rubin, *Freedom Summer: The 1964 Struggle for Civil Rights in Mississippi* (New York: Holiday House, 2014), 86.

Chapter 12

59. Chris Crowe, *Getting Away with Murder: The True Story of the Emmett Till Case* (New York: Dial Books, 2003), 112.
60. Christopher Mettress, ed., *The Lynching of Emmett Till: A Documentary Narrative* (Charlottesville: University of Virginia Press, 2002), 216.
61. Dave Tell, *Remembering Emmett Till* (Chicago: University of Chicago Press, 2019).
62. Tyson, *Blood of Emmett Till*, 52.
63. Ibid., 210.
64. Jeanne Theoharis, *A More Beautiful and Terrible History: The Uses and Misuses of Civil Rights* (Boston: Beacon Press, 2018), 45, 62.
65. Crowe, *Getting Away with Murder*, 112.
66. James Hicks, quoted in Mettress, *Lynching of Emmett Till*, 157.
67. Mettress, *Lynching of Emmett Till*.
68. Tyson, *Blood of Emmett Till*, 124.
69. "Muddy River Gives Up Body of Brutally Slain Negro Boy," *Commercial Appeal* (Memphis, TN), September 1, 1955.
70. Tell, *Remembering Emmett Till*, 100.
71. Transcript of the Trial of J. W. Milam and Roy Bryant, September 19–23, 1955, *https://fsu.digital.flvc.org/islandora/object/fsu%253A390158/datastream/OBJ/view/J_W__Milam_and_Roy_Bryant_Trial_Transcript.pdf*, 104.
72. Tyson, *Blood of Emmett Till*, 29.
73. Ibid., 63.
74. Crowe, *Getting Away with Murder*, 68.
75. "Muddy River Gives Up Body of Brutally Slain Negro Boy."
76. Transcript of the Trial of J. W. Milam and Roy Bryant, 113.
77. *The Untold Story of Emmett Louis Till* (Beauchamp, dir.), Velocity/Thinkfilm, 2005.
78. Tyson, *Blood of Emmett Till*, 62.
79. Mamie Till-Mobley and Christopher Benson, *Death of Innocence: The Story of the Hate Crime That Changed America* (New York: One World, 2003), 131–32.
80. Ibid.
81. Tyson, *Blood of Emmett Till*, 71.
82. Crowe, *Getting Away with Murder*, 111.
83. Anne Moody, *Coming of Age in Mississippi: The Classic Autobiography of Growing Up Poor and Black in the Rural South* (New York: Bantam Dell, 1968), 132.

84. Metress, *Lynching of Emmett Till*, 276.
85. Crowe, *Getting Away with Murder*, 111.
86. Tyson, *Blood of Emmett Till*, 179.
87. Metress, *Lynching of Emmett Till*, 177.
88. Ibid., 64.
89. Sam Johnston, "Uncle of Till's Identifies Pair as Abductors of Negro Boy," *Greenwood (MS) Commonwealth*, September 21, 1955.
90. Metress, *Lynching of Emmett Till*, 121.
91. Ibid., 105.
92. Till-Mobley and Benson, *Death of Innocence*, 189.
93. David M. Oshinsky, *Worse Than Slavery: Parchman Farm and the Ordeal of Jim Crow Justice* (New York: Free Press, 1997), 235.
94. Jerry Mitchell, "'They Just Want History to Die': Owners Demand $4 Million for Crumbling Emmett Till Store," *Clarion-Ledger* (Jackson, MS), August 29, 2018.
95. Jim Carrier, *A Traveler's Guide to the Civil Rights Movement* (New York: Harcourt, 2004), 263–64.
96. Tyson, *Blood of Emmett Till*, 83.
97. Metress, *Lynching of Emmett Till*, 121.

Chapter 13

98. Paul Robert Walker, *Remember Little Rock* (Washington, DC: National Geographic Society, 2009), 9.
99. David Halberstam, *The Fifties* (New York: Random House, 1993), 667.
100. Doris Kearns Goodwin, *Wait until Next Year* (New York: Simon & Schuster, 1997), 234.
101. Melba Pattillo Beals, *Warriors Don't Cry: A Searing Memoir of the Battle to Integrate Little Rock's Central High* (New York: Tantor eBooks, 2011), 462.
102. Kekla Magoon, *Today the World Is Watching You: The Little Rock Nine and the Fight for School Integration, 1957* (Minneapolis: Twenty-First Century Books, 2011), 39.

Chapter 14

103. "Henry Loeb, 71, Memphis Mayor at Time of King's Assassination," Associated Press, September 10, 1992.
104. Peter J. Ling, *Martin Luther King Jr.*, 2nd ed. (New York: Routledge, 2015), 294.
105. Nikita Stewart, "'I've Been to the Mountaintop': Dr. King's Last Sermon Annotated," *New York Times*, April 2, 2018.
106. Michael K. Honey, *Going Down Jericho Road: The Memphis Strike, Martin Luther King's Last Campaign* (New York: W. W. Norton & Company, 2007), 415.
107. Jennifer Biggs, "Soul Food Restaurants Fed Bellies and Souls in Civil Rights Movement," *Commercial Appeal* (Memphis, TN), April 2, 2018.

Chapter 15

108. Carson et al., *Eyes on the Prize Civil Rights Reader*, 154.
109. Diane McWhorter, *Carry Me Home: Birmingham, Alabama: The Climatic Battle of the Civil Rights Revolution* (New York: Simon & Schuster, 2001).
110. Gaillard, *A Hard Rain*, 132.
111. McWhorter, *Carry Me Home*, 341.

112. *Eyes on the Prize: America's Civil Rights Years (1954–1965)*, "Episode 3: No Easy Walk (1961–1963)" (Crossley and DeVinney, dirs.), PBS Video, 1987.

113. Jonathan Rieder, *Gospel of Freedom: Martin Luther King Jr.'s Letter from Birmingham Jail and the Struggle That Changed a Nation* (London: Bloomsbury, 2013), 152.

114. Weisbrot, *Freedom Bound*, 70.

115. McWhorter, *Carry Me Home*, 370.

116. "Outrage in Alabama" (editorial), *New York Times*, May 5, 1963.

117. Rieder, *Gospel of Freedom*, 158.

118. McWhorter, *Carry Me Home*, 372.

119. Rubenstein, *American Story*, 254.

120. Claude Sitton, "Rioting Negroes Routed by Police at Birmingham," *New York Times*, May 8, 1963.

121. Owen J. Dwyer and Derek H. Alderman, *Civil Rights Memorials and the Geography of Memory* (Chicago: Center for American Places at Columbia College, 2008), 62.

122. "Virgil Lamar Ware, a 13-Year-Old Unsung Soldier of the Civil Rights Movement," BlackThen, July 11, 2018, *https://blackthen.com/virgil-lamar-ware-13-year-old-unsung-soldier-civil-rights-movement/*.

123. Rieder, *Gospel of Freedom*.

124. Ibid., 141.

125. Henry Hampton and Steve Fayer, Voices of Freedom: An Oral History of the Civil Rights Movement from the 1950s through the 1980s (London: Random House, 2011), 125.

126. John Lewis, Facebook post, October 5, 2011, *https://www.facebook.com/RepJohnLewis/posts/the-rev-fred-shuttlesworth-is-the-last-of-a-kind-he-was-a-fearless-determined-co/260684340637407/*.

Chapter 16

127. Sam Roberts, "Bob Adelman, Whose Vivid Photos Captured Civil Rights Struggle, Dies at 85," *New York Times*, March 16, 2016.

128. Elizabeth Griffin Spears, "Memorializing the Freedom Riders," Southern Spaces, June 29, 2009, *https://southernspaces.org/2009/memorializing-freedom-riders/*.

129. Anthony Cook, "The Ride," *Anniston (AL) Star*, May 11, 2011, special section.

Chapter 17

130. Alex Haley, "Martin Luther King: A Candid Conversation," *Playboy*, January 1965.

131. Taylor Branch, *Parting the Waters: America in the King Years, 1954–63* (New York: Simon and Schuster, 1988), 606.

132. Cobb, *On the Road to Freedom*, 187–88.

Chapter 19

133. Carrier, *Traveler's Guide to the Civil Rights Movement*, 268.

134. Weisbrot, *Freedom Bound*, 94.

135. Tyson, *Blood of Emmett Till*, 119.

136. Bobby Delaughter, *Never Too Late: A Prosecutor's Story of Justice in the Medgar Evers Case* (New York: Scribner, 2001), 111.

137. "Ex-Ole Miss Student Sentenced for Noose on Statue," *Clarion Ledger* (Jackson, MS), September 17, 2015.

138. Vollers, *Ghosts of Mississippi*, 94.

139. Ibid., 27.

140. Dana O'Neil, "A Game That Should Not Be Forgotten," ESPN.com, December 13, 2012, *https://www.espn.com/mens-college-basketball/story/_/id/8741183/game-change-mississippi-state-loyola-cannot-forgotten-college-basketball.*

Chapter 22

141. Bryan Bowman and Kathy Roberts Forde, "How Slave Labor Built the State of Florida—Decades after the Civil War," *Washington Post*, May 17, 2018.

Chapter 23

142. Tom Wolfe, *The Right Stuff* (New York: Picador, 1979), 111.

143. Benjamin Hedin, "Keep Your Eyes on the Prize," *Oxford American*, no. 107 (Winter 2019), *https://www.oxfordamerican.org/magazine/issue-107/x201c-keep-your-eyes-on-the-prize-x201d.*

Chapter 24

144. Gaillard, *A Hard Rain*, 3.

145. Cobb, *On the Road to Freedom*, 105.

Chapter 25

146. Frederick Douglass, "Speech on the Dred Scott Decision," May 1857, *https://teachingamericanhistory.org/library/document/speech-on-the-dred-scott-decision-2/.*

147. "Books: Will the Real Nat Turner Please Stand Up?," *Time*, July 12, 1968. The quote is from the Author's Note to *The Confessions of Nat Turner.*

148. Daniel Rasmussen, *American Uprising: The Untold Story of America's Largest Slave Revolt* (New York: Harper Perennial, 2012).

Chapter 26

149. Eric Foner, *Reconstruction: America's Unfinished Revolution, 1863–1877*, updated ed. (New York: Harper Perennial, 2014), 437.

150. See complete lyrics at *http://www.metrolyrics.com/a-change-is-gonna-come-lyrics-sam-cooke.html.*

151. Peter Guralnick, *Dream Boogie: The Triumph of Sam Cooke* (New York: Little, Brown and Company, 2005), 526.

Chapter 30

152. Nancy C. Curtis, *Black Heritage Sites: An African American Odyssey and Finder's Guide* (Chicago: American Library Association, 1996), 391.

153. James W. Loewen, *Sundown Towns: A Hidden Dimension of American Racism* (New York: New Press, 2005), 55.

154. Ibid, 90.

155. Jamie Munks, "Prospective Owner Wants Moulin Rouge Revival in Las Vegas," *Las Vegas Review-Journal*, May 29, 2018.

156. *I Am Not Your Negro.*

Abbreviations

AARLCC	African American Research Library and Cultural Center
ACMHR	Alabama Christian Movement for Human Rights
ACRI	Albany Civil Rights Institute
APEX	African-American Panoramic Experience Museum
ASM	Atlanta Student Movement
AUCC	Atlanta University Center Consortium
BCRI	Birmingham Civil Rights Institute
BSCP	Brotherhood of Sleeping Car Porters
CAAM	California African American Museum
COAHR	Committee on Appeal for Human Rights
COFO	Council of Federated Organizations
CORE	Congress of Racial Equality
DCVL	Dallas County Voters League
EJI	Equal Justice Initiative
ETHIC	Emmett Till Historic Intrepid Center
ETIC	Emmett Till Interpretive Center
ETMC	Emmett Till Memorial Commission
ETMP	Emmett Till Historic Memory Project
FBI	Federal Bureau of Investigation
FCC	Federal Communications Commission
FOR	Fellowship of Reconciliation
HMAAC	Houston Museum of African American Culture
IAAM	International African American Museum
ICRCM	International Civil Rights Center & Museum
IOSL	Independent Order of St. Luke
LRCHS	Little Rock Central High School
MCRM	Mississippi Civil Rights Museum
MDAH	Mississippi Department of Archives and History
MFDP	Mississippi Freedom Democratic Party
MLK	Martin Luther King, Jr.
NAACP	National Association for the Advancement of Colored People
NAAM	Northwest African American Museum
NCNW	National Council of Negro Women
NCRM	National Civil Rights Museum
NHP	National Historical Park
NHS	National Historic Site
NMAAM	National Museum of African American Music
NMPJ	National Memorial for Peace and Justice
NPS	National Park Service
NSM	Nashville Student Movement
OMCA	Oakland Museum of California
PBS	Public Broadcasting System
RCNL	Regional Council of Negro Leadership
SCLC	Southern Christian Leadership Conference
SNCC	Student Nonviolent Coordinating Committee
SPLC	Southern Poverty Law Center
UKA	United Klans of America
UL	University of Louisville
UMCC	University Museum and Cultural Center (University of Arkansas)
WCC	White Citizens' Council
YNCL	Young Negroes Cooperative League

Photo Credits

All photos are © John J. Hanrahan except for page 2 © Abernathy Family, Public domain, via Wikimedia Commons; page 12 © National Park Service (NPS); page 18 © Carol M. Highsmith, Public domain, via Wikimedia Commons; page 20 © Peter Pettus, Public domain, via Wikimedia Commons; page 24 © Equal Justice Initiative (EJI); page 25 © Mississippi Department of Archives and History (MDAH); page 26 © Beth Perkins; page 44 (left) © National Public Radio (NPR) used with permission; page 44 (center) © EJI; page 44 (right) © Seizing Freedom, a podcast from VPM. Artwork by L.A. InkWell; page 45 © Emmett Till Memory Project; page 58 © The Library of Congress, no restrictions, via Wikimedia Commons; page 60 © "1 - The U.S. Civil Rights Movement" by U.S. Embassy The Hague is licensed with CC BY-ND 2.0; page 61 © "4 - The U.S. Civil Rights Movement" by U.S. Embassy The Hague is licensed with CC BY-ND 2.0; page 62 © National Civil Rights Museum; page 66 (top row left and center) © Simon & Schuster, (top row right) © Penguin Random House, (bottom row left) © Little, Brown Books for Young Readers, (bottom row middle two) © Simon & Schuster, (bottom right) © Scholastic Books; page 68 © Yoichi Okamoto, Public domain, via Wikimedia Commons; page 81 © NPS Digital Image Archives, Public domain, via Wikimedia Commons; page 88 © JJonahJackalope, CC BY-SA 4.0, via Wikimedia Commons; page 90 © The Badass Women Project by Us & We Art; page 102 © Ser Amantio di Nicolao, CC BY-SA 4.0 via Wikimedia Commons; page 110 © Historical Marker Database (HMDB) - Fair use; page 121 © DiAnna Paulk; page 128 © Ron Cogswell, CC BY 2.0 via Creative Commons; pages 144 and 145 © Photos by Mark Levy, Mark Levy Papers, Queens College Special Collections and Archives, City University of New York; pages 150, 154, and 155 © Federal Bureau of Investigation, MIBURN files; page 161 © NPS; pages 163 and 167 © MDAH: page 187 © ynet, CC BY-SA 4.0, via Wikimedia Commons; page 191 (left) © "Bryant's Grocery and Meat Market, Money, Mississippi, 1955" (2021). Emmett Till. 4. https://digitalcommons.memphis.edu/speccoll-mss-mpressscimitar6/4; page 191 (right) © Carlapbatchelor at the English-language Wikipedia, CC BY-SA 3.0 via Wikimedia Commons; page 209 © Emmett Till Interpretive Center; page 218 © Warren K. Leffler, Public domain, via Wikimedia Commons; page 232 © "Little Rock Nine" by Steve Snodgrass is licensed with CC BY 2.0; page 234 © photo courtesy of Little Rock Convention & Visitors Bureau; page 235 © "Congressional Gold Medal," Clinton Digital Library, accessed October 30, 2021, https://clinton.presidentiallibraries.us/items/show/56833; page 243 © National Civil Rights Museum; page 251 © Unknown author, Public domain, via Wikimedia Commons; page 253 © WillyBearden, CC BY-SA 4.0, via Wikimedia Commons; page 273 © "Bethel Was the Movement..." Rev. Fred L. Shuttlesworth – Historic Bethel Baptist Church 33rd and 29th Sts. North Birmingham (AL) February 2019" by Ron Cogswell is licensed under CC BY 2.0; page 274 © "3 - The U.S. Civil Rights Movement" by U.S. Embassy The Hague is licensed with CC BY-ND 2.0; page 278 © Farm Security Administration - Office of War Information photograph collection (Library of Congress); page 291 (program) © Unnamed organizers of the March on Washington for Jobs and Freedom, Public domain, via Wikimedia Commons; page 291 (photo) © "Martin Luther King Jr. - I Have A Dream Speech" by e-strategyblog.com is licensed with CC BY 2.0; page 294 © Michael Rivera, CC BY-SA 4.0, via Wikimedia Commons; page 297 © Steven W. Sabourin; page 301 © National Portrait Gallery, CC0, via Wikimedia Commons; page 303 © courtesy of Visit Mobile; page 305 © Mark S. Hilton (HMdb.org); page 308 top © "sojourn to the past" used by permission of Wayne Taylor; page 308 bottom fair use; page 313 © Marion S. Trikosko, U.S. News & World Report, Public domain, via Wikimedia Commons; page 316 © The Clarion-Ledger and Jackson Daily News, Public domain, via Wikimedia Commons; page 318 © courtesy of Amoz Eckerson; page 320 © NPS; page 323 © National Museum of African American Music; page 330 © Opinion in Case 16cv2725(DLC), 221 F. Supp. 3d 396 (S.D.N.Y. 2016); page 332 © Hampton House per Wayne Anderson; page 335 © Photo by Bob Sandberg, Look photographer, Restoration by Adam Cuerden, Public domain, via Wikimedia Commons; page 338 © Unknown, Public domain, via Wikimedia Commons; page 339 © Unknown photojournalist, CC BY-SA 4.0, via Wikimedia Commons; page 343 © "File:Home of assassinated Florida NAACP President Harry Moore, Mims, FL.jpg" by Unknown is marked under CC0 1.0; page 345 © Icon Books; page 348 © Hampton House per Wayne Anderson; page 354 © Ed Dwight, sculptor; page 355 © Historic Columbia; page 361 © w_lemay, CC0, via Wikimedia Commons; page 369 © Woodcut artist not listed; W.J. Moses, printer; stereotyped by Dennis Bro's & Co., Public domain, via Wikimedia Commons; page 374 © Cewatkin, CC BY-SA 3.0, via Wikimedia Commons; page 376 © Alexisrael, CC BY-SA 3.0, via Wikimedia Commons; page 380 © Unknown derivative work: MagentaGreen, Public domain, via Wikimedia Commons; page 389 © Virginia Tourism Corporation; page 390 © Erik Soderstrom, CC BY-SA 4.0, via Wikimedia Commons; page 393 © Public Domain; page 394 © Virginia Tourism Corporation; page 397 (both) © MarmadukePercy, CC BY-SA 3.0, via Wikimedia Commons; page 402 © Cupreous, CC BY-SA 4.0, via Wikimedia Commons; page 407 RCA Victor Records, Public domain, via Wikimedia Commons; page 412 © Proof377, CC BY-SA 4.0, via Wikimedia Commons; page 417 © Schlesinger Library, RIAS, Harvard University, No restrictions, via Wikimedia Commons; page 418 © Historical Marker Database (HMDB); page 423 © NPS; page 426 © Frances Benjamin Johnston, Public domain, via Wikimedia Commons; pages 431 and 435 © Ed Dwight, sculptor; page 440 © © USMC, Public domain, via Wikimedia Commons; page 443 © Frank Schulenburg, CC BY-SA 4.0, via Wikimedia Commons; page 444 Ed Dwight, sculptor; pages 450 and 451 © NPS; page 454 © Library of Congress; page 457 © NPS; page 468 (both) © Fort Des Moines Museum and Education Center; page 469 © Ed Ford, World Telegram staff photographer, Public domain, via Wikimedia Commons; page 470 © NPS; page 473 © Bentai at English Wikipedia, CC BY-SA 3.0, via Wikimedia Commons; page 477 © Simmons, William J., Public domain, via Wikimedia Commons; page 481 © (left) NPS; page 481 (right) © Official White House Photo by Pete Souza, Public domain, via Wikimedia Commons; page 482 © Jason Flakes.

Map Credits

Destination city maps were created by John J. Hanrahan using Google My Maps. State and regional maps were created by John J. Hanrahan using Adobe Stock Images licensed by Bookwrights.

Acknowledgments

Acknowledgment pages stand out more while writing a book. At least that is true of me. As I read relevant books on civil rights history, I was struck by the pages of thanks many authors had recognizing helpful individuals by name. Fearing I'd forget someone, I'm not doing that, with a few key exceptions.

My sincere appreciation goes out to:

- Every teacher who took a red pen to my writing to improve it.
- Everyone who said "Maybe you should write a book" after hearing about the 2018 trip my wife and I took to explore this important history.
- Everyone who offered encouragement as I wrote.
- Everyone who read a query letter or proposal from me and actually responded back.
- Everyone who read a chapter or two along the way.
- Every writer whose work expanded my knowledge of African American and civil rights history.
- Everyone at the museums, NPS facilities, historic churches and homes, interpretive centers, libraries, archives, and more who answered my many questions.
- Every photographer, sculptor, illustrator, and other artist whose work graces the book's pages.
- Ehren Foley whose encouragement and thoughtful feedback propelled the project just at the right moment.
- Robert Land, for his editing and our enjoyable banter.
- The ever-patient Mayapriya Long for guiding this first-time author through the process of designing the book and creating the perfect cover for it.
- My parents who taught me tolerance, patience, and persistence.
- My wife Lisa who endured not only the trek to this important history but also the day-to-day ups and downs that accompanied this writing project.

Lastly, thanks to everyone purchasing the book. Your support helps two nonprofits fight for social justice: the Equal Justice Initiative in Montgomery and the Legal Aid Justice Center in Charlottesville. They split the profits.

Index

Italic page numbers refer to photographs. Page references including *t* or *f* refer to tables or figures, respectively

About the Author

John J. Hanrahan grew up in Cranston, Rhode Island. Better known as Jack, he received his undergraduate degree from Boston College and two master's degrees and a Ph.D. from Indiana University. His career in marketing took him to Chicago, Atlanta, and New York City. Jack and his wife, Lisa, retired to Charlottesville, Virginia where they volunteer with several community service organizations.

Jack has volunteered at the Legal Aid Justice Center in Charlottesville for a decade. That organization and the Equal Justice Initiative in Montgomery, Alabama will share any profits generated by *Traveling Freedom's Road: A Guide to Exploring Our Civil Rights History.*

Made in the USA
Monee, IL
27 June 2024

60843873R00292